CZECHOSLOVAKIA

CZECHOSLOVAKIA

Anvil of the Cold War

John O. Crane and Sylvia Crane

Foreword by Corliss Lamont

 PRAEGER

New York
Westport, Connecticut
London

Library of Congress Cataloging-in-Publication Data

Crane, John O., d. 1982.
   Czechoslovakia : anvil of the Cold War / John O. Crane and Sylvia
Crane.
         p.   cm.
   Includes bibliographical references and index.
   ISBN 0-275-93577-9 (alk. paper)
   1. Czechoslovakia—Politics and government—1918-   I. Crane,
Sylvia E.   II. Title.
   DB2188.7.C73   1991
   943.7'03—dc20   90-39146

British Library Cataloguing in Publication Data is available.

Library of Congress Catalog Card Number: 90-39146
ISBN: 0-275-93577-9

First published in 1991

Praeger Publishers, One Madison Avenue, New York, NY 10010
An imprint of Greenwood Publishing Group, Inc.

Printed in the United States of America

The paper used in this book complies with the
Permanent Paper Standard issued by the National
Information Standards Organization (Z39.48-1984).

10 9 8 7 6 5 4 3 2 1

To the Spirit of Tomáš G. Masaryk

Contents

Foreword by Corliss Lamont ... ix

Acknowledgments ... xiii

Introduction ... xvii

1. The Independence Movement Commences ... 1

2. Founding of the Legions: Entrapment in Anti-Bolshevik Intervention ... 11

3. The Legion's Anabasis to the Sea ... 30

4. Masaryk in America ... 50

5. Drawing the Frontiers ... 63

6. Internal Stabilization ... 72

7. The Beneš Succession: Storm Warnings ... 85

8. The Sudeten Fires Flare ... 103

9. Summer Turmoil ... 124

10. The Runciman Mission ... 131

11. Munich   151

12. Aftermath of Munich   172

13. War on Two Fronts   187

14. Wartime Conferences and Treaties   205

15. The Slovak Uprising: The Government's Return Home   218

16. The Government Reconstituted on Home Ground   235

17. Nationalities Transfers and Allied Army Withdrawals   247

18. Democratic Socialization   257

19. Cold War Beginnings   273

20. Storm Signals   290

21. The Communist Coup   308

22. The Death of Jan Masaryk   320

     Abbreviations   333

     Bibliography   335

     Index   343

     About the Authors   353

Illustrations follow page 150

Foreword

Sylvia Crane's interest in Czechoslovakia was provoked by her personal anguish over its sell-out at Munich. She was a politically alive senior majoring in history at Brooklyn College, where she and her colleagues seethed in outrage at the betrayal. Devotion to democratic liberties and social justice were cardinal values for her depression-ridden New Deal oriented class.

She learned more about European history during her graduate studies at Columbia University, where she took courses conducted by many of the celebrated scholars of the time, such as professors James T. Shotwell, that great internationalist; Harry J. Carman, in American history; Carleton J. H. Hayes, in German history; Shepard B. Clough, in French and Italian history; René Albrecht Carrié, in international relations; and Geroid Robinson, in Russian history. She later returned for more of this scholarly enterprise when she came under the tutelage of professors Henry Steele Commager, Richard B. Morris, Dumas Malone, the great Jeffersonian, Allan Nevins and others. The latter had started his career as a journalist in Chicago for the short-lived newspaper *The Day*, which had been underwritten by Charles R. Crane.

John O. Crane and Sylvia Engel met socially in New York in 1942 soon after his return from a long expatriation in Europe. They were promptly drawn together by magnetic attraction, fortified by their interest in history and their shared views on politics. She was employed professionally in political public relations. Inspired by a strong desire to contribute to the war effort, she had relinquished her cherished goal of a career teaching history to promote favorable public attitudes toward the war.

It was quite natural for John to solicit her interest in helping the Czechoslovak cause; she had, in his judgment, the requisite training and talent. He had been approached by Ambassador Vladimir Hurban, an old friend, to find someone to arrange private receptions and a notable public demonstration for President Eduard Beneš, who had just communicated his intention to come to the United States from his post of exile in London to see President Franklin Delano Roosevelt to clear up some knotty problems in their relationship. Probably because of Beneš's pro-Soviet stand, the State Department was not as friendly to the Czechoslovak government-in-exile as in days of old. Moreover, Beneš found it expedient to go to Moscow shortly to discuss border and nationalities questions at issue between the two countries for postwar settlement. He wanted to explain in advance to FDR his reasons for this projected trip. In this tenuous circumstance, Beneš deemed it would be useful to have an enthusiastic display of public sentiment accompanying his visit to Washington. This was the path trod at the close of World War I by Tomáš G. Masaryk, when courting the favorable attention of President Woodrow Wilson.

John sketched these considerations to Sylvia and asked if she would be prepared to undertake the task. Would she meet again soon to discuss the project with him and Ambassador Hurban, who was coming from Washington to New York expressly to meet with her? She assented readily, eager to confront the challenge. It was an invitation for her to step through an open door to exciting opportunities. When the ambassador requested her plan of procedure the moment they sat down to lunch, she appreciated his serious intent. She advised that among other receptions, a public rally, which she would manage in consultation with John, should be held in prestigious and not overly large Carnegie Hall. Thus commenced a lifelong collaboration with John Crane, whom Sylvia married on July 7, 1945. Foreseeing political difficulties that might be made by public figures and journalists, she proposed an acceptable formula to the ambassador: they should solicit sponsorship from all people representing Allied unity and exclude only the appeasers. Hurban agreed willingly.

The meeting was held on May 27, 1943, in Carnegie Hall under the auspices of the American Friends of Czechoslovakia, chaired by William Jay Schieffelin, formerly head of the International Red Cross. Mayor Fiorello La Guardia gave President Beneš a cordial private reception at City Hall and he sent his deputy mayor, Newbold Morris, to preside over the meeting. It was a smashing success. Beyond "Standing Room Only" notices for a week, it drew almost 1,000 frustrated supporters clamoring for entry. Sylvia Crane set up a public address system in the lobby to accommodate these hopefuls, after she had placed the maximum of 150 chairs on the stage. She accommodated the last-minute arrival of Beneš's Czechoslovak Air Force Color Guard, numbering ten, by standing them around the rear of the central boxes, thus successfully conforming to the fire law restrictions.

In addition to the stirring effect of Beneš's speech, a dramatic script based on the exploits of the Resistance Movement, which she had arranged to be written by Norman Corwin, aroused sentiment to fever pitch. At the close, the emotional response culminated in the fervent singing by the standing audience of the Czechoslovak National Hymn, signifying the rebirth of freedom and independence, to follow an Allied victory expelling the occupying Nazis. The banner newspaper headlines on the next day's front pages reflected the charged atmosphere and audience response accurately.

When President Beneš visited President Roosevelt in the White House, he was accorded a fine reception. He informed Roosevelt of his forthcoming trip to Moscow and stated his reasons for going, hoping to forestall Cold War reprisals. The Czechoslovak legation was upgraded in status to an embassy, and presumably cordial relations were restored.

After the war, when travel permitted, John and Sylvia visited Prague to see their friends. Jan Masaryk, installed in the Czernin Palace as foreign minister, greeted John with a hearty embrace of fraternal love. He welcomed Sylvia cordially as befitted an adopted "sister-in-law." President and Madame Beneš expressed great pleasure to see them again. Straight off at the beginning of their two hour conversation, the president thanked Sylvia abundantly for the successful meeting which had played so important a role in his achieving his objectives in Washington during the war. They returned to Prague several times in later years and spent one unforgettable weekend with Hana Beneš at Sezimovo Usti, the Beneš home near Tabor. On that occasion, Hana took Sylvia upstairs to her late husband's study to show her that the souvenir program of the famed meeting rested atop his papers on his desk, undisturbed over the years.

One evening at dinner in the fifties, when Sylvia Crane had resumed her graduate studies at Columbia, she told her friend Alice Masaryk, Tomáš Masaryk's daughter, about her interesting course with Professor Dumas Malone on Thomas Jefferson and his time. Alice promptly responded eagerly and begged for permission to accompany her to audit the lectures. Malone consented graciously, and so it transpired that Alice came to the Crane home for early dinner every Tuesday evening, rain, snow, or shine, and walked briskly with Sylvia to class throughout the academic year. Malone would nod his head in polite acquiescence when Alice's chin dropped to her chest in a brief after-dinner drowse. She loved the course and she explained that her father had been enamored of Jefferson's views and ideals; she had been reared in this tradition.

Alice, who never married, took an active interest in the two Crane sons, the younger one named after her father. She directed them to call her Aunt Alice.

In later years, John and his wife played an active role in organizing and supporting the Masaryk Publications Trust, which engaged in translating and publishing Volume III of Tomáš Masaryk's *Spirit of Russia* and underwrote Ruth Crawford Mitchell's biography of Alice Masaryk.

Sylvia Crane's dedication to Czechoslovakia's freedom and independence persisted. She collaborated with John on this book on Czechoslovakia from the beginning. After his death from cancer in May 1982, she courageously took up the remaining job, as John had earnestly requested, of pursuing the archival researches necessary to authenticate the unfinished manuscript, to rewrite where necessary, and to complete it. By this time she had gained the experience wanted for this task by the publication of another heavily researched historical work. Interestingly, she found nothing in all the archival material that she unearthed to contradict any of John's assertions and conclusions.

The chapter on Jan Masaryk's death was written collaboratively from the outset. John and Sylvia together interviewed all the close friends and relatives of Jan they could locate, including his sister Alice, Hana Beneš, and Alice's former secretary in Prague, as well as numerous others.

CORLISS LAMONT
New York, March 1989

Acknowledgments

I am deeply grateful to many friends for their valuable suggestions for this manuscript. Limitations of space necessarily confine my statement. Straight away, I want to give my heartfelt thanks to my keen and discriminating editor, Dan Eades, who liked what he read in these pages and accepted them for publication. His continued confidence was balm through the grind of production. I wish also to thank my beloved friend and colleague, Corliss Lamont, for writing his gracious presentation of me for the Foreword.

Having decided that this book was to be constructed on the building blocks of the archival materials, I plunged into the extensive research. The British archives became my first quest. I was cordially and courteously received in the Public Records Office in London by the Keeper of the Public Records, George Martin, who promptly issued my reader's card. His assistant, Mr. Chalmers, and the other staffers provided ready help, initiating me into the intricacies of their file codes and computerized system for calling up documents.

Eva Verdi, a native Czechoslovak of long residence in London, expressed interest in this work following my presentation of a paper on the Crane/Masaryk Connection at the International Conference on Tomáš Masaryk at the School of Slavonic Studies of London University. She generously undertook to search the records for the war years and beyond for 1941-1948, sending me packing to other a rchives. Hers was a most useful and pleasurable collaboration.

Prof. Arthur S. Link graciously eased my way into the immense 49-volume collection that he edited of Woodrow Wilson Papers at the Firestone Library of Princeton. The staff at special collections was ever courteous and helpful. They also permitted my use of their microfilm reading machines.

I thank my friend Prof. Robert Tucker of Princeton for his interest in the manuscript and for supplying his summary paragraph from his own manuscript about Russia in the Stalin years.

The staff of the Library of Congress epitomized courtesy and expertise. Dr. George Kovtun, director of the Central/East European Division, was most solicitous to guide me to the right sources. He gave me generously of his time and attention. The National Archives, that giant storehouse of our public records, has a commendable staff who steered me efficiently.

Above all, I want to thank my readers, who generously gave the manuscript their discriminating attention and imparted sage advice. Linda Abegglen and Joseph Jay Deiss made editorial suggestions at the beginning. Prof. Arno Mayer at Princeton told me how to scale down the original overwritten work. To him, for his encouragement and for his wise guidance, my deep gratitude. Prof. Dennison Rusinow, a longtime friend also of John from Central Europe and the Institute of Current World Affairs, now at Pittsburgh, made innumerable suggestions in the text for which I am most grateful. My thanks also to his wife, Mary, for her important suggestion for change.

I was very touched by the interest of our old friend, Jiři Hájek, whom we had met years ago at the United Nations. He had returned home to head the Foreign Affairs Ministry in the Prague Spring Cabinet of Alexander Dubček. After the invasion of 1968, he was under strict police surveillance and occasional detention for 21 years. He courageously headed the Charter 77 Movement which President Václav Havel joined. In the midst of their revolutionary activities last fall, Hájek read this manuscript. His numerous suggestions for changes, as he delicately phrased it, were "purely cosmetic" to conform to Czechoslovak perceptions. Happily, he loved the manuscript, especially pleased that it made "an important contribution to restoring Masaryk and Beneš to their rightful places in Czechoslovak history." He shared the manuscript with his friend, Dr. Jaroslav Opát, the famous Tomáš Masaryk scholar, who concurred, to our delight.

To our son, Thomas, my thanks for his skillful editorial revisions in the chapter on the death of Jan Masaryk. His keen lawyer's eye and judicious judgment of evidence came into play. The authors early on consulted their close friend, Dr. Kurt Alfred Adler when gathering evidence in Prague about Masaryk's death. Dr. Adler carefully weighed our facts of the case for suicide before he eventually agreed that suicide was likely. My gratitude extends also to our longstanding

Slovak friend, Paul Rohon, for instilling in me consciousness of including Slovakia in all references to Czechoslovakia.

For the technical production of the book, I thank Nina Neimark for her conscientious editing and Evelyn Connolly for her excellent typing, handling the foreign names and places with striking precision. Without Gardner Miller's patient initiation of me into the mysteries of using my computer, I may never have progressed to completion. My deepest gratitude goes to my esteemed comrade, Henry Hemmendinger, who gave priority over his own work unstintingly to meticulous editorial assistance on the final form of the manuscript. His expert knowledge of wordprocessing technology was of crucial importance to the technical production.

SYLVIA E. CRANE
September 1990

Introduction

I was prompted to write *Czechoslovakia: Anvil of the Cold War* by the circumstance of my lifelong association with that keystone country in the heart of Europe.

The title of this book is self-explanatory. It is the contemporary story of how this Slavic nation located astride the East-West watershed innocently and for no reasons of her own became involved in the Cold War on four successive occasions and emerged as its principal victim. These turning points in modern Czechoslovak history occurred during the year of its founding in 1918 in the midst of the Bolshevik Revolution, in the Munich betrayal in 1938, in the Communist coup of 1948, and in the Soviet occupation in 1968. We leave the last episode to other historians, as my personal attachment with the Masaryk family precluded later access to people and archives within the country. We terminate this account with the death of Jan Masaryk in March 1948.

My family's relationship with Czechoslovakia commenced in 1896 when, during one of his perennial visits to Russia, my father, Charles R. Crane, president of the Chicago-based Crane Company, stopped off in Prague to call on the 46-year old scholar and Slavic expert, Professor Tomáš G. Masaryk, in his modest apartment in ancient, colorful Malástrana (Old Town). Their interest in Russia fostered a mutual attraction, which was strengthened over the years by frequent reciprocal stopovers and numerous family exchanges. Five years later my father founded a chair in Slavonic studies at the University of Chicago, which was filled in the second year by Masaryk.

While Masaryk was lecturing in Chicago about the smaller nations of Central and Eastern Europe, my father made arrangements to enable Masaryk's eldest daughter, Alice, to complete her social studies by working in the great settlement house of Jane Addams and Mary McDowell, Hull House.

In 1906 the second Masaryk son, Jan, came to New York in search of a career as a pianist. But he soon relinquished his musical aspirations for lack of steady employment and meager earnings, and he accepted my family's offer of work at the Crane Valve Company in Bridgeport, Connecticut. There, he formed an affectionate lifelong friendship with my brother, Richard, who was plant manager. Jan was placed in the personnel division of the company, where he acquired two additional languages, Polish and Hungarian, to supplement his native trilingual fluency in Czech, German, and English.

At that time the American setting of the Czechoslovak independence movement proceeded in numerous cities of heavy ethnic concentration. The tide also swept through my family circle. My father and brother were deeply involved in obtaining recognition of the new independent republic. Masaryk and my father had last met in revolutionary Russia in the summer of 1917, and my brother, then secretary to Secretary of State Robert Lansing, transmitted reports of both Slavicists for the President's attention.

In his autobiographical *War Memoirs,* Tomáš Masaryk detailed the helpful role played by my father and brother in 1918 to initiate contacts with President Wilson and members of his administration. On May 8, 1918, my father wrote Wilson: "I hope you can set aside a little time with Professor Masaryk." He recommended Masaryk as "the wisest and most influential Slav of our day . . . I believe he could materially aid you in a technical way with your program."[1] A couple of weeks later, Crane wired Joseph Patrick Tumulty, the President's secretary, "Please congratulate him for me in the decision in regard to the small peoples in the Austrian Empire. It is timely."[2] Early in June, he again requested a presidential interview with Masaryk. "I believe no one else in Europe could make so valuable a contribution as he," wired my father to Wilson from Woods Hole, Massachusetts.[3]

While I was still a history student at Harvard, I observed expressions of concern by my father and some of his friends about the success of the Czechoslovak independence cause. I witnessed their conversations with Tomáš Masaryk both at our New York apartment and in Richard's Washington home during Richard's tenure in the State Department. Richard then went on in May, 1919, to be the first U.S. minister to the fledgling republic.

At the end of my father's tour of duty as U.S. ambassador to China in May 1921, my father and I departed Peking. We traversed Siberia on the Trans-Siberian Railway, virtually the first foreigners to gain access to that route in its entirety following the chaos of civil war and destruction. We delighted in our reunion in Prague with my brother Richard. The next day, father indulged his choice pleasure in reporting our observations of the situation to his trusted friend Masaryk, now president of the republic.

The exchange of views took place in the relaxed ambience of Lany, the presidential country residence outside Prague. Zamek (Chateau) Lany, situated at a comfortable remove from Prague, is an Italianate villa that once served as the hunting lodge of Prince Karl Furstenberg, an intimate of Kaiser Wilhelm. To meet the simple tastes and modest needs of the Masaryk family, Alice had supervised some modernizing, overseeing the installation of bathrooms and electricity, and had effected several other internal improvements.

The talk commenced in a family setting over the luncheon table on the terrace. The two friends, who shared a deep-rooted knowledge of old and new Russia and sympathized with her plight, sought in vain for an appropriate Western response to the country's reorganization out of postwar and revolutionary chaos. Whatever course the smitten country would take, it was certain that patient planning and meticulous organization over long years were required to resolve its problems. Meanwhile, the best policy for her well-wishers, in their view, was "Hands Off." The conversation was impressive to my youthful, inexperienced ears and all the more fruitful for emanating from those two experts, who possessed such diverse backgrounds and personalities: Masaryk, the probing scholar and responsible statesman, and Crane, the pragmatic ex-businessman turned diplomat and philanthropist.

I returned to Harvard in September with a dizzyingly enlarged perspective for my senior year, when I pursued the mysteries of history and political science. I had no premonition that I would ever return to Prague to work. Just prior to my graduation from Harvard, life took a radical turn as a result of a chance conversation between my father and President Masaryk in the spring of 1922. Arriving from what was then called the Near East for his annual "cure" at Carlsbad, my father drove the two hour's distance to Lany to stop again to compare notes.

Masaryk inquired, as usual, about family news. "And John, what does he intend to do after he has finished at Harvard?" asked the president. "I'm not sure, but from last reports I believe he intends to continue with his history studies at Oxford or the Sorbonne," replied my father.   "That sounds interesting," commented his friend, "but perhaps John would find it more interesting to come here and observe history in the making. He can have a room here and he can take part in anything we're doing. He can pursue his studies as well; we have a fine German university in town."

And so it was that I went to Lany and Prague on a sort of exchange fellowship in residence with the president and his family. I drove over in the car that Jan had dispatched for me on September 22, 1922, from Carlsbad, where I had gone at my family's insistence for the "cure." My mind was filled with eager anticipation and my eyes feasted on the riotous autumnal colors of yellow, red, green, and brown in the prosperous looking countryside. I arrived in the midst of a diplomatic luncheon honoring 79-year-old Pašič, prime minister of Serbia, and an old acquaintance of Masaryk's. The president showed no reluctance to interrupt this state occasion to receive me. He greeted me as an old friend, smilingly and simply, saying, "I am pleased to meet you."

I found myself face to face with the medium-tall, gaunt 72-year-old president in fine physical trim for his age. His truly noble dome, almost completely bald, was rounded and symmetrical; his friendly eyes sought to establish direct contact with mine. His innate kindliness and warmth beamed a hearty welcome, moderating the awesome impression upon me of his striking appearance.

The cordial personal greeting by the solemn, dignified president and the sophisticated luncheon talk provided a heady and somewhat overwhelming experience for this young novitiate. After a brief rest in Jan's room, I took a walk in the villa's wooded park with the president's secretary, Vladimir Kučera. About 4 P.M., the president came up to my room to inquire whether I was comfortably installed.

He showed me my spacious office, where we decided there would be plenty of room for my personal library, and he then explained my duties. These would be kept to a minimum so as to leave me time to socialize with all sorts of people, especially those in the international set now living in Prague. As soon as I became acclimated, I would handle the president's social duties in this milieu, take over his foreign correspondence, particularly that with Americans, and facilitate visits of American friends and journalists to the exciting new Czechoslovakia of the 1920's. For the present, I would be in charge primarily of reading, summarizing, and clipping the international press in English and French. I would extend these tasks when I gained proficiency in German, which I needed in any case to attend the university. He recommended for my benefit a sensible program of courses and gave me the names of men to consult. My honorarium would be 2,000 crowns monthly, a comfortable stipend in those days, especially in view of room and board being subsumed with my inclusion in the family.

Alice, the eldest daughter, handled the duties of first lady with natural grace in the absence of her stricken mother. She paid special attention to acclimating me within the household, starting with the rangy third floor where my bedroom was located. She informed me I could take any meals I desired with the family, especially when they entertained interesting guests. Whenever I chose, I could eat in the kitchen with the staff and deepen my acquaintance with the knowledgeable Kučera, who doubled to cover reports about Central Europe for the Associated Press. Kučera was most helpful in orienting me into my work and filling in the numerous gaps in my information. He suggested books and articles I could read for this purpose.

Jan's bedroom suite adjoined my single room both at Lany and at the Hradčany Castle in Prague where the presidential entourage spent the midweek days of each week. Jan and I often read the continental press together over breakfast, and we dined together frequently in Prague's colorful and excellent restaurants, either before or after some performance we had chosen from the many available for an evening's entertainment. His affection for my brother, Richard, and especially for my sister, Frances, whom he later married on my birthday, December 28, 1924, spurred him to treat me with fraternal solicitude, and indeed, it was he who primarily eased my way into the bosom of the family.

The morning following my arrival at Lany, Jan drove me into beautiful, baroque Prague, where we stopped at the imposing gate to admire the commanding cityscape before entering the ancient Hradčany. Jan introduced me to the staff of the castle before I called on the U.S. legation in the Schonborn Palace in Malástrana. Richard, as the first U.S. minister to Czechoslovakia, had chosen this site for the ministry. The historic palace was sufficiently commodious in those days also to accommodate his residence. He was now in the process of purchasing the palace and assigned to me its management and the final negotiations for the transaction. Jan also introduced me at the Živnostenská Bank, where after the usual initial fuss I opened an account and changed some money. We returned to Lany for the evening, glad to escape the city's confusion.

The atmosphere at Lany allowed President Masaryk a relaxed routine of work in family surroundings. In his private suite overlooking the rosy horse chestnut allée, he would arise before seven and, while breakfasting, scan carefully a dozen or so domestic and foreign publications. By nine he would arrive at his downstairs office, which was an ample room lined with bookcases on one side and cubbyhole shelves for clippings on the other, altogether a homey workroom. In an hour or two, he would dispatch with his tall swarthy private secretary, Kučera, the more urgent official business. Office routine and official visitors were, for the most part, relegated to the two or three days that Masaryk spent weekly in town at the Hrad.

At about eleven in the morning, he would take an hour and a half of horseback riding as his daily exercise. He had discovered his taste for that sport long ago at the Villa Borghese in Rome. Usually, Jan and I would bring up the rear. Mounting his steady-footed Viktor and accompanied by his Austrian-trained equestrian companion, Krejčik, he would ride out into the nearby countryside or fields. When Krejčik was absent, I was selected to ride alongside. Actually, Masaryk preferred the open fields, for he felt a mystical affinity with the farming peasants, as witness the colorful reproduction of Jean-François Millet's *Angelus*, depicting a young girl listening to the song of the lark at sundown, that hung in his studio. When questioned as to why he would risk a handicapping accident from riding at his age, Masaryk would reply succinctly: "I ride so I can read more." He felt at no risk on horseback; his physical fitness attested to his claim.

At Lany, for our regular exercise, we also had a tennis court, which the president considered as beneficial for those of us who preferred this sport. The youngest Masaryk daughter, Olga, who in her earlier days had been women's runner-up in the prewar Prague championships, was still a smashing player. On her occasional visits, she partook of doubles with the resident group. I frequently played singles with Eduard Beneš, who was a formidable opponent despite his short stature. He was by nature highly competitive on the court. Although Jan had the build for tennis, being taller than my own six feet and much huskier, he preferred to indulge in Prague's brilliant night life. I was continually amazed to see how much he could drink of an evening, or on successive ones, without detracting from his handsome looks or dimming his normally bright, piercing eyes.

Alice was principally concerned with reorganizing the rigid social services of Austria. She expanded the almost nonexistent Hungarian services in the eastern provinces, working happily with her personally imported colleagues Ruth Crawford and Mary Hurlbutt to found the Czechoslovak Red Cross. She also took a prominent interest in the famous Russian Action, an organization that was personally sponsored by Masaryk and Beneš, as well as Karel Kramář. When I arrived,

Alice was mobilizing the organization of the Russian Cultural Center with Princess Volkonsky, whom I soon met and liked very much.

Whenever Eduard and Hana Beneš were not traveling abroad on some foreign mission, they would join the Masaryk family at Lany for Sunday luncheon. Arriving at midday, Edka, as Eduard was familiarly called, loved to go outdoors before lunch, either to ride or play tennis with me, and also with Olga when she was present. Hana, or Hanci, Beneš was apt to pair off to chat with Alice, a natural outgrowth of their intimate relationship, developed during their years together in prison during World War I.

The family would gather for a three-course lunch at one-thirty. At the table, Beneš would informally begin a report to the president of his week's work. This discourse would broaden into an exchange of views afterward over coffee before the fireplace, with the entire family participating. Black Viennese coffee and water would be served on the round glass-top table before the corner fireplace.

Masaryk would sit in his customary leather armchair on the left side of the fireplace, his hands easily clasped in his lap, a picture of kindliness and benign attentiveness. On ordinary occasions he would not take an active part in the conversation, but if a significant point arose, he would sit forward, stroking his long grey-white moustache which drooped around his full mouth. In his responses he would rarely raise his voice, but might stress a point with the index finger of his right hand. Masaryk was a courteous listener—a habit cultivated in his professorial days—whose reactions typically summed up the essential facts set forth in logical synthesis. He restrained any impression of having spoken the last word.

On these occasions, Masaryk would pay particular attention to the quiet reactions of Hana Beneš, whose innate common sense both he and Edka respected and valued. I attribute Masaryk's attentiveness to Hana largely to his customary behavior with his own prescient wife, with whom he had discussed his every activity and plan before arriving at any decision. Their loving and affectionate relationship was inter-laced with mutual respect. Today one could say that Masaryk was a premature feminist.

Soon after I came to Lany, Jan was posted to London as counsellor of the Czechoslovak legation, but owing to the rapid deterioration of his mother's health and her tragic death in May 1923, he actually spent more time at home than at his foreign post. He was sorely missed when away. At the family gatherings when at home, Jan would sit quietly, always alert to fill in the few dull points with a pithy story. When he was present at some semiofficial meeting that his father was having either with Beneš or with Prime Minister Antonin Švehla, a wry smile might flicker around his lips while the principals were discussing a course of action. Often his intense father would turn to him with a gentle gesture to solicit his advice on how to implement a certain move. In his social contacts, too, he complemented his father. As the older Masaryk's inner circle more naturally embraced his Socialist and Radical friends, Jan often found it useful to maintain countervailing breadth and balance by cultivating more conservative associates. In Prague, he was likely to see Karel Loevenstein, managing director of the Škoda Works, over a bottle or two of cognac, which they drained, drinking into the early morning hours.

It was Jan who introduced Robert Bruce Lockhart into our circle. Bruce Lockhart was presently representing the Anglo-Czechoslovak Bank in Prague. This British agent had met Tomáš Masaryk in Moscow during the Bolshevik Revolution and had intervened for him with Léon Trotsky, to whom he had enjoyed access. Bruce Lockhart became an intimate friend of Jan's; their friendship deepened over the years both in Prague and in London as drinking and political companions. [4]

After post-lunch discussions, Tomáš Masaryk would withdraw to his private quarters. Throughout his presidency, he pursued his scholarly bent and continued to be a prodigious reader and writer. In this period he preferred to keep abreast of Anglo-American letters, particularly those written by women. Willa Cather was his favorite author that fall. He spent three or four hours toward the end of the day reading current literature. He often told us: "When I was younger, I studied history by reading the great texts, but now I find I learn more of how the people live and think by reading novels." [5] He even confessed to having started writing a novel himself, more than once, but he acknowledged contritely a marked lack of success. At fireside talks Masaryk often referred to difficulties he was encountering in putting the final touches on his manuscript of *War Memoirs,* which, nevertheless, he soon completed.

During a holiday break in Lomnice in the high Tatras in Slovakia in 1923, I had the supreme pleasure of dining several times entirely alone with President Masaryk. He talked at length about the politics and political theory of the time of the American Revolution, a period that fascinated him. In the course of one conversation, he speculated on the reasons it was better for Czechoslovakia to set up a republic rather than a monarchy, which many people had favored. Aside from his personal preference, he drew an illuminating comparison of his position in the fall of 1918 with that of Washington 150 years earlier in America. As I wrote in my diary of that period, he reasoned:

If Czarist Russia had come out of the war victorious, the idea in Bohemia was, I suppose, to have a Russian King of one kind or another. But after the collapse and withdrawal of Russia, it would have been impossible to set up a monarchy here . . . Who would have been King? [speculated the President]. Absolutely no one was fitted for the Kingship . . . In order to have a King, there must be some idea, some traditional foundation behind it . . . It was the same matter in America at the time of the Revolution. Washington could not have been King . . . there was no foundation for a Kingship under American conditions and besides, he had no children . . . In both our countries, there was no aristocracy, in fact, nothing to back up a Monarchy. So I decided shorthand in favor of a Republic. This will save Czechoslovakia from the necessity of another Revolution later on, I hope. [6]

Often, for relaxation, he talked to me about his many other ideas. While retaining deep personal faith in his mission, he skeptically discounted the popular enthusiasm for the newly won freedom. He acknowledged pragmatically that the ordinary people focused on their daily lives and living conditions and cared little for political theory or institutional forms. In any case, democracy sounded pretty good, even if the poor still had not won suffrage. Masaryk thought the new republic's constitution provided the guidelines of a new social contract. His ideals defined in the simplest terms were social justice and tolerance, which he found paralleled those of Jefferson. In modern terms, they were social democratic, encouraging class harmony as opposed to class conflict.

He rejected the equality of communism for lacking the motivation of profits under capitalism, and he pondered frequently how to utilize and integrate in current context the historical humanist traditions of the Hussite Reformation and the Moravian Brethren, to whom he credited important national influences. Masaryk felt that political independence, and even classical freedom, would not suffice to guarantee a democratic evolution. Influenced by his American wife and his concentrated study of her country's history, he had discovered his essential building blocks for this goal in the principles and practices of Thomas Jefferson and Abraham Lincoln.

In those early years, Masaryk was wont to express in the family circle his fervent hope that his newly reunited and liberated nation be granted at least 50 years' respite from war to develop along its indigenous traditional lines. In the end, the First Republic enjoyed only a skimpy two decades to sink its democratic taproots in the Masaryk concept.

One lesson I learned later from the turmoil of Munich was the need of an accurate reading of the term "appeasement." It originated in the context of Hitler's time as a disparaging, even opprobrious term, meaning accommodation by the Western powers to a right-wing, aggressive dictator in an effort to prevent war or to deflect it eastward against Soviet Russia. At Munich, it signified the selling out to Hitler of democratic Czechoslovakia's independence and liberties by the Great Powers, who did not consult Czechoslovakia's leaders, and would gain but another year of peace before the caldron of war ignited, engulfing them too.

In the post World War II epoch of Cold War, appeasement was twisted to focus against the USSR, which was erroneously equated with Nazi Germany. In our view, despite their many similarities, these states were basically different. Verisimilitude does not make for sameness. We find the comparison loose and inaccurate, also dangerous for its implication of the necessity to fight a war against the "evil Empire," which was justified in the name of humanity when the enemy was Nazism and Fascism. In the nuclear age, when the stakes have accelerated to menace all of civilization with destruction, the implication of appeasement is frightening and unacceptable.

This review of Czechoslovak history, in the light of Cold War pressures and forces, accords with those of other scholars of the Cold War, namely D. F. Fleming[7] and André Fontaine,[8] in tracing its origin to the Bolshevik Revolution. My objective is to distill the lessons of her history, which in the early years of the republic, I was privileged to witness at close range for several years, not merely to learn the truth for myself, but also to recount as a guide for the sake of historical accuracy and world survival.

JOHN O. CRANE
Rome, January 1982

NOTES

1.   Charles R. Crane letter to Woodrow Wilson, May 8, 1918, Crane family archive.

2.   Charles R. Crane to Tumulty, wire, May 30, 1918, Crane family archive.

3.   Charles R. Crane to Woodrow Wilson, Woods Hole, June 8, 1918, Crane family archive.

4.   John O. Crane Diary, November, 1922, Crane family archive.

5.   Ibid.

6.   Ibid.

7.   D. F. Fleming, *Causes and Origins of the Cold War*, 2 vols. (New York: Doubleday, 1961).

8.   André Fontaine, *History of the Cold War*, 2 vols. (New York: Random House, 1969).

CZECHOSLOVAKIA

1

The Independence
Movement Commences

The Czechoslovak independence movement commenced with the first volleys fired against Belgrade in the summer of 1914, when Archduke Ferdinand and his wife were assassinated at Sarajevo on June 28th. Tomáš Garrigue Masaryk, on holiday with his family at Schandau in Saxony, promptly detected the possibility, even the likelihood, of the Austro-Hungarian Empire's dismemberment in the event of a defeat. He was heartened in contemplating the opportunities engendered by the war. He hurried home to explore the reaction among his friends and colleagues at Prague to the chances of launching a national independence movement. Although he was theoretically a dedicated pacifist, he knew that national independence would not sprout automatically, nor necessarily alone by peaceful diplomacy in courting the support of the Great Powers. It would have to be painstakingly organized at home and abroad. On the train homeward bound, he was encouraged by overhearing strains of anti-Austrian sentiment among the soldiers he encountered.

He proceeded cautiously in his soundings among his parliamentary and political colleagues, foremost among whom were Antonín Švehla, the Agrarian leader, and Václav J. Klofáč, founder and for many years the leader of the National Socialist Party and editor before his arrest of its daily paper, the *Czech Word*. Eduard Beneš signed on in September 1914 on his own initiative, when he joined the editorial staff of the independence organ. Beneš felt impelled to move beyond the passivity of the nationalist group to a more positive attitude. He approached Masaryk, who assured him he had already started working and proposed their collaboration, which became lifelong. Other prominent political leaders joined in the effort, among whom the most important were Karel Kramář, notable leader of the Young Czech Party, which he represented in the Reichsrat, and Alois Rašín, a Prague lawyer with important banking connections.[*]

Masaryk encountered an acquaintance at a political dinner party in Prague on July 4th, Emanuel Victor Voska, a successful Bohemian-American businessman on a visit from his residence in New York. Because of his nationalist pronouncements in the general conversation, Masaryk propositioned Voska warily and promptly recruited him. Voska had been encouraged to learn recently in embassy circles in Budapest that despite every Austrian precaution, Czech soldiers were surrendering in large numbers, thereby showing their disinclination to fight for the empire. He stopped in London on September 2, 1914, at Masaryk's request, to see an old friend of Masaryk's, H. Wickham Steed, foreign editor of the *London Times*, to apprise him of the professor's plan of national liberation. Steed specifically undertook to convey word to the Russians to treat the Czech soldiers as friends, indeed as allies, rather than as enemy Austrians. Steed accomplished this task that very day through the friendly Russian ambassador in London, Count Beckendorff.

Voska organized a service of special couriers among his personal and business contacts in neutral countries and among Czechs returning home to Prague for visits. Voska also undertook the crucial mission of raising substantial sums for the revolutionary effort for the duration among his large acquaintance of wealthy émigrés in America. He and his son later joined the Czechoslovak Legion in Russia, and extended his intelligence service there. His work proved invaluable in the national cause.

Masaryk took advantage of the departure from Prague of his American sister-in-law, Espie, to escort her in the fall of 1914 to her steamer at Rotterdam. He tarried there from the 12th to the 16th of September 1914. From this safe haven, he wrote to his old academic colleague at the Sorbonne, Ernest Denis, an historian of Central Europe, and to his British friends Wickham Steed and Robert William Seton-Watson, an eminent Central European historian at London University, whom he asked to meet with him for an important talk. The latter responded with alacrity and joined Masaryk on his second trip to Rotterdam. Masaryk discoursed on the potentially disruptive

---

[*]Before the war, Kramář and Rašín were arrested and sentenced to death for high treason, but were afterwards amnestied. Kramář was to become the first prime minister in the Czechoslovak Republic and leader of the National Democratic Party.

internal Austrian situation and set forth his perspective for liberating his country. On his return to London, Seton-Watson composed a memorandum on Masaryk's appraisal and plans for action, which he sent, as requested, to the Allied governments in London and Paris. He dispatched it to St. Petersburg by hand with Ambassador Pavel Vinogradoff who handed it personally to the Russian foreign minister.

Masaryk returned to Prague filled with optimism. He called a meeting of his friends in the Progressive (Realist) Party to elicit their interest in his long-range project. Enlisted was an honor roll of prominent intellectuals and political leaders including the entire editorial staff of *Čas*, comprising Adolf Kunta, Sasek, Fisher, and Čvetisa. Josef S. Machar, a poet and author living in Vienna at the outbreak of the war, agreed to write articles for publication in *Čas* and elsewhere and to perform various other unique favors for the group as opportunities arose at his excellent vantage point. Of prime importance was Kramář, who joined despite his disagreement with Masaryk's liberation plan. Kramář thought independence could be achieved only with Czarist Russian support, rather than with the backing of the Western powers, England and France.

Bohumír Šmeral, a decisive personality in the nationalist camp, abstained from participation because he thought the liberation plan fantastic. He told Beneš that in his opinion, Masaryk was leading the nation to another White Mountain. He demanded Entente guarantees and assurances beforehand, and he thought Masaryk and company foolhardy to proceed without them.

At the first meeting, the group decided to band together for action and called their organization the *Maffia*. They decided that a nationalist objective was insufficient to arouse effective opposition to the imperial government; their program had, of necessity, also to include social reforms. These would provide substance for popular motivation. Beneš felt it was "immoral" to support Austria in any way, even by a passive attitude. He thought greater appeal could be generated by posing an ideological struggle against absolutism such as those reigning at Berlin, Vienna, and Budapest. This line may have appeared more idealistic than pragmatic at the time, but Beneš's views helped shape and define the democratic basis of the nascent Czechoslovak Republic. All present were optimistic that success would derive from the social upheaval that would result from the military defeat of Austria-Hungary. This outlook was an ambitious perspective for that time, when some of their members were still drenched in monarchist notions.

Early in December 1914, Masaryk resolved to go abroad to obtain greater freedom of movement for his "seditious" undertaking than was possible at home. The project of creating an independent democratic Czechoslovak republic out of provinces of the Austro-Hungarian Empire would inevitably involve some measure of dismemberment. Such a project would incur heavy penalties at the hand of the Empire if discovered prematurely. On the other hand, economic discontent nurtured political and religious stirrings against repression at home; all converging favorably for the movement. Masaryk determined as his more fruitful personal course a quest for allies abroad, where a number of conflicting forces in war-disrupted Europe would provide fertile ground for his operations. Moreover, his talents, experience, and international contacts fitted him more uniquely for the required diplomatic maneuvering than for political organizing at home, which suited Beneš's talents to a tee.

Prior to his departure, Masaryk convened the *Maffia* members to map their public relations strategy at home, looking toward broadening their contacts and obtaining vital funding. At this initial juncture, these goals indicated the need of constant publication of articles in their house organ, *Čas,* or in other reviews. Maintaining contact was essential; they had to weave an information network between the group in Prague and Masaryk abroad. The discussion was so precise as to include their notions about frontiers for the new nation. Masaryk was explicit in pointing to the necessity of an anti-Austrian campaign abroad, accompanying anti-German propaganda, to forestall any separate peace maneuvers. These would be hinged on coming to terms with the Habsburgs and preserving, perhaps even aggrandizing, Austria.

Events in the Italian provinces and passionate nationalist aspirations among the various South Slavic peoples would contribute significantly to the Empire's disintegration, hence were desirable and to be nourished. It would moreover gratify the aging Masaryk, who at age 64 empathized so deeply with his brother Slavs that he even contemplated volunteering for active military duty—manifestly a romantic notion for his advanced years. Practically, he chose to bend his efforts toward working for unity among these patently hostile forces in opposing imperial rule. He pinned high hopes for his cause on the disruptive nationalisms among the Empire's Slavic peoples.

Just before Christmas, on December 18, 1914, Masaryk slipped over the border into neutral Italy on a mere parliamentary document. His first move in Rome was to request a valid passport from the Royal Serbian Legation, where he felt assured of a friendly reception due to his help during the 1908 Bosnian annexation crisis and the subsequent Agram treason trial. His estimate proved accurate.

His success was fully appreciated by the Austrian ambassador in Rome, Baron Macchio, who reported censoriously to Vienna in detail on Masaryk's movements. Especially interesting at the imperial court were Masaryk's "seditious" activities with Supilo and Ante Trumbič, both members of the imperial parliament and prominent in their native independence movements. News of Macchio's confidential reports to Vienna was transmitted to Beneš in Prague by Machar and his friend Kovanda, both *Maffia* members working within the government bureaucracy in Vienna.

After the New Year inaugurating 1915, Masaryk transferred his locus from Rome to Geneva. In and out of neutral Switzerland, various intelligence networks functioned almost openly, providing unrivalled sources of war information. A student named Lavička acted as courier for Masaryk. On January 10, 1915, Lavička returned to Prague with messages, the most pertinent being an inquiry from Masaryk whether he could safely risk border crossings into Prague. Beneš, armed with the intelligence report of Machar in Vienna, vetoed the idea. Instead, he volunteered himself for the reverse trip to Switzerland in February during the university semester break, to devise further plans with Masaryk. He took care to ferret out an old school chum at the Vinohrady police headquarters to obtain his passport.

They met at the Hotel Victoria in Zürich early in the year. Masaryk was accompanied by Vsevolod Svatkovsky, a Russian journalist, who afterwards rendered numerous services to the Czech cause in government circles at Petrograd and in diplomatic Russian groups in Western Europe. Prior to the war, Svatkovsky had spent some years as a journalist in Vienna, where he had imbibed the intricacies of imperial politics and adopted a favorable attitude toward Czechoslovak independence. At once, he was willing to place at their disposal his network of journalistic and diplomatic contacts. Upon arrival, Masaryk informed Beneš that he had begun to organize the first modern group of Czech political émigrés, who would work in concert with the politicians at home for overt actions against Vienna.

They decided it was premature to contact the Allied governments, who took little interest in their cause at this point; they must work hard to merit such attention. Beneš was to carry home news of their international contacts to encourage the *Maffia* members, and he was also to relay credible war bulletins, amplifying the heavily censored ones at home. Beneš was entrusted to establish a secret printing press, for which he would recruit double personnel in case any of the first echelon were apprehended. He was further charged with the responsibility to maintain the connections between Prague and abroad and to coordinate all activities at home. He would collect materials and dispatch these abroad by couriers. Whenever necessary, he would undertake similar journeys himself again.

Beneš returned with his international news and a large number of military and political books, which he secreted successfully in the train's lavatory among the railway employees' belongings, through two inspections between Zürich and Vienna. His problem was magnified by the confiscation of his passport at the Austrian consulate at Zürich, in exchange for which he had been given one that was valid one way only, for the return to Prague. Safely at home, he resorted to a variety of stratagems to evade the censors in carrying on his tasks. He often hid his special reports destined for abroad within book bindings, and he would secrete similar messages between two postcards pasted together. Occasionally, whenever possible, relevant items were published openly. Chiefly, he relied on trusted messengers.

Soon he had to give Masaryk the sad news of a police sweep of Prague in May 1915, which had been occasioned by the stepped-up *Maffia* activity. The German spring offensive was clearing the Russians out of Poland, permitting the Austro-Hungarian advance into the Ukraine. Although this military success was offset for the imperial power by Italy's entry into the war with the Western Entente, Viennese police had moved in to smash the resistance ring in Prague, beginning with the most prominent pro-German conservatives, who were already under severe restrictions. The most distinguished leader, Kramář, and his chief aide, Rašín, were arrested, joining the Czech socialist leader and Reichsrat member, Klofáč, who was already similarly charged with treason. Rašín's imprisonment hit the *Maffia's* purse severely, as he was their principal fund raiser at home. The police surveillance penetrated Beneš's cautious movements, but he proceeded undeterred. For communications abroad, they had established coded names and a large number of addresses in Switzerland. Beneš exercised vigilance in coordinating with other *Maffia* members in Prague by resorting to frequent walks in the park with one or two, or laboriously calling on them individually at home. The burden on his energies was stressful, and his evasions were only partially successful.

Masaryk was considerably saddened by the news of the arrests in Prague of his dear colleagues, some of whom he prized also as friends. On December 27, 1914, already in a dejected mood, he communicated to Voska on a personal note: "In Moravia two men were executed for keeping and distributing the Russian Manifesto. In Prague, our editor Kusek . . . was arrested; it is not permitted to publish it . . . The first case that an editor was imprisoned by military authorities, who now have the upper hand over the civilians." [1]

Masaryk then had to absorb the blow of the news that his daughter, Alice, and Beneš's wife, Hana, had been caught in the police dragnet and imprisoned. Charlotte Masaryk, his wife, strangely, eluded apprehension. She shared her husband's concerns and his grief at the death of their eldest son, Herbert, a painter, who had been stricken with typhus while working with a medical team among Galician refugees from the Eastern front. The negative organizational fallout from these losses was the eradication of two precise sources of information that had simultaneously dried up: that of Herbert reporting regularly from the front lines, and those emanating from the women's groups, which Alice and Hana had organized for social and hospital work.

Along with Charlotte, there remained at liberty her favorite son, Jan, who was now fighting on the eastern front with his Hungarian Hussar regiment. He had by chance returned from the United States in 1913, in time to attend the celebrations of the 500th anniversary of the Jan Hus martyrdom. To escape the danger posed by the name of Masaryk if he served in an Austrian regiment, he had enlisted in the Hungarian army, which had, among other advantages, a quite relaxed discipline. Exploiting this fortunate circumstance, he was able to obtain home leave almost every month, and to carry back to his mother food and other supplies from the regimental commissary. These more or less regular expeditions replenished the dwindling supplies of Charlotte and her group and literally sustained them in good health to survive the winter's rigors.

In Geneva, Tomáš Masaryk also marked the 500th anniversary of Hus's execution at the stake for defying the Council of Constance. Dismissing as premature a public announcement of his liberation campaign at the rally held in the Reformation Hall, Masaryk confined himself to noting that the Hussite Reformation had signaled the birthright of the Czech nation. Another speech on this occasion was delivered by Professor Denis, who provided inestimable assistance to Masaryk's and Beneš's work within the intellectual community in Paris.

Early summertime saw Masaryk in Paris and London on a scouting mission for the best location for his permanent committee abroad, after realizing that it had become too dangerous for Beneš to risk another border crossing with intelligence reports. The framework of the future Czechoslovak National Council was established in Paris where Beneš was now stationed and could count on help from the Slovak intellectual Milan Rastislav Štefánik and his journalistic and academic contacts, among whom was Beneš's former Sorbonne professor Louis Eisenmann.

Denis, Masaryk's old acquaintance, was a Rock of Gibraltar for trustworthiness, discretion, and work. He now undertook to edit a new Czech political journal, *La Nation Tcheque,* that supplemented its counterpart in London, *New Europe*, launched by Masaryk and his cohorts and edited by Seton-Watson. These journals carried articles of high literary or historic merit and included at least one political-military piece on the war situation. Decisions on contents were made at regular conferences, in which the entire staff participated until arriving at a consensus. Current news, based on direct intelligence reports from Central Europe, was fed to Czech and Slovak newspapers and magazines throughout the world, while international political and military news was siphoned to the widely read *Čas* in Prague. Truly secret and significant intelligence items were privately shared with 10 Downing Street in London and the Quai d'Orsay in Paris.

Masaryk and Beneš themselves undertook full schedules of public lectures and press interviews. By late September 1915, Masaryk had positioned himself at headquarters in London, which he deemed the political capital of the war, from where he could simultaneously follow military developments. London proved an excellent base where he could work with his well-placed university friends for the next 20 months, until the first Russian Revolution toppled czarism and radically changed all war calculations.

The fall term at King's College of London University opened with Professor Masaryk filling a new chair of Slavonic studies that had been arranged by Seton-Watson. His inaugural lecture on October 19, 1915, was sponsored by Prime Minister Herbert Asquith and was attended by intellectuals and journalists of high standing and some government officials as well. The introductory session outlined Masaryk's views on the role of small nations in European history, fixing upon their rights and their culture as the roots of their potential democratic contribution to building a new Europe.

Although deprived of Asquith's presence at the last moment by a sudden illness, Masaryk was nevertheless honored by the attendance of a prestigious audience. In the chair presiding was Under-Secretary of State Sir Robert Cecil, who later worked closely with Beneš at the League of Nations in Geneva. The renowned Greek scholar Gilbert Murray, who was to receive him officially later at Oxford, was present along with the Slavicist Sir Robert Young. Of course, both Seton-Watson himself and Steed came, having already performed handsomely behind the scenes as the principal organizers of the occasion. Steed's help was assisted by the activities of his inimitable companion from his Vienna days, Rose, who presided in Steed's home, Landsdowne House, London's smartest political salon. In fact, whenever Steed published an especially brilliant lead article in *The Times*, the wags declared it had been written *sub rosa*.

The founding meeting of the Czechoslovak National Committee, later the National Council, took place in Paris only one month later. The event was enhanced by the arrival from Prague of Josef Dürich, Agrarian leader in the Reichsrat and representative of the conservative Kramář group, which was now semiparalyzed by the imprisonment of its leaders. When Dürich accepted the vice-presidency under Masaryk, the union of the foreign and domestic branches of the national movement was formalized, bridging the political spectrum from socialists, social democrats, and liberal democrats to monarchists. They could all agree with the concluding proclamation, declaring clearly for total independence. The form of the state was left undefined for the sake of unity, in the face of overwhelming monarchist sentiment at home in Czechoslovakia.

Masaryk was soon brought over from London to add his prestige with top government officials, through doors opened by Štefánik at the Quai d'Orsay and the War Ministry. Accompanied by Beneš in February 1916, Masaryk penetrated barriers for a brief interview with Foreign Affairs Minister Aristide Briand, from which he emerged triumphantly with a communique declaring the support of the French government for the Czechoslovak National Council. From this oblique recognition rippled a domino effect, creating new access in British government circles as well.

Europe was approaching its third winter of bleak stalemate. Ninety year-old Emperor Franz Josef, who had mounted the Habsburg throne in 1849 after crushing the revolution, died in Vienna on November 16, 1915. Archduke Carl, his successor, promptly decreed a general amnesty, under which the Prague *Maffia* prisoners were freed. Alice Masaryk and Hana Beneš emerged first, followed by Kramář, Rašín, and Klofáč, who gained a measure of restricted freedom. Perhaps because of international intercession, the treason charges against them were not pressed.

Renewed Austrian peace feelers naturally gave Masaryk his greatest concern about the danger of perpetuating the Habsburg Monarchy. The military deadlock produced widespread demoralization, and the inevitable fissures in the national resistance evoked numerous secret offers and counter-proposals. The National Council in Paris focused on demonstrating as illusory the hope that Austria could be effectively detached from her German ally. Actual facts lent credence to the hypothesis. Germany's civilian government was effectively in control of overall policy and in a strong enough military position to make offers of settlement in return for lifting the British blockade. If this halt were to find acceptance in London and Paris, the Habsburg monarchy could be salvaged.

NOTES

1.   Letter of Tomáš G. Masaryk to E. V. Voska, Dec. 27, 1914, John O. Crane (henceforth JOC) private file.

2

Founding of the Legions: Entrapment in Anti- Bolshevik Intervention

Tomáš Masaryk joined with numerous other close observers of the Russian Bolshevik Revolution to detect in its early stages a break from centuries of czarist tyranny and a modicum of hope for a democratic evolution. A measure of optimism was also generated favoring the Czechoslovak drive for national independence.

Masaryk realized that he, as president of the Czechoslovak National Council, had personally to complete and formalize the negotiations initiated by Col. Milan Rastislav Štefánik to organize a Czechoslovak army out of the Druzinas, as the local groups formed in 1914 were called. Intuitively, he knew that a pillar of his liberation movement would rise from an independent national fighting force, which could be recruited from the tens of thousands of Czech and Slovak prisoners of war now being released from detention in Russia.

Immediately after the March Revolution, Štefánik hastened to Russia to resume his high level talks to gain recognition for the Druzinas as an Allied fighting force. Masaryk's arrival in Petrograd on May 16, 1917, coincided with the concluding plenary meeting of all Druzinas, which voted to accept the authority and program of the National Council. The consolidation of Masaryk's leadership abroad, paralleling the developing liberation movement at home, provided an early building block in the movement for independence from Vienna.

In the formation of the Czechoslovak Legions, Masaryk stumbled upon another subtle justification for his anti-Austrian program. He saw in the nationalist military units the fallout benefits of offering greater personal safety and better treatment for his sick or injured countrymen. Had they gone home, he reasoned, they would have been conscripted into the Austrian Army, where they would have fared worse while swelling the forces of the Central Powers fighting the Allies.

Masaryk spent his first fortnight in Russia completing the military arrangements for the Czechoslovak units. Having concluded a pact a year earlier in Paris, providing for the transfer of these forces to the French front, his mission now was to procure permission and transport facilities for their exit from Russia via Vladivostok. In Petrograd, he had the help of Robert Bruce Lockhart and of Albert Thomas, a leading French socialist sent to Russia to reinforce the request on behalf of the French government. The Czechoslovak National Council leaders backed this plan for the speediest transport of the Legions to France. Masaryk succeeded in his initial efforts on June 13, 1917, when he signed an agreement with the French military mission providing, as a first installment, that 30,000 prisoners should be sent to France, including some thousands of Southern Slavs. This treaty was the first official one concluded by the National Council with a state body. In it, he promised that some of these prisoners would work in French factories, thereby releasing French workers for the fighting front. A month earlier, on May 14, 1917, the Russian foreign ministry and General Staff had pledged to get the convoy out as quickly as possible by way of Archangel. But in consequence of delays, the first contingent started six months later, in November 1917, and its numbers were much smaller than anticipated.

The first Czechoslovak corps was granted independent status on October 9, 1917, by the Russian chief of staff, Gen. Alexieff Dukhonin, in recognition of its spectacular fighting prowess, manifested in the assault on Zboroff Heights in the Carpathian foothills on July 3, 1917. This victory had enabled the Alexander Kerensky regime to survive the pro-czarist coup organized by Gen. Lavr Kornilov the following month. General Dukhonin stipulated that this force "should only take action against the foreign enemy," confirming Masaryk's principle of neutrality in Russian internal affairs. Unfortunately all around, the Czechoslovak Legions were caught in the maelstrom of the revolutionary tide.

On February 10, 1918, Masaryk negotiated with Mikhail Muravieff, chief of staff of the Red Army, in his railway saloon car in the presence of Allied representatives. On February 7th Masaryk had signed a treaty with the Council of the Ukraine, which was now abruptly replaced by Red Army forces. On the 16th, Muravieff confirmed the agreement in writing, guaranteeing that the Czechoslovak Legions might leave from Kiev, where they were concentrated, to France by way of Siberia. This arrangement was subsequently endorsed by the central Soviet authorities on March 26th. Masaryk acknowledged that it was a fantastic plan but that there was not much choice; the troops could not remain in Russia, and France was their "magnetic pole." The accord was approved by the British Foreign Office, which authorized the payment of £36,000 to Procop Maxa, representing the Czechoslovak National Council, "to assist it financially in dispatching the Czechoslovak Army from Russia to the French Front".[1]

The 40,000 Czechoslovaks in the Kiev areas, 5,000 of whom were Slovaks, met in free assembly formally to found the Legion and to transfer the supreme command from Russian into French hands. There was open debate, in which Bolshevik representatives participated. Masaryk, as President of the Czechoslovak National Council, authorized Gen. Maurice Janin to become commander-in-chief of the Czechoslovak armies in all countries, some units of which were already fighting on the French and Italian fronts. The Russian general, Mikhail Konstantinovich Dieterichs, who had been General Dukhonin's chief of staff, was appointed by Masaryk as commander of the First Corps. The soldiers, save for 218 dissenters, ratified the nonintervention agreement. The left-wing dissenters defected a fortnight later and formed the Soviet of Czechoslovak Soldiers in Russia.

Right off, the evacuation from Kiev to the marshalling points of Kursk and Penza was blocked by German forces at the railway hub of Bachmach, forcing the Czechoslovaks to fight their way out of encirclement. Their escape from the Ukraine was managed by engaging superior German forces in a four-day battle, losing "about 600 men," in contrast with the enemy's 2,000 dead whom they buried "in one day."[2] This military engagement confirmed the already high reputation of the Legion's fighting capacity that had been established at Zboroff Heights.

Another difficulty, of a diplomatic nature, hampered the withdrawal. The French military mission and the British general, Frederick C. Poole, commanding Britain's North Russian expedition, met "with great difficulty in securing permission to leave Russia for the Czechs," according to the British counsellor of embassy, Francis Oswald Lindley, in Moscow. This contingent was heading to embark on the S.S. *Port Arthur* at Murmansk. Lindley proposed to London that the "most practical way out of the difficulty" was to threaten the local authorities with refusing to disembark the Russians they were bringing home "unless [Czechoslovak] units are allowed to embark."[3] The trade-off worked, and the Czechoslovaks were permitted to depart via the northern port. These few hundred troops were lucky enough to arrive in France and Italy in time to join the anti-German action at the front.

The Czechoslovak troops were trapped in the complicated fluctuating Russian situation of revolution and counterrevolution. The Soviet Russian government had confronted a huge dilemma upon taking power with the slogan of "peace, bread, and land." The Russian Army, which U.S. Ambassador David R. Francis had estimated to have conscripted 16 million men, was melting away. Francis calculated that "2,000,000 had been captured and 2,000,000 had been killed or died from disease," leaving some 12 million men in the field at the time of the armistice. [4] Francis explained that the Russian Army had been threatening to cease fighting and had opened "debating societies, not only at every front, but [in] every division and brigade, and even in every regiment." [5]

The peasant army disintegrated into a disorderly long march home in search of bread and land. It took to looting the great estates on the way. V. I. Lenin's peace proclamation of November 1917, based on "no annexations and no indemnities," was countered by "outrageously onerous" terms by the Germans, amounting to approximately one-sixth of the Russian lands and material resources. [6]

Secretly, Lenin counted on fraternal revolutionary support, especially within Germany. On Sunday, March 3, 1918, the Bolsheviks signed the Brest-Litovsk Treaty, which was scheduled for ratification within a fortnight. The All Union Congress of the Soviets was set to convene on March 12th but was inexplicably postponed to the 14th.

Berlin's strategic imperative was to transfer the bulk of its 100 Eastern divisions [7] to the Western front for its planned spring offensive against the British and French armies.

From the outset, the fate of the Czechoslovak Legions hinged on the decisions of the Big Powers. Although the French assigned top priority to the gridlocked Western front, in which decision they were joined by Great Britain, Germany, and the United States, in late March Gen. Ferdinand Foch still submitted a plan to stop Bolshevism by force. President Wilson's contrary response was succinct. He wrote, "In my opinion, trying to stop a revolutionary movement by troops in the field is like using a broom to hold back a great ocean." [8] Japan was poised on the brink of Siberia's borders, ready to plunge across, but was obliged to await a go-ahead from Washington because of the well-attested anti-Japanese feelings of the Siberian population.

The British were pressing the Bolsheviks unremittingly to reconstitute the Eastern front, not only to relieve the added burdens soon to fall on their embattled forces in the West, but also to retrieve the vast hoard of military stores deposited at Vladivostok and at the northern ports of Archangel and Murmansk. At the least, these were the reasons given by the Foreign Office as a cover for its undeviating determination to intervene. [9] The chief spokesman for the British at Petrograd and later at Moscow was their unofficial representative, Bruce Lockhart, who had learned fluent Russian during a previous tour of duty, when he had fallen in love with a beautiful Russian aristocrat and also worked his way into close and trusting terms with both Lenin and Léon Trotsky. His relationship with them was abruptly severed when the British landed several hundred troops at Murmansk, in contradiction to his promises to the Soviet leaders that no intervention was intended or planned. He was clapped into a dungeon for a month due to their construal of his information, which proved misleading on its face. He was eventually liberated by friendly intercession, and the misunderstanding was cleared away. [10] He later returned as unofficial British representative at Petrograd and retrieved his former position of confidence with the Soviet leaders. He employed his connections to smooth Masaryk's mission, and he never wavered subsequently in his friendship and fidelity to the Czechoslovak leaders and their new democratic republic.

From the very outset, the Czechoslovak Legions ran into clashing rivalries among the Great Powers, with significant negative consequences for the small, nascent democratic state in Central Europe. The British government reacted swiftly to the November Revolution. On December 14, 1917, a short month following the November 7th overturn, the War Cabinet decided secretly to pay any anti-Bolshevik Russians such money as they required for "the purpose of maintaining alive in South Eastern Russia the resistance to the Central Powers." [11] During the interval of the peace negotiations, the Germans attacked and then hardened their terms. Several sympathetic Allied observers at Petrograd lent their prestige and efforts to help the beleaguered Soviet leaders. The dean of the group, Col. Raymond Robins, chief of the American Red Cross mission, was joined in this mission by Wall Street banker William Boyce Thompson, a recent convert to opposing intervention. The two Americans had the support of Jerome Davis, representing the YMCA, and Unitarian minister Albert Rhys Williams. These Americans were seconded by the socialist lawyer Capt. Jacques Sadoul of the French military mission, and by Albert Thomas, all joining with Bruce Lockhart in seeing the

Soviets as the sole force capable of organizing a government in the midst of the wartime chaos. They encouraged Lenin to delay signing and then ratifying the separate German peace treaty on the disadvantageous terms offered. Lenin and Trotsky heeded their advice and stalled for time. The Russian correspondent of the *Manchester Guardian* reported in August 1918: "The Soviet Government not only showed no desire of bringing the negotiations to a speedy conclusion, but they did everything possible to drag on indefinitely." [12] These astute Russophiles wanted time to make a stab at changing their governments' positions. On March 15th, War Commissar Trotsky handed a note from the Soviet government to roundly trusted Colonel Robins for transmission to his government. It was carried home by his colleague, Thompson. [13] In it, the Soviet government queried the possibility of serious U.S. aid along with recognition of the Soviet regime. Lenin asked: If the All-Russian Congress of Soviets should reject ratification of the separate peace treaty, and if consequently, the Germans renewed their military offensive, what real assistance could the Soviets anticipate from the Allied Powers, specifically by way of military and transportation supplies, food, and so on?

While U.S. consul Gen. DeWitt C. Poole, who was notably hostile to the Bolsheviks, stood aside, Thompson took off on November 28th for London, where he sought out his old well-connected friend, Thomas Lamont, a J.P. Morgan Bank partner, for assistance. Lamont willingly complied and "took him the rounds of British officialdom in London." [14] They were courteously received at "a long breakfast" at 10 Downing Street by Prime Minister David Lloyd George, on whom they pressed the case for recognition in exchange for reconstituting the eastern front against the Germans. Lloyd George said he was "strongly in favor of attempting more active contact and cooperation with the new Soviet Government." He would go along if Wilson agreed to send a "joint Anglo-American Mission" to explore "aid to Russia in keeping her in the war . . . [and] to arouse the war-weary Russians to the German menace." Lamont agreed to accompany Thompson home to the United States to lend his considerable weight with the President. By the time the pair had overcome innumerable delays to arrive in Washington late in December, President Woodrow Wilson had been swayed to delay any overt declaration, and adamantly refused to see them.

Wilson had had a plethora of advice on the subject. Besides his secretary of war, Newton D. Baker, he listened chiefly to expert Kremlin watcher and friend Charles R. Crane, who advocated "hands off!." He soon had confirmation for this stand from Masaryk, who "doubted the value of military intervention" from the outset and also advocated massive civilian aid. [15] On May 7, 1918, Richard Crane, son of Charles R., serving then as secretary to Robert Lansing, transmitted Masaryk's enclosure to the President, which stated: "I cannot see that military intervention would be of any use to European Russia, even if Siberia could be saved." [16]

Beneš in Paris shared Masaryk's estimate of intervention, despite the divergence from the stand of his trusted military adviser, Štefánik, and of several British and French officials whom he was courting.

Before submitting the Brest-Litovsk Treaty for a ratification vote by the All-Union Congress of Soviets on March 15th, Lenin inquired of Rhys Williams and Bruce Lockhart whether they had received any news of change from their governments. Both shook their heads sadly in the negative, and Lenin made a forceful speech in favor of ratification. The vote, which occurred after midnight, making the ratification date March 16th, gave a large preponderance, 784 votes, in favor, against 261 opposed, with 115 abstentions. [17]

On March 16th, coincidentally with the ratification vote on the separate peace on the Eastern front, Lord Curzon, Earl of Kedleston, Lord President of the Privy Council, submitted a report in secrecy, titled *The Russian Situation*, to the Foreign Office for its serious consideration. Curzon emphasized the contradictory public policies of the British government. On the one hand, he said, it was encouraging, through Bruce Lockhart in Moscow, "the creation of a new Russian revolutionary army [which would obtain] Allied assistance" and promising "No Allied or Japanese intervention at Vladivostok" and "No Allied or British intervention at Murmansk or Archangel." Meanwhile, "we have Gen. Poole advising the occupation of Murmansk and Archangel . . . [and moving] in the direction of Japanese intervention in Siberia." Curzon asked pointedly, "Ought we not to decide between the two policies?" [18]

It is no wonder that confusion on the subject reigned at Whitehall, at the Quai d'Orsay, and in Washington. The British ambassador to the United States, Lord Reading, wrote to the Foreign Office requesting clarification. He received a reply two months later, on May 18th, not from his chief, Sir Arthur James Balfour at the Foreign Office, but from the War Office, in a curt message dated March 16th and marked "Secret Operation" which said: *"The Supreme War Council had made a declaration in favor of intervention in Siberia on 15th March*, when the views of the Permanent Military Representatives set forth in Joint Note 16 were noted and it was agreed that a joint telegraphic dispatch should be sent to President Wilson, advocating

Japanese intervention in Siberia." [19] The War Office respondent was "not clear whether the Supreme War Council dispatched any such Joint Note to Lord Reading" and now conveyed the substance of this declaration of the Supreme War Council to Lord Rufus Reading. [20]

Despite endless talk and negotiations in Moscow and elsewhere, the British War Cabinet met again in another secret session on April 20, 1918, and fortified its interventionist decision of March 15th, without prior consultation with Masaryk, Beneš, or any other leader of the Czechoslovak National Council, unilaterally nullifying their accord with the Bolshevik leaders for the dispatch of the Czechoslovak Legions via Vladivostok to the western (French) front. It declared to Bruce Lockhart:

The War Cabinet have had under consideration the question of utilizing to the best advantage the Czechoslovak Corps, which is probably the only force in Russia ready to fight against Germany. It is considered that Corps can be *most usefully employed in opposing German aggression and intrigues at Archangel and Murmansk and along the railways leading to those ports.* Thus employed, the Corps would *serve to protect Russian as well as Allied units and you should endeavor to obtain Trotsky's authorization for making necessary arrangements in conjunction.* [21]

Bruce Lockhart complied with the directive to take immediate steps about the change in conjunction with the French Mission. [22] Trotsky wanted the Czechoslovak corps out of the country at the soonest and posed no objection to their evacuation via the northern ports if evacuation were indeed the purpose of the switch. But the British War Office, which now wanted the Czechoslovaks "for fighting against German aggression within Russia," failed at this early stage to consult with the Czechoslovak leaders about the change of destination from Vladivostok. This brusque alteration of plan was not, however, the only thing that went wrong concerning the evacuation of the Czechoslovak Legions.

The British government's secret decision threw into a cocked hat the arrangements made by Masaryk, with the approval of the National Council, for the neutrality and withdrawal of the Legions via Vladivostok for transportation to France. Despite his own personal antipathy to communism, Masaryk's intentions toward the Russian Revolution were unequivocal: the Russian civil war was not his concern or that of his national forces. He desired to have them withdraw from Russia via Vladivostok and to be transported to the western front. For this, they required assistance by way of trains from the Soviet government. Having made such arrangements with Soviet Commander-in-Chief Muravieff, he was ready to move on to his next challenge, in the United States. He saw no possibility, moreover, of occupying and holding the immense territory of Eastern Russia with only 50,000 men. On taking leave of Russia, Masaryk cautioned his Legions to maintain, as hitherto, strict neutrality in the Russian conflict, although he did not forbid vigorous self-defense if attacked.

An arrangement was reached at Penza providing the prototype of disengagement which allowed the dispatch eastward in 100 railway cars of some 10,000 men, comprising the First Corps, commanded by Dieterichs. At each station along the 4,500-mile trip, the Czechoslovaks encountered a mixture of frenzied welcome from most of their fellow Slavs, combined with some sullen suspicion of them as class enemies. Overcoming numerous obstacles and harassments, the First Corps began pulling into Vladivostok during the last days of April 1918. They camped on the heights overlooking the city, where they were cheered to spot a few small Allied warships riding at anchor in the port below.

They quickly established working relations with the local Soviet authorities, having no intention of interfering with Russia's internal affairs. Indeed, they refused to obey the advice and appeals of the various anti-Bolshevik elements, which comprised both White Russians and Allied officials. [23]

The Legions were welcomed and provisioned by the Allied missions as provided in the agreements with Masaryk. During the four weeks of quiet waiting outside the city, however, they detected not one single sign of the promised Allied transports to convey them to France. What had not been communicated to the corps or to its commanders in the field was news of the searching review in London of the terms initialled in these accords.

The first overt sign of the revised British policy showed up on April 29th, only a week following the April 20th British War Council meeting, when the Supreme Allied War Council adopted Joint Resolution No. 25 at Versailles, containing three clauses revising the terms agreed to by the British and French governments with Masaryk. At this time, "the Military Representatives" agreed "that the Czech troops should be *transported as expeditiously as possible and those who are already east of Omsk should be used in Siberia* in cooperation with the Allies as was recommended in Joint Note 20." The Allied War Council then divided the Czech forces gathered at Omsk and directed that "those who have not proceeded east of Omsk by the Trans-Siberian railway should be sent to Archangel and Murmansk, it being possible to transport them in the quickest manner from these ports." While awaiting embarkation, *"they could be well employed in defending the same and guarding the Murman railway."* [24] Gen. Lavergne observed that it was "almost impossible to find provisions in the city itself" and suggested that foodstuffs "on the two ships already at Archangel . . . shall be allocated to the Czechs." [25]

A few days later, on May 1 and 2, 1918, a meeting of the Supreme Allied War Council was held in the Chambre des Notaires at Abbéville, France, which considered the "transportation of Czech troops from Russia." The terms of dividing the Czech forces at Omsk were ratified, adding the proviso that the British should take charge of transporting the troops while the French undertake their provisioning. The British, with Bruce Lockhart in mind, further volunteered to secure Trotsky's approval of the change "to transport the remaining troops to the northern ports." [26]

Gen. Jan C. Smuts filed a report on May 11, 1918 about a secret meeting of the Supreme Allied War Council (409A) at which a committee was appointed comprising himself, Lord Milner, and the First Sea Lord "to consider the . . . steps which *could immediately be taken to organize military resistance to the enemy in Russia."* The committee met that very afternoon of May 11th and took cognizance of advice from the shipping controller that "any transport of Czechoslovak troops would simply divert tonnage from the equivalent number of American troops." They came to the conclusion that "the Czechoslovak troops now at Vladivostok or on their way should be taken in charge of there and *be organized into efficient units by the French Government . . . and pending their eventual transport to France, they might be used to stiffen the Japanese as part of an Allied force of intervention in Russia."* [27]

As for the remaining Czechoslovak forces in Russia, the committee recommended: "They should be collected at Murmansk and Archangel preferably the latter, and organized by the British Government and *pending their transport across the sea, they should be used to hold these places and to take part in any Allied intervention in Russia."* [28] The secretary of state for war undertook to inform French Premier Georges Clemenceau of this proposed shift of British policy, which was announced in response to an anxious inquiry by Clemenceau about "the transport of the Czechoslovaks from Vladivostok in execution of the [Allied] Supreme War Council resolution on the subject." [29]

The British War Council affirmed the order given the previous day, May 10th, by the War Office that Gen. Poole should proceed as soon as possible to Russia *"as our representative* in order to take charge of military affairs so far as the British Government was concerned." Poole was directed as follows: *"Your immediate duty in this respect is the organization and operations of the Czech and other contingents en route to Archangel for the defence of the northern ports."* [30]

Poole was also ordered to report directly and only to the War Office. He was told further to consider, "while holding and safeguarding the positions at Murmansk and Archangel . . . and organizing the Czechoslovaks and other forces of intervention, . . . how far he could work up from Archangel towards Vologda with the forces at his disposal." [31]

The General Staff was to be asked to ascertain "whether anything effective could be done in Siberia . . . using as a nucleus the Czechoslovak force, reinforced perhaps by other forces." The War Council dispatched Lord Robert Cecil to see Beneš in Paris to "ascertain definitely *whether the Czechoslovaks were willing to be used for the purpose."* [32] Belatedly, they realized the need to consult the Czech leader!

Without awaiting Beneš's response, the War Office on May 15th was charged by Balfour to inform all its British Military Representatives in Russia that "in view of the latest decision of the War Cabinet . . . these [Czechoslovak] troops should remain for the present at Vladivostok, where they will be organized by the French into *efficient units for possible use in connection with Allied intervention in the East."* It postponed for the while any approach to the Japanese government on the subject. [33]

During all of these meetings, Bruce Lockhart was requested to do his best to persuade the Soviet authorities to join the Allied plans to reconstitute the eastern front against the Germans. Both Lenin and Trotsky were sorely tempted, despite the withholding of Allied recognition and military assistance. In mid-May, however, Bruce Lockhart detected a sudden sharp alteration of the war situation affecting these proposals. The Germans at this time announced precipitately that "their military operations in Russia are completed and that they have no intention of occupying Petrograd or Moscow, and that they are anxious to cooperate economically with the present Russian government." [34] Bruce Lockhart's explanation was reasonable. The Germans were encountering great difficulty in the Ukraine, from which they had anticipated huge quantities of grain to feed their armies, and their armies were stalled on the Western front, compelling them to retain their fullest complement of soldiers there. The economic chaos in Russia required "far larger forces than they were able or willing to spare [to] reorganize the country." Bruce Lockhart concluded that "as long as the Bolsheviks feel themselves safe from the Germans, they will never accept Allied intervention." And, he added, "There is no party in the country strong enough to turn Lenin out," despite ubiquitous hunger, chaos, discontent, and numerous White Russian military operations led by generals Petr Wrangel, Anton Deniken, Alexander Kolchak, and the wily Cossack leader, Grigorii Semenoff.

The British War Cabinet meeting on May 17th reviewed at length "the *question of using Czechoslovak troops now at Vladivostok as a nucleus of a force on which to base Allied intervention.*" Lord Alfred Milner, undersecretary of state, explained that "*Gen. Poole was leaving that day with a Military Mission for Archangel and Murmansk, with a view to organizing such Czechoslovak forces as might be sent to North Russia,* as well as any others that might volunteer for the defense of that district." [35]

Balfour observed that "the Japanese would not consent to an enterprise in Siberia being undertaken without their taking a leading part . . . and once the Japanese joined the Expedition, [he] did not think American cooperation would be long withheld." [36]

Lord Milner declared that *"the French were very keen that the Czechoslovak forces should be transported to France and he had a long telegram from M. Clemenceau on the subject that morning."* He continued: "All our information tended to show that the *Czechoslovaks themselves were unwilling to be involved in the internal strife in Russia. Their desire was to fight Germans, not Bolsheviks."* [37] Former Prime Minister Bonar Law revealed at the meeting the duplicitous British tactic, saying, "We had told the French that we could not get sufficient ships at the moment for this purpose . . . [and] *it would be better to use these troops in an Allied Expedition into Siberia."* [38]

It was noted that the remainder of Czechoslovak forces "had not yet arrived at Vladivostok—approximately 50,000 out of a total of 70,000 might go to Archangel." Cecil "thought that once we had taken definite *steps in regard to intervention in Siberia, the rest of the Allies would soon conform.*" Milner argued that *"as the Czechoslovak force was entirely the creation of the French, it was imperative that we should obtain their cooperation before employing such force [otherwise]."* In any case, however, he would "prefer to have *10,000 Americans in Siberia than in France,* if such an exchange could be made for the sake of intervention." [39]

Beneš, secretary of the Czechoslovak National Council, was informed in Paris on May 18th by Cecil of the policy reversal, creating a dilemma for Beneš, whose job it was to court Big Power support for his national aspirations. He could ill afford to thwart them at any stage. He greeted the news coldly, fortified by top-level French government assurances of their assigning the highest priority to obtaining the Czechoslovak forces to relieve their desperate manpower shortage in their stalled Western trenches. French Foreign Minister Stephen J. M. Pichon later reported to the British at a special meeting on the subject of leaving the Czechoslovaks in Siberia that "he had had a conversation with M. Beneš, who had made it clear that in all his reports, the Czechoslovaks did not wish to be mixed up on Russian affairs or to remain in Siberia."

Beneš later admitted that he had told Cecil that "if appealed to as Allies, and *recognized as an independent force,* they would be prepared, as a great sacrifice, to remain." In further conversations with Pichon, Beneš said he had made it "quite clear that the Czechoslovak Council did not wish to leave their forces in Siberia," and he added that Štefánik and Masaryk "were in full agreement . . . on this point." Pichon himself agreed with the Czechoslovak leaders that their forces "could not intervene effectually in Siberia."[40] Pichon said that although he personally had become a strong advocate of intervention, "the French government were absolutely certain that intervention by the Czechoslovak division would effect nothing."[41]

Beneš responded to Lord Cecil with utmost diplomatic tact. Without modifying his preference for non-intervention, he replied that the Czechoslovak forces were disciplined and would do as directed by the leaders of the National Council. If the Allies insisted on using the Czechoslovak forces in Russia, however, he set two conditions for compliance. "(1) Some sort of declaration should be made by the Allies asking the Czechoslovaks to assist the Allied cause in Russia as Allies . . . (2) Care should be taken to recognize that any Czechoslovak detachment to Russia was part of the Bohemian National Army." In other words, the legions would then be fighting for their own national aspirations. Beneš then insisted in stalwart loyalty to his French friends, as a matter of utmost importance, that "a considerable number of Czechoslovak troops, say 20,000, should be transported from Archangel or some other Russian port to France," because of the primary importance of the Western front. Beneš then requested "recognition in public of the Czechoslovak involvement and [of] their National Council . . . [which] should be *acknowledged as a nationality with just claims to independence.*" Finally, he "offered to send Col. Štefánik out to Siberia to see that [his directives] were carried out."[42] There is no indication that the Foreign Office was willing to commit itself this far publicly in favor of Czechoslovak independence as a price of their military collaboration.

Cecil repeated the revised British stand in Paris to Clemenceau and his ministers. He put the case bluntly to the French leaders. "The question is the best use that we can make of the 20,000 [not 70,000] Czechoslovaks who will be in the near future at Vladivostok. If they are transported to France, they cannot possibly reach the fighting line for three or four months. If they can be employed . . . to produce effective intervention, with or without the consent of the Americans, they would be fulfilling a far more important service to the Allied cause." [43]

When Clemenceau reiterated to Cecil his insistence on the terms of the Abbéville Accord, Cecil backed down and asked Lord Edward Derby, the British ambassador to France, to report home. Derby wrote, "M. Clemenceau believed that he was promised at Abbéville that we should have the whole of the Czechoslovak force transported to France and he altogether refuses to allow even a fraction of them to be used for intervention in Siberia." Clemenceau expressed fury at the unilateral British shift. Derby was instructed to tell the premier "that vehement letters at this stage were futile." [44]

An emergency Anglo-French meeting was held by the British War Cabinet at 10 Downing Street in London at 11 A.M. on Tuesday, May 28, 1918, at the behest of Clemenceau, who sent Pichon to attend. Pichon was accompanied by Paul Cambon, his ambassador in London. The agenda contained only two points, the first being "the transport of the Czechoslovakian forces from Russia and Siberia." The second point, which was never reached was "the policy of the Allied coalition toward the Polish-Czech-Slovak question."

Pichon opened the meeting, referring to Cecil's letter summarizing the British Government's proposal "that the Czechoslovaks should not be transported from Vladivostok to the Western front, but should be left in Siberia as a nucleus of an Inter-Allied force there." This letter had "greatly preoccupied M. Clemenceau who considered it a matter of first importance to transport the Czechoslovaks as agreed at Abbéville, and was unwilling to change this decision. He had therefore asked M. Pichon to come here to press for the maintenance of the Abbéville decision." Pichon cited the leaders of the Czechoslovak National Council, Beneš, Štefánik, and Masaryk, as "all agreed that they could not intervene effectively in Siberia."

Cambon then confronted Cecil, asking whether "supposing the tonnage was actually available at Vladivostok, he would not prefer to transport them to the Western front?" Cecil just as candidly replied "he would not." In his calculation "the most important thing at the moment [was] to re-establish the [Allied] position in Russia." Then he added: "In any case, some Czechoslovak troops, sufficient to *secure the political advantage named* should remain." Cambon thought he settled the dispute when he said: "to use the Czechoslovak forces was useless if only because the Czechoslovak National Council had shown clearly that the Czechoslovaks did not wish it."

Balfour concluded the meeting, summing up "that if the French did not agree with our proposals, the Abbéville policy should stand." He easily conceded that "the Allies had not enough manpower on the Western front. They had, however, still less manpower in Russia . . . One of the greatest difficulties of the Allies was tonnage . . . [They sought] some belligerent activity [to] be maintained in Russia . . . to tie down some German divisions there." [45]

Surprisingly, they were all informed by Sir Joseph Maclay, heading the Ministry of Shipping, that he calculated that "5,000 men could be transported from Vladivostok to the United States between now [May] and July [and] another 4,000 to 5,000 troops . . . by the end of July" for transport through the Suez Canal. [46]

President Wilson sided with Clemenceau against intervention in Siberia as the Western front was the primary battleground against the Germans. His secretary of war, Baker, and his naval chief, Admiral Knight, both opted against intervention, preferring economic assistance and trade. They argued that the Russian people were starving and needed food rather than guns.

Trouble arose on May 24th, impelling a quick meeting of the War Cabinet in London, at which the cabinet was informed by the Japanese ambassador of the discovery by the Bolshevik authorities in Moscow that the marauding Cossack general, Semenoff, was being supported by the British. The British had denied their covert subvention of the general and now the Japanese ambassador "wished to know what our attitude was in regard to Semenoff." Lord Cecil replied that "he thought we should deal perfectly frankly with the Soviets. He himself was prepared to back Semenoff, provided that his activities were part and parcel of an Allied movement." [47] The cabinet decided to say nothing to Trotsky, although they recognized "that this would not be dealing frankly with the Soviets," as "to recognize Semenoff now . . . was to recognize an avowed enemy of the Bolsheviks." [48]

Initially, the behind-the-scenes differences among the Allied governments over the uses of the Czechoslovak Legions in Russia and Siberia shielded the troops for a while. Clemenceau opposed unilateral British maneuvers to revise the agreements for their transportation to the French front for the sake of utilizing them for anti-Bolshevik intervention in Siberia and at the northern ports. In any case, trouble developed directly for the Czechoslovak Legions as clashes erupted with the Soviet forces.

NOTES

1. Received from Consul Wardrop, Moscow, April 1, 1918, Foreign Office (henceforth FO) 371/v. 3323, p. 325.

2. 4-page report by Capt. Vladimír Hurban, April 9, 1918, p. 1, War Office (henceforth WO) 106/v. 683. Hurban, belonging to that force, had returned recently from Vladivostok to the United States. He was subsequently stationed in Washington to represent the Czechoslovak National Council. He was later appointed as minister, then ambassador, to the United States from Czechoslovakia.

3. Francis Oswald Lindley, Jan. 15, 1918, FO 371/v. 3297, p. 153.

4. David R. Francis: *Russia From The American Embassy, April 1916-November 1918* (New York: Scribner's, 1921), pp. 224-25.

5. Ibid., p. 148.

6. Report of Russian representative of the British United Shipping Co., Ltd. in Petrograd, Mar. 13-26, 1918, FO 371/v. 3331:

If there were any doubt about the onerous terms imposed by the Germans on the Soviets at Brest, these were comprehensively analyzed for the British Foreign Office by a long time resident Russian representative of the British United Shipping Co., Ltd. in Petrograd, who reported on it as follows:

"Russia loses" Poland, or rather the Russian Polish provinces, also Lithuania (Kovno, Grodno, and Vilna governments) Courland, Livonia, Esthonia, and the Ukraine—the governments of Bolhynia, Podlia, Jekaterinoslav, Kiev, Tchernigoff, Poltava, Cherson, Kharkoff and Bessarabia, the governments of Kharkoff, Minsk, and Vitebsk or part of them.

The loss of these regions represents the loss of:

4% of the whole territory of Russia,
26% of the total population of Russia,
27% of the total arable land,
37% of the average crop,
26% of the railway system,
33% of the total value of manufactured articles, say of production,
39% of the total Horse Power of the country, N.B. Machinery,
75% of the total coal production, and
73% of the total pig iron production.

Three separate Republics are being proposed:

1) People living on the south side of the Caucasus Mountains.
2) Another Republic in the districts occupied by the Cossacks.
3) Third Republic comprising the Governments of Ufa, Orenburg . . . where a Tartar majority exists.

4) Siberian Republic, where White Russian governments are working to establish their independence.
5) Republic of what remains of the Russian Empire comprising Moscow and Petrograd.
6) Finland an independent country and the governments of Olomutz and Archangel with an outlet on the Murman coast.

The only conclusion one can come to is that Russia does not exist any longer as an Empire. [The reporter foresees ahead] . . . great difficulties and endless disputes before even the boundaries of the various Republics . . . as well as with regard to the ownership of State Railways and other property . . . the country will continue in a state of ferment.

See also George Kennan, *Russia Leaves the War* (Princeton, N.J.: Princeton University Press, 1956), p. 370.

7. Francis, *Russia*, p. 225.

8. Arthur S. Link, *Wilson, The Diplomatist* (Baltimore: Johns Hopkins, 1957), pp. 117-18; Link, Ed., *Woodrow Wilson and a Revolutionary World, 1913-1921,* (Chapel Hill, N.C.: University of North Carolina Press, 1982), p. 82.

9. Richard H. Ullman, in Volume II of his excellent 3-volume study of Anglo-Soviet Relations entitled *Britain and the Russian Civil War, Nov. 1918-Feb. 20, 1920* (Princeton, N.J.: Princeton University Press, 1968), argues that "few [in the British Cabinet] felt that the solidification of Bolshevik power in Russia would be fundamentally harmful to the interests of the British Empire. Only Churchill warned that by not crushing Bolshevism in its infancy, the Allies were storing up for themselves a vastly more costly confrontation in the future" (p. 359). "Political will was lacking," he continues (p. 361). This was not consistent with archival documents and the inaccuracy of this conclusion is demonstrable in his own volume: "Milner, as well, gave his support. Bolshevism was the greatest danger faced by the civilized world, he said . . . [He advocated] keeping the Bolsheviks out of Siberia, the Don country, and Turkestan" (p. 93).

Lord Robert Cecil declared "himself prepared to back Semenoff" (War Cabinet 417, May 24, 1918, FO 371/v. 3286). Similarly, Lord Curzon favored intervention, as did others whose arguments favoring intervention fill scores of reports on the subject in the Foreign Office archives.

Ullman concludes in his epilogue at the end of vol. 1 (*Intervention and the War*), "Intervention in Russia was a policy born of a desperate feeling that something, anything, had to be done to relieve the pressure on the Allied forces in the West. Basically, it was a policy aimed at getting something for nothing, recreating an Eastern Front, without sacrificing any Allied resources which might have been brought against the enemy in the West" (p. 333). Ullman continues his epilogue: "After the Armistice [by the Great Power Allies] the intervention which had been conceived as part of the war against the Germans had lost its raison d'être. All the old arguments by which intervention had been justified were thus invalidated, and it could be continued only as an operation admittedly aimed at the destruction of the Bolshevik regime" (p. 334). "The decisive influence was to pass from the hands of the soldiers into those of the politicians" (p. 335). "In large measure, [Churchill] was to be responsible for the transformation of intervention into an operation avowedly anti-Bolshevik in purpose" (p. 335).

This conclusion of a progression of British motives falls by the weight of contrary evidence, of strong anti-Bolshevik opinions of the entire group of British leaders who participated in the Cabinet debates. It also omits consideration of British subsidies to White Russians fighting the Bolsheviks as early as December, 1917, which never ceased during Ullman's first phase. The British supported the Whites throughout the Civil war in Russia as a counter-revolutionary force. Moreover, wherever the Czechoslovak forces took over, either alone or in conjunction with the White Russians, Soviet administration was deposed and White Russian governments installed. The delays in interventionist activity were occasioned by French and U.S. opposition, for the most part. Winston Churchill, of course, led the pack at home to whip up enthusiasm for intervention. General William S. Graves, commander of the American Expeditionary Force in Siberia thought it evident. "England, France and Japan went to Siberia with the distinct idea of fighting bolshevism . . . they tried to cover up this design by advocating the formation of an Eastern front" (Graves, *America's Siberian Adventure* [New York: Jonathan Cape, 1931], p. 334).

10.   Robert Bruce Lockhart, *Memoirs of a British Agent* (London: Penguin, 1950).

11.   *"Russia in Turmoil,"* pamphlet, 1919, FO 371/v. 3321, p. 220.

12.   M. Philips Price, *"The Truth about Allied Intervention in Russia,"* pamphlet (Moscow: August 1918), p. 6, FO 371/v. 3317, pp. 232-40. Also quoted in George Kennan, *Russia Leaves the War* (Princeton, N.J.: Princeton University Press, 1956), p. 497.

13.   *Congressional Record*, June 29, 1919.

14.   Thomas Lamont, *Across World Frontiers*, (New York: Harcourt Brace, 1961), pp. 86-90. Also George Kennan, *Russia Leaves the War*, p. 245.

15.   Arthur S. Link and Betty Miller Unterberger, State Dept. Records, 861.00/2721. Masaryk also wrote Charles R. Crane on this subject, April 10, 1918.

16.   Woodrow Wilson Papers (henceforth WW), May 7, 1918.

17.   Richard Ullman, *Intervention and the War* (1917-21), p. 127. Albert Rhys Williams recounted this report personally in the 1950's to the authors.

18.   Lord Curzon. March 16, 1918, FO 371/v. 3285, p. 291. This report was held 50 years under a *secrecy* order.

19.   Military File, FO 371/v. 3323, p. 327. Italics added.

20.   Ibid.

21.   FO 371/v. 3285, p. 301. Italics added.

22.   Moscow, No. 114, FO 371/v. 3285, p. 307.

23.   Hurban Report, pp. 1-4, WO-106/683-Xc/A 65181 .

24.   FO 371/v. 3323, p. 321. Italics added.

25.   Ibid., p. 365.

26.   Text of Abbéville Accord, Ibid., p. 334:

a) The British Government undertake to do their best to arrange the transportation of those Czech troops who are at Vladivostok or on their way to the Port.
b) The French Government undertake the responsibility of these troops until they are embarked.

c) The British Government undertake to approach M. Trotsky with a view to the concentration at Murmansk and Archangel of these Czech troops but not belonging to the Army corps which has left Omsk for Vladivostok.

27. Whitehall Gardens, May 11, 1918. Secret. FO 371/v. 3285 p. 513. Italics added.

28. Ibid. Italics added.

29. Ibid.

30. British War Council May 10, 1918, WO 106/v. 1161. Italics added.

31. Ibid.

32. British War Council FO 371/v. 3443, p. 53. Italics added.

33. Arthur Balfour, Decision of War Cabinet FO 371/v. 3323, p. 349. Italics added.

34. Robert Bruce Lockhart to Foreign Office, 371/v. 3286, pp. 41-42. Bruce Lockhart was unofficial British represenative of Foreign Office to Moscow, enjoying access to Foreign Commissar Georgyi Chicherin and Defense Commissar Léon Trotsky.

35. FO 371/v. 3443, pp. 51-53. Italics added.

36. Ibid, p. 51.

37. Ibid. Italics added.

38. Ibid, p. 53. Italics added. Bonar Law, Member of British Supreme War Council.

39. Ibid. Italics added.

40. Lord Edward Curzon Report, p. 2, FO 371/v. 3334, p. 84A.

41. Ibid.

42. FO 371/v. 3443, pp. 55-56. Italics added.

43. FO 371/v. 3323, p. 375

44. Robert Cecil to Edward Geoffroy Derby, May 25, 1918, FO 371/v. 3323, pp. 82-84

45. Arthur Balfour FO 371/v. 3334, p. 82-84.

46. W. Langley for Secretary of State for Foreign Affairs, July 8, 1918, FO 371/v. 3324, p. 193.

47. Robert Cecil FO 371/v. 3286, p. 113.

48. Ibid.

3

The Legion's Anabasis
to the Sea

By the terms of the troop withdrawals, negotiated by Tomáš Masaryk with Soviet Commander-in-Chief Muravieff on February 10, 1918, and confirmed by the Moscow authorities on March 26th, the Soviets agreed to provide trains to transport the Czechoslovak troops across Siberia to Vladivostok. From there, they would be evacuated to Vancouver or Seattle by ships to be furnished by England. The Czechoslovak troops would relinquish most of their military equipment, retaining only minimal sidearms for self-defense. The last proviso removed what had proved to be a major sticking point for Defense Commissar Léon Trotsky, who did not want foreign troops wandering across Soviet soil heavily armed.

When communications between the Czechoslovak leaders and their troops were disrupted, the Czechoslovak Legions gradually became involved in anti-Bolshevik fighting in the field, contrary to the arrangements negotiated by Masaryk and approved by the Czechoslovak National Council. The field commanders subsequently seized control of military operations and affected political realignments.

According to an important Czechoslovak military leader, Capt. Vladimír Hurban, in exchange for their unmolested passage eastward, the forces were "determined to leave Russia without a conflict."[1] Straightaway, however, the Czechoslovak Legions had no choice but to fight their way out of German encirclement at the railway junction of Bachmach against heavy odds. Hurban noted in his report that "relations with the Bolsheviks were still good . . . We refrained from meddling with Russian internal affairs and we did not react to the appeals of the different anti-Bolshevik circles."[2] In accord with the agreement, for "personal safety" they withheld 10 rifles for each 100 men.

Eduard Beneš had an ampler estimate of the arms retained by the men. Realizing that "the troops succeeded in hiding in their luggage a certain number of machine guns and probably also of rifles," he calculated that "it may be assumed that on departure, every transport was provided with 15 or 20 machine guns in consequence of capture, and each Czechoslovak now also had a rifle."[3]

As they were proceeding eastward in 80 trains with Captain Hurban in the lead car, Hurban stated that they were subjected to "constant abuse and difficulties . . . Our trains were attacked in different stations by Soviet troops formed mostly of German and Magyar prisoners . . . Unending negotiations [were] repeated in every seat of a local Soviet . . . After 57 days of such tiresome travel, our first train arrived at Vladivostok, where we were enthusiastically received by the Allied units stationed there."[4]

Captain Hurban described graphically the incident along the way at Irkutsk, which alarmed all the Allied governments:

Our train—about 400 men—armed with 10 rifles and 20 hand grenades was surrounded by a few thousand Red Guards, armed with machine guns and cannons. The Commander gave our men ten minutes to surrender their arms or be shot . . . We began negotiations . . . heard the German command "schiessen" and Red Guards began firing on the train. Czechoslovaks descended and fought. In five minutes, they had all the machine guns, etc.[5]

Hurban charged the Siberian government at Irkutsk with having ordered the attack. We are now fortunate to have discovered the "other side" of this episode. Buried in the British Foreign Office archive lies an official communication from the Central Siberian Foreign Commissariat at Irkutsk to Moscow, which had obviously been intercepted by British intelligence. Written by M. Geysman, it reads:

Having received orders from Moscow to pass Czechoslovak Army through [to] Vladivostok aboard the Supreme Siberian Power, Central Siberie [sic] took measures to rapidest furtherance of mentioned army to the East, but . . . regret due to catastrophic conditions of transport and supplies, we could not pass them forward so fast as we wanted. When railroad communications was [sic] threatened by Semenoff, we were compelled to stop the passing of the Czechoslovaks . . . misinterpreted by Czechoslovaks and used by reactionary elements as agitation against present Russian Government.[6]

Intervention by the American and French consuls prevented the destruction of the city in reprisal. New negotiations proceeded by which "the Siberian government guaranteed [them] . . . unmolested passage to Vladivostok."[7]

The first Corps of the Czechoslovak Army was reported to the Foreign Office to be "arriving from Kieff . . . at Vladivostok" late in April. The rest began pouring in shortly thereafter.[8]

The Anglo-French agreement struck at Abbéville in early May generated much confusion. Convoked on British initiative, the talks produced a decision to divide the Czechoslovak forces at Omsk; those who had already passed eastward would continue to Vladivostok, while those remaining would be shunted northward to Archangel and Murmansk. While awaiting embarkation, "they could be well employed in defending the same and guarding the Murman railway."[9] The French, taking the British at their literal word, went along.

Soon, the Foreign Office was delighted to learn that "a second Czechoslovak Corps . . . was formed in the neighborhood of Omsk." It informed Robert Bruce Lockhart that "the Supreme Council [of Great Britain] has decided that this Corps whose strength is reported as some 20,000 men should if possible be concentrated at Murmansk and Archangel."[10]

At this time, the ministry of shipping claimed a shortage of ships for the transport [from Vladivostok] of the "estimated 50,000 men," or perhaps 60,000. The larger the number, the better for their interventionist plans. Inadequate shipping provided an ostensible reason for detaining the Czechoslovak forces, reinforcing the other cover reasons, which were to recreate an Eastern front against the Germans and to guard the military stores they themselves had deposited. The shipping ministry now declared, in response to a query: "We are quite unable to furnish the necessary tonnage [to convey these troops to France] except by withdrawing it from the North Atlantic and thereby reducing materially the transport of American troops to France."[11]

On May 10th, when Gen. Frederick C. Poole was appointed by the War Office as commander of all British forces in Russia, he was directed "to organize and direct operations of all Czechoslovak contingents . . . now en route to Archangel *for the defense of the northern ports.*"[12]

The British War Cabinet, acting as though the Czechoslovak forces were freely at its disposal, next day decided that the British general staff should explore possibilities for British intervention *"using as a nucleus the Czechoslovak forces."*[13] This was followed on May 14th by the clash at Chelyabinsk between the Czechoslovak forces and the Red Guards over a quarrel involving a released Magyar prisoner of war. The self-constituted Czechoslovak Revolutionary Army, meeting in democratic session at the time, voted to retain their arms for self-defense. Moscow's reprisal was instantaneous. Trotsky issued a strict order for disarming the Czechoslovak forces. The Czechoslovaks saw little choice in the matter. If they complied with Moscow's orders, reinforced by those of their own National Council, to lay down their arms, they risked being shot as traitors if captured by Austrian or German troops, even if they were fighting against the Bolsheviks. On the other hand, they risked being shot if caught with arms by Soviet Guards.

When Trotsky's order to disarm became known, the Czechoslovak Revolutionary Army Assembly on May 23rd voted overwhelmingly to defy it, despite the order of their own National Council. Trotsky's reinforcing directive on May 26th transcended disarmament; it was also punitive. It commanded Red Guards to shoot anyone in possession of arms and to detain the trainload including such persons in a prison camp, subject to military service. Local Soviets were charged to execute the order. Procop Maxa, chief of the Russian division of the Czechoslovak National Council, responded formally to the Moscow authorities on June 4th that disarming his national forces would constitute an hostile act. The confrontation was joined.

Two conflicts between Czechoslovaks and Bolsheviks erupted in late May as a result of the latter's effort to disarm the former. [14] The first occurred at "Irkutsk station where seven Czechs and some ten Bolsheviks were killed." The Bolsheviks had confronted a unit of Czechoslovak artillery to disarm them. The Legion responded in "self-defense." A second incident took place ten kilometers before Irkutsk, when "five Austro-German prisoners captured by Czech officers were shot," thus equalizing somewhat the score of captured soldiers who were peremptorily killed. Captain Hurban later explained in his report that such executions of their own captured men was a very sore point for the Czechoslovak troops. He wrote: "The Austrians hanged all our wounded . . . in Siberia. The Czechoslovaks decided on reprisals, to give no quarter to German-speaking troops falling into their hands . . . who were fighting with the Red Army and caught by them carrying guns." [15] A U.S. officer, Col. Emerson, attached to the corps of railway engineers, accompanied by U.S. Consul-General Ernest L. Harris at Irkutsk, joined with the French consul to intercede, and an armistice was struck on June 10th.

The report by the Central Siberian foreign commissariat at Irkutsk attributed the clash to "misunderstanding or provocation." It deplored that "human blood was shed for neither reason nor purpose." Government representatives arrived to settle the differences quickly "to [the] satisfaction and conviction of both sides." They said, "There was no reason for quarrel between Soviet Representatives and Czecho-Slovak Army." [16]

This account was affirmed by the reporter for the foreign commissariat of the Government of Irkutsk, who claimed that "Chief Commanders are exceedingly dissatisfied with the situation and categorically *ordered their fellow countrymen located in the West to submit to the Soviets and instantly proceed east.*" [17]

The self-proclaimed autonomous leaders in field command of the Czechoslovak forces at Chelyabinsk disregarded their National Committee's directive to disarm in compliance with Trotsky's threatening order. The troops were discontented too with their bread rations, demanding an increase and "departure for Vladivostok." [18] Their spontaneous uprising at Chelyabinsk disassociated them from their own accommodating National Council. On May 26th, when they seized control of the city, they dislodged the local Soviet administration and instituted their own anti-Bolshevik government with the support of the Social Revolutionaries and cadets. This uprising "soon spread East and West." [19]

Consul General Wardrop confirmed the political takeover at Chelyabinsk, where "Czech Committee formed [a coordinating pact] with Cadets, Right Social Revolutionaries, Mensheviks . . . [They were] assisted by Cossacks, Kirghiz and White Guards . . . They were attempting to cut off retreating Soviet troops from Tiuman and Katerinburg and threatening the Tiumen line." [20]

Bruce Lockhart verified this state of affairs, as described also by Consul General Francis Oswald Lindley in his report home from Petrograd. On June 1st, he informed the Foreign Office: "Czech National Council has been disbanded by Czech troops themselves for being too moderate and too conciliatory towards the Bolsheviks. Troops who now control large parts of Siberian railway from Penza to Irkutsk seem determined to fight their way through towards the Far East." At the same time, he wrote that the "Bolsheviks [at Irkutsk] are anxious to come to terms. General Lavergne and French Ambassador are against disarmament of Czechs . . . [who] now hold valuable parts of Siberian railway." [21]

On June 3rd, a joint note of the U.S. section of the Supreme (Allied) War Council, entitled *Allied Intervention at the White Sea*

Ports, spoke of the German military threat to Murmansk and Archangel as having become "more definite and more imminent." It recommended "a military effort . . . by the Allies to keep possession" of these Northern ports as vital economic Russian outlets with Western Europe. [22]

The Bolshevik leaders at Moscow, underestimating the threat posed by the Czechoslovak forces, resolutely proceeded in their futile effort to disarm them. On the 4th of June, Bruce Lockhart informed his superiors of a new order, prohibiting "their further use of Russian railways eastwards until they lay down their arms." [23]

The following day, Consul General Wardrop wired from Moscow that the "district railway Kurgan, Chelyabinsk [was] closed." [24] The British censor intercepted a telegram from Trotsky to his London ambassador informing him of "violent collision [of Czechoslovak forces] with Soviet troops at Penza . . . The lines [that] are forbidden to the Czechoslovaks were Penza, Pouzaewka, Oufa, Tcheliabinsk, and Omsk." [25] A perilous situation was developing, but Bruce Lockhart cheerfully assured his superiors that "they can fight their way to Vladivostok." [26]

It defies logic that Czechoslovak troops in Russia provoked worry abroad over their security, as they were advancing steadily and giving an excellent account of themselves. Bruce Lockhart was the sole Western diplomat stationed in Moscow to remain cool to the embroilment of the Czechoslovak Legions with the Soviets without clamoring for reinforcements to rescue them.

He admired their stupendous performance and extolled their magnificent spirit and wonderful discipline. He attributed their excellence to their high level of education and observed that the Legion was composed of "men of intellectual class, 50% have received a higher education, 30% middle education . . . not an illiterate amongst them." His description of their camp life is illuminating:

They live in trains—study French and [do] daily Swedish exercises . . . They have secured a considerable number of guns and are more than a match for anything the Bolsheviks can send against them. Two Lett regiments who were ordered to leave Moscow to fight against the Czechoslovaks refused to go. Fate has given us in the Czechoslovaks [the] last chance of regaining Russia. [27]

Despite their triumphs in the field, Lord Edward Derby learned in Paris that "all parties involved in the situation realize that the Czechoslovak troops at this juncture desire above all things to be transported to France." [28] He also heard from his French sources that a revolutionary council had been organized in Moscow to effectuate the Soviet campaign against "the Czech camp." [29]

London's Foreign Office was still giving lip service to its Abbéville Accord with the French, despite its behind-the-scenes plans to land a sizable force shortly at one of the northern ports.

The reported "serious situation" at Omsk "was resolved by the Czechoslovak occupation on June 9th and a provisional government [being] established there." [30]

Bruce Lockhart observed from Moscow: "Far from leaving Russia, the Czechoslovaks now controlled a vital part of her communications. The Czechoslovaks were now in full possession of all the railway system from Omsk to Krasnoyarsk (800 miles)." Soviet officials in Moscow placed the blame squarely on the Allies, meaning Great Britain in particular. [31]

Samara was also taken on June 9th, by two Czech regiments commanded by a French officer, Selitzer. Communications between Viatka and Vologda were cut. At the commencement of hostilities, Allied representatives stated that "the fate of Czechoslovaks [was a] matter of lively interest . . . Allied Powers [were] much concerned . . . Soviets expressed readiness [to] allow Czechoslovaks to leave Russia, but only unarmed." [32]   Eventually, said Gen. William S. Graves, the Soviets conceded so far as to permit "the Czechoslovaks [to] proceed fully armed." [33]

In the face of the resolute refusal of the Czechoslovak troops to disarm, perhaps the Soviet leaders were oversensitive about allowing foreign troops to wander through their country armed. General Graves explained that "The Soviets not only were filled with anxiety as to the Czech's intentions in Siberia, but they apparently felt that for foreign troops to pass through the country armed, would lower their dignity and would be an infringement of their sovereign rights." [34] Actually, Colonel Emerson told young Capt. Rudolf Gajda "that nothing would be gained by fighting if the Czechs really wanted to get to Vladivostok." Gajda responded "that as soon as the new Government comes into power, it will stop the Soviets." [35]

Bruce Lockhart amplified on the situation from his box seat in Moscow. He wired home his news:

At present, there appear to be about 10,000 Czechs around Samara and altogether about 26,000 between Samara and Chelyabinsk. At Samara, *they have been joined by local counterrevolutionary force of about 4,000 White Guards,* whilst 1,000 Serbians have also offered to accompany them. They have come easily victorious out of all their encounters with Bolshevik forces. [36]

On June 21st, the British consul at Vladivostok was authorized to advance such funds as necessary for "maintenance of the Czech Corps in Siberia." [37]

Matters were now definitely transferred to the battlefront for settlement, posing a threat of far greater significance to the Soviets, which they stubbornly ignored. The most charismatic and audacious of the anti-Bolshevik officers at Chelyabinsk was Capt. Rudolf Gajda. Before the final decision of defiance was voted by the Legions' assembly, Gajda had played a leading role in forcing the outbreak of hostilities. General Graves attributed the fault indubitably to Gajda, and the Soviets also blamed the Czechoslovak leaders. Graves recorded in his war memoir: "There was a clear indication that the Czechs were involved in driving the Soviets out of the towns and substituting . . . a new Government," [38] to which Gajda alluded in his reply to Colonel Emerson.

Several Allied diplomats tried to deflect the political machinations, according to General Graves, to forestall the fighting. For example, the French consul general had wired Gajda from Chita, "Do not let yourself be implicated in the internal political fight." A couple of days later, on June 4th, American Consul General Thomas directed a message to Gajda that "he must only consider the movement of these Echelons East . . . and that he must not forget the important and explicit instructions of Professor Masaryk" for neutrality in the Russian Civil War. [39] Graves detected collusion by the Czechoslovaks and the reactionary anti-Bolshevik Russian forces in Siberia and European Russia, which were being subsidized monetarily by both England and France.

Gajda had organized a personal commando squad, improvised an armored car, and dashed out of town from Chelyabinsk under the noses of the Red garrison. He passed through Isil Luk, just west of the rail hub of Omsk, where the U.S. consul general had invited the Omsk Soviet commander to negotiate the peaceful passage through Siberia of the Gajda-led Czechoslovak groups. Gajda's commando forces instead proceeded, and by June 21st reached the Angara River some miles upstream from Irkutsk.

The commander did not deign to stop until he had reached the Siberian capital city of Novo Nikolajevsk. His arrival coincided with the plans of the Right Social Revolutionaries to attempt seizing control of the city. The political takeover occurred simultaneously at Chelyabinsk. Gajda's plunge across Siberia proceeded relentlessly, assisted by his developing the fine art of guerrilla tactics, which simultaneously outflanked the diplomatic efforts expended to moderate his excessive zeal. Gajda was making steady, spectacular progress, entering critical points such as Omsk, Krasnoyarsk, Nikola-jevsk, Marinsk, and finally, Irkutsk.

There seems to have been no military necessity for the Czechoslovaks to advance to the regional capital city of Irkutsk, indicating a clear political motive. The city became the seat of the new government, which was nurtured by Britain's commanding general, Alfred Knox. Kiakhovitch, a leading Octobrist, was installed as president, and Admiral Alexander Kolchak was named as war minister.[40] Czechoslovak General Gajda, contrary to protests by the Czechoslovak National Council at Vladivostok opposing the political coup, became for a time Admiral Kolchak's principal military adviser and strategist. He also married the admiral's daughter. He accepted official command from Kolchak of the First Army, which comprised five Czechoslovak regiments. The U.S. military attaché at Vladivostok, Major Walter Drysdale, observed that the new government "depends . . . entirely upon the Czechs," with salutary results. He reported that the peasants "are again bringing in supplies and offer food to the Czechs without payment . . . pleased at the removal of the Bolsheviks . . . Food is more plentiful . . . The Legions planned to arm the peasants in case of trouble with the Red Guards."[41]

The British admiralty, hardly a source of pro-Bolshevik sentiment, reported that

The Czechoslovak detachments . . . arrested and changed local authorities . . . [refused orders to] disarm, they fired against [Soviet] troops . . . [and] restored the Administrations where [they] were abolished . . . [and] collaborated openly . . . with White Guards and counter-revolutionary officers . . . followed everywhere by the arrest of Soviet authorities and by the formation of counter-revolutionary organizations, which have proclaimed themselves Regional Governments. [They stirred a] mutiny which leans on Czechoslovak armed forces.[42]

Bruce Lockhart confirmed the news that "they are evidently working in close connection with Cadets and Social Revolutionaries which have set up a new government . . . [and that they] received certain help from Cossacks and from various Russian sources."[43]

As for the forces of the Cossack leader, Grigorii Semenoff, a secret memorandum in the Foreign Office archive reveals that "France and ourselves are supplying £10,000 a month and guns to Capt. Semenoff, who commanded a Regiment of trans-Baikal Cossacks. Japan has helped him with machine guns and gunners . . . All this help is supposed to be secret, but it must be known to the Bolsheviki . . . Semenoff's methods are looting and terrorism . . . He harms the Allied cause in Siberian Russia. Everyone in Siberia . . . wants peace and trade and safety from Japan." [44]

Bruce Lockhart, in a mid-June report home, delineated the French involvement supportive of the counterrevolutionaries. He wrote that the French "hope that Allies will be in Russia before the end of the month. French have also informed General Anton Deniken's representative in the same sense and have promised him support in money." [45]

The coalition of the broad spectrum of counterrevolutionary forces was organized by the local Czechoslovak field commander, Gajda, who shielded the Social Revolutionary take-over of Nikolajevsk in the Western Siberian wheatlands in early June, while Capt. Stanislav Čeček entered Samara in the Volga basin almost simultaneously. These coordinated actions also guaranteed a regular supply of food and provisions to the Czechoslovak troops from cooperative stores under a carefully drawn contract. These cooperative stores had been set up by the Right Social Revolutionaries at Samara and at Nikolajevsk.

At just this time, two representatives of the Czechoslovak National Council, Vladimír Girsa and his colleague Jiři Špaček, in charge of affairs at Vladivostok, arrived at Irkutsk on June 22nd to survey the military battleground at first hand. They were accompanied by three local commissars. The Girsa-Špaček report was sent directly to Masaryk. Indulging in some self-serving praise, it said, "In spite of all obstacles that the Bolshevik Authorities placed in our road, 13,000 of our soldiers have accomplished the journey all through Russia without dispute and have been living for the past two months in Vladivostok in correct and loyal relations with Bolshevik authorities here." They also affirmed, however, that "the only object and most ardent desire of the Czechoslovak troops is to arrive as soon as possible upon the French Front." They then added: "Should the Allies . . . esteem that the final result of the war would best be attained under present circumstances, by the return of our troops to the Russian [Eastern] Front to be created, then our Army would obey the order of its supreme political leader, Professor Masaryk." [46]

Meanwhile on June 23rd, the British landed another 600 of their troops at Murmansk. This did nothing to help the rapidly deteriorating situation in Siberia, which was developing into the major battleground against the Bolsheviks.

In view of the assemblage in Vladivostok of so vast a force of well-provisioned, experienced fighting men, and of their comrades in arms being reportedly hardpressed in the field on the western front, it appeared that the time for action had arrived. So thought Gen.

Mikhail Dieterichs, commanding the Czechoslovak forces in the city, who made the decision. Vladivostok had to be taken to secure the rear so a portion of the Czechoslovak troops there could depart westward to aid their countrymen. Dieterichs obtained assistance of men and materials from both British and Japanese vessels anchored in the harbor. Even the U.S. naval vessel *Brooklyn* sent 20 marines at the behest of the U.S. consulate, which had been authorized in advance to help. [47]

The Czechoslovak Legions took possession of Vladivostok on June 29th, assisted by 200 men from the British ship of war *Suffolk*, stationed in the harbor, and 100 Japanese from their vessel, assisted by their regular shore parties of 450 men, who proceeded to surround the Allied consulates for their protection against the Red Guards. The Czechoslovaks issued an ultimatum to the Red Guard demanding disarmament. "Six hundred sailors in the barracks laid down their arms as did 400 Red Guards at the first request. The fortress headquarters was reduced by 5 P.M. with the loss of two killed. Red losses in killed and wounded [were] about sixty." It was reported that the "population welcomed [the] action of the Czechs." Captain Hurban in his report described the takeover of the Siberian administration as urgent due to the "influx of masses of men into the newly reorganized Red Army, which the military leaders in the field saw as threatening." [48]

The city was peacefully administered by the municipal militia, which resumed its functions. Almost immediately, detachments of the Legions would be "moving on Nicolsk and Habarovsk and Harbin." [49] The Japanese were willing to provide the Czechs with rifle ammunition, machine guns, and airplanes for their new expedition westward. [50]

The British War Cabinet met on July 2nd to assess this major development at Vladivostok. It considered that the occupation of Vladivostok "has transformed the Siberian situation." Now, the War Cabinet declared it feared that "this Czechoslovak force . . . is in great danger of being cut off at Irkutsk." [51] This was an odd deduction in view of the Legion's control of the railways in Siberia. [52]

Meanwhile, Gajda's commando forces had reached the Angara River on June 21st, some miles upstream from Irkutsk, a military center as well as the most important city of central Siberia. He took some time out to rest his forces, while the friendly Soviet commissar importuned U.S. Consul General Harris to make one more effort to avoid bloodshed and spare the city. Gajda spurned the humanitarian offer. Taking a gunboat and an armored car, Gajda's group divided into mobile units and ultimately lured the Soviet garrison into attacking the commandos across the river from the city. Although grossly outnumbered, the Czechoslovaks dispersed the garrison with little damage or loss of life, and the city fell on July 11th. The capture of Irkutsk yielded immense booty, but the six-week campaign was also costly in lives and was devitalizing to Gajda's exhausted troops.[*] General Dieterichs in Vladivostok realized he had to mobilize immediate reinforcements for the strung-out, embattled Czechoslovak forces.[53]

Leaving a small contingent in the port to cover his rear, Dieterichs took the bulk of his corps and backtracked up the Ussuri River to where it converges with the Amur. He fought two engagements against Red forces, the first with heavy losses. On the Amur River, "All steamers [were] taken over by the Bolsheviks . . . and several of them had arrived [at Nikolajevsk] at the mouth of the Amur River." This development gave rise to anxiety aboard HMS *Suffolk*. The captain alerted the Japanese admiral, "who . . . telegraphed to Tokyo asking that destroyers be sent immediately to watch Mouth of Amur River."[54] This rapid deployment improved the Czechoslovak forces' capability for maneuvers.

A War Cabinet meeting was convened on July 10th to review the Czechoslovak victory at Nikolsk and found the "Czechs urgently in need of medical assistance in the firing line . . . reinforcements of 50 to 100 thousand forces [wanted and the] immediate dispatch of at least one American Division to Siberia."[55] The U.S. military attaché undoubtedly sent a similar report to his commander-in-chief, Gen. Peyton C. March, who would relay the urgent request to President Wilson.

General Dieterichs's forces had hard work, but they cleared the rail line up the valley of the Amur. The battered army reached Chita in the last days of July, where it made juncture with Gajda. On their way, they "defeated an enemy force near Spasskoe." Dieterichs was reported to "intend to leave Spasskoe guarded by a small force and proceed with remainder via Harbin towards Chita,"[56] where "their comrades were heavily engaged with enemy forces."[57]

After taking a few days to rest and recoup, Dieterichs led his corps to Irkutsk and westward, ultimately to join in the Ural region the Čeček forces after they had been driven out of the immense Volga

---

[*]Ironically, Gajda was indicted for high treason in Prague later on for offering his services to Soviet intelligence in 1919, following his return from his brilliant anti-Bolshevik career in Russia.

basin. Neither in that area when they held it, nor in Siberia, however, did Czechoslovak–Social Revolutionary control embrace many miles beyond railway stations in this early phase of the fighting, and the extended armies were always exposed to flank attacks.

For Gajda, there remained Lake Baikal, the largest fresh water body in the world, athwart his entry into the Soviet far east. The great railroad ran around the precipitous southwestern shores, through no fewer than 39 tunnels. Gajda dashed to the Amur River's mouth before the Reds could effectuate any dynamiting plans. Meanwhile, the main body of troops under the White Russian general, Ushakov, reinforced by the Cossacks, outflanked the Red forces and bent around the southern shore of the lake. Other Czechoslovaks, seizing any lake-going vessel in sight, ferried across and joined the Ushakov contingent, all converging on the rail junction at Kerkne Udinsk. Ushakov himself lost his life in an infiltrating action, and the Red Army of the Far East broke up and fled into the lakeside mountains or down the rail spur toward the Mongolian frontier.

Such was the military situation in Siberia when President Wilson issued his Aide Memoire on July 17th, announcing his dispatch of the U.S. expeditionary force under the command of General Graves.

At an Allied conference held on August 5th, the Czechoslovak general explained the "present situation [regarding] enemy forces from information he had just received." He estimated that "three divisions are necessary to support him in his advance towards Irkutsk." He proposed to move forward immediately. "In addition to this, 8 battalions are necessary for defense of Ussuri front."[58]

The first U.S. troops, the 27th Infantry, consisting of 53 officers and 1,537 enlisted men, arrived in Siberia from Manila on August 16, 1918, followed a few days later by the 31st Infantry, comprising 46 officers and 1,375 men. General Graves himself did not arrive in Siberia until September 1, 1918. His instructions from Secretary of War Newton D. Baker, were to help the Czechoslovak forces extricate themselves and not to intervene in the internal political squabbles. He became disillusioned quickly. From Colonel Emerson's report, Graves decided that the "Czechoslovaks were the aggressors . . . The Soviets wanted to get the Czechoslovaks out of Siberia."[59] He continued, "Col. Emerson's report shows that . . . Czechs were never in any danger as long as the Czechs stuck to their announced purpose of going through to Vladivostok on the Trans-Siberian Railway." This course was directed by their own National Council officers. General Graves concluded that, "relative to the safety of the Czechs, as drawn from Colonel Emerson's report, [their vulnerability] differs . . .

radically from the generally accepted idea that they were in grave danger."

Graves was especially critical of U.S. Consul General Harris for telling Colonel Emerson "that he had received confirmation of the report that the Allies and the United States were going to intervene in Siberia two days before the U.S. government announced its policy on July 17th. . . . The Consul General of the United States in Siberia, Mr. E. L. Harris, a representative of the State Department was telling the people of Siberia that the United States was a party to the contemplated intervention in the internal conflicts of the Russian people." This flatly contravened "the policy statement of President Wilson, who explicitly prohibited intervention in the internal affairs of Siberia or Russia." The consul's statement also contradicted Graves's own orders from Secretary of War Baker. [60]

As for the Japanese, Graves wrote that on October 18, 1918, "I reported to the War Department that Japan had at least 60,000 troops in Siberia and it was disclosed later, that I had underestimated the number by 12,000. There was no military situation demanding this increase . . . Japan was indulging in both political and military maneuvers . . . at cross purposes with the announced policy of the U.S." [61] Graves further recorded that the Allied Supreme War Council had concluded that the Japanese "always hoped to occupy Eastern Siberia"; and he resigned himself pragmatically, "she will [in any case] take part of Siberia." [62] After inspecting the battlefield, the intelligence officer with the U.S. forces decided that the strength of the "enemy," meaning the Red Army, as estimated by the Japanese general staff, was greatly exaggerated. [63]

Although the Japanese were willing and anxious to commit as many as 250,000 troops in Siberia by negotiation, President Wilson attempted to keep them, more or less, to a pledge not to exceed the number of U.S. troops, at 7,000. Almost immediately, reports arrived that the Japanese were putting in 12,000 troops, and they later added to these, as noted. In various accounts of the actual fighting, the Japanese were not mentioned as playing any special role. The Czechoslovak Legions accomplished the major share of the anti-Bolshevik action.

Graves vented his anger against the general official duplicity in his memoirs in which he confided: "At least one month before I received my orders . . . [to intervene] the Czechs were not in need of help," as was well known to Consuls General Harris and DeWitt C. Poole. "They had taken the Trans-Siberian Railway and had driven the Soviets out of the towns along the railroad and had organized new governments for these towns; and . . . they did not intend to leave Siberia, as confirmed by the Czech National Council in Washington." He continued, "It is difficult to believe that Professor Masaryk, head of the Czech National Council functioning in Washington, [64] was not consulted as to the move of the U.S. troops to go to the assistance of the Czechs in far-away Siberia." [65]

In this conclusion, Graves seems to have been carried away, as these authors could not turn up any evidence that Wilson had consulted Masaryk in formulating his decision to dispatch his Expeditionary Force. Toward the end of the deliberative period, Masaryk did seem to be swayed by the Girsa-Špaček report to request assistance for his embattled forces. But, for the historical record, he was again not consulted.

"By this interference" in the internal affairs of Russia, resumed Graves, "the United States helped to bolster up by its military forces, a monarchistically inclined and unpopular Government . . . The U.S. gained by this act the resentment of more than 90% of the people of Siberia . . . There were no beneficial results . . . flowing from intervention . . . Colonel Emerson's report that the Soviets had been trying to get the Czechs out of Siberia for two months before I received my instructions, and that they would not go . . . creating the immediate necessity for helping the Czechs . . . was an error, or a deliberate misinterpretation." [66]

In the end, Gen. Graves concluded that while the U.S. troops did not participate in any military engagements, they did maintain and operate the trans-Siberian railway over which hostile armies traveled. Consequently, we did intervene internally to that extent. [67] Graves found solace, however, in observing that the eventual withdrawal of U.S. forces put the Japanese under pressure to do likewise, thereby saving Siberia for the Russians and in that respect, retaining Russia's territorial integrity.

Eduard Beneš came to a similar judgment of the events. He wrote, "The Trans-Siberian Railroad is of vital military, as well as economic and administrative importance . . . and consequently the Czechoslovaks in the field were intervening in Russia's internal affairs to bolster the reactionary Government under Kolchak." [68]

As for the dangers to the Czechoslovak forces from the "German menace," Gen. Graves scrutinized these reports as well. U.S. Ambassador David R. Francis, acting through Col. Raymond Robins, had questioned Trotsky as to the truth of the reports of Soviet intentions to arm German and Austrian prisoners of war held in camps in eastern Siberia. Trotsky suggested that the United States send its own responsible men to probe the accuracy for themselves. These men were dispatched: the American Red Cross representative in Moscow, Webster; Captain Hicks of the British Army; and Maj. Walter Drysdale, U.S. military attaché in Vladivostok and later in Peking. They went to eastern Siberia to investigate the prison camps. Webster and Hicks sent the following telegraphic report from Irkutsk on April 1, 1918:

There are in all Siberia not over 1,200 armed prisoners . . . used for guarding other prisoners and especially German officers in whom Soviet places no confidence. The Soviets state they would not think of placing arms at the disposal of [these] prisoners . . . The Soviets further gave us their official guarantee that no more than a maximum of 1,500 prisoners will be armed in the whole of Siberia. [69]

Drysdale conducted his own separate investigation and reported: "The Soviets did not release their German war prisoners from the prison camps, and . . . rumour that the Germans were forming a battle front in Siberia was propaganda designed to influence the United States in the question of military action." [70]

For Masaryk, the problem was analogous to Wilson's; he had to depend on his own countrymen as informants, and many of these were decidedly prejudiced against acceptance of the Soviet regime. After his Legions became engaged against the Soviets, contrary to his wishes and to those of his National Council, which had requested them to disarm and withdraw, the leaders lost control of events in the field. The decisions passed to anti-Bolshevik commanders, exemplified by Rudolf Gajda. Eager for a reliable report, Masaryk sent Gen. Milan Rastislav Štefánik to Siberia to investigate the situation at first hand. Crossing Siberia with Gen. Maurice Janin, Štefánik arrived at Omsk a week following the Kolchak coup. The new government was composed of Right Social Revolutionaries in varying local combinations with Mensheviks and Cadets. Although it imposed brutal treatment of workers and peasants, nonetheless the Czechoslovak Legions assisted the local regimes to rehabilitate civilian life and to resume economic production. Harsh conditions of life deprived the new government of any popular base of support. Štefánik found the reactionary nature of the new dictatorship so distasteful that he avoided personal contact with Admiral Kolchak during the entire month's duration of his mission.

To counter further Czechoslovak political embroilment, Štefánik incorporated the Legion into his new Ministry of National Assembly, which had a dual function as the Legion's government body and its military command. It failed to thwart Gajda, however. Štefánik also eliminated the Hussite egalitarianism established at Kiev and reinstituted the traditional authority of the officers. Ultimately, the other Allied troops also became war weary and rebellious in the Allied camps abroad.

The Czechoslovak troops eventually withdrew from Siberia, beginning in 1919. They used their own resources to charter seven Japanese vessels and two Russian ones. The first to go were the sick and wounded; the thirteenth ship, which left Vladivostok in December 1919, carried the first military formation. The repatriation took an entire year, some ships sailing through the Suez Canal to European ports such as Trieste or Naples; others headed for Canada. After landing at Vancouver, the troops crossed the continent by rail to Halifax. Their accommodations were modest, clean, and economical. They began arriving home during 1920. [71]

The question may be reasonably posed whether the interventionist role of the Czechoslovak Legions advanced their movement's objective of gaining foreign Allied recognition of their national aspirations. Their compliance with British intentions undoubtedly ingratiated them with British leaders, but in the end, the British exacted a high price for their friendly support of Czechoslovak independence. The fate of the Czechoslovaks hinged on the decisions of the Great Powers, whose support they required in their struggle for national independence. At best, the fighting confirmed them as an Allied force.

President Masaryk emphasized his policy of strict nonintervention in the internal affairs of Russia, [72] despite his Legion's involvement in the civil war.

NOTES

1. Capt. Hurban Report, April 9, 1918, War Office (hereafter WO) 106/v. 683; also *WW Papers*, v. 49, p. 197.

2. Ibid.

3. For a more complete report, see Capt. Hurban, FO 371/v. 3324, pp. 269-82.

4. Ibid.

5. Ibid.

6. M. Geysman, Chief Central Siberian Foreign Commissariat, Irkutsk, June 9, 1918, FO 371/v. 3323, pp. 411-13.

7. *WW Papers*, v. 49, p. 197-98

8. Hodgson at Foreign Office (hereafter FO) to Robert Bruce Lockhart, FO 371/v. 3323, p. 319.

9. FO to Bruce Lockhart, FO 371/v. 3323, p. 321.

10. Ibid.

11. Ministry of Shipping to Foreign Office, May 10, 1918, FO 371/v.3323, p. 343.

12. WO 106/v. 1161, 91670, Secret. Italics added.

13. British War Cabinet meeting, FO 371/v. 3443, p. 53. Italics added.

14. Cecil Greene, British Consul General, Tokyo, to Foreign Office, May 25, 1918, FO 371/v. 3443.

15. Capt. Hurban report, *WW Papers*, v. 49, p. 199

16. M. Geysman, Foreign Commissariat, Irkutsk, June 9, 1918, FO 371/v. 3323. Italics added.

17. Ibid. Italics added.

18. Francis Oswald Lindley, British Consul General, Murmansk, June 21, 1918, FO 371/v. 3333, p. 407.

19. Ibid.

20. Wardrop, Moscow, June 9, 1918, FO 371/v. 3323, p. 288.

21. Bruce Lockhart, Moscow, June 1, 1918, FO 371/v. 3323, pp. 438-39.

22. Records of the American section of the Supreme War Council, 1917-1919, *WW Papers*, v. 48, p. 287.

23. Bruce Lockhart, Moscow, June 4, 1918, FO 371/v. 3323, p. 441.

24. Consul General Wardrop, Moscow, to FO, June 5, 1918, FO 371/v. 3323, p. 244.

25. Foreign Office to Edward Derby, Paris, June 5, 1918, FO 371/v. 3323, p. 403.

26. Bruce Lockhart to Foreign Office, June 5, 1918, FO 371/v. 3323, p. 443.

27. Bruce Lockhart, Moscow, to Foreign Office, FO 371/v. 3286, pp. 321A-321B.

28. Derby, Paris, to Foreign Office, June 8, 1918, FO 371/v. 3323, p. 418.

29. Ibid.

30. Consul General Lindley, Murmansk, June 21, 1918, FO 371/v. 3333, p. 407.

31. Bruce Lockhart, Moscow, to Foreign Office, June 10, 1918, FO 371/v. 3321, p. 10.

32. Lindley, Murmansk, to Foreign Office, June 30, 1918, FO 371/v.3324, p. 107.

33. William S. Graves, *America's Siberian Adventure* (New York: Jonathan Cape, 1931), p. 47.

34. Ibid., p. 45.

35. Ibid.

36. Bruce Lockhart, Moscow, to Foreign Office, June 18, 1918, FO 371/v. 3324, p. 15. Italics added.

37. Treasury Chambers to Under Secy of State, June 10, 1918, FO 371/v. 3324, p. 23.

38. Graves, *America's Siberian Adventure*, p. 46.

39. Ibid., p. 46.

40. Lindley, Murmansk, June 21, 1918, FO 371/v. 3333, p. 407.

41. Extract of report of Maj. Walter Drysdale, American Military Attaché, Vladivostok, June 25, 1918, FO 371/v. 3324, pp. 579-84.

42. British Admiralty Report, June 16, 1918, WO 106 v. 681, Series 5047.

43. Bruce Lockhart, Moscow, to Foreign Office, June 12, 1918, Received June 23, 1918, FO 371/v. 3286, p. 324.

44. Foreign Office Memorandum on Capt. Semenoff, FO 371/v. 3297, p. 581.

45. Bruce Lockhart, Moscow, to Foreign Office, June 10, 1918, FO 371/v. 3286, pp. 452-53.

46. Vladimir Girsa and Jiri Spaček, Vladivostok, June 25, 1918, FO 371/v. 3324, pp. 545-48. A similar report was forwarded by telegram from the British Consul at Vladivostok, dated June 14, but message was not received until June 28th. *WW Papers*, v. 49, pp. 44-46, sent as enclosure with letter from Masaryk to Wilson. See also Sir M. Jordan, Peking, June 26, 1918, FO 371/v. 3324, p. 44.

47. Lord Reading, Washington, D.C., July 11, 1918, FO 371/v. 3324, p. 203.

48. Capt. Hurban Report, *WW Papers*, v. 49, p. 199.

49. Report to Admiralty from Hong Kong, July 1, 1918, FO 371/v. 3324, pp. 166-68, Secret. See also FO 371/v. 3324, p. 158.

50. Hong Kong to Admiralty, June 26, 1918, FO 371/v. 3324, p. 5l.

51. Report, FO 371/v. 3286, pp. 480-83.

52. Ibid.

53. C. Greene, Consul General, Tokyo to Foreign Office, July 22, 1918, FO 371/v. 3324, p. 245.

54. Hong Kong to Admiralty & Commander-in-Chief, FO 371/v. 3324.

55. War Cabinet Meeting, July 10, 1918, FO 37l/v. 3324; also Sir J. Jordan, Peking, July 11, 1918, FO 371/v. 3324, p. 197.

56. Telegram from Rear Admiral Hong Kong to Admiralty and Commander-in-chief, July 20, 1918, FO 371/v. 3324, p. 268.

57. Ibid.

58. Telegram from Rear Admiral Hong Kong to Admiralty, August 7, 1918, FO 371/v. 3324, p. 388.

59. Graves, *America's Siberian Adventure*, pp. 51-52.

60. Ibid., pp. 51-53.

61. Ibid., p. 64.

62. Ibid., p. 65.

63. Ibid., p. 62.

64. Ibid., p. 343.

65. Ibid., p. 344.

66. Ibid.

67. Ibid., p. 347.

68. FO 371/v. 3324.

69. Webster, Hicks, Drysdale report. Graves, p. 25.

70. Telegram Webster and Hicks, Irkutsk, to Gen. Graves, April 1, 1918, Graves, *America's Siberian Adventure*, pp. 26.

71. Baerlein, Henry, *The March of the Seventy Thousand* (London: Leonard Parsons, 1926), pp. 276-79.

72. John O. Crane, *Diary*, November 4, 1922, Crane family archive.

4

Masaryk in America

Even as his Czechoslovak Legions were being embroiled by Allied duplicity concerning the eastern front, Tomáš Masaryk traveled to the United States to gain President Woodrow Wilson's support for Czechoslovak independence. This, he felt, should inevitably follow the defeat of the Central Powers and the subsequent dismemberment of the Austro-Hungarian Empire. Wilson's backing was crucial to insure the favorable attitudes, just short of public commitment, that were already expressed privately in London and Paris government circles.

Masaryk entered the United States from Vancouver where he had landed on the last day of April 1918 from his Pacific crossing. He was met by his Czech-American secretary, Charles Pergler, who for years had been organizing the Bohemian and Moravian communities to advance the goal of Czechoslovak independence politically in America. Now, Pergler crisscrossed the United States with Masaryk, renewing his contacts with their leaders, long activated to further Masaryk's aims. The exiles had earlier responded unstintingly to the call for volunteers issued by Col. Milan Rastislav Štefánik who was commanding some national units in France. Without a clear statement of their objective, however, official foreign support could not be won.

Masaryk pondered the dilemma for a long while and decided the time had come to risk the increased dangers posed by this course for his beloved family and *Maffia* colleagues at home. Weighing the advantages against the hazards before leaving Vladivostok, he chose to move ahead. "Revolutionary conditions in Russia dictated categorically the principle of non-interference [in the Civil War] . . . nor was it possible to occupy and hold the immense territory of European Russia with 50,000 men," he decided. The die was cast, prodded by necessity. His troops had to "get away from Russia," as had been agreed, and be transported to France. He took leave of his troops on March 7, 1918, and departed from Moscow that evening, bound for Vladivostok. [1]

In Chicago, with its dense Czechoslovak population, Masaryk received a hero's welcome, including a noisy tickertape parade and a reception at City Hall. He went to the University of Chicago to renew friendly ties formed there in 1902, when he had filled the Crane Chair of Slavonic Studies. His next stop was Pittsburgh, a metropolis of heavy Slovak concentration. It proved excellent strategy for Masaryk to demonstrate the popularity and unity of his cause before approaching Washington. All his interviews and public speeches were designed to convince his public that "the first thing the Allies ought to understand is that the destruction of Austria-Hungary is the first step to victory." [2]

His message to Czechs, Slovaks, Serbs, Croats, and Slovenes alike focused on the break-up of the Austro-Hungarian Empire at the war's end, which would permit the establishment of two independent states of Czechoslovakia and Yugoslavia, comprising the oppressed nationalities. His theme fused perfectly with President Wilson's concept of self-determination for all subject peoples.

In Washington, Masaryk soon established close relations with Secretary of State Robert Lansing and his staff and with other cabinet members as well. He found it handy to encounter Richard Crane, eldest son of his old friend Charles R. Crane, serving as secretary to Lansing. Masaryk's press coverage was embarrassingly favorable. Jean Jules Jusserand, the French ambassador to Washington, monitored Masaryk's progress and reported his findings to his superior at the Quai d'Orsay, Foreign Minister Stephen J. M. Pichon. At the end of May, Jusserand wrote: "Mr. Masaryk, who has not yet seen the President, has published a new interview in the *New York Times*, May 27th, in which he still insists on the necessity of working with the Bolsheviks who, he claims are 'more and more anti-German.' All speak against military intervention and recommend industrial and economic aid." [3] In this interview, Masaryk warned President Wilson and the other Allied leaders against intervention in Russia as futile. The advice bolstered Wilson's own bent. Moreover, it repeated what Wilson had already heard from his trusted friend and foreign policy adviser, Charles Crane.

Crane had written the President from his summer home on Cape Cod on June 9th recommending Masaryk, whom he had known for nearly 20 years as "one of the wisest" experts on central European and Russian affairs—practical too, having "organized the Bohemian Army in Russia last year—the only organized thing there—and, with all the anarchy around him . . . He is certainly the outstanding Slavic leader of the world." Crane told the President: "Professor Masaryk plans to spend two weeks in Washington after June 16th and I hope at some time within that period you and he can have a good talk."[4] President Wilson responded promptly on June 11th. "My dear Friend," he wrote, "Of course I will try to see Professor Masaryk. I had been planning to have a joint conference with him and one or two others in order to work out a scheme for the relief of Russia."[5]

Woodrow Wilson lost little time to honor his promise. He received Masaryk at the White House on June 19th, three days after the eminent nationbuilder arrived in town. A further incentive for Wilson to talk with Masaryk was the latter's recent return, fresh from the Russian revolutionary scene. Wilson listened avidly to Masaryk's presentation of his case for recognition of his projected independent, democratic, constitutional republic, which predicated rejection of a separate peace with Austria-Hungary. Wilson also heard at length the multiple pragmatic reasons against intervention in Soviet Russia and against detaining the Czechoslovak Legions in Russia for intervention purposes, contrary to compelling British pressures in favor.

Coincidentally, British general George Tom M. Bridges, military attaché in Washington, directed a pertinent message to his chief, British Ambassador Lord Reading, on June 18th, saying, among other things: "Masaryk has arrived and I saw him this afternoon because I was very anxious that he should not confuse the issue [of anti-Bolshevik intervention] with his Czechoslovak views, especially as I believe he will carry great weight with the President having been recommended to him by Mr. Crane as the best informed man he is likely to get on the Russian problem."[6]

Wilson was under a heavy barrage of persuasion from Whitehall to join in the contemplated anti-Bolshevik intervention. Wilson kept abreast of events independently and had no real need of Masaryk's briefing on the subject. Another fresh arrival from Russia was Capt. Hugh S. Martin, a former American assistant military attaché there, who joined in an interesting morning briefing session at Col. Edward House's office. Unsurprisingly, they "discussed Japanese and Allied intervention in its every phase."[7] In a letter to the President from his country home on June 11, 1918, House informed his chief of his talk with the French ambassador about "the old story of Japanese intervention, . . . assuring him that you knew it in its every phase." [8]

Some days later, Charles Crane gave a packet of papers to Joseph Patrick Tumulty, secretary to Wilson, for the President's attention, saying it was "a sort of composite of views by Russian experts . . . thoroughly informed about the actual state of affairs in various parts of Siberia." [9] Wilson sent them to his secretary of war, Newton D. Baker, for study by Gen. Peyton C. March, his chief of staff. Steadfast in his aim to mobilize U.S. resources in manpower and production for maximum support of the western front against the Germans, the President, through General March, instructed his representatives on the Allied Supreme War Council to oppose all interventionist schemes, however distasteful he personally found the Soviet regime. Wilson required no prodding from Masaryk for a neutralist stance in the internal Russian civil war.

There were other useful contacts for Masaryk to make in Washington, especially in Congress, where Pergler, Capt. Voska, and others had opened the doors since 1914. Of special interest was Bohemian-born ranking Democrat Adolph Sabath, who represented a solid Czech-based constituency in Chicago. Colonel House, Wilson's chief foreign policy adviser, gave Masaryk a cordial lunch, and David Franklin Houston, secretary of agriculture and Crane's close friend, took Masaryk on an expedition to the battlefield at Gettysburg.

Masaryk now contacted several prominent Jewish leaders whom he had met during his 1907 visit to the States, and who had enlisted in the cause. These were chiefly: Rabbi Stephen S. Wise, Supreme Court Justice Louis D. Brandeis, and Judge Julian W. Mack. Charles W. Eliot, ex-president of Harvard, an old academic friend, and President Nicholas Murray Butler, of Columbia University, also signed on publicly as supporters.

The first sizable Czech emigration overseas during the nineteenth century had been instigated by the political repression following in the wake of the short-lived 1848 revolution. Moreover, glowing opportunities beckoned in America throughout the decades, in contrast with mounting economic distress at home. The migrants generally employed their skills or resumed their professions in the New World and many launched small businesses in New York, Chicago, Cleveland, and other cities in the Midwest.

The greatest majority of the Slovaks, Catholics of uneducated peasant stock, were driven out in the tens of thousands by the economic stagnation and political repression imposed by Magyar rule in the late nineteenth century. These gravitated to the coal mines and industrial, chiefly steel, factories of Pennsylvania, centering around Pittsburgh. While throughout the national revival Slovak intellectuals like Štefánik had kept in touch with their Czech counterparts and occasionally led them, Imperial Hungary held a tight rein on indigenous political and cultural developments in this province and drove out the dissidents.

Popular stirrings were of course fostered by President Wilson's doctrine of self-determination, which was announced at the core of his Fourteen Points speech on January 8, 1918. The Fourteen Points stopped short of endorsing the break-up of the Habsburg realm, a necessary prelude to Czechoslovak independence. It served, nonetheless, as a conceptual framework for liberation of the subject peoples. At the moment, self-determination indicated at the least the promise of full local autonomy. Wilson was taking his time, as Masaryk had done for three years, to weigh the full consequences of demolishing the old Empire, which ruled over multiple clashing peoples. This American caution was not manifestly influenced by David Lloyd George's and Winston Churchill's shared aspiration to preserve the Empire as a bulwark and potential instrument against the spread of Bolshevism.

Wilson's declaration of war on Austria-Hungary in December 1917 implied to Czechoslovak leaders a possibility of his treating separately with this aggressive Central Power. It would require intense effort by the Czechoslovaks both in Europe and in the United States to dispel the dangerous delusion of a separate peace with the Dual Monarchy and to relegate it to the background.

In April 1918, a Congress of Oppressed Nationalities was convened in Rome, which propelled the Wilson Administration to tilt closer to the Czechoslovak cause. As Masaryk expressed it, the question was no longer whether it was desirable to dismember Austria-Hungary. The Empire was inexorably breaking up through centrifugal disintegration and required a new order to fill the power vacuum.

The congress was largely an outgrowth of the policy of cooperation between Czechoslovaks and Yugoslavs long ago initiated by Masaryk. After Masaryk's departure from London in May 1917, the task of mediating nationalities conflicts devolved upon H. Wickham Steed, who put the key Yugoslav leader, Ante Trumbič, into working contact with high-ranking Italian diplomats before the congress convened. Trumbič would attempt to compromise the ethnic contentions seething between Italy and the Yugoslavs over irredentist claims, whose diplomatic settlement would take years more to accomplish.

An American counterpart Nationalities Congress was convoked in

Pittsburgh. This congress assembled representatives of the spectrum of patriotic organizations supportive of Czechoslovak independence. It produced an agreement between the Czech National Union and the Slovak League, signed by both parties on May 30, 1918, registering uncommon unity and widespread support, both prerequisites of foreign recognition. Masaryk signed the Pittsburgh Agreement as president of the Czechoslovak National Council based in Paris. [10]

The Agreement underwrote support of Masaryk's program for the union of Czechs and Slovaks in a free and independent democratic republic. It explicitly granted the new province of Slovakia an autonomous status, with its own Diet, schools, courts, and "complete cultural freedom." It also decreed "its own financial and political administration, all to be conducted in the Slovak language of the State." [11] The eventual definitive structure was left to the elected representatives of the new nation, who would promulgate its constitution.

A chord to these positive developments toward independence was sounded with a renewal of political activity in the homeland. The collapse of the German spring offensive, followed by the repulse of a summer campaign on a broad front, spurred upsurges both in Prague and at Turčiansky Svätý Martin in Slovakia, led by Vavro Šrobár. In mid-April, Foreign Minister Ferdinand Czernin came over to open endorsement of independence. A new unity was forged between the National Socialist Party, led by Masaryk and Beneš, and the old Social Democratic Party, which had been led by vacillating Bohumír Šmeral, now replaced by František Soukup, who spoke outrightly for independence. Part of the *Maffia* joined with the Social Democrats, who projected beyond national independence to a socialist character for the nascent Czechoslovak state. The new Czech Democratic Party, led by Karel Kramář, attracted the Catholics to its banner. Confidence in the movement toward independence grew visibly at home, as at Washington. This new optimism led Secretary Lansing to authorize the use of State Department channels on June 25th to transmit to Russian Foreign Commissar Georgyi Chicherin a sharp Czechoslovak rebuke and protest at the maltreatment of their Legionnaires in Russia.

In any case, Wilson sought a means to react favorably by some public gesture or statement following Masaryk's first visit to the White House. On June 29th, the Wilson Administration recognized the right of all Slav peoples to freedom and independence. It was a significant first step in the President's progress toward intervention to protect the Legions, which would be followed inevitably by recognition of the

Czechoslovak National Council's drive for an independent republic.

Four days after the Wilson-Masaryk interview, on June 23rd, British contingents landed near Murmansk on the Kola peninsula. Wilson was now parrying the escalating prointervention pressure on the home front. Business interests involved in the Russian market had become notably aggressive, although initially they had been inclined to deal with the Soviets. The press, with little exception, willingly gave voice to virulent anti-Bolshevik propaganda. An information association founded by George Kennan, known as the Friends of Russian Freedom, counseled intervention on humanitarian and trade grounds. The neophyte Russian expert, Samuel N. Harper, who had studied in Russia during the 1904-1905 revolution and observed events there at firsthand in 1917 for the State Department, registered his opinion favoring involvement. Thomas Lamont, senior partner of the J. P. Morgan Bank, was the leading Wall Street voice to oppose and then to denounce intervention.

On July 15th, Lord Reading spoke to Lansing "about sending a garrison battalion from Hong Kong to Vladivostok . . . [as] reinforcement of the forces already there . . . again with Mr. Polk [the assistant secretary of war] next day . . . about it . . . I did not say anything about the French sending troops." [12]

Wilson made his public announcement of his about-face of policy in the Aide Memoire issued by the State Department on July 17th, setting forth his reasons and conditions for dispatching the U.S.expeditionary force to Siberia under the command of General William S. Graves, as noted in Chapter 3. As we have already seen, his primary motive was "to assist the Czechoslovaks," for whom he saw "immediate necessity and sufficient justification." The document gives solemn assurances of abstaining from any intervention in Russia's internal affairs or "any impairment of her territorial integrity either now or hereafter." [13] Britain's Foreign Secretary, Sir Arthur James Balfour, deemed the limitation in the number of troops to 7,000 as vastly insufficient, although the number was to be matched by the Japanese. At the same time, Balfour concurred heartily with Wilson's proposal to send an economic mission through Vladivostok to supply material assistance. [14]

Wilson anticipated "obtaining a rapid and radical solution on the Western front." [15] He intensely disliked meddling in other countries' internal affairs, preferring his policy of self-determination for all peoples and respect for their territorial integrity. Wilson's apprehensions about Japanese intentions in Siberia matched his premonitions, not without justification. A few months later, Japan's expeditionary force was increased tenfold from the agreed level of 7,000, to exceed, in General Graves's opinion, 72,000 men. In the process, the Japanese displaced the Czechoslovaks in policing the mainline of the Trans-Siberian Railway all the way to Lake Baikal. Captain Voska wrote with alarm from Paris on July 17th, suggesting taking immediate steps to prevent Japanese intervention in Russia, as it "would throw into the arms of Germany the whole Russian element which is now anti-German because Japan as a nation is more hated by Russians than any other race." [16]

The buildup, constituting the most flagrant violation of the intervention agreement, culminated Japan's expansionist policy, which had begun at the turn of the century. Both before and following the principal Japanese landings in August 1918, one paralleling the U.S. landing on August 6th and another several days later, the Japanese had been supporting and actively subsidizing the most brutal of the White Guard leaders, Cossack Gen. Grigorii Semenoff, who had also gained surreptitious support from various Allied representatives for his "band of scoundrels," as Graves perceived them. [17] The U.S. commander was personally revolted when he witnessed the cold-blooded murder of several war prisoners by Semenoff's men.

During the summer of 1918, the Czechoslovak Legions were gradually integrated into Allied plans for Russian intervention. Italy had already in April signed a treaty permitting the creation of a local Czechoslovak Legion. Great Britain and France proceeded cautiously but unswervingly to acknowledge the right to independence for the Czechoslovaks. The Czechoslovak National Council in Paris was duly recognized by the French government on June 29th as the Czechoslovak provisional government, and as the government of an associated power at war with the enemy Central Powers. On the following day, the French government presented military colors to the legion corps fighting in France. Great Britain recognized the provisional Czechoslovak government on August 9th; Japan on September 9th; and Italy on October 3rd. [18] Secretary Lansing told President Wilson that these acts "are assumed to be a full recognition." He stated further: "I feel strongly that Austria-Hungary as an Empire should disappear . . . [as the] keystone of Mittel-Europa." [19] Eduard Beneš diplomatically emphasized that this provisional government was only a partial one, to be completed by its Prague representatives when they could be absorbed.

Movement toward that end was taken in Prague on July 13th with the founding of a new National Committee by the 30 Czech members of the Reichsrat. The chairman was the prestigious Kramář, leader of the Nationalist Young Czechs, while the real organizational work was undertaken by Antonín Švehla, the emerging Freeholders' leader, who became a vice-chairman, along with Václav J. Klofáč, who was named second vice-chairman. Soukup became secretary. Food shortages gave Švehla, the foremost Agrarian spokesman, potent political leverage.

The Czechoslovaks were undoubtedly earning their upgraded status by their multiple contributions to the Allied cause, beyond the Siberian fighting by their Legions. They provided intelligence reports to the foreign ministries from the heart of Central Europe. Counter-intelligence by the Czechoslovaks against German disinformation was another vital function performed by their network, especially when it exposed a newly launched Save Austria movement as a German subterfuge. [20]

Secretary Lansing proposed on August 19th that "we might recognize the belligerency of the Czechoslovak revolutionists in view of their military organization operating in Siberia and Eastern Russia against Austrian loyalists and their German allies . . . I think it would be proper . . . to recognize Czechoslovak Council with Masaryk at its head as a de facto Revolutionary Government and give it as much aid as seems expedient." [21]

Although Allied policy now doomed the Austro-Hungarian Empire, Emperor King Carl of Habsburg was in no mind to relinquish power. He began to scout his best chance for a separate peace by extending the olive branch of federalism to the various nationalities within the Empire. Internally, recognition of the autonomous rights of the Kingdom of Bohemia could prove attractive to Prague Conservatives, but the offer of federalism foreclosed acceptance in Hungary, the population of which was but half Magyar, the rest being suppressed. Aware of the dangers implicit in these splitting intrigues, on September 3rd President Wilson granted the National Council full recognition as the provisional government of the emerging independent state.

In mid-October, Masaryk received a warning from his Paris-based organization of Emperor Carl's preparation to issue a Peace Manifesto of his own, based on his offer of federalism couched in terms paralleling Wilson's declaration of self-determination for all subject peoples. On October 14th, the National Council moved decisively to outflank the Emperor. It reorganized itself as the provisional government. Beneš was designated as foreign minister and Štefánik became war minister under the presidency of Masaryk. Beneš was soon able to represent the Czechoslovaks in the forthcoming armistice negotiations, an honor that was withheld from the Poles but granted also to Allied co-belligerents and existing states.

Secretary of State Lansing was consulted regarding the timing of an early announcement of Czechoslovak independence to forestall any corrosive consequences in Europe of Emperor Carl's imminent Vienna manifesto. President Wilson readily agreed to dispatch a diplomatic note to the Emperor on October 18th, rejecting the separate peace overtures. On the same day, October 18th, Masaryk in Washington and Beneš in Paris coordinated their proclamations of Czechoslovak independence in a document prepared by Masaryk in consultation with the Bohemian-born Justice Brandeis and also with legal counsel in the State Department.

The Washington declaration epitomized Masaryk's concept of a democratic republic, which guaranteed progressive social legislation and granted equal rights to women and to the national minorities. Inherited rights signifying the class privileges of the landed gentry were abolished; large entailed estates were broken up; and the Catholic Church was disestablished. What amounted to a bill of rights revealed the hand of Brandeis in the drafting. There was, lastly, this significant pledge on foreign policy: "The Czechoslovak nation [will] accept its full responsibility for the re-organization of Eastern Europe."[22]

Masaryk's solidarity campaign with fellow Slav leaders was promoted in November 1918 at a great rally at Carnegie Hall in New York, at which pianist Ignaz Paderewski, premier of reborn Poland, played the leading role. Despite inevitable frictions of personalities, the meetings evolved a program of common aims for democratic collaboration and solidarity. In the face of this overt pledge for reducing national rivalries, this platform held hope of leading to a loose federation of the states situated between Germany and Russia.

Emperor Carl now came under the dual threat of his armies' military rout and widespread social and national upheaval at home. On October 28th, he capitulated to President Wilson's conditions of peace without actually renouncing his throne in Vienna. Violent revolutions had erupted in Budapest and Vienna, calling for independent socialist republics. In Prague, the Czech leaders declared their independence. The bloodless overturn constituted the Czechoslovak revolution, for on the following day the Imperial authorities turned over military control of Prague to the governing committee.

On October 30th, the Slovak parties announced the severance of all ties with Budapest, and a joint Czechoslovak delegation, led by Kramář, left for consultative conferences in Geneva, coordinating with Beneš coming from Paris, as representative of the Allied countries recognizing the provisional government.

The two-way fusion talks in Geneva were dominated from the outset by Beneš. The first reason for Beneš's ascendancy was his personal representation of President-Designate Masaryk, the acknowledged leader of the new state and the manager of the campaign for international recognition. Secondly, Beneš, as foreign minister, was already an accepted member in the councils of the Big Powers sitting in Paris. The Czech Socialist and Social Democratic members, combined with the Agrarians, who altogether comprised virtually the entire popular base within the new country, were thinking along far more radical lines than those evinced by the Slovak Democrats. Lastly, Beneš presented the National Council's program with such logical persuasion that his resolution carried by acclamation.

In the end, Kramář accepted nomination as Czechoslovakia's first prime minister under his old associate and rival, Masaryk, the president-elect. Beneš and Štefánik were duly confirmed as ministers of foreign affairs and war, respectively, in an all-party coalition government that was determined to establish the new regime by peaceful rather than forceful means wherever possible. Never before or since in history did a newly emerging state get a more highly qualified or experienced minister of foreign affairs, straightaway.

President Masaryk directed a letter on November 9th from Washington to "all military authorities and Czechoslovak Legion Commanders," conforming his new government's Russian policy to that of Wilson. He wrote: "On the basis of the agreement reached between the Czechoslovak National Council and the High Command and General Staff to the effect that Czechoslovak troops may not be used in internal Russian conflicts, but solely to combat Russia's internal enemies, I demand that Czechoslovak military formations should not in any way be involved in the present conflict between the [Russian] parties." [23]

A week later, on November 16th, President Masaryk returned to the White House to take leave of Woodrow Wilson. The two intellectual statesmen, as Masaryk later told his intimate circle, had discovered a large number of common interests, but with no occasion to explore these interests in depth, they had focused on the business at hand. Masaryk reported that he had deliberately kept their meetings brief and to the point, rarely exceeding a half hour. Genuine cordiality existed between the two, as witness their exchange of letters. After extending recognition to the new provisional government, Wilson took pleasure in having been of service to the Czechoslovak peoples. His interest in their fate and his best wishes for their success never waned.

Toward the end of his five-month stay in Washington, Masaryk, who had been prolific in turning out memoranda and conducting interviews concerning the significance of war developments, took a bold initiative. He privately ventured the suggestion to Wilson of a radical turn of policy, stemming from his apprehensions about the Allied Powers. He estimated that after the long years of bloodletting and destruction, the Allies would go soft on the enemy in their peace accords. In the closing days of the war, Masaryk advocated that Marshal Foch advance his armies deep into the German heartland and not stop at the Rhine barrier. The German people, he warned, would never realize that they had lost the war until they witnessed foreign armies on their soil. Such a military occupation was destined to wait 27 years, following a bloodier and more devastating holocaust.

In politics, Masaryk hewed sharply to his cool pragmatism, while the U.S. president turned ideological in forging peace terms. Masaryk's style was to govern through discussion, always in search of consensus.

On his way home, Masaryk continued to make useful contacts for his nascent state. He met with some important leaders of Wall Street who were eager to assist Czechoslovakia's embarkation on its experiment in democracy and independence. He had earlier been in touch with Bernard M. Baruch, chairman of the War Industries Board, to arrange a loan for the purchase of supplies and equipment, arms and munitions for his Legions in Siberia. Now, he met with the secretary of the navy, Josephus Daniels, and his assistant secretary, Franklin D. Roosevelt, about providing early transport for the Legions out of Vladivostok. He urgently needed to arrange a reconstruction and rehabilitation loan of $10 million.

The next stop on his homeward journey was in London to call on Foreign Secretary Balfour, to thank him personally for his help. In London and then in Paris, he sought out close friends and associates to express his gratitude and to elicit their continuing interest. He paid particular homage to the triumphant Tiger, Premier Georges Clemenceau of France. On his last lap, he met in Padua with King Victor Emmanuel II of Italy. In the last two places, the new president passed in review Legion units that had fought on the French and Italian fronts. The Legion divisions were soon to form the military core of the new republic; those in France and Italy began to move on their way.

Masaryk's round-the-world expedition culminated in Prague amidst thunderous acclaim four years, almost to the day, after his unheralded departure.

NOTES

1. Tomáš G. Masaryk, *The Making of a State* (New York: Frederick Stokes, 1927), pp. 190, 176, 199.

2. Vera Olivova, *The Doomed Democracy: Czechoslovakia in a Disrupted Europe, 1914-1938* (London: Sidgwick & Jackson, 1972), p. 85.

3. Washington, Letter received May 19, 1928, Woodrow Wilson Letters (hereafter *WW Letters*), v. 48, pp. 202-3.

4. *WW Letters*, v. 48, p. 273.

5. Ibid, p. 283.

6. Letter, June 18, 1918, Washington, *WW Letters*, v. 48, pp. 352-53.

7. "Diary of Col. Edward House," June 11, 1918, *WW Letters*, v. 48, p. 283.

8. Magnolia House, Mass, June 11,1918, *WW Letters*, v. 48, p. 283.

9. Wilson to Newton D. Baker, June 19, 1918, *WW Letters*, v. 48, p. 357.

10. The Pittsburgh Agreement, FO 800/106, p. 367.

11. Ibid.

12. Lord Reading, Washington, July 15, 1918, FO 371/v. 3324.

13. William S. Graves, *America's Siberian Adventure* (New York: Jonathan Cape, 1931), pp. 7-10.

14. Telegram, Sir Arthur Balfour to Lord Reading, July 22, 1918, FO 371/v. 3287, p. 419.

15. Henry Bergson to Stephen J. M. Pichon, *WW Letters*, v. 49, p. 113.

16. Letter E. Voska, Paris, to Wilson, *WW Letters*, v. 49, p. 41.

17. Graves, *America's Siberian Adventure*, p. 86.

18. Richard Lansing to Wilson, August 19, 1918, *WW Letters*, v. 49, p. 387.

19. Ibid.

20. Frank L. Polk to Wilson, *WW Letters*, v. 49, p. 41.

21. Lansing to Wilson, August 18, 1918, *WW Letters*, v. 49, pp. 287-88.

22. Masaryk, FO 800/306, p. 367.

23. Olivova, *The Doomed Democracy*, pp. 43-44.

5

Drawing the Frontiers

The treaties drawn at Versailles by the victorious Western Allies organized the peace and gave the new Europe its legal framework. Soviet Russia, still rent by civil strife and intervention, was excluded. Four treaties were produced by prolonged negotiations, delineating new borders for the liberated nations that were carved out of the domain of the defeated Central Powers and Czarist Russia.

The Versailles system was ultimately dependent for enforcement on French military power. This presence, combined with a network of alliances, provided the keystone of the new order that welded the outlines of Czechoslovak independence. With English and French backing, Czechoslovakia was positioned to reorganize trade and political relations among the successor states of Central Europe. Her territorial perimeters presented the first set of her problems at Versailles concerning Czechoslovakia. [1]

President Masaryk and Foreign Minister Eduard Beneš made clear from the outset of their negotiations with the Allies that they would insist on realizing in the West the historical frontiers of the Kingdom of Bohemia. Within these natural boundaries, Slavic tribes had lived far earlier than the time of Charlemagne. The territory now also held more than 3 million Germans, whose native land had lost the war; consequently, the occupation of Czechoslovakia's three western provinces presented no political obstacles at Versailles. The definition of the three Slovak borders, however, provoked ethnic and strategic clashes deriving from the dismemberment of royal Hungary.

Preceding the armistice in Europe, on October 30, 1918, the Bohemian German nationalist leader, Rudolf Lodgmann, headed a delegation to Prague in quest of food and supplies. Three days later, a German Social Democratic group arrived on the same mission. Both rejected out of hand the invitation to join their Reichsrat colleagues in the new government. Lodgmann was destined, however, to survive in Czechoslovak politics.

Beneš, as Czech delegate to the Paris conference, protested an Anschluss proposal on the ground of its giving defeated Germany a significant increase of territory. On December 19th, France, taking her cue from the Beneš formulation and without consulting her Allies, vetoed the proposed Anschluss. Full French support was then given to Czechoslovakia's request for guarantees of security within her historic frontiers. Germany, afflicted by postwar turmoil, paid little heed to this territorial setback.

The Prague government of Karel Kramář, provisional prime minister, had already in early November called for volunteers among the Sokols* to venture forth and occupy the frontier districts where most of the Germans lived. Only one brief skirmish occurred, and within a month, without further overt resistance, the demoralized German population submitted to the authority of the new republic. Moderate German parties, the Social Democrats and Agrarians, soon initiated talks with their Czech counterparts, with whom they had collaborated in Vienna. Following the first municipal elections in May 1919, they took their seats, first in local bodies and soon in the national parliament.

Hungary did not contain a Slovak province, although the predominant majority of the Slovaks lived in northern Hungary. The delineation of the new frontiers for Slovakia, therefore, encountered special intricacies. To begin with, the Allied armistice with Austria and Germany, signed at Padua on November 4th, concerned itself primarily with Italian matters. It omitted any provision for Hungary, a Central Power ally, to evacuate the minority-populated territories that were stirring in revolt against the new central government. And the republican regime of Count Mihály Károlyi in Budapest faced an external threat of Allied invasion from the south. It sued for and obtained at Belgrade an armistice with French General d'Espery, commander-in-chief of the advancing, mostly Serbian, armies. The resulting agreement provided the provisional border between Hungary

---

*The Sokols (Falcons) were the national gymnastic society, which, lacking a national army, the Czechs had founded in 1860, modeled on the German Turnverein. Every four years, the Sokols held a giant outdoor rally in Prague, which was in fact a great patriotic demonstration symbolizing national liberation.

and the new kingdom of Yugoslavia. But Károlyi, supported by the French representative at Budapest, also interpreted the Belgrade armistice as allowing Hungary to retain control over the restless Slovak districts, and those in the province of Transylvania, which contained a large Romanian majority.

Meanwhile, Prague had chosen Vavro Šrobár, chief Slovak representative of the Geneva conference, as its minister for Slovakia. Heading a four-man team of administrators, Šrobár, with 70 gendarmes, moved into western Slovakia, where he encountered opposition from the Hungarian authorities. It was not, in fact, until December 19th that French Foreign Minister Stephen J. M. Pichon issued an order to the Károlyi government to withdraw its officials and army units from what it still considered as northern Hungary.

Kramář had simultaneously reinforced Šrobár's mandate in Slovakia by dispatching a contingent of legionnaires, who had just returned to Prague from Italy with President Masaryk. Imperial authority melted away after the declaration of independence on October 28, 1918, when the top Austrian army officers withdrew with their men to Vienna. It took the mostly Czech Sokol cadres, backed by the legionnaires and the French Army, to fill the gap and to police public order. A veteran French general, Maurice Pellé became Czech chief of staff. By January 20th, a month after the western provinces were fully occupied, Slovakia was integrated into the republic.

A divisive policy of these early days was that of staffing the new Slovak province with Czech officials recently returned from Vienna. After the elimination of the prewar Magyar administrators in the eastern lands, the returning bureaucrats served as a reserve pool for the newly created posts in all the provinces. Charges were levelled reflexively against Prague for "colonizing" these provinces with Czech officials, school teachers, police officers, and tax collectors, in betrayal of the Pittsburgh agreement.

The practice was especially offensive as it contravened the promise made by all the successor states when they subscribed to a Special Convention for Protection of Minorities, which Beneš himself had initiated, guaranteeing equal civil rights to minority peoples living within their borders. This convention specifically guaranteed the use of the mother tongue in state and local administrations, in the courts, and in the schools, as well as in state employment. Presumptive violations could be taken up in hearings before the League of Nations, with ultimate appeal to the World Court.

According to the 1921 census, Czechoslovakia was not as polyglot a state as Austria-Hungary had been, where roughly half the population was neither German nor Magyar. In Czechoslovakia, out of a total of more than 13 million people, 8.8 million, or 63% were Czechoslovaks, including 2 million Slovaks. The Bohemian Germans did not reside in a compact bloc. They were concentrated in the big cities and were scattered over a 600-mile area bordering on Austria, Bavaria, Saxony, and Polish Silesia. About half a million Magyars lived on the Great Rye Island, which was assigned to Slovakia, and along the eastern frontier with Sub-Carpathian Russia.

Drawing the frontiers with Hungary presented difficulties due to internal differences. During the month between two French warning notes to Budapest, Milan Hodža, Czechoslovak commissioner at Budapest, conducted unauthorized negotiations with the Hungarian government relative to the frontier to divide them. As Hodža's proposals were more favorable to Hungary than Beneš's as set forth on his map, the Hungarian withdrawal created an awkward situation for the diplomats at Paris.

There Beneš invoked a combination of economic and strategic considerations to uphold his proposal for a Danubian border in the south of Slovakia including the city of Posony (Pressburg). The immediate hinterland of Posony, soon renamed Bratislava, was solidly Slovak, but only some 20 percent of its population, mostly workers, was Slovak; the rest was equally divided between Magyar and German. An important river port, Bratislava was extended with a bridgehead on the south side of the Danube and became the capital of Slovakia.

From that point, the frontier line was drawn down the river's mainstream, leaving the Great Rye Island, wholly Hungarian populated, to Slovakia. From where the Danube bends to the south, the new boundary runs irregularly in a northeasterly direction, cutting south of the Hungarian city of Kassa, renamed Košice. This key railway junction in eastern Slovakia contained a mixed population of Magyar officials and residents and included Jewish tradesmen and Slovaks.

The eastern frontier of Slovakia, lacking any geographic definition, presented a primarily ethnic problem. In that area, the Slovaks shaded into a Ukrainian people, known locally as Ruthenians, whose language blended with Slovak. The Mid-Eastern Union, speaking for Ruthenian immigrants in the United States, petitioned the peace conference for incorporation of these people into Czechoslovakia as an autonomous province, eventually taking the name of Sub-Carpathian Russia. Beneš inserted a security argument seconding this recommendation before the Czechoslovak Commission in Paris. Czechoslovakia and Romania, as allies in the proposed Little Entente, demanded a common frontier, which was secured by including the rail line eastward from Košice through the fertile Magyar-populated plain into northern Transylvania and continuing southward to the capital city of Cluz.[2]

To the north and west of Czechoslovakia there were clearly defined lines of demarcation. The Tatra Mountain ridge naturally divided the province of Polish Galicia from old Hungary, and in the west there was a historic frontier with Moravia. There remained to be settled at Paris the acrimonious dispute between Czechoslovakia and Poland over the former Bohemian Crown land of Teschen. Although it had never been part of Poland, Teschen contained a mixed German and Polish population. It was valuable as a rail hub, which formed the connecting link between northern Moravia and Slovakia. The Poles were outraged when their Slav brothers to the south, chiefly with French backing, occupied the city of Teschen.

The Polish Foreign Minister, Roman Dmowski, came to Paris to meet with his friend Beneš to discuss the controversy. The entire matter was moved from the peace conference to a separate direct negotiation, where it subsequently stalled, and again moved to a conference of ambassadors. Ultimately, the controversy was adjudicated favorably to Czechoslovakia by the Court of International Justice at the Hague in 1925. Here, behind the scenes, the French supportive role was crucial.

Several threats to Czechoslovak survival emanated from Budapest after the armistice. The revolutionary takeover by Béla Kun was met by the imposition of martial law from Prague, while it reaped broad popular support in Slovakia. The regime might have moderated and survived longer had it not exceeded its Versailles boundaries to recapture ground shorn from Hungary in Slovakia. Beneš and Šrobár took a stern nationalist stand, combined with help from General Pellé, commanding the new Czechoslovak army to repel the irredentist Hungarians. Marshal Ferdinand Foch sent an ultimatum for withdrawal to Budapest.

The final blow was administered to the Kun revolutionary regime in Budapest by an Allied blockade, soon followed by the intervention of 300 Romanian Army troops ordered from Paris. Before withdrawing, the Allies installed the first protofascist regime, headed as regent by the unimpressive Admiral Miklos Horthy, who was bolstered in power by the ruthless "resurrected Hungarians" under Julius Gömbös, later to become prime minister. This early conflict perpetuated historically hostile feelings in Hungary that would later come home to roost menacingly. Budapest's irredentist claims upon its Little Entente neighbors were its overriding preoccupation.[*]

The next threat to Central European stability was posed by the attempted Habsburg restoration in Budapest. Ex-King Charles of Habsburg arrived in Budapest over the Easter weekend of 1920 to the great embarrassment of the government. Charles certainly had more legitimacy than Horthy. Backed by the mutual assistance treaties that Beneš had had the foresight to conclude with his neighbors, Romania and Yugoslavia, the Little Entente was well placed to take firm action. Beneš now declared a *casus belli* and called on his allies to join in demanding and securing the immediate expulsion of King Charles. The ex-king repeated his foray in October, in Western Hungary. With the full backing of his Allies, Beneš threatened a Little Entente mobilization. A series of intense negotiations ensued, resulting in Hungary's acceptance of humiliating terms imposed by the Allies; a dethronement act covering not only Charles but all Habsburg princes. Charles was banished to the Madeira Islands, where he died two years later.

The Little Entente pact with Romania and Yugoslavia was confected by Eduard Beneš and supported by France to enhance Central European security. Final signing of the treaty was postponed due to frontier raids by Macedonian terrorists, whom the progressive Bulgarian government of Prime Minister Alexander Stamboliski was powerless to control. Probably for this reason, the mutual assistance treaty was extended to cover the contingency of an unprovoked attack by Bulgaria. Czechoslovakia held aloof from this enlarged commitment, to give Beneš a chance to promote inter-Slavic rapprochement in the Balkans by mutual consent.

In the final analysis, France became the general guarantor of the Versailles system of alliances, from which she also profited when concluding her own interlocking treaties of friendship and mutual assistance separately with each of her eastern Allies. French friendship and support was a mainstay of security for the new fledgling Czechoslovak republic in Central Europe, situated between Soviet Russia and Germany, looking east and west, and between Poland and Hungary, looking north and south, all neighbors with historic designs on segments of her corpus. The Czechoslovak leaders

---

[*]Hungary's irredentist claims were as follows: Slovakia from Czechoslovakia; Transylvania from Rumania; Voivodine from Yugoslavia; also Burgenland from Austria. Hungary favored a Habsburg restoration. These ambitions were thwarted by firm Little Entente opposition, to the extent of mounting a military mobilization in Czechoslovakia and Yugoslavia.

counted on their dealings with Soviet Russia to provide counter-balancing security against a possible German resurgence under rightist leadership. This pro-Soviet foreign policy of Beneš and Masaryk was then, and often later, misconstrued by hard-liners both at home and in the West as being ideologically inspired.

Masaryk soon undertook extended visits to Paris and London, accompanied by Beneš, to smooth over the impediments to completing their network of foreign alliances. In Paris they sought a treaty of friendship and alliance, short of undertaking a commitment to give automatic assistance in the case of unprovoked aggression against France from Germany. In October 1923, they argued before Premier Raymond Poincaré and President Alexandre Millerand that the French position in Central Europe would be strengthened by having a truly independent friend and ally there, while France would be protected militarily because a French general staff officer was serving as Czechoslovak chief of staff. The Czechoslovak leaders wished to avoid the trap of their country's being turned into a French satellite.

In London, the Czechoslovak leaders could flatly disclaim any secret military commitments. This was a primary sticking point at the moment for the British, who were anxious to resist French militarism and continental predominance. They deemed French policy as dangerously tending to overextend itself militarily, and they calculated its overexacting reparations demands as blocks to European economic reconstruction. All of the Powers, however, would profit by the proposed Franco-Czechoslovak treaty. This treaty of friendship and alliance was eventually signed in Paris on January 25, 1924. Openly based on the peace structure erected in Paris and on practical realities of French continental policy, the pact compromised on the lesser ground of automatic consultations, rather than automatic military response, in the case of unprovoked aggression.

The Czechoslovak leaders employed the same caution when they were being pressured to mediate differences between Britain and France over the settlement of debts and reparations from Germany. In early January 1924, Premier Poincaré ordered French troops into the Ruhr basin to exact direct collections in coal and other commodities. They then deferred to the Americans, who evolved the Dawes Plan for the reduction of war debts and reparations, and this spurred a German resurgence. This improvement sparked the convening of an international conference at Locarno on October 16, 1925, which provided a limited settlement for western and eastern Europe on regional lines. Germany recognized the inviolability of the Versailles western frontiers for France and Belgium and agreed to the permanent demilitarization of the Rhineland. Both frontier guarantees were underwritten by Great Britain and eventually also by Italy.

As for Eastern European security, only treaties of compulsory arbitration were granted by Germany. These were formally under-written by France, which further extended the provision of her Czechoslovak alliance by inserting a military clause to respond automatically in case of unprovoked aggression by Germany. Despite the high hopes evoked by the overpublicized spirit of Locarno, as symbolizing a definitive peace settlement, in the end the lack of Eastern frontier guarantees proved a fatal flaw.

On the whole, Czechoslovakia, a multiracial nation of robust farmers, skilled workers, and thrifty shopkeepers, benefited from the fruits and protection of the French-dominated Versailles system. In its exposed geographical position, Czechoslovakia could not hope to attain full independence in its foreign policy. To the east, even as Czechoslovak units were still embattled in Siberia in 1919, Masaryk and Beneš at once established working relations with the Moscow regime and sought to reaffirm their traditional policy of neutrality in internal Russian affairs and cooperation with the established Soviet government.

In pursuing his bilateral negotiations, Beneš had already opened trade talks with Warsaw and then with Moscow. His early efforts at Warsaw met with success. His announcement on May 1, 1925, of resuming talks with the Soviets was strengthened by the approval of his Little Entente partners. Clamor against these accommodations again erupted in Prague, the loudest protest emanating from the new Fascist Party. Seven months later, Masaryk reiterated his explicit instructions to his foreign minister to renew efforts also to secure full diplomatic relations with the USSR. Beneš, meantime, with an eye to rallying public support for his Eastern policy, organized business and trade delegations, including German and Magyar representatives, to visit the new Russia.

NOTES

1.   The best short account of drawing Czechoslovakia's frontiers at Paris in 1919-20 can be found in Isaiah Bowman, *The New World* (New York: World, 1928), pp. 329-44. For the negotiation of the treaties of peace concerning Czechoslovakia, see H. W. V. Temperly, Ed., *History of the Peace Conference of Paris,* Institute of International Affairs, Vol. 4 (London: Hodder & Frowdie & Stoughton, 1921).

2.   John O. Crane, *The Little Entente* (New York: Macmillan, 1931). The four key railway hubs for which the Czechs took a determined stand are clearly shown on the map at the end of the book. These were Cheb (Eger), a small enclave taken from Bavaria; Teschen, which controlled the northern rail link with Slovakia; Bratislava, a Danube outlet; and Košice, providing connection through Sub-Carpathian Russia, the link with Transylvania, Rumania.

6

Internal Stabilization

The new Czechoslovakia was richly endowed with natural resources, comprising three-quarters of the industrial capacity of the old Empire. Although she was saddled at the Paris Peace Conference with half of the Empire's debt of 20 million gold crowns, she was still far ahead of the other successor states. The Czech and German workers and peasants also had a higher level of literacy and greater urbanization than the others. [1]

The skilled German workers predominated in the export production of high quality glass, porcelains, and textiles, whereas the heavy industries, mines, and engineering plants were chiefly manned by Czechs. German farmers raised most of the famous Bohemian hops, and the Czechs grew the sugar beets. The mixed population in the west at Pilsen worked the famous beer emporium and the immense Škoda engineering and armaments works.

General farming on the large entailed estates of Bohemia was impeded by feudal land-holdings, which had been owned from the time of the Counter-Reformation mostly by the Austro-German nobility and Catholic institutions, deriving from the tragic annihilation of Bohemian nobles at the Battle of the White Mountain in 1620. The greater industrial complexes were owned and controlled largely by banks in Vienna. The industrial and landed wealth in the German community gave the people an aristocratic and bourgeois orientation that was singularly absent among the Czechs.

The Czechs were an unique people, virtually lacking in landed aristocrats or an upper class. The Czech middle class was emerging coincidentally with their attainment of nationhood. Owing to the lack of nobility and upper bourgeoisie, the Czechs had by tradition an egalitarian society and a democratic outlook, which was bolstered by their Hussite religion. Not more than two or three generations removed from the soil, the Czechs were generally a petit bourgeois people residing in the cities and towns. They constituted a society of the little man, a nation of shopkeepers, artisans, and peasants.

Whereas more than half of the Czechs lived in towns and cities, the Slovaks were predominantly a rural peasant people. They tended their pastures and small family farms on the hillsides and mountains, but the forests and fertile land in the plains were held in large entailed tracts by the Magyar nobility and the Catholic Church. The Slovaks historically had been disadvantaged in educational facilities; only in parish schools could they study in their native tongue. This condition had been exacerbated when Count Albert Apponyi became minister of education at the turn of the century. In 1907, he decreed further Magyarization by suppressing Slovak elementary schools. Before the adoption of Apponyi's laws, the 267 primary schools and Slovak districts had permitted partial instruction in Slovak.[2] In 1914, the 59 secondary schools were giving no instruction in Slovak and no university existed in Slovakia. The Magyarization had first become relentless following the Austro-Hungarian compromise of 1867, when an entirely Hungarian administration displaced the more tolerant Habsburg state apparatus. At that time, tens of thousands of Slovaks went abroad in search of work, freedom, and equality, also escaping their forced naturalization as Hungarians.

By consensus there were not more than a thousand families to be found among the Slovak intelligentsia. Most of these had gained their higher education in Budapest, but a few of their number, such as Vavro Šrobár, had attended Charles University in Prague; another outstanding exception, Milan Rastislav Štefánik, had studied in Paris. In view of the pitiable conditions prevailing in Slovakia before World War I, it is notable that Slovak intellectuals had played a prominent role in the Slavic revival which had begun a century earlier during the late eighteenth century enlightenment.

At the time of independence, Slovakia had two principal parties; the pro-Czech Hlasists led by Father Andrej Hlinka, or Populists, and the autonomists. Soon the Populists moved to protest the Czechization of the public administration and the public schools. Exasperated feelings provoked the unhappy alienation of a segment of Slovak popular opinion from the Prague government, an alienation that would later come home to roost. Distress among unemployed workers and peasants in Slovakia disposed them to swallow the demagoguery that attributed all their acute troubles to Czech mismanagement and exploitation.

At Prague, the newly organized land office, established under the Land Control Act of April 16, 1919, provided for expropriations of landed estates. The complicated mechanism of property allocations to landless or small cultivators was administered by the conservative Agrarian Party, led by Antonín Švehla, enhancing his political power. The vested landowners, who for the most part retained control of the productive core of the large estates containing the agricultural industries, tugged the administration rightward as well. Although the state took over vast tracts of indivisible forest lands, the old owners managed to retain roughly a third of their holdings. Despite the conservative pressures generated, however, Švehla remained loyal to his coalition with the Social Democrats, honoring his commitment to promote the progressive social legislative program. At the same time, Švehla deftly handled the spate of political issues behind the scenes in the five-man Agrarian executive committee called the Pĕtka. His political skills were keenly appreciated by President Tomáš Masaryk who esteemed Švehla highly for contributing thus to the nation's consolidation.

The government agenda comprised labor laws establishing factory councils (soviets), an eight-hour day, and a comprehensive social security system implementing the partial coverage provided in old Austria. The extension of these social reforms into Slovakia went far to ease tensions there as well. Despite early revolutionary agitation, factory councils in Czechoslovakia never pressed beyond the organization of work and the supervision of working conditions in the plants. They did not acquire a political dimension until 1945, and they were eliminated after the Communist takeover of 1948.

The concluding act of the provisional assembly, sitting also as a constituent assembly, was to adopt the permanent constitution. This fundamental charter, created by the prewar parliamentary representatives, was manifestly the instrument of the Czechoslovak people. The preamble began; "We the Czechoslovak nation . . ." Although no minority group participated in the drafting, all nationalities were guaranteed equal rights and treatment under the law.

The constitution provided for parliamentary rule, with a Cabinet responsible to the parliament. The duties and rights of citizens were delineated; social rights were provided; all inherited privileges were abolished; and the Catholic Church was disestablished. The powers and structure of the state were centralized in Prague, and local administration was divided into counties and townships organized through elected councils.

A federal state was explicitly rejected by the deletion of provincial diets. This proviso was a decisive setback for Slovak autonomists, who charged a violation of the Pittsburgh Convention. Their rivals, the Hlasists, on the other hand, asserted that Slovak progress now could only be realized through close cooperation with Prague.

In the general elections held on April 20, 1920, the catch-all Social Democrats of the prime minister, Vlastimil Tusar, won twice as many votes as any other party, mirroring the leftward mood of the electorate, which was now enjoying universal and equal suffrage. The first act of the new Czechoslovak parliament was to elect Masaryk as chief of state, a triumph over the candidates of the various minority parties, who had rallied to cast their ballots for the Moravian-Slovak president.

Postwar food shortages, however, gave rise to protracted food riots in Bohemia and Moravia, fanning out from the mining town of Kladno, near Prague. The acute scarcity was worsened by hoarding and speculation. Agitators mounted protests, which soon spread to embrace metal and railway workers. To alleviate the food shortage and to curb the extremists, President Masaryk appealed directly to the Social Democratic shop stewards.

The famous private nationalization law of December 12, 1919, greatly strengthened the Czech business and financial community by requiring foreign firms to register as national companies. It ultimately resulted in 231 business firms being taken over by Czech interests. The principal corporate beneficiary was Prague's privileged Živnostenská Bank, which enjoyed large French participation. For national security reasons, French capital representing the Schneider-Creussot arms firm was permitted to purchase a half-share of the Škoda works, which made the famous Austrian 155 howitzer. Unhappily, however, the French then removed several patented machines and transported them to France to copy the patents and float them on the French market. Czech patent rights were thus violated without recourse by the fledgling republic. These were the facts of the widespread rumor about French "dismantling" of the Škoda plant. The machines that were removed were subsequently returned to Pilsen.[3] The government bit its collective lip and absorbed the big-power offense; it could ill afford quarrels with its chief international sponsor.

Within the big financial and industrial circle of the new country, Jaroslav Preiss, managing director of the Živnostenská, a political moderate of National Democratic persuasion, and Škoda's general corporate director, Karel Loevenstein, maintained close working relations with the government at Prague. The other heavy industrial complex of the former Empire was the Witkovitz works of Moravska

Ostrava, which attracted Czech participation and remained under the control of Viennese capital.

Czechoslovakia's contributions to Austrian reconstruction bore a high stake of self-interest. Austria had long been the natural outlet for Bohemian-Moravian-Silesian manufactures. The obvious advantages of closer relations were not lost on certain nationalist groups representing new economic interests in Czechoslovakia. These elements, however, were lukewarm toward Beneš's plan to participate in rehabilitation measures for the Austrian economy. Beneš prevailed, and on December 16, 1920, he negotiated with Austria cooperation and arbitration conventions. Between them, Germany and Austria would soon absorb more than 40 percent of Czechoslovakia's exports, including transit trade to the free-trade cities of Hamburg and Trieste, which would inspire severe political repercussions after the rise to power of nationalist Hitler.

A fundamental clash of interest became manifest as a divisive influence in Central Europe between the northern tier of manufacturing export states, namely Czechoslovakia and Austria, protecting the elevated living standards of their farmers, and the southern tier, comprising Hungary, Yugoslavia, and Romania, which produced farm surpluses that the richer countries could only partially absorb. To worsen matters, Hungary blocked bilateral tariff reductions between Czechoslovakia and her Little Entente partners, Romania and Yugoslovia.

During the winter months of 1919-1920, economic distress instigated agitation by the labor unions. By June 1920, social unrest exploded in a wide strike originating among railway and steel workers in the Moravska Ostrava area. An early demand in the walkout was a halt to French arms and munitions shipments to Warsaw, just as the Red Army was approaching its gates. The strike spread quickly throughout Slovakia against the Hungarian-owned factories and estates that were supported by Hungarian President Julius Gömbös's irredentist campaign. The reinforced government of Vlastomil Tusar reacted with renewed resolution.

Martial law was reinstituted, and frontier posts were occupied by army units. One of the rising extremist leaders in Slovakia, Vojtech Tuka, emerged into prominence at this time. He and his coterie were never expelled from Hlinka's party and later turned to embrace Hitler's banner. The Slovak people rallied to the republic, and Czech labor, adhering to Socialist Bohumír Šmeral's stand, again eschewed extremist adventures. With the concurrence of President Masaryk and with labor support, on August 7th Foreign Minister Beneš stood up to the pressure of a special French mission and declared Czechoslovak neutrality in the Polish-Soviet war.

The Marxist Socialists under Šmeral's leadership were galvanized by the successful though eventually suppressed strike wave that erupted during the spring and summer months. The previous December they had already founded a left-wing club within the Social Democratic Party, while the proceedings of the Third Congress of the Comintern, convened in Moscow in July-August 1920, prompted them to press agitation among their militant members. The following month, the group held an organizing meeting that caused such tension within the Social Democratic ranks that government business ground to a virtual standstill.

Confronted with Tusar's inability to conduct normal business, President Masaryk stepped beyond his constitutional position and made a personal appeal to the workers to rally behind the government. Masaryk did not hesitate to say that his ten months in revolutionary Russia had given him a low estimate of Soviet Communism. His firm stand left no doubt of his determination to spare the nation any such proletarian experiment, which he felt to be a poor model for Czechoslovak democracy.

The government sought to contain the crisis of social unrest by modified martial law. In Slovakia, it yielded to Catholic autonomists a larger role in public education, which had been secularized in exchange for support and pacification.

Tusar proceeded with plans to convene the thirteenth Social Democratic Congress in December. Early on, Tusar discerned that he had been outmaneuvered by his Party's Marxist wing, led by Šmeral. The latter organized his left control of a newly elected Central Committee, which occupied Social Democratic headquarters and seized the large printing press from which then issued the first number of *Rude Pravo*. Tusar appealed to the courts and called a general protest strike on December 10th. He was bested by the government, which proclaimed martial law. The strike was suppressed by police force; civil liberties were curtailed; and protest meetings were repressed. The police opened fire on workers' gatherings in Prague and elsewhere, killing, by official admission, at least one person and wounding scores of others. The courts released those arrested after imposing light fines, and the government stopped short of following the example of neighboring countries to outlaw the newly organized Communist Party.

Out of the months-long crisis, the new proletarian party was formed, which promptly joined the Comintern and subscribed to Lenin's twenty-one conditions. In practise this commitment enjoined member parties everywhere to accept and execute the decisions of the International, dominated as it was by the Soviet Central Committee. As for Czechoslovakia, the new revolutionary party was indeed the only political entity set up on an interracial basis and dedicated to the promotion of international proletarianism and world revolution.

The text of Šmeral's speech founding the Czechoslovak Communist Party on March 21, 1921, was discovered among Lenin's papers. It conformed to Lenin's New Economic Policy introduced that very month in Moscow, which downgraded perpetual revolutionary action and gave priority to economic development. At home, in successive street confrontations, Šmeral came to realize that his revolutionary party could not count on the workers, especially those in the processing industries, to follow the more militant leaders to the barricades. On the whole, Šmeral's political influence undoubtedly had a moderating effect, inhibiting extremist tactics.

In the course of its early national consolidation, the ethical egalitarianism of Masaryk prevailed over the revolutionary socialist path of Lenin, whose war-torn country had endured massive destruction and privation to the extent of famine. Masaryk's political style succeeded in shaping his decisive imprint on the stabilizing process which charted a centrist course, steering between French and Soviet pressures. The democratic, petit bourgeois nation exemplified the pluralistic roots of its combined peoples; it came forth with overwhelming majorities to accept and support the new democratic and egalitarian republic.

A modest foreign loan assisted public finances, which were managed with a measure of conventional conservatism. However, the old policy of Finance Minister Alois Rašín, of fixing a high value on the Czech crown, again sharpened social distress and induced unemployment. Modest capital investments and expanding credits from abroad had eased the earlier recession, and now Czechoslovakia's economy profited further from the general upswing following the Allied stabilization loans to Austria and Germany.

Unemployment continued to plague the country throughout the decade, menacing the government's stability. The massive protest demonstrations were generally suppressed by the police. The political turmoil came to a head on the eve of the quadrennial congress in 1924. Tens of thousands of members of the National Gymnastic Society were gathering in Prague from all parts of the country and from abroad, when suddenly Gen. Rudolf Gajda, of Legionnaire fame and dazzling performance, emerged as heading the new fascist groupings. He was stripped of his uniform for threatening a coup d'état and was tried and jailed for three years for this offense against the state.

The Social Democrats dropped from first to fourth place in the popular vote and Czechoslovak politics were polarized between the Agrarians on the right and the Communists on the left, each polling around 13 percent of the vote in 1924.

The conservative trend in Czech politics assisted fascist movements to arise. Fueled by acute social distress, they sprouted in all three ethnic groupings and were nourished from abroad with subsidies. Their programs demanded the overthrow of the Democratic Republic, or its weakening.

The Gajda group, inspired by Mussolini's fascist Italy, was reorganized in 1927 with the assistance of rightist National Democrats. following the general's release from jail, This group attacked the Masaryk-Beneš foreign policy and social programs. Troops under Gajda's influence were thwarted in an attempted takeover of their barracks in Brno. Although the process of Slavicizing the public services and educational system progressed through the 1920's in Slovakia, Father Hlinka's aides intensified their anti-Czech agitation and hatred.

The Sudeten Nazis were originally an insignificant offshoot of pan-German nationalism that came under aggressive youthful leaders, who became an integral part of the Hitler apparatus next door. They were financed, trained, and armed in Germany. They mimicked Hitler's successful demagogy in their vitriolic anti-Communist rallies.

By the end of the 1920's, before Hitler's rise to power, Czechoslovakia had no visible external enemies threatening her national existence; her multilateral diplomatic arrangements seemed sufficient to assure her security. Masaryk was reelected as President in May 1927. When he celebrated his eightieth birthday, while still in office on March 7, 1930, the Czechoslovak nation, shielded by the French system of alliances, had maintained its democracy and expanded its considerable economic plant. But it failed to deal adequately with its sizable and uncomfortable level of unemployment.

The Great Depression was spreading in Czechoslovakia. The industrial slowdown, following on the heels of collapsing farm prices, was accentuated by the loss of foreign markets for the famous national export products, notably glass and textiles. In three years, exports dropped to 26 percent of the 1929 level, while unemployment rose to the point that one family in four lacked direct means of livelihood. The crisis hit with particular severity the Sudeten industries and the weak economies of Slovakia and Ruthenia, portending grave political consequences.

In the midst of these problems, Švehla suffered a disabling stroke, leaving the aged president to cope alone with the affairs of state. Masaryk confessedly was not adept at the political game. He was too impatient to deal with meticulous details, and he loathed the necessity of what he called "kuh-handlung" (cow trading), meaning logrolling and compromise, the essence of successful political dealings. President Masaryk kept his hand firmly at the helm nevertheless.

In the bitter winter of 1931, the growing crisis swelled the ranks of the unemployed, giving the Communist Party a foil for fomenting strikes and mass rallies. Protest demonstrations were mounted throughout the country. In Prague, one of these attracted 200,000 people, mostly workers. Class conflicts were sharpened noticeably as a result of the decisions of the VIIth Plenum of the Third International, convoked in Moscow during March and April 1931. A total break with Social Democracy was decreed for all socialist and communist parties. "Social fascism" was held to be a tool of imperialism. In Czechoslovakia, Masaryk was portrayed as head of a fascist dictatorship parading in the guise of parliamentary democracy.

At the Locarno-inspired economic and disarmament conferences convened in Geneva in 1927, Beneš found an opportunity to intensify his contacts on a higher level. Both these conferences saw the Czechoslovak foreign minister in frenetic activity. Sensing the supreme importance of having France agree to multilateral disarmament, Beneš became the official reporter of this conference, where he was also active in technical matters at the economic talks. At these sessions, Beneš personally met with the Soviet foreign minister, Maxim Litvinov, the successor of Georgyi Chicherin. When the French foreign minister, Louis Barthou, was present at Geneva, Beneš saw to it that the three statesman laid the groundwork for the triangular mutual security system that was eventually finalized after the Nazi regime took power.

Czechoslovakia was, by its very position as an exporting nation, poorly prepared to deal with the coming storm. The political consequences of the rising Nazi star were to be of such magnitude that Czechoslovakia could not protect her internal or external security without the loyal adherence of her friendly allies. The two pillars of the 1935 alliance, France and Soviet Russia, would of necessity have to remain intact.

France and Czechoslovakia opposed the Customs Union declared at Vienna on March 19, 1931, as a veiled threat to give Germany dominant control in the Danubian basin. As a countermove to rehabilitate Danubian trade and economy, Beneš in January 1932 revived the idea of a Danubian Federation, which was incorporated into the André Tardieu Plan. To eight countries in this group, including Poland, France extended political loans amounting to $250 million, averting treasury disasters in Austria and Hungary. The plan was designed to reduce interzonal tariffs preferentially by 10 percent. Unhappily, this French push for dominance in Central Europe was vetoed by Great Britain and Italy as undermining their business interests. Thus the most serious effort to counter German economic penetration of Central Europe failed, and Czechoslovakia was thrown back to the more limited possibilities of increasing trade with its Little Entente partners.

Whatever countermeasures Czechoslovakia took with French backing, it could not save her bilateral arrangements from being overwhelmed by the immense productive power of Germany. Germany won the race to penetrate weaker Balkan economies. Hitler dispatched his right-hand man, Hermann Göring, on a Balkan tour in May 1935, starting in Sofia, Bulgaria, which had a German royal house. Göring was followed there in 1936 by Hjalmar Schacht, former president of the German National Bank, who became the financial wizard of the rising Nazi regime and now turned his talents to making inroads into the Yugoslav economy and integrating it into the expanding German clutches.

The Czechoslovak government pursued anticrisis economic measures. State controls were instituted over industry, and the government launched a large public works program. The reforms were designed to counter the class-oriented, Agrarian-promoted grain monopoly under which the Czechoslovak people were paying twice and three times world prices for wheat that was readily and cheaply available next door in Budapest.

While Czechoslovakia was grappling with the foreign and domestic aspects of the world economic crisis, the Nazi coup in Berlin occurred abruptly on January 30, 1933. The Geneva Disarmament Conference had collapsed in late 1932, giving Hitler the excuse he sought to withdraw Germany from the League of Nations. Despite the ingenuity of Barthou and Beneš, no formula could be devised to persuade France to dismantle her military preparations in return for what she held to be inadequate security safeguards.

New laws for the defense of the Czechoslovak republic became necessary, providing for press censorship and curtailing other civil liberties to contain native fascist threats to public order. The promoters of the threatening Brno rally, who had failed to escape to home base in Germany, were jailed, but the Slovak fascists continued their trouble-making activities with relative impunity.

Shortly after Nazi Germany left the League, Hitler scored his first diplomatic breakthrough. In January 1934, Poland, now under Marshal Jozef Pilsudski's dictatorship, agreed to enter the proffered nonaggression pact with Germany. A year later, in 1935, Great Britain became the first Western power to make an appeasement move, by signing a naval pact with Germany.

Although Masaryk had suffered a slight stroke on May 1, 1934, he reluctantly agreed, after his full recovery, to run again for the presidency in November. He felt no confidence that Beneš, his designated successor, could win sufficient votes in the National Assembly for an assured victory. In any case, Masaryk drew his largest majority, failing to attract only the votes of the extremist parties, the Slovak Populists and the Sudeten Nazis. The militant Communist leader, Klement Gottwald, fled to Moscow to avoid arrest, but the Communist Party remained legal, the only one in Central/-Eastern Europe.

Although economic circumstances and working conditions improved, the Sudeten Deutsche Heimatsfront, now the Sudeten Deutsche Partei (SdP), covertly an integral branch of Hitler's Nazi Party, made rapid progress in its reorganization under Konrad Henlein. He gained international prestige from an invitation to London as a guest of the British government. The mass hysteria flooding the Sudeten districts from across the border was another factor in the Henlein party's polling some 70 percent of the German Bohemian votes. This stunning victory brought it within one vote in parliament of the dominant Agrarians, who had lost some ground. Fortunately for democracy, the Czech Populists had declined to invite the Slovak extremists to appear on a joint ballot.

The Communist Party, very likely in response to the new popular front strategy of the Comintern, soon dropped its innate hostility to the bourgeois-socialist republic. On May 25, 1935, Czechoslovakia and the Soviet Union extended each other de jure recognition and signed four treaties to outline their pact of mutual assistance in the event of German aggression. The prolonged negotiations leading to the triangular Franco-Soviet-Czechoslovak Alliance gained the approval of both Romania and Yugoslavia.

The unique feature of the Czechoslovak-Soviet-French treaty was the provision that exempted Prague from the automatic obligation of coming to the military aid of the Soviet Union in the event that France did not first honor its commitment. Beneš thus avoided any need for Czechoslovakia prematurely to fight a war at the side of its Soviet ally.

Beneš paid his first visit to Moscow to exchange instruments of ratification with Joseph Stalin on May 16, 1935. Three days after the foreign minister's return, John O. Crane had an hour's interview with him in the Hrad. Beneš reported his astonishment at the visible development of the awakened Russian giant and was truly impressed with ubiquitous signs of its military and industrial prowess.

The Little Entente reacted to the Hitler menace with a new spirit of solidarity by accepting Beneš's plan to set up an executive permanent council under rotating chairmanships.

Three months later, the 85-year old Masaryk suffered another and more severe stroke. By this time, the vexing problem of the Beneš succession had skated to far more favorable ground. Beneš had gained popularity in Communist circles due to his having negotiated the Soviet alliance, and was further bolstered by an even more decisive factor, that of the popular front resolution of the seventh Comintern congress, which opened in Moscow on July 25th. This congress directed its members to participate in broad-based governments around the globe. The Czech Communists turned full circle and threw their weight behind an anti-Fascist, popular front alignment in Prague, as elsewhere.

At the same time, the new Agrarian leader, an attractive Slovak, Milan Hodža, underwent a change of position. Although conservatively oriented, he was alarmed by the pro-Fascist swing in his party under the ascending leadership of Rudolf Beran. On November 5th, 1935, Masaryk appointed Hodža as prime minister, while Beneš gained the backing of the three socialist parties and of some Communist leaders too. On December 14, 1935, Masaryk resigned office with a fervent plea to the nation that Beneš be chosen as his successor. With the broad anti-Fascist coalition in his favor, Beneš was elected as second president of the republic by a vote that surpassed even that of Masaryk's last triumph.

During the election campaign, the country became aware that Beneš had grown up in an utterly poor peasant family, in contrast with Masaryk's advantages of having lived on an imperial estate under the tutelage of his exceptionally able and endowed mother, who had encouraged Tomáš's intellectual proclivities. People appreciated Beneš's having overcome his impoverished and deprived youth to take advanced studies at the Sorbonne in France. They welcomed his return to Prague thoroughly imbued with the humanist traditions of the Western Enlightenment, which fused so naturally with those of the Hussite Reformation. It emerged that he had become a pacifist, as had Masaryk, and the voters approved. Campaigning with Masaryk's hearty backing, his more rapid acceptance than Masaryk's of cooperatives and central planning now gained him the strong approval of the voters.

NOTES

1.   Ivan Derend and Gyorgyi, *Economic Development in East Central Europe in the 19th and 20th Centuries* (New York: Columbia University Press, 1974), p. 182.

2.   Victor Mamatey and Radomír Luža, *A History of the Czechoslovak Republic 1918-1948* (Princeton, N.J.: Princeton University Press, 1973), p. 78.

3.   Ms. letter to JOC from Frederick R. Kuh, Hotel Beranch, Prague, October 7, 1920, Crane family archive. Kuh was a famous and reliable U.S. journalist based in Central Europe, most frequently in Prague.

7

The Beneš Succession: Storm Warnings (1935-38)

When the 51-year old perennial foreign minister, Eduard Beneš, succeeded to the presidency on December 14, 1935, he was bitterly aware that his longtime efforts to build the League of Nations had been virtually nullified. The League's collective security edifice was significantly crippled. The first crack had appeared when the Japanese invaded Manchuria with impunity in 1931. Fascist Italy and Nazi Germany had then proceeded to unravel the fragile collective security system at the core of the League. These Western European dictatorships soon created a clear and present threat to Czechoslovakia's security, as well as to world peace. As pointed out by Henry Ashby Turner, Adolf Hitler's first speech upon his installation as chancellor reflected among the country's industrialists "mounting dissatisfaction with republican institutions."[1] When the dictators demanded justice and lebensraum, they meant a revision of the Versailles system implying territorial gains for themselves.

Czechoslovakia's geographic position, wedged between Germany and the Soviet Union, rendered her especially vulnerable to aggressive revisionism. The internal rightward political drift impeded closer arrangements with the growing Russian giant for counterweight against the Germans. British and French backup became crucial. Beneš was directly challenged to give top priority to his country's security via a military buildup and treaties of alliance.

Beneš forthwith formed the Supreme Council for the Defense of the State, directed to review and overhaul the defense establishment. The army needed modernizing; it required, above all, mobile armored units and a technologically improved weapons system. The air force wanted upgrading in all sectors. Special training courses to improve staff coordination were instituted for young officers. More importantly, the government erected a series of fortifications along its extensive, vulnerable frontier facing Germany.

On March 7, 1936, scarcely three months following Beneš's accession to the Hrad, Adolf Hitler, eager to counter the encircling Franco-Soviet-Czechoslovak alliance of 1935, threw his skeletal army into the demilitarized Rhineland "in defiance of all treaties."[2] The Locarno order, sponsored and underwritten by Germany herself in 1925, was automatically demolished.

In a note of stiff protest to Berlin, speaking also for the Little Entente and Soviet Russia, Beneš declared the Rhineland occupation an act of war. The Tripartite Alliance, however, ruled out responsive action in the West without France's invocation of an act of aggression. The timid government of Premier Camille Chautemps, in fear of affronting the pacifist mood of his country, was unwilling to risk a tough reaction. Nor would France now lift a finger to force Hitler to cancel his recent conscription order, an act both warlike and "contemptuous of all treaties."[3] The inaction of France found an unmistakable chord of sympathy in equally cautious Great Britain, itself under the influence of a strong peace movement.

Hitler himself later said of this episode: "If France had marched then, we should have been forced to withdraw."[4] Churchill heartily agreed, writing in his memoir: "A firm stand by France and Britain under the authority of the League of Nations would have been followed by the immediate evacuation of the Rhineland, without shedding a drop of blood."[5] This proved a watershed decision for the Western Powers; had they responded sharply, they might have nipped Hitler's aggressive plans in the bud. In occupying the Rhineland, Hitler erected an armed barrier capable of blocking any French Army force from reaching an attacked eastern ally, Czechoslovakia in the first instance.

Allied dalliance over the Rhineland provoked Soviet consternation and loss of confidence in the French alliance. The Soviets turned their focus to their own defenses, or should have. Security-anxious Stalin unleashed his drastic purge trials upon the old guard Bolsheviks. More damaging was his military purge in June 1937, which disastrously eliminated the foremost hero of the Soviet army, Marshal Mikhail Tukhacevsky. According to Czechoslovakia's intelligence chief, Gen. František Moravec, "Stalin liquidated 75% of the members of the Supreme War Council, including three marshals and thirteen generals, an estimated 1,500 high ranking officers, while thousands of others disappeared into prisons and labor camps."[6]

Dilatory responses in the West to Gen. Francisco Franco's assault on the Spanish republic in 1936 further encouraged the rising dictators. The advent of Léon Blum's Popular Front regime in France also did little to assist the beleaguered Spanish republic. The Western democracies, including the United States, passively took umbrage behind a shield of nonintervention; in contrast, Mussolini had five Italian Army divisions engaged alongside General Franco's battalions.[7]

Already in September 1935, the Czechoslovak chief of staff, Gen. Ludvik Krejčí, looked eastward to the Soviet Union for security balance. He had personally attended the annual Red Army maneuvers, held that year in the strategic province of the Ukraine. Gen. Krejčí returned to Prague with a positive assessment of Soviet equipment, notably the armored units and excellent staff work; he also reported a fine overall esprit de corps.[8]

This favorable appraisal of Soviet military strength, which matched Beneš's nonprofessional estimate, was flatly contradicted by General Moravec after his military mission to Moscow in the summer of 1936. Moravec noted the necessity to avoid hostile Polish territory, when he and five other staff officers traveled a long detoured route by train to pass through friendly Romania. In two weeks of intensive meetings with their Russian counterparts, they emerged with withering criticisms. They discovered that the Soviet military's knowledge of the situation in Germany during the "rapid build-up of the German armed forces and of unmistakable signs [of] practical preparations for war . . . was not only incomplete, but also inaccurate." The Soviet military leaders displayed "great gaps in their knowledge of . . . the number and location of German higher units . . . of armoured units and their armament, the motorization of German armed forces, and the build-up of the German Air Force . . . [the further] increase of the Reich's war potential . . . about the strategic plans for the German High Command." Moravec found that "a further weakness of the Soviet Intelligence service was the ignorance of foreign languages . . . [of] their top men at our conference . . . The service's analysis of its raw information was inadequate . . . lack of first-hand knowledge . . . of the . . . evaluators . . . They were working on information likely to be colored by political bias . . . rather than objective reality."[9]

On this occasion, Moravec met with Marshal Tukhacevsky, whom he rated as "the architect of the Red Army."[10] He credited Tukhacevsky with all the Red Army reforms of 1934–1936, such as mechanization and the use of paratroopers.

To deepen the new friendly relations between the two countries. Czechoslovakia and the Soviet Union instituted exchanges of technical and business delegations, as well as military delegations. Journalists undertook reciprocal visits, while Soviet staff officers were invited to inspect the new frontier fortifications being erected first in northern Bohemia. The Russians visited important arms and chemical plants, which were increasingly supplying the Little Entente countries to replace waning French deliveries. First among these was, of course, the Škoda works, comprising the largest engineering and armaments production facilities in Central Europe.

Little Entente solidarity was dealt its first severe jolt as a consequence of the assassination of Yugoslavia's King Alexander in October 1934. The sovereign was felled by Croatian Ustachi assassins as he was passing through Marseilles on his way to prop up lagging French relations. French Foreign Minister Louis Barthou, who had come to meet the royal visitor, was killed at his side. The death of Barthou brought to an end the Raymond Poincaré–Aristide Briand–André Tardieu line of French statesmen who, with Beneš and others, had created the collective security system of the League of Nations. Successor to the late king in Belgrade was his pro-Fascist brother, Prince Paul, who became president of the regency council and ruler in the name of the young heir, King Peter.

President Beneš became aware that the Nazi and Fascist powers were also abetting the covert rearming of Austria and Hungary, besides destabilizing Yugoslavia with Ustachi assassins. Beneš, intent on countering these aggressive threats, convened two meetings of the Little Entente early in his presidency, in 1935.

Hermann Göring's Balkan trip in 1935 solidified Yugoslavia's about- face in alignment. A few days after his departure, Prince Paul discharged his pro-French prime minister, Bogoljub Jevtić, and designated in his place Germanophile Milan Stojadinović. Pan-Serb Stojadinović expanded the secret policy to inaugurate a reign of repression. It soon emerged that the new dictator of Yugoslavia had potent German support.

Hjalmar Schacht's economic mission through the Balkans the following year reinforced Göring's results. Schacht was an authoritative and powerful Nazi German representative. He had built the financing mechanism for Germany's rearmament program, then in full swing, and had mobilized the necessary work force from the large pool of unemployed remaining from the Great Depression, whose numbers had risen and whose conditions had worsened following the crushing of the left-dominated unions.

Germany concluded bilateral trading arrangements throughout the Danubian and Balkan areas, which enabled her to expand her purchases of raw materials and farm products without the unavailable hard currencies. Subsequent trade produced large credit balances in Berlin for the agrarian states, which enabled them to purchase German machinery and other manufactured goods. Political pressure was applied by the Germans where necessary to attain the goal. Taking the year 1933 as base 100, German imports from southeastern Europe jumped in 1937 to 282 and its exports there rose to 283. [11]

Small Czechoslovakia, although approaching self-sufficiency in food production, could not complete with the monopoly position of her towering neighbor, especially in view of Germany's subsidies of her exports. Czechoslovakia's successful export drive was necessarily beamed to the Western countries, where the commodities were paid for in hard currencies, enabling her to buy in return raw materials such as iron ore, raw cotton and wool that she required for her processing industries. In her case, bilateral agreements in the Balkans could not reap the complementary advantage to her foreign trade that Germany could obtain.

At the annual mass rally held by the Nazi Party at Nuremberg in September 1936, Hitler made a qualitative leap in his expansionist policy. He preemptively announced the assumption of protective custody of all Germans living beyond the borders of the Third Reich. He threatened his neighbors Austria, Czechoslovakia, and Poland that Germany would not idly witness her sons who lived abroad being humiliated and deprived of their rights.

It transpired during this 1936 Nuremberg rally that young Konrad Henlein was chosen as the new leader of the SdP. The former school teacher was assigned the task of consolidating the in-fighting Bohemian Nazi formations, a task at which the older Sudeten leader, Deputy Karl Hermann Frank, had failed.

Taking direct oversight of the Sudeten problem, Hitler dispatched two secret envoys to Prague in November. Ostensibly, their mission was to offer Czechoslovakia a treaty of amity and nonaggression patterned on those with Poland and Austria, as an extension of the 1925 arbitration convention. Their real intention was to persuade President Beneš to resolve the Sudeten issue by granting autonomous rights to the Bohemian German minority. Beneš parried these demands by submitting a draft of his own based on the principles of collective security and recognition of existing treaties, especially those of Locarno.

Right wing groups in Prague soon got wind of Beneš's unyielding response to Sudeten demands for self-government and accelerated their agitation also to force a drastic change in foreign policy aimed at scuttling the Soviet Alliance. Led by the Agrarian chief, Rudolf Beran, they were pressing for an eventual realignment in harmony with the reality of German power. They raised the spectral Hitlerite theme of the country's becoming a base for Soviet infiltration of Central Europe. Czechoslovak Foreign Minister Kamil Krofta, Beneš's right-hand man in the foreign ministry, scotched their fulminations in the parliament. Although Beneš won a rousing vote of confidence, Nazi circles at home and abroad bent their efforts to overthrow him by a rightist coup in Prague.

On the initiative of Prime Minister Milan Hodža, a parliamentary committee that omitted representatives of the Sudeten German Party was appointed at the end of 1936 to study solutions to the problems of discriminations against the German minority raised by Henlein. Henlein's representatives in the Parliament stated their case in a memorandum submitted to the committee detailing charges of economic, linguistic, and cultural discrimination.

Coincidentally, Heinz Rutha, Henlein's "foreign representative," went to England to advance the party's fortunes with Nazi sympathizers there. He found articulate and strategically placed supporters among conservatives in London, led by the prominent Cliveden set, and generated considerable press attention.

Opposing Henlein's disruptive maneuvers, the German Democratic Party participating in the government agreed with its Czech cohorts to enter into negotiations on the German minority. These resulted on February 18, 1937, in acceding to most of the nationalities' demands. The concessions may be summarized as follows:

1. Economic concessions: Increase of public works for the relief of admitted economic want in the German-speaking districts; local labor and firms to be employed in such work.

2. A greater measure of local control over social welfare, youth organizations, etc.

3. Reintroduction of the principle of "proportionate" equality of opportunity into competitions for Government Service . . . stipulation of requisite unconditional loyalty to the State.

4. Linguistic concessions in official correspondence before the courts . . . to the extent of supplying free translations of relevant documents;

5. Maintenance of the "constitutional rights" of the minorities, related to tuition in schools. [12]

Henlein greeted these significant concessions with reserve in a speech on February 28th. He pressed for full control over the

Sudeten German population, while Prague rejected local autonomy as unacceptable, "as it would involve handing over 350,000 Czechs to Sudetic German jurisdiction." [13]   In April the SdP introduced six bills into Parliament, which were disparaged by British Minister Basil C. Newton as "verbose and ambiguous" and a priori unacceptable to the government. On the other hand, "the ceasing of police abuses, such as illegal arrests and detentions which were forbidden, and equal opportunity of employment in public service" stood for Newton as justifiable demands. The bills were referred to appropriate parliamentary committees and in November Prime Minister Hodža promised that they would be submitted to Parliament. Newton's appraisal, forwarded to London, favored the government, which was not prepared to accept SdP's main principles because "they were in direct contradiction to the basic principles of democratic and parliamentary government . . . [being] racial in tenor and totalitarian in spirit." [14]

Beneš made a tour of the predominantly German-speaking districts in the spring and summer of 1937 to test sentiment at first hand. He made several conciliatory speeches, promising "further recognition of the claims . . . [of the] minorities who were prepared loyally to cooperate with the Czech majority." [15] Loyalty to the state became an overarching ingredient of national security.

Discriminations persisted, however, against the employment of Germans in public works such as the military fortifications under construction. [16]   Under Defense Minister František Machnik's decrees of 1936, discrimination against Germans was necessarily written into government contracts. How could the Czechoslovak government trust intimate knowledge of its fortifications to the German workmen in these heated circumstances? The SdP in January 1937 organized a petition to protest these discriminations nonetheless.

To make matters worse, distressing economic conditions were reported in the German districts, despite a revival in international trade that was partially stimulated by world rearmament. [17] Resentment against the discriminations within the National Defense Law of 1936 continued and crested by November 1937. The defense minister then took cognizance of them and promised alleviation by a lax application of the law. The following May, the law was upheld in Prague because of general appreciation that nothing short of complete territorial autonomy would ultimately satisfy Henlein's SdP and its Nazi supporters abroad. Beneš and his government held firmly that these matters could not even form a basis of discussion. The situation had deteriorated beyond "nationalities" concessions. A confidential interview between accommodating Prime Minister Hodža and recalcitrant Henlein in September 1937 was inconclusive, leading to a hardening of positions on both sides.

Hitler revealed more far-reaching plans at the 1937 Nuremberg Congress, which was attended officially by the British and French ambassadors in Berlin for the first time. The foreign diplomats soon joined in the search for ways to mount increasing leverage on Prague.

In obedience to orders from Berlin, Henlein called a Sudeten Party rally for October 17th at Teplice in northern Bohemia, at which the noisy street demonstrators were illegally clad in brown shirts. It seemed a bald provocation, inviting a police crackdown. Henlein then sent an open letter to Beneš denouncing the ensuing police brutality, a letter that was announced over the German radio well before its delivery to the Hrad. The letter proclaimed that "liberation" was at hand by means of intervention vowed by German Nazis from across the frontier. Territorial autonomy was the Sudeten rallying cry. Czechoslovak intelligence responded by leaking to its press outlets the information that the prime instigators of the disturbances lodged in Berlin.

The Czechoslovak government informed the world in a public declaration of the gravity of the subversive Nazi menace to it, to Europe, and to world peace. It simultaneously ordered appropriately stern measures in the German districts of Bohemia, such as a ban on political meetings. This crackdown was soon withdrawn, because the government realized that the confrontations could provide the German government with a pretext for intervention.

At this point the Foreign Office in London requested its Prague envoy to press President Beneš for more concessions to the Sudetens. The interview took place on January 24, 1938. Beneš responded easily that if autonomy were interpreted to mean "that all officials in their areas should be German," he would concede that much, although Czechs comprised a large segment of the population in those districts. Newton queried about "the right of selection" in the appointment of SdP people. Beneš again found no difficulty, provided "they were ready to cooperate with the State." Then the president demonstrated to his visitor with maps that "territorial autonomy was . . . admitted to be geographically impracticable" because "the German population is diffused over six areas." Beneš further observed dryly "that neither the Reich nor the Henlein Party really know what they want."

He attached great importance to the prohibition of receipt of money from abroad. He also thought the power to suppress local associations was necessary, as a means of "checkmating disturbances at election[s]." Beneš affirmed that the "bill would apply equally to the Communists," and he explained, "it would not apply to [bona fide political] parties in the interest of freedom to engage in political activity." [18]

In refuting the allegations that schools were used for the "Czechization" of Germans, continued Newton in his report, "Dr. Beneš gave me a few interesting figures." He said, "Of some 433,000 German children attending schools, 409,000 went to German schools, 8,000 to mixed schools, and only 15,000 to non-German, Czech, or Magyar schools. Children were sent by German parents to Czech schools often to learn the language. Some 6,000 Czech children attended German schools for the same reason." Newton was persuaded and urged Beneš to publish these facts, which would be useful to allay the bitterness engendered by "mischievous exaggerations or distortions" in the press. [19]

In the spring of 1937, the intelligence chief, Moravec, fell into the good fortune and had the temerity to pursue what appeared to be a high-echelon offer of first-hand intelligence: classified intelligence information about the "detailed battle order and deployment; German defence plan for the Saxonian border; information on German armament, tanks, planes, and airfields; information on Sudeten activities and *their support from official German sources;* information on German espionage in Czechoslovakia." [20]

Although the potential agent's services would cost extravagantly, Moravec promptly decided to meet the man and test his authenticity with a view to accepting his offer even at the inflated price. If he proved indeed as highly placed as the information indicated, he would be an incalculable asset. They met at the German's suggestion in a frontier town in Saxony. Moravec decided it was worth the risk of going into Germany to obtain "a number of vital secrets of the Reich." [21] The would-be agent, named Karl, "brought along a packet of materials so valuable" as to establish his bona fides; it would "speak for itself . . . 'I don't like the regime myself,'" responded Karl to a query about his motives, which he said were "'not entirely pecuniary.'" [22]

In addition to providing Moravec with the German frontier defense plan for the border of Saxony, the agent produced documents to prove that German intelligence had penetrated the Czechoslovak apparatus to learn Czechoslovakia's defense plan for its northeastern region. The Czechoslovak chief of staff, General Krejčí, was ill for two days when later informed that this vital data had been betrayed to the

Germans, a betrayal of far greater consequence for the defenders than for the aggressor. Karl also "produced two original documents from the Abwehr [German Intelligence Agency] Headquarters" in Berlin to its local branch in Chemnitz on the border *"which proved the Abwehr's role in directing and organizing 'incidents' in the Sudetenland,"* that violent Nazi propagandists had blown up out of proportion. [23]

The arrest in mid-October 1937 of Henlein's "foreign minister," Rutha, because of his objectionable behavior abroad in his "advocacy of the Sudetic German cause," exacerbated feelings. The anger reached fever pitch when, three weeks later, Rutha was found hanged in the cell where he was being detained awaiting trial. His friends and sympathizers doubted the official verdict of suicide. Apparently, it had been a disgruntled Sudeten Party member who had denounced Rutha to the police. Henlein conducted a purge of "disloyal" members who had been working within the party toward "more extreme and Socialist channels." [24]

The Sudetens aired loud complaints of maltreatment in both the press and Parliament. A Henlein deputy, Wolfgang Richter, in a speech to Parliament in January 1938, challenged government statistics about unemployment between September and December 1937, which had practically doubled, from 230,000 to 451,000. He wanted to demonstrate that the Prague government's "constructive economic policy" had failed utterly to mitigate "the hardships of the greater measure of unemployment in the German areas" as compared with the intensively industrialized Czech region. He said that for every 100 Czech unemployed, 240 Germans could be found. [25]

What Richter omitted from his presentation was supplied privately by Beneš to Newton during a late January interview. Beneš said that prior to the world economic crisis in 1929, Czechoslovak export and import trade with Germany had amounted to roughly 25 percent of her total foreign trade. As a result of the upheaval, trade with Germany had sunk to about 10 percent, but by 1937, it had risen to 14 percent. Her big neighbor wanted more, but Czechoslovakia preferred to maintain the 14 percent ratio. [26]

Daily press reports in *Die Zeit* and other influential German-language papers fueled the discontent. Now they charged Czech economic encroachment in Sudetenland through "infiltration of Sudeten districts by the acquisition of German properties." The Czech press denounced these accusations as gross exaggerations. [27]

The Socialist paper *Pravo Lidu* publicized an inquiry made at the National Bank as to whether Henlein drew foreign exchange from them for his trips abroad. The National Bank had replied that

"Henlein had never asked for any 'devisen' from them . . . In two years, Henlein had spent 200 days abroad." Where did he get the money for his expenses? "It was natural to assume that the German Government or the Nazi Party put up the money." The French government instituted inquiries of its own to get at the source of these funds, as Germany herself was short of hard currency. "It was felt that London might be one of the places from which funds were derived, either through organized sympathizers or by payment of expenses for a lecture." [28]

Meanwhile, the War Office in London took note that the completion of the Czechoslovak fortifications along the German frontier was proceeding at a brisk pace. It observed "considerable headway . . . with their re-armament program . . . and the frontier defences vis-à-vis Germany [are] nearing completion . . . The reorganization of the Army . . . [has] been carried out . . . and armament factories are being moved to less vulnerable positions." [29] They also remarked that "the original plan of constructing defence works in the so-called Moravian quadrilateral had been extended to include all the main approaches from Germany into Bohemia. We believe that they will now put up a determined resistance in the recently constructed fortifications near the German frontier." [30]

Toward the close of 1937, when the Sudeten complaints of discrimination were cresting, the Polish government added its own fat to the fire. Foreign Minister Jósef Beck charged before the Polish foreign office's Commission of the Polish Sejm discriminations against the Polish minority in Czechoslovakia. The press reports found that

guarantees [of] equal treatment for all citizens regardless of race . . . [were flouted, and] mis-application of that legislation . . . [by] chauvinist local and police authorities . . . Polish workmen and peasants were continually oppressed in a diversity of ways solely because of their desire to remain Poles . . . They were doing the same thing to the Slovaks . . . This unfriendly policy toward the Polish minority [is] regarded as distinctly unfriendly toward Poland. [31]

The Polish minority numbered merely about 70,000 living chiefly in the Teschen area. The charges of discrimination embraced three major complaints, those of enforced "Czechization," inadequate Polish schools, and exclusion from higher administrative posts. However justified, the British minister thought the charges grossly exaggerated. The Czechoslovak government offered to refer these accusations to the League of Nations in Geneva for adjudication, but "the Warsaw government entertained small sympathy for the League," which it saw as "an ideological association of anti-Fascist States of a strongly leftward tendency . . . harboring a natural bias in favor of Czechoslovakia." [32]   Hodža thought that "the demands could be satisfied within the framework of the Constitution and in the spirit of the Government Resolution of the 18th February comprising a series of concessions to all the national minorities." [33]

Great Britain's prime minister, Neville Chamberlain, in the fall of 1937 was primarily concerned with the need of a clear understanding and joint action with the French in response to the increasingly menacing tones emanating from Berlin. At the same time in Berlin, uppermost on Hitler's mind, as perceived by London's Foreign Office under Sir Anthony Eden, was the restoration of the German colonies that had been wrested from Germany as a consequence of her defeat in the Great War. Eden declared his readiness, in conversation with his French counterparts, "to discuss the colonial question with Germany." [34]   Lord Halifax was dispatched to Berchtesgaden to explore this question.

This was not the first British effort to probe a peaceful settlement in Europe with Hitler. A year earlier, in the autumn of 1936, Schacht had "had conversations with M. Blum and other French Ministers, and in February 1937 with F. Leith-Ross," according to a Foreign Office memorandum, in which Schacht is reported to have suggested that "secret discussions might be initiated between representatives of the United Kingdom, French, and German Governments, with a view to a general settlement of outstanding questions between Germany and the Western Powers." Dr. Schacht contemplated "a comprehensive settlement, covering certain economic and financial concessions to Germany, the most important of which related to the transfer of colonies" in return for "the acceptance by Germany of the political desiderata of the United Kingdom and French Governments." [35]

The terms proposed by Schacht and circulated to the cabinet committee on foreign policy on March 15, 1937, which were labeled "To be kept under lock and key," with a note requesting secrecy appended, were as follows:

1. Colonies. "Germany must have colonies." He mentioned the Cameroons and Togoland under German management and using German currency.
2. Economic. Arrangements to be made as regards adjustment of currency, debts, relaxation of exchange controls, starting with commercial operations.
3. Political. Germany was prepared to contemplate some kind of pact for the whole of Europe, and to give indirect assurances of nonaggression as regards Russia. Germany would accept a nonaggression and noninterference pact with Czechoslovakia subject to the German minority being reasonably well treated.

Germany would be willing to rejoin the League, but would want the covenant separated from the Treaty of Versailles and sanctions cut out. [36]

The Foreign Office dispatched instructions to its ambassador in Paris, Sir Eric Phipps, "to obtain from the French Government the terms of a reply." The suggested wording follows:

Before the governments can judge whether the proposed tripartite conversations would be useful, as a first stage of negotiations . . . would include the following objectives . . .

a. The conclusion of a treaty or treaties of non-aggression and guarantees for Western Europe to replace the Treaty of Locarno.

b. Measures by Germany, in treaty form or otherwise, which will satisfy the Governments of Central and Eastern Europe with regard to Germany's intentions with respect to the territorial integrity and sovereign independence of all Central and Eastern European States . . . Germany's readiness to negotiate a non-aggression and non-interference treaty with Czechoslovakia and to enter into some arrangement with regard to the Soviet Union.

c. The return of Germany to the League of Nations . . . still as described in their Peace Plan of March, 1936 . . .

d. An international arrangement for the limitations of armaments. [37]

The precise methods of arriving at these agreements were left open, while His Majesty's Government declared "a genuine desire to cooperate in achieving agreement upon these points." These would be "the readiness of the German Government to adopt the measures necessary to restore internal economic equilibrium, to reassure capital, and to play their part in a general relaxation of trade restrictions." [38]

Sir Eric was instructed to explore the French attitude "to contemplate the transfer of their mandates in the West African area, i.e. Cameroons and Togoland." The British blandly acknowledged that

The French would be making the sacrifice of (their) colonial mandates, and not the British . . . If therefore, further concession was required from His Majesty's Government, it would have to take the form of economic measures . . . His Majesty's Government would be prepared to consider what could be arranged in this direction. [39]

The British ambassador in Paris executed the directive on May 3, 1937 and reported unsurprisingly, in level bureaucratese, that "the suggestion that France should be required to make a sacrifice of colonial territory so much greater than that of Great Britain was strongly opposed by the French Ministers." On May 9th, "the French Ministers stated that after reflection and consultations they thought that conversations should be renewed with Dr. Schacht when he came to Paris later in the month, but they rejected sending the proposed British communication to the German Government." After some deliberations, the French foreign minister for the Popular Front government, Yvon Delbos, and his British opposite, the conservative Lord Halifax agreed that "it should be made clear to Dr. Schacht that neither the French nor the British Government were prepared to consider the colonial issue unless and until agreement had been reached in principle on all the other elements [of] a general settlement . . . [and] to explore further economic and financial questions."[40]

The French Premier, Blum, accordingly talked with Schacht May 28, 1937, in Paris and duly reported on the conversation to the British Foreign Office. He had insisted that "a general political settlement must be reached, after which economic discussions with or without possible colonial concessions would follow." Blum said further, "If serious prospects were apparent on the political plane, economic discussions might begin." In the margin, Blum appended by hand the question: "Why only our colonies?"[41]

It was acknowledged freely in Paris by the French government, as well as by Whitehall, that under the then circumstances "it would in fact be much more difficult for the French to render assistance . . . to Czechoslovakia in the event of German action."[42]

Items were forwarded to London's Foreign Office from Berlin's at this time as feelers about mutual limitations of armaments as regards aerial bombardments. The Germans declared they were impelled by a desire for an agreement for the "humanization" of war.

Analysis of Schacht's proposals and the Allied responses can only rest on speculation. Did Schacht speak for the industrial-military interests in Germany who wanted to avoid the destructions of war? Or did Schacht speak for Hitler, seeking a bargain in the satisfaction of his claims without resort to a costly war? Or did Hitler hope to deflect his potential adversaries' attention to the economic terms in his "peaceful intentions" while he aggrandized his military machine for use as blackmail, or for victory in the impending war of his own making? Were Schacht's proposals communicated to Czechoslovak officials, or did Jan Masaryk in London or Moravec's intelligence service glean this Hitlerian gambit? Any of these interpretations would fit this picture, while Hitler's expansive drive eastward persisted.

Instead of exploring collective security alternatives, Neville Chamberlain, uneasy about Hitler's intentions, dispatched his trusted, pro-German emissary, Lord Halifax, again to visit the Nazi leader at

Berchtesgaden on November 29, 1937, an event that emboldened the Führer in his tactical movements. On this occasion, Halifax agreed with Hitler on the desirability of certain changes in Central Europe, with but one proviso, that his government would insist upon "peaceful processes."

Apprehensions pervaded Prague, which Newton reported home: "The visit was regarded with nervousness by the Czechs, who feared that some deal might be afoot, which would adversely effect their interests," he wrote and explained that "the anxiety was vastly increased" by a *London Times* article dated November 29th. Newton observed that "Public opinion seemed aghast at the extent of pro-German feeling in Great Britain." The Czechoslovak "press continued to harp on the alleged desire of certain circles in Great Britain to reach an agreement with Germany at the expense of this country," generating widespread fear. Newton made it a special point to thank Eden for making a speech in Parliament on December 21st containing "a formal denial that His Majesty's Government were seeking a resolution of Europe's differences at the expense of other powers." Newton cited "the anxiety of the Czechs to have the moral support of Great Britain." [43]

The British ambassador in Berlin, Sir Nevile Henderson, apparently swayed by the atmosphere in the Nazi capital, took decided issue with Beneš's statements to Newton and to the press regarding Germany. Henderson unreservedly saw definite justification for Hitler's demands, arguing with his superiors at home: "These 3-1/2 million Germans [Sudetens] were incorporated in the Czechoslovak State against their will and in defiance of their rights of self-determination." He said that "Czechoslovak promises of full equality of rights in the new State . . . have never been granted although they are the national due of every national group." [44] Such hearty agreement with Hitler by Britain's envoy could not fail to add grist to Hitler's mill.

Newton attended a parliamentary debate in Prague early in March 1938 and reported on it to his superiors. He wrote that "the Czech parties showed remarkable unanimity in support of the Prime Minister's [Hodža's] statement and his assertions of Czechoslovak independence." Newton related sympathetically, in marked contrast with Henderson, that the leaders of the government coalition spoke supportively on the following points:

1. There were no reasonable grounds of complaint against the treatment of the German minority, and foreign interference on their behalf would not be tolerated;

2. . . . Germany was not interested in the German minority, as such; only as an instrument of policy . . . [of] German expansion to the East;
3. England fully realized the danger which such expansion would constitute for her;
4. The Czechoslovak population were determined to resist to the last any attack on their independence and would never submit to any change of their frontiers. [45]

The Agrarian Party spokesmen were "less provocative in their manner of expression" but were equally insistent that "Germany . . . must be no danger to the independence of Czechoslovakia." The German activist parties also supported the government's willingness for the SdP to join the government coalition, provided "loyalty to the State were demonstrated, and would pursue their aims within the framework of the State." Even the leader of the Slovak People's Party, Sokol, who favored collaboration with the SdP, declared that "his party regarded the frontier of Czechoslovakia as eternal and inviolable," although he took issue on foreign policy and religious grounds with the Soviet pact. [46]

Henlein had been busily organizing in Slovakia to attract to his banner the German population, numbering 147,000, most of whom he assumed were inclined in his favor. The focus of attack on his tours of Slovakia was the pro-Beneš activists. [47]

Sokol, on the other hand, declared his party's willingness to enter the government coalition provided the Slovak demands were met, namely, "acceptance of the Pittsburgh Agreement." On the whole, "the Slovak people would defend the State," judged Newton. Newton declared that Father Andrej Hlinka alone demanded autonomy as a prerequisite for cooperation with the government; in opposition were only the "Sudetic German Party and the Magyar opposition," in the Senate, and the Communists, who voted negatively in the House. The Slovak People's Party and the Communists abstained in the Senate vote. [48]

In the estimation of the British Foreign Office, Hitler's aggressive intentions in Central and Eastern Europe "were driven by his determination upon domination in the economically independent inter-Danubian basin [and] Bohemia-Moravia quadrilateral." [49] "The agriculture of Czechoslovakia would be of considerable assistance to Germany . . . and even more important [were] her coal, pig-iron, chemicals, and munitions." [50] These economic riches of Czechoslovakia were indeed potent motivation for German attempts to grasp and keep by whatever means; they would go a long way to alleviate economic problems within the Reich itself.

NOTES

1. Henry Ashby Turner, *German Big Business and the Rise of Hitler* (New York: Oxford University Press, 1985), p. 46.

2. André Fontaine, *History of the Cold War*, vol. 1, (New York: Random House, 1969), p. 83.

3. Ibid.

4. Nuremberg Documents (London: His Majesty's Stationary Office), Part 1, p. 249, quoted in Winston Churchill, *The Gathering Storm*, (Boston: Houghton Mifflin, 1948), p. 263.

5. Churchill, *The Gathering Storm*, p. 266.

6. Frantisek Moravec, *Master of Spies, Memoirs* (London: Bodley Head, 1975), p. 108.

7. Churchill, *The Gathering Storm*, p. 256.

8. Personal report later given to JOC by Ambassador Vladimir Hurban, based on Foreign Office memos.

9. Moravec, *Master of Spies*, pp. 70, 76 .

10. Ibid., p. 108.

11. Based on JOC reports to Institute of Current World Affairs from Prague. JOC archive.

12. Annual Report of Basil C. Newton, Prague, to Anthony Eden, January 14, 1938, p. 2 of report, FO 371/v. 22336.

13. Ibid.

14. Ibid., p.3 of report.

15. Ibid.

16. Ibid., p. 6 of report.

17. Ibid.

18. Newton to Eden, Prague, January 25,1938, FO 371/v. 22336, pp. 221-25.

19. Ibid.

20. Moravec, *Master of Spies*, p. 77. Italics added.

21. Ibid., p. 78.

22. Ibid., p. 84.

23. Ibid., p. 87. Italics added.

24. Ibid., p. 23.

25. Newton to Eden, January 27, 1938, FO 371/v. 22338, pp. 192-99.

26. Ibid.

27. Newton to Eden, February 3, 1938. FO 371/22338, p. 241.

28. E. B. M. Ingram, Foreign Office to British Legation, Prague, February 10, 1928, FO 371/v. 22338, p. 238.

29. FO 371/v. 22339, p. 432.

30. War Office, Whitehall, to Ingram, Foreign Office, January 3, 1938, FO 371/v. 22336, p. 270.

31. British Ambassador, Warsaw, to Eden, January 15, 1938, FO 371/v. 22336, pp. 167-68.

32. Foreign Office Memo, *"Polish-Czech Differences in Regard to the Polish Minority in Teschen,"* January 1938, FO 371/v. 22347, pp. 107-11.

33. Ibid.

34. Ibid.

35. Memo, January 22, 1938, Prem 1/330, especially Annex 11, pp. 8-9.

36. Ibid., Annex I of document.

37. Ibid., Annex 1.

38. Ibid., p. 10 of report.

39. Ibid., p. 10 of report, based on Eric Phipps's telegram of May 4, 1937.

40. Ibid.

41. Foreign Office report, January 22, 1938, Prem 1/330.

42. Foreign Office, Noble for Secretary of State to Phipps, Paris, March 12, 1938, FO 371/v. 22337, p. 95.

43. British Legation, Prague, to Eden, December 30, 1937, FO 371/v. 22336, p. 17.

44. Nevile Henderson, Berlin, to Foreign Office, repeated to Prague, March 8, 1938, FO 371/v. 22337, p. 55.

45. Newton, Prague to Foreign Office, FO 371/v. 22338, pp. 28-29.

46. Ibid.

47. Troutbeck, Prague, to Foreign Office, February 21, 1938, FO 371/v. 22336, p. 315.

48. FO 371/v. 22338, p. 219.

49. Frank Ashton Gwatkin, Foreign Office, Memo on Czechoslovakia, March 15, 1938, FO 371/v. 22338, p. 217.

50. *The Economist*, March 12, 1938, FO 371/v. 22338, p. 219.

8

The Sudeten Fires Flare (1938)

The Führer's expansionist plans were initiated explicitly in July 1936, when he instructed the German general staff to draw up a plan called "Case Otto," for later use in the occupation of Austria. On November 5th, he gathered his principal collaborators, including the military, to inform them that he "wanted to finish rapidly with Austria and Czechoslovakia."[1] He issued a special directive regarding actual preparations. His eventual objectives in Eastern Europe, according to Churchill, were particularly Poland, White Russia, and the Ukraine.[2] The gate to the east was located in Central Europe; the path opened through Austria and led unmistakably through Czechoslovakia. Hitler rearmed with all possible speed. On February 4, 1938, he reorganized his army command, giving top slot to generals Werner von Blomberg and Werner Von Fritsch; topmost chief was pro-Nazi Marshal Wilhelm Keitel. At the Foreign Office, he replaced the moderate diplomat Konstantin von Neurath with Joachim von Ribbentrop.

Hitler constantly watched West European reactions to his early moves, lest the West Europeans feel their own security threatened. On November 6th, the French ambassador to Berlin sent a telegram home about a meeting there, speculating that it was motivated by "a problem of raw materials" for the growing war machine.[3] Von Ribbentrop was in Rome attending the ceremony of initiating Italy into the Anti-Comintern Pact. The watchword at Whitehall and the Quai d'Orsay was to avoid doing anything to provoke an aggressive response, a line that was interpreted in Berlin as weakness. Guided by his political intuition early in 1938, Hitler overrode his own staff officers who felt he was moving ahead of their preparedness; he believed the Western Powers would not force a confrontation that would erupt into conflagration.

Hitler had prepared his fifth column in Austria well. Starting with the assassination of Chancellor Engelbert Dollfuss in July 1934, Austria was inundated with subversion by native Nazis, while surface relations on the diplomatic level appeared "normal." On February 12, 1938, Hitler summoned the new Austrian chancellor, Kurt von Schuschnigg, to Berchtesgaden and subjected him to the heaviest possible pressures, such as threats of invasion and challenging the latter's "mistaken" estimates that England and France would move to assist him. French diplomacy gleaned this gambit in advance, but failed to move, [4] even though Foreign Minister Yvon Delbos of the Popular Front Blum government, in conversation with British Ambassador Sir Eric Phipps and also in a telegram to his London ambassador, Charles Corbin, did warn: "The Führer counts on our passivity." [5] Phipps and Delbos even talked of an economic pact between Vienna and Prague that would include all the Danubian countries. Next day, according to Alexander Werth, a weary and discouraged Delbos addressed the French chamber of deputies expressing disquiet over Austria and affirming the loyalty of France to its Czechoslovak alliance. The chamber sustained his policy statement by a vote of 438 to 2, with 163 abstentions. [6]

By 11 P.M. Schuschnigg had caved in. Three days later, on February 15th, he met Hitler's deadline and appointed the Führer's henchman Seyss-Inquart as minister of interior and chief of police, with a post in the cabinet. Mussolini sent a message complimenting Schuschnigg on his exemplary behavior, while the British legation in Prague reported that "Dr. Schuschnigg's capitulation has been a genuine shock to Czechoslovakia's Government." [7] On March 9th Schuschnigg announced he would organize a plebiscite to affirm popular support of Austria's independence. [8]

The German minister to Prague had a long audience with President Beneš on February 16th, in which he undoubtedly set forth explicit terms of a settlement that was tantamount to total capitulation, especially in his demands for abrogation of the Soviet pact and the inclusion of Konrad Henlein in the cabinet, as prerequisites to "improve relations with Germany." [9] Beneš sat unruffled. He felt obliged, he responded, to keep France informed, and as for the German minority, that was an internal question beyond the scope of any foreign government's appropriate concern. Regarding the proposal to revise Czechoslovakia's frontiers by ceding to Germany some of the Sudeten areas, Beneš was equally adamant against any revision.   The British minister, reporting on this meeting, stated bluntly: "Germany's aim was to use three million Germans to get control of Czechoslovakia and her resources . . . to create a sphere of influence down to the Black Sea." [10]

Three days later, the scene shifted to Berlin, where Hitler told the Czechoslovak minister that "while insisting on 'revision' of the status of the Sudeten Deutschen he had no desire to violate the integrity of Czechoslovakia," and he offered to concretize this guarantee of Czechoslovak independence in an official pact. [11]

On February 20th at midnight, Anthony Eden resigned as Foreign Minister over a dispute with Neville Chamberlain about negotiation with Mussolini's government for a "Gentlemen's Agreement." That same day, the outlook was sufficiently auspicious for Hitler to go before the Reichstag and issue to Austria, Czechoslovakia, and the world this resounding tocsin: "It is unthinkable for a self-respecting world power to stand by and see members of its nation continually humiliated on account of its sympathies and their oneness with their motherland, its destiny, and its world view." [12]

Hitler was encouraged to tell the world openly, and his own people, that the Third Reich felt obliged to rectify the wrongs to its nationals living beyond Germany's frontiers to assure their liberties and well-being.   His own foreign office, headed by Von Neurath and his military chiefs, advised contrarily at this point.   Hitler's claims of responsibility beyond his national confines clearly imperiled his immediate neighbors.   The British legation in Prague duly reported home the strong negative reactions of the Czechs.   On February 22, Newton's deputy, Troutbeck, wrote: "Government circles [are] depressed by Hitler's speech," enclosing a spate of critical press clippings as evidence. [13]

Apparently, before the Anschluss, internal conflicts within the German ruling circles were visible; the industrialists, the army generals, and German Intelligence Chief Wilhelm Franz Canaris comprised the moderate faction, as against the extreme political elements.

The German press exulted with "satisfaction that they have the power to exercise a decisive influence on the settlement of those problems in which they are concerned.   The ease of the Austrian change encouraged them," according to the British Consul at Liberec. [14]

President Roosevelt wanted to do something significant to show his support of beleaguered Czechoslovakia and his opposition to the Fascist dictators, despite the continuation of his nonintervention policy toward Spain. Early in January 1938, he sent a secret message to Chamberlain via the British ambassador in Washington, proposing a Big Four conference in Washington to explore solutions for the deteriorating European situation. Chamberlain turned him down flatly, saying he feared further irritating the aggressive dictators in case of failure. Foreign Secretary Eden was "deeply perturbed" at Chamberlain's response and he was joined in this by Winston Churchill. [15]

Wishing in any case to make a public demonstration favoring Czechoslovakia, Roosevelt on March 7, 1938, signed a U.S.-Czechoslovak trade agreement, strengthening the most-favored-nation provisions which were already in effect for three years, and improving opportunities for the expansion of trade in products of special interest to each country by 10 percent to 50 percent reduction of duties. Shoe exports from Czechoslovakia to the United States were greatly enhanced in exchange for reduced duties on U.S. goods into Czechoslovakia. [16] The new treaty, which had been under negotiation for three months, was greeted with glee in the Prague press as a "considerable breach in the tariff walls, giving to Czechoslovak exports a substantial margin of preference over their German competitors" as well as "holding out prospects of a further substantial increase in their trade." [17]

On March 11th, Hitler ordered the German armed forces to occupy Austria militarily with sizable forces, comprising 40,000 to 50,000 troops, 20,000 armed police, and 200 aircraft. [18] The mobilized units were to have made a triumphant entry into Vienna on Saturday, the 12th, but to Hitler's chagrin, they became snarled in heavy traffic jams on the road, forcing the postponement of the event to the next day. While Hitler was being photographed in his car entering the city amid cheering throngs, he is said to have remarked to Gen. Franz von Halder, riding alongside, "this will be very inconvenient to the Czechs." [19]

Joseph Paul-Boncour, succeeding the discouraged Delbos, now headed the French foreign ministry for the Popular Front government of Léon Blum. He sought to evoke a spirit of resistance to Hitler's easy success in his aggressions, especially since the disaster of the Anschluss. [20] He convoked a meeting on March 15th of the chiefs of defense and war, including Léon Blum; generals Philippe Pétain, Robert Jacomet, and Maurice Gamelin of the armed forces, and Alexis Léger. The meeting readily acknowledged the vast superiority in numbers of the German Army over that of France; 900,000 to 400,000 according to General Gamelin. Pierre Cot of the Air Force was a black pessimist. Paul-Boncour faulted Delbos for his weak, noninterventionist stance in Spain. The meeting explored some possible actions against Franco, which were vetoed by the generals as giving Germany and Italy a *casus belli*. From Rome came reports of fury over the Anschluss; it was said that only Mussolini was willing to give a good face to the provocative event. [21]

In Berlin, on the eve of the Anschluss, when asked by the French Ambassador about Germany's intentions, Marshal Hermann Göring had declared unblinkingly Germany's having "no evil intentions towards Czechoslovakia." [22] To mollify the Czechoslovak minister in Berlin, Göring said on the 12th "that Reich troops in Austria had been ordered not to go within 10 kilometers of the Czechoslovak frontier so long as there was no mobilization in Czechoslovakia." [23] Two days later, the British military attaché in Prague seconded his French counterpart's skeptical appraisal that the reassuring statements of Marshal Göring and Hitler meant less than nothing.

Diplomatic assurances notwithstanding, the situation looked grim to the democratic world and especially to Czechoslovakia. The German armies had gained access to the southern frontier of Czechoslovakia, where the German fifth column was concentrated. Moreover, within Sudetenland lay the main anti-German military fortifications. In ex-Austria, the SS troops and the Gestapo not only unleashed a campaign of violence against the Heimwehr (home guard), but also inflicted the "final solution" on any entrapped Jewish and Socialist groups, while in Czechoslovakia, the Sudeten Germans were told "it was their duty to increase their influence in Czechoslovakia." [24]

A secret intelligence report from Germany to the British Foreign Office disclaimed any "immediate likelihood of a German attack on Czechoslovakia, but the Führer was always capable of taking a sudden decision." Another secret source stated that "while there was no intention of making an immediate move, if the Czechoslovaks did not give a suitable degree of autonomy to the Sudetendeutsch, more active steps would be considered . . . in two or three months' time." A third source vouchsafed the opinion that "action against Czechoslovakia is probable after the harvest." [25]

Coincidentally with the invasion, the British Foreign Office directed its minister in Prague to brief President Beneš on its position at this critical moment. The friendly exploration of possible further conciliation took place on March 14th. Basil C. Newton explained that his government "desired concessions to be made to the Sudetens . . . to gain time." Beneš went along. Both men agreed that "the

Germans should be given no excuse whatever for intervention on [the Sudeten's] behalf." Observing that 22 percent of the population of Czechoslovakia was German-speaking, "Beneš offered that 22% of all government officials will be drawn from this section of the population. This cannot be done at once," he said, "since the Germans themselves agree that sufficient candidates are not available immediately." The SdP wanted only German-speaking officials in their districts, but Beneš held that "this could not be conceded . . . [either, as it would be] equivalent to autonomy." They compromised; in these districts Germans and Czechs would alternate as prefects and deputy-prefects. [26]

In an ethnic study made by parishes, Czechoslovakia's statistical office found that in Bohemia's 12,665 parishes, 8,451 had a Czech and 4,211 a German majority. In Moravia's 3,867 parishes, 2,852 had a Czech, 952 a German, and 55 a Polish majority. "These figures," said the *Prager Tagblatt* article, "do not fully show the extent to which the population is mixed . . . In Bohemia, there are twice as many Czechs living in places with a German majority as there are Germans living in places with a Czech majority . . . In Prague alone, there are 41,701 Germans, the result of great changes brought about by industrialization." [27]

As for schools, Beneš affirmed, "facilities for schooling for German-speaking children are actually better in Czechoslovakia than in Germany, in that classes are smaller." The demand for cultural autonomy could not be conceded, but "separate school boards would be set up in Prague for each nationality with complete control over the schools, including appointing teachers of the nationality of the children." A system of traveling inspectors would be created to investigate complaints. "Dr. Beneš will do everything in his power to gain time," assured Newton, "to give France time to emerge from her present difficulty . . . and the Balkan countries time to react against Germany." [28]

In their military defenses, Newton reported, they were "still somewhat sketchy in the south and there is an unfilled gap in the north and some of the secondary lines of defense need completing." The British emissary expanded: "By August, the aviation will be considerably more advanced . . . Czechoslovakia should have 1,000 first line machines, for which aerodromes are prepared . . . More equipment is anticipated from Russia . . . The morale of the whole nation is so staunch . . . it must be seen to be believed." [29]

Checking further into the military situation, Newton relayed the observations of his military attaché that the "Czechoslovak Army [had]

17 ordinary and four mechanized divisions . . . [occasioning] no [need of] change in [their] disposition at present to meet [the] new threat which was anticipated . . . [Although] not complete, [they were] considered by General Staff adequate to check infantry attack by armoured forces." The attaché concluded: *"Consider Czechoslovakia will stand, if given time to mobilize."* [30] Returning to the interview with Beneš, Newton continued: "The attitude of the Czechoslovaks is one of profound attachment to France . . . They dislike the Poles," he wrote. "But the unity of France is anything but certain . . . Antimilitarism is rife."

Despite the pervasive gloom, President Beneš was optimistic. "The Western Powers," he deemed, were "in a far more favourable position than . . . in 1914 . . . Germans [then] had the resources of Austria, and Turkey was their ally. Today, France is relatively much stronger, a million Czechs bar the way to the East . . . Germany today is very short of materials and of cadres . . . very short of guns, but she will be sufficiently ready to tackle France in 1940 . . . Germany's ultimate aim," as foreshadowed in *Mein Kampf.* Beneš saw that "the only means of gaining time, perhaps a year, is that Great Britain should declare her support of France, if the latter has to go to the aid of Czechoslovakia . . . [That] would rally the countries in South-Eastern Europe . . . The people would prefer to fight, even with 90% of the chances against them to preserve their full liberty, rather than become a puppet of Germany . . . We are prepared to fight to the last," declared Beneš with conviction, "but we must make sure that people not get massacred in vain . . . The Nazis have such great powers of repression" [31]

A *London Times* article noted that "the feeling of isolation in Czechoslovakia is quite dreadful, but is concealed." Great Britain could ease this apprehension by "the immensely powerful weapon of the blockade," Beneš was quoted as saying. The isolation of Czechoslovakia was also detected by Churchill, who spoke in the House of Commons as reported in the *Times* on March 14th, signaling the dangers in southeastern Europe. [32]

Beneš had discreetly made an urgent plea to Newton to nudge his government toward a public statement assuring both Czechoslovakia and the French, and warning Germany, that the British would rise to support France in assisting Czechoslovakia in case of a German invasion. British silence at this moment "might have disastrous results," warned Pierre Étienne Flandin, the French foreign minister, who was preparing on March 15th "to repeat . . . M. Delbos' recent statement . . . that France was resolved to carry out her treaty obligations if Czechoslovakia were attacked." [33]

Phipps underscored "the great disappointment in many quarters [of Paris] that Mr. Chamberlain's speech contained no declaration of the readiness of Great Britain to go to the aid of Czechoslovakia if she were attacked by Germany." [34] Phipps said this omission was "noted with regret" in official offices and the press, while at the same time, "MM Blum and Paul-Boncour renewed to [Czech Minister Štefan] Osuský previous French assurances that Czechoslovakia could count on France's military assistance in the event of her being attacked by Germany." [35]

While the Prague government had to avoid any appearance of military movements in the vicinity of the Bavarian-Saxon frontier, its military intelligence observed on March 16th that "the German troop strength in Austria appears far in excess of requirements . . . and frontier garrisons have been placed on a footing of preparedness," while "reserve officers in Saxony and Bavaria have been called up." [36]

The invasion of Austria gave the Yugoslavs impetus to break away from the Little Entente. At a recent session of the alliance, Prince Paul of Yugoslavia had been joined by King Carol of Romania in thwarting the resolute effort of Beneš to present a solid front of the Little Entente against Nazi expansion. Both were opposed to calling another immediate meeting of the alliance as Beneš desired. [37] Beneš had already directed a vain appeal the previous December (1937) to the new Yugoslav prime minister, Milan Stojadinović, who had come to Prague to attend the state funeral of Tomáš Masaryk. As a result of the subsequent Stojadinović-Göring understanding, Yugoslavia reneged on its opposition to the Anschluss. The British Foreign Office had noted the recent drift of Romania and Yugoslavia toward neutrality, "though they remain formally bound by obligations of mutual assistance." [38]

Another meeting was later called in May by the Czechoslovak foreign minister, Kamil Krofta, where "Roumania and Yugoslavia shared with Czechoslovakia a recognition of certain common interests and dangers." In any case, they all found the time "unlikely" to commit themselves. [39] The Little Entente alliance, which Beneš had built painstakingly, had eroded into insignificance by May 1938. A parallel report to the Foreign Office from the British legation in Bucharest confirmed that "the Roumanians and Czechoslovaks found Stojadinović very slippery and it was a decidedly difficult job getting out a nice looking final communique." [40]

Soviet Russia and Czechoslovakia alone vigorously protested the seizure of Austria, to the point of reiterating their readiness to abide by the military provisions of the alliance should France invoke their implementation. This stand was unflinchingly affirmed by Maxim Litvinov at Moscow's foreign ministry to Viscount Aretas Chilston, Britain's ambassador to Russia. Litvinov said he was sure that Hitler "would soon proceed to deal with Czechoslovakia," being "not afraid of any active opposition owing to the weakness shown by Great Britain and France in various stages of German menace in the past and the absence of collective security and the failure of the League."[41] At this juncture, on March 17th, Moscow formally proposed the convocation of an international conference, including the Soviet Union and Czechoslovakia, "to seek a diplomatic settlement of the Czechoslovak crisis."[42]

Even the Popular Front government of Blum, adhering to its nonintervention policy in Spain and taking its cue from England, moderated its diplomatic protest against the Austrian Anschluss. The conservative regime of Premier Edouard Daladier, succeeding Blum's Popular Front to office on April 12th, seemed more disposed to yielding gradually to Hitler the Western bastion in Central Europe, Czechoslovakia.

The new foreign minister of Daladier, Georges Bonnet, was a celebrated Paris attorney with long ties to the ruling circles. Although more cynical than his British colleague, Bonnet's attitude toward fascism appeared as a mirror image of Lord Halifax's. They were each responsible representatives of their respective establishments, which at the moment were predominantly concerned with striking peaceful terms with the unruly power of Nazi Germany, as the bulwark against the terrifying menace of Bolshevism. They failed to see, as conservative Churchill did, that their own security interests were closely bound to those of Czechoslovakia. With the resources of central and southeastern Europe at his command, Hitler's accretion of resources would be significant. And the only way to deflate the aggressive Nazi leader was to create for him the necessity of fighting a two-front war when he should decide to turn on the Western European powers. That meant an effective Czechoslovak, French, and British alliance with Soviet Russia. Churchill was willing and eventually did create just that arrangement when Hitler invaded the Soviet Union. Chamberlain and Daladier and their foreign ministers fell short of deciding on these necessities for the long run.

Bonnet's standing rule of thumb at the Quai d'Orsay was not to engage France without British backing, which implied disengaging France from her eastern alliance. Right off, it meant aborting the grand alliance of France–Great Britain–USSR at the soonest possible moment. Although warned of the change by his minister to Paris, Osuský, in April 1938, the trusting Beneš continued to respect the French alliance overtly, as did Daladier. Each knew that their respective public statements were dissimulations. Discovered in Daladier's papers, not Bonnet's, was a statement added in the premier's own hand that he had told Osuský on July 20th that "the Czechoslovak government must know clearly our position: France will not make war over the affair of the Sudetens . . . although publicly we will affirm our solidarity according to the desire of the Czechoslovak government." [43]

Beneš expounded his theme during an interview on March 17th with the *London Times* correspondent and with Bruce Lockhart, when he told them that the defense of Czechoslovakia was vital to British interests. He argued that Germany would be greatly strengthened by Czechoslovak resources and those of Southeast Europe for her eventual war against Britain and France, "upon whose Empires Germany had ulterior designs." [44]

Western intellectual circles, similarly attuned to peaceful means, went equally astray in succumbing to Hitler's siren song as he bludgeoned his way to attaining his desired "lebensraum" in the East. Moreover, the British were incessantly being wooed for an "Anglo-German understanding," for which Marshal Göring asserted that "never had conditions been more favorable," as he explained to G. Ward Price in private conversation over a three-hour lunch in his home at Karinhall, near Berlin, on March 23rd. In exchange, Göring was prepared to pledge Germany's "entire strength to the defense of British interests throughout the world." Göring took this occasion to avow that "Germany had only three national aims to fulfill, that the first of these, the Anschluss, had just been achieved . . . remaining (a) the redemption from oppression of the German minority in Czechoslovakia, and (b) the recovery of some of Germany's former African colonies, or of satisfactory substitute territories." Göring pledged Germany "to respect Czechoslovakia's independence if full autonomy is granted to the Sudeten Germans." [45]

It was archly hoped by the prevailing Western establishment leaders, moreover, that the two dictatorial colossi might fatally weaken each other in deadly combat in the East, while the West stood aloof observing the mayhem. Collaboration between British and German industrialists had been vaguely rumored since the first World War, as explaining the drift toward appeasement. The Foreign Office archive contains one document supporting the assertion. A letter from the manager of the Armaments Contracts Department of Vickers-Armstrong to an under-secretary of state at the War Office, dated May 3, 1938, requests official permission for a mutual exchange of personnel with a counterpart company in each of their plants. These exchanges were made customarily under license agreements issued by the War Office in London. The arms manufacturers palpably applied no political litmus tests to determine the convictions or behavior of their purchasers. [46]

In the evolving scenario, independent Czechoslovakia was increasingly viewed in the West as an obstacle rather than a treasured ally. If only the Prague government were more resilient, was the attitude! Hitler had little trouble stirring up enough turmoil to give the Sudetens a prima facie case for their grievances. Czechoslovak intelligence sources shared with Newton their estimate that "the Reich will doubtless soon tackle the next item on their programme, Czechoslovakia . . . They will at first seek to achieve their aims by friendly diplomacy . . . Later on, they may attempt to use Henlein as the Seyss-Inquart of Czechoslovakia." By habit and necessity, intelligence sources must be accurate in their forecasts; in this case, the prophecy was widely shared. Hitler's verbal guarantees of peaceful intentions gained him the time his war machine required for a state of readiness. Meanwhile, Newton in Prague observed bleakly: "Should war come, nothing that we or France can do would save Czechoslovakia from being overrun." He then bluntly asked his superiors whether Britain could undertake "such commitments or risks as will enable Czechoslovakia . . . to preserve her independence against brute force or economic strangulation." If so, the sooner, the better. After he informed the Foreign Office blandly that "Czechoslovakia would welcome definite promises of support," he demurred, "*HM's'G are entitled to decline the risk of involving Great Britain in a fresh war* . . . to shore up the present position which seems to us fundamentally unsound." [47]

This was the unvarnished reasoning of one of Czechoslovakia's best advocates within the British official circle! His news bulletin took into account widespread popular reluctance at the moment to risk a war over a distant threat, however much this reaction overlooked the long-run British and French national interests.

Newton explained to his superiors that Beneš was "very anxious to get some sort of reciprocal guarantee from Great Britain, or if possible an alliance," although he suspected a negative answer. In all conscience, it was Newton's duty to transmit Beneš's message to the Foreign Office. Beneš pressed his point with Newton: "He believed

Herr Hitler, knowing Germany was not ready for a major war, would commit no act of aggression if we made it clear that we should oppose it by force." [48]   On the next day, Beneš told Newton of his earlier fear that "the Germans were secretly mobilizing . . . We are now satisfied that Czechoslovakia was in no immediate danger." The British military attaché on March 19th reported that "they were not anxious" for the moment concerning German troop movements in the vicinity of the frontier. [49]

A sorry turn was reached on the 19th with the appearance in the *London Times* of a report of a speech by the parliamentary secretary to the labor minister, which anticipated with equanimity that "Germany would absorb Czechoslovakia and Great Britain would remain secure . . . [that] Chamberlain would not think he would make a move to give a guarantee of that kind, [respecting] the frontiers of Czechoslovakia." Sir Orme Sargent of the foreign office characterized the statement by a high government official as a "most indiscreet speech [that] no member of the Government ought to make." There was great need "in the present delicate state of international affairs . . . for circumspection." [50]   Britain was maneuvering in a rocky channel between Scylla and Charybdis. But the camouflage cover was off and the direction of Chamberlain's policy stood revealed.

Prior to the Anschluss, Prime Minister Milan Hodža had nimbly assuaged Sudeten public opinion while establishing talking relations with moderate Bohemian Germans, Socialists, and Agrarians. The resulting Nationalities Statute broadening self-government, which had been under discussion for two years, was finally presented by the Agrarian Party to parliament on March 26th, 1938. These bills would provide for equal nationality rights for the Sudetens, national self-administration, protection for agriculture, and redress of injustices. [51] At this late date, however, the concessions were too little, too late. The Sudeten moderates panicked, and along with other pro-Nazis, joined the SdP to create a landslide favoring Henlein that now constituted 83 percent of the Sudeten vote.

Meanwhile in Slovakia, taking advantage of the central government's new conciliatory stand toward the German demands, Father Andrej Hlinka added fuel to the already roaring fire. On April 14th, he proclaimed to the Slovak nation his threat "to sever all parliamentary cooperation with his opponents unless Slovak autonomy was granted." Newton saw Slovakia as a "backward and unbalanced" province under the "influence of a "fanatical priesthood, and [belonging] to the 19th rather than the 20th century, [with] leaders so irresponsible and immature" that their behavior provided "excellent propaganda value for Czechoslovakia's enemies."[52]

At the same time, a noted German businessman in Prague, known to London (but whose name is not recorded), was doing what he could to persuade his hesitant fellow nationals to support Henlein's Nazis without delay. H. Wickham Steed of the *London Times* sent Lord Halifax a memo on April 24th revealing the mentality in this circle. These people saw in the Austrian Anschluss evidence of the speed of German advances in Central Europe, enhancing Germany's position. They agreed there were "no differences upon the aims of Italy-German policy."[53]

It is amazing that the business interests in the Allied camp failed to draw similar lessons from the growing fascist alignment, while political circles also misconstrued their significance. The diplomatic situation at this time had seriously degenerated for Czechoslovakia, especially in her relations with Poland. Early in April the British military attaché in Warsaw had reported "widespread apprehension that fundamental changes may be imminent in Czechoslovakia now that the Anschluss is an accomplished fact." Although it was noted that "an independent Czechoslovakia would be most unpalatable to the Poles," the government deluded itself that "Germany would not wish to absorb Eastern Czechoslovakia, but only the German districts of Bohemia, and this would not seriously increase the [military] dangers of their position."

The lack of a firm stand by France had a ripple effect in Poland. The Poles, as observed by the British ambassador to Warsaw, "are more than ever convinced of the impotence of France as an ally." It was no surprise that "they should show signs of preferring to descend on the German side of the fence . . . Short-sighted in the extreme, but the reality of the moment . . . But perhaps they hope they would share in the spoils if Czechoslovakia were dismantled." It was said in Warsaw that "Beck is very much moved by his personal dislikes . . . and he suffers from a strong aversion to [Romanian Prime Minister Nicholas] Titulescu, Beneš, and the French in general."[54] Some weeks later, the same source reported that "Poland's interest in Czechoslovakia is understandable . . . Their solidarity with the Slovak Autonomists is one of their favorite methods."[55]

Henlein utilized his improved rating at the polls to escalate his terms in a speech at Karlovy Vary on April 24th, terms he had coordinated with Berlin. He demanded full equality between Czechoslovaks and Germans, the designation of German regions with German officials therein, and territorial autonomy. Both Henlein and his bosses in Berlin understood full well that Czechoslovak acceptance of these extreme terms would dismantle the democratic structure of the state and lure the Sudetens into a right-wing government. Chamberlain had observed in his parliamentary speech, "It must be realized that if war broke out it was unlikely to be confined to those who had assumed legal obligations." [56]

In recognition of the developing crisis over Czechoslovakia, an Anglo-French meeting was held in London over April 28 and 29th. Present were Chamberlain, Lord Halifax, Sir Robert Vansittart, Sir Alexander Cadogan, Sargent, Robert Strang, and Roberts for the British, and Daladier, Bonnet, Corbin, Léger, Charles Rochat, and Roland de Margerie for France. Chamberlain led off palpably respecting Britain's engagements to France: "They would not extend in case France entered a war to come to the assistance of her Czechoslovak ally." This stand was backed by the Dominions; the risks of entering would be enormous. He continued, "Together, they must obtain appropriate concessions from Beneš to satisfy Germany." Chamberlain did not think Hitler would want to annex 3.5 million Sudeten Germans. Henlein himself had limited his demands to a transformation of Czechoslovakia from a national state into one of nationalities. Chamberlain, seeing Beneš as the chief stumbling block, declared it was necessary to overcome the reservations of Beneš to assure the peace of Europe.

Daladier disagreed. He esteemed Beneš as a man of wisdom; at the least he proposed that France and Great Britain should sustain Czechoslovakia and impede her dismemberment. He felt that Hitler wanted to destroy those countries covered by the treaties and to destabilize Europe's equilibrium in order to dominate her as Napoleon had. He ended, saying that France, for her part, considered her "alliance with Czechoslovakia has a vital importance" and she is resolved "to execute her obligations." Chamberlain responded that he did not think these two countries had sufficient strength to impose their will on Germany. Daladier said that for four years in the French infantry, he had seen German atrocities and was dedicated to prevent their return.

Bonnet did not think it possible to satisfy Hitler by giving autonomy to the Sudetens, as Hitler wanted to erase Czechoslovakia from the map of Europe. And he added that "France must respect her word and her signature." The meeting ended in an impasse. [57] On May 7th, nevertheless, the British and French Ambassadors in Prague presented a joint demand requesting full compliance by the government to Henlein's outrageous demands at Karlovy Vary, which had been so clearly backed by Berlin. [58]

The Prague government parried the Anglo-French ultimatum and diverted attention to an intelligence report warning the West that Nazi troops were again on the move in bordering Saxony. These were confirmed by French consuls in Saxony and also by the French military attaché in Berlin, Gen. Gaston Renondeau. The Czechoslovak intelligence sources reported transports moving toward Silesia and others toward Austria. French Ambassador André François-Poncet heard the news in Prague with high skepticism, which was overcome by a report from the French consul general in Dresden. [59] British military intelligence in London was convinced that the "Germans were in fact contemplating action against Czechoslovakia, but dropped the project after the diplomatic uproar," pretending that "nothing abnormal was taking place." [60]

The reports were angrily refuted by German Foreign Minister von Ribbentrop on May 20th, who simultaneously threatened onerous punitive measures to protect Sudeten rights. Facts were demanded of Sir Nevile Henderson by the Foreign Office. Henderson telegraphed that "no really extensive troop movements took place," but he conceded that "no one investigated the Bavarian frontier where movements had also been reported." [61]

Meanwhile, intelligence sources informed the Czechoslovak government that an SdP coup, in coordination with Berlin, was being prepared in Sudetenland, coincident with the first round of municipal elections set for May 22nd. The Wehrmacht was to march in to support. [62] Henderson was requested to check this out promptly. He dismissed the threat and vouchsafed his opinion: "I do not believe that the Germans were prepared lightheartedly to risk another coup in Czechoslovakia, so soon after the German success." [63]

Henderson's assurances placated Whitehall, but it was too much to believe that Prague would trust these disclaimers, nor was Prague privy to them. The Hodža government, next day on May 21st, ordered a partial mobilization in self-defense. Ambassador François-Poncet strongly counseled against mobilization; Bonnet from Paris merely advised "prudence." Prof. Jean-Baptiste Duroselle, the Sorbonne's eminent authority on the Foreign Ministry's archives, judged that "the role of France is practically nil." [64] In the face of massive Western public opinion, which rallied to the manifestly menaced Czechoslovakia, Hitler backed down from the intended coup d'état and Henlein requested reopening negotiations with the Czechoslovak prime minister.

Bonnet took stock at the Quai d'Orsay at this point in the European diplomatic situation. He knew he could not count on Poland in a crisis with Germany, and the support of the Soviet Union was at best not efficacious, even if the British should turn to collusion in this quarter; although this was possible, it was not likely. He took cognizance of the Italo-English Easter Accords, signed on April 16th, and opened his own negotiations with Rome on April 22nd. Hitler quickly made his countering move; he went to Rome personally on May 5th and remained there until the 9th to shore up his friendly relations with Mussolini and to forestall his pro-French move. The early result came in a speech by the Italian dictator at Genoa on May 14th, when he informed his public that he would cut short his conversations with France, a move that further isolated France diplomatically. [65]

While strongly disclaiming reports of military mobilization or intentions of a Sudeten coup, on May 30th the Führer, in fury over the backdown, overrode his military leaders' objections to pen his famous secret directive to the Wehrmacht for the implementation of Operation Grün. The army was ordered to speed all preparations for war, to begin not later than October 1st, to fulfill Hitler's unalterable intention to destroy the independent Czechoslovak nation. [66] Hodža, in resuming his talks with Henlein, stood by the generous provisions of the Nationalities Statute of March 26th, and Henlein, in turn, followed Hitler's instructions to insist on the Karlovy Vary program prescribing total autonomy. Although the latest Henlein demands did not appear drastic to the British and French governments, who were restive at the snail-paced negotiations, in tandem with Germany they exerted heavier pressure on Prague for the complete acceptance of the Sudeten demands.

The political crux for the Sudeten Nazis was how to break the indomitable spirit of national unity forged around President Beneš in reaction to the Anschluss and to the May mobilization. The central figure in rallying anti-Hrad sentiment, aside from the Slovak fascist Father Hlinka, was Rudolf Beran, who headed the rightist Agrarian elements. These were of one mind with Czech fascists and Slovak populists who were demanding exclusive control of the German-speaking areas. The propaganda machine of German minister Joseph Goebbels opened a scurrilous campaign, picked up in the appeasement press in London and Paris, fingering Beneš as the sole instigator of Czech obduracy and unreason. Accompanying these attacks at home and abroad came the stunning diplomatic rebuff to Beneš delivered by his chief ally; French Foreign Minister Bonnet pointedly neglected to finalize the long-laid plans for President Beneš's first state visit to Paris. Even more mortifying was the anger that the normally contained Neville Chamberlain vented against Beneš in a Parliamentary speech on June 29th.

The Czechoslovak government exerted every effort to resume its talks with Henlein's negotiators.   To rebut the Nazi charge of sabotage, Beneš offered to publish the record documenting that he had yielded political ground to a point infringing on State sovereignty. The Sudeten principals refused the public airing, a stand upheld by a final British veto on any publicity.   Beneš's offer was seen at Whitehall as a maneuver to appeal to the mass of public opinion in the West.

Aiming to pierce the wall of isolation around Czechoslovakia, Soviet Foreign Minister Litvinov on June 23rd issued a timely declaration of solidarity, offering to honor any collective action upon request, either through the League of Nations or under its alliance, and again pledged to defend Czechoslovak sovereignty. As France had abjured response to repeated invitations to organize joint defense talks, Prague and Moscow alone proceeded with high-level consultations, and the Soviet military mission continued to inspect installations and plants.   New contracts were stipulated with Škoda and other Czechoslovak arms manufacturers, of great value to Russia.

The political interplay of early summer in Prague moved around the pliable figure of Prime Minister Hodža. This Agrarian Slovak leader, under pressure from right wing groups, intermittently conducted talks with Henlein. who continually backed off, while escalating his demands. Hodža kept Beneš apprised of the course of the negotiations and also of the extent of his being cultivated by the British and French ambassadors, who kept pressing him to accept the accelerated Karlovy Vary program.

The British Foreign Office appeared willing to accept Czechoslovakia's neutrality shorn of fortifications, as a bulwark against the expansion of Soviet influence. Steed, in anticipation of these fresh Anglo-French pressures on Czechoslovakia, presented his pro-Czechoslovak view directly to Lord Halifax in a letter dated May 5, 1938. He had just compared notes with a "competent British observer returned this week from a visit to Czechoslovakia . . . whose memorandum accorded with his own analysis." Steed found the main arguments essentially sound. He wrote:

The peace of Europe and ultimately the safety of this country may depend on the nerve of the Czechoslovak Government. If our policy should help to break that nerve . . . or lead to a collapse of the Czechoslovak resistance to pan-German aims, we may find that the two or three million troops which Germany would need to overcome Czechoslovak resistance will be thrown against France and Great Britain . . . I know that the Secretary of State for War [Leslie Hore-Belisha] informed an audience of American correspondents at a private luncheon in London last week that *British policy will be to let Hitler eat his belly full of Europe.* Echoes of this disastrous statement may have already reached me from the U.S . . . Nothing more deplorable than a member of the Cabinet . . . spoken thus at the very moment when the Prime Minister and the Foreign Secretary of France were in London. [67]

In a private and confidential note next day to Hore-Belisha, Lord Halifax confessed he was "a little bit disturbed" by Steed's letter, but he did not call for Hore-Belisha's resignation, As Halifax saw it in his letter,

Czechoslovakia could not possibly stand up against German economic and political pressure . . . quite apart from any military measures . . . Germany might take . . . *We have a very complicated line to ride in this matter and it is of great importance . . . that we should not allow the impression to get back to Berlin that we are in fact taking a view so realist* . . . We must constantly be putting to the Czechs and French privately that our object will risk being defeated if the knowledge that we are doing so became current in Berlin. [68]

Convinced that Hodža was more amenable than Beneš, the British prime minister approached him to have his government request the British to send a special envoy to mediate the internal Sudeten question. Early in June, British policy definitely changed to "mediation of HM's Government, followed by direct talks between British and Germans for a general understanding." Sargent at the Foreign Office questioned the wisdom of this decision. He feared this stance would be "interpreted in Berlin, Prague, and Paris as meaning . . . that *Great Britain had decided to collaborate with Germany* in bringing *pressure to bear on the Czechoslovak Government to submit to Germany's demands, in return* for which Great Britain would obtain from Germany assurances and undertakings accruing to the benefit of Great Britain alone," exactly as had been proposed earlier by Göring via Ward Price. Sargent continued: "France and Czechoslovakia will again complain of our perfidy in regard to the Czechoslovak problem." [69]

When Hodža presented the idea of accepting British mediation with Germany to the Czechoslovak cabinet, Beneš vehemently objected that "such foreign mediation would infringe on Czechoslovak sovereignty and violate her constitution." The British vetoed the president's counterproposal to submit the issue to the judgment of the British parliament, because of assurances given by Sir Robert Vansittart to Masaryk in London that "English public opinion was completely favorable to the cause of Czechoslovakia." [70]

From Berlin, Sir Nevile Henderson reported that he had told the Czechoslovak ambassador, Vojtech Mastný, that Beneš had committed a fatal error in failing to transform the centralized unitary state into the Swiss model of cantons based on nationalities. Short of this unfeasible change, the only recourse would be a plebiscite, also unacceptable to Prague. Beneš, seeking rescue, had his minister to Paris, Osuský, check out alternatives at the Quai d'Orsay with Foreign Minister Bonnet. Osuský said that a strong French response was key to the Czechoslovak decision. He continued: "If the French Government should declare that it has certain political or military interests in Czechoslovakia, and [that] it intends to defend them," such a statement would permit Prague to refuse the proffered British intervention, which prejudiced "the political and military independence of Czechoslovakia."[71] On July 25th Bonnet counseled acceptance of the intervention without reservations or conditions. Beneš had no alternatives.[72] He was isolated and accepted the British dictation. He issued the required official invitation to the already designated Lord Runciman in London.

NOTES

1. Jean-Baptiste Duroselle, *La Décadence, 1932-1939* (Paris: Imprimerie Nationale, 1979), p. 325. This book was compiled by the Sorbonne's outstanding expert on the Foreign Ministry's records which for 1933-1939 were burnt on May 16, 1940; See: A. J. P. Taylor, *The Origins of the Second World War* (London: Penguin, 1962), p. 37.

2. Winston Churchill, *The Gathering Storm* (Boston: Houghton, Mifflin, 1948), p. 260.

3. Duroselle, *La Décadence*, p. 325.

4. Ibid., p. 326.

5. Ibid.

6. Ibid., p. 327.

7. Troutbeck, Prague, February 18, 1938, FO 371/v. 22336, p. 278.

8. Duroselle, *La Décadence*, p. 328.

9. Basil C. Newton, Prague, March 1, 1938, FO 371/v. 22337, p. 8.

10. Notes on a conversation between Eduard Beneš and Richard Keans, March 2, 1938, FO 371/v. 22337, pp. 60-61.

11. Talk held around February 19, 1938, FO 371/v. 22337 pp. 77A-78.

12. *Documents on International Affairs, 1938* (London, 1942), Vol. 2, pp. 12-13, quoted in Vera Olivova, *The Doomed Democracy: Czechoslovakia in a Disrupted Europe, 1914-1938* (London: Sidgwick & Jackson, 1972), p. 214.

13. Troutbeck, Prague, February 22, 1938, FO 371/v. 22336, p. 299.

14. British Consulate, Liberec, Czechoslovakia, February 25, 1938, FO 371/v. 22337, p. 18.

15. Churchill, *The Gathering Storm*, pp. 151-53.

16. U.S. Dept. of State, March 7, 1938, FO 371/v. 22340, pp. 222-23.

17. Newton to Lord Edward Halifax, March 21, 1938, FO 371/v. 22340, p. 227.

18. Newton to Foreign Office, March 14, 1938, FO 371/v. 22337, p. 129.

19. Churchill, *The Gathering Storm*, p. 281.

20. Duroselle, *La Décadence*, p. 329.

21. Ibid.

22. Churchill, *The Gathering Storm*, p. 281.

23. Newton, Prague, March 12, 1938, FO 371/v. 22337, p. 90.

24. Secret Intelligence report from Germany, FO 800/309, p. 151.

25. Intelligence report from Germany, FO 800/309, p. 152.

26. Newton, Prague, March 14, 1938, FO 800/309, pp. 130-31.

27. *Prager Tagblatt*, May 8, 1938, FO 371/v. 21578, pp. 126-27.

28. Newton, Prague, March 14, 1938, FO 800/309, pp. 130-36.

29. Ibid., p. 133.

30. Newton to Foreign Office, March 20, 1938, FO 371/v. 22338, p. 138.

31. Newton to Foreign Office, March 14 1938, FO 371/v. 22337, pp. 129-36.

32. *London Times*, March 14, 1938, FO 371/v. 22338, p. 222.

33. Foreign Office to Prague, March 15, 1938, FO 371/v. 22337, p. 132.

34. Phipps, Paris, to Foreign Office March 15, 1938, FO 371/v. 22337, p. 150.

35. Ibid.

36. Newton, Prague, March 16, 1938, FO 371/v. 22337, p. 173.

37. Newton, Prague, March 15 1938, FO 371/v. 22349, p. 1.

38. Foreign Office to Prague, FO 371/v. 22349, pp. 7-9.

39. Report of Little Entente meeting May 8, 1938, FO 371/v. 22349, p. 18.

40. British Legation, Bucharest, May 6, 1938, FO 371/v. 22349, p. 28.

41. Viscount Chilston, Moscow, to Foreign Office, March 15, 1938, FO 371/v. 22337, p. 166.

42. Jiri Hochman, *The Soviet Union and the Failure of Collective Security* (Ithaca, N.Y.: Cornell University Press, 1984), p. 165.

43. Duroselle, *La Décadence*, pp. 331-35.

44. Newton, Prague, March 17, 1938, FO 371/v. 22338, p. 14.

45. Memo from G. Ward Price to Foreign Office, FO 800/313, pp. 54-57.

46. Letter, May 3, 1938, FO 371/v. 21760, p. 35.

47. Newton, Prague, March 15, 1938, FO 371/v. 22337, pp. 188-90.

48. Newton, Prague, March 17, 1938, FO 371/v. 22338, p. 14.

49. Newton, Prague, March 19, 1938, FO 371/v. 22338 p. 35.

50. *The London Times*, March 19, 1938, from Orme Sargent, FO 371/v. 22338, p. 53.

51. Newton, Prague, March 17, 1938, FO 371/v. 22338, p. 27.

52. Newton to Halifax, April 19, 1938, FO 371/v. 21578, pp. 82-84.

53. H. Wickham Steed to Halifax, April 24, 1938, FO 800/313, pp. 101-03.

54. British Ambassador, Warsaw, to Sargent, May 4, 1938, FO 371/v. 21808, p. 70.

55. British Ambassador, Warsaw, to Sargent, May 25. 1938, FO 371/v. 21808, p. 91.

56. Extracts from *Parlimentary Debates*, Foreign Relations, May 25, 1938, FO 371/v. 21776, pp. 119-23.

57. Duroselle, *La Décadence*, pp. 336-37.

58. Extracts from Parliamentary Debates, May 25, 1938, FO 371/v. 21776, pp. 119-23.

59. Duroselle, *La Décadence*, p. 337.

60. Orme Sargent, Foreign Office, to Nevile Henderson, May 25. 1938, FO 371/v. 21768, pp. 53-55.

61. Henderson, Berlin, to Halifax, May 24, 1938, FO 800/313.

62. Hochman, *Soviet Union*, p. 151.

63. Henderson, Berlin, to Halifax May 24, 1938, FO 800/v. 313.

64. Duroselle, *La Décadence*, p. 337.

65. Ibid., p. 339.

66. Ibid., p. 338.

67. H. Wickham Steed to Halifax, May 5, 1938, FO 800/v. 309, pp. 162-63.

68. Halifax to Hore Belisha, May 6, 1938, FO 800/309, pp. 169-70.

69. Minutes of Foreign Office, June 3, 1938, FO 371/v. 21776, p. 125.

70. Eduard Beneš, *Munich*, French ed. (Paris: Stock, 1969), p. 131.

71. Ibid., p. 108.

72. Ibid., p. 109.

9

Summer Turmoil
(1938)

Summer is usually associated with holiday expeditions, but not in Czechoslovakia this summer of 1938, which witnessed Hitler's aggressive maneuvers across the border. The summer months of June and July were replete with divisive activity in both Sudetenland and Slovakia. Hostile activity by the Polish government increased, posing rising threats to the Prague government. The disruptive domestic outbreaks cut the ground from under President Eduard Beneš and Prime Minister Milan Hodža in their negotiations with the dissidents.

Bratislava was the scene on June 5, 1938, of the Slovak People's Party Jubilee celebration of the Pittsburgh Agreement which had set forth guarantees of equal rights for Slovaks, then joining the new Czechoslovak State. This was followed the next day by a demonstration twice as large, organized by the Slovak Agrarians. Both were attended by an American Slovak delegation that declared, "National, political, cultural, and economic interests can best be developed within the Republic." They spoke as "friends of the Czechoslovak Republic," but insisted upon the "application and fulfillment of the terms of the Pittsburgh Agreement," to wit, self-government by their own officials, Slovak as the official language in their administration and schools, Slovak soldiers to serve only within the province, and a provincial diet to approve national laws affecting them, such as finance. The national assembly at Prague would have jurisdiction over constitutional questions, foreign affairs, and national defense. Prime Minister Hodža, a Slovak himself, emphasized national unity in the face of foreign threats. He welcomed Slovak support of the besieged state to preserve the republic. Even Father Andrej Hlinka's

Autonomists declared their loyalty to the Czechoslovak state at this time.[1]

During the summer of 1938, the central government in Prague was beset on all sides, internally as well as externally, by her Great Power allies in the West. It would seem that whatever measures Prague took to advance its interests, such as concessions to the nationalities or improving its defenses, would be declared insufficient *a priori*. For example, on June 10th a fund for national defense, known as the Jubilee Fund, was inaugurated by the governor of the Czechoslovak National Bank, Karel Engliš, to receive voluntary contributions. Protests arose from the Sudetens on two grounds: (1) that it was unconstitutional, and (2) that "from an economic point of view, [it] will reduce the amount of liquid capital on the market," decreasing investment capital available for Sudeten industry and consequently will also be "harmful . . . to labor." For these feebly contrived reasons, the SdP opposed the voluntary arrangement. The SdP undoubtedly had ulterior motives, such as, perhaps, hamstringing the defense buildup.[2]

Reports arrived from Poland to London's Foreign Office alerting it to "the notable increase in armament and fighting efficiency of the Polish army." British diplomats, sounding sentiment in Warsaw, found "that the Poles were determined, if something approaching autonomy were granted to other minorities, that the Polish minority in Teschen would fare no worse . . . [that there would be] equal treatment of the Polish with the Sudetendeutsch minorities . . . [that they are] not to be fobbed off with fewer concessions than [those to] the Germans."

They evinced only peripheral interest, however, in the Polish minority in Slovakia. The British military attaché in Warsaw opined that "provided no untoward incidents occurred, and provided the Czechoslovaks made really important concessions, the Germans would not force the crisis." But he harbored grave doubts about the military strength of Czechoslovakia due to its military personnel comprising 50 percent minorities, 20 percent of whom were Germans. He also disparaged the "Czech mentality [for being] so obstinate."[3]

A complicating military factor for Czechoslovakia was observed by the Polish chief of staff, Gen. Waclaw Stachiewicz, who told the British military attaché on June 14th:

Soviet Russia could only give serious help to the Czechoslovaks by land . . . [over] the railway system of southern Poland . . . [This] would inevitably be resisted by Poland . . . The Polish General Staff do not believe that the Soviet Government are now able . . . to give military help to Czechoslovakia by land, and they think Russian help will be restricted to the supply of aeroplanes . . . The Czechoslovak Government have already obtained a number of bombers from Russia. [The unfriendly Poles gave them chase with fighters but] . . . the planes got through [using various routes] . . . [and the] bombers traveled by night. [4]

Toward the close of June, Lord Halifax penned a confidential letter to Viscount Astor, the most prominent member of the pro-German Cliveden Set, in response to praise sent by Astor of a speech Halifax had delivered. Expressing interest in Astor's conversation with the German ambassador in London, Halifax wrote: "Like you, I am continually turning over in my mind ways and means of improving Anglo-German relations." But the moment was not politically propitious "so soon after the Austrian Anschluss." He continued: "The P.M. [Neville Chamberlain] had closed the door to further negotiations" in a speech following the invasion. Halifax regretted the fact that "*the Germans never seem able to grasp the dire effect of their actions on public opinion here. The Anschluss, or rather the methods . . . by which it was brought about, shocked this country profoundly.* Such methods will always be likely to block attempts to bring the two countries together . . . German action itself closed [the door] for the time being." [5]

Behind diplomatic secrecy, the Germans, following Göring's proposal to G. Ward Price in March, kept pressing British Ambassador Sir Nevile Henderson in Berlin to move toward "a general understanding" or even an alliance. Henderson spent most of the afternoon of June 22nd at Karinhall, Göring's splendid home outside Berlin, listening to the Nazi leader argue the necessity and desirability of a good "understanding with Great Britain." Henderson agreed this was vital for "peace and quiet in the world," but everything "depended on the solution this year of the Spanish and Czechoslovak questions, and particularly the latter." If, on the other hand, reported Henderson, "Germany were to resort to force again . . . the last chance of an understanding would vanish." Henderson said he thought "it would be marvelous if the French were to come to an understanding with Germany." [6]

Henderson said the tensions over Czechoslovakia militated against "complete confidence" and rendered the moment unfavorable. "If the Czechoslovak problem is solved peacefully and satisfactorily . . . there might be a . . . good opportunity for attempting a settlement of many other questions," even if a resolution became likely "in the event of *the Germans refraining from any form of direct action or use of force.*" Weidemann, an army officer on Marshall Göring's staff, responded that he was authorized (by Göring) to give Henderson the "most binding assurance . . . that in present circumstances, the German government were *planning no kind of forcible action, and so far as one could see into the future . . . had no intention of resorting to such methods . . . limited to a definite period.*" Weidemann doubted whether they could give it for all time. There were long delays in the settlement of the Czechoslovak crisis; "at any moment [there could] occur incidents which a great State like Germany would be unable to overlook." [7]

At this eleventh hour, Hitler was still officially avowing peaceful means in Czechoslovakia to settle the Sudeten claims. Captain Weidemann was dispatched to London, undoubtedly at the initiative of Göring, to seek an understanding with Britain that would pave the way for an alliance. He was received by Prime Minister Chamberlain on July 18th for a conversation that explored improving Anglo-German relations, to be followed by a visit to London of "an eminent German personality," meaning Field Marshal Göring, whose project this was, "on a carefully chosen occasion." Although Weidemann's visit was to be "highly secret, the Prime Minister thought the better of secrecy," given the possibility of leaks. On the 20th, he addressed the House of Commons with a report on his conversation with Captain Weidemann, [8] followed the next day with another report to the House of Lords, wherein he "welcomed the recent contacts between HMG and the German Government."

Hitler's game at this stage patently was to gain freedom for his expansions in Europe without resort to costly and destructive war, repeating the terms as originally proposed by Göring to Ward Price in March, in exchange for guarantees, whatever they were worth, to protect British interests around the globe. The rumors of behind-the-scenes deals were palpably not entirely unfounded.

Later, on July 18th, Henderson wrote Halifax in his own hand in a state of high agitation. "I do not like the atmosphere here. It has greatly deteriorated during the week I was away." He blamed a speech in Parliament by Kamil Krofta, the Czechoslovak foreign minister, and the *News Chronicle* campaign[*] for "a great deal of harm." [9] Henderson continued at length:

---

[*]The *News Chronicle* at that time was published and edited by Walter Layton, who had served as right hand to Lloyd George and Winston Churchill at the Ministry of Munitions in the First World War, and then as the first economics and finance director of the League of Nations Secretariat and editor of the *Economist*. Layton at the *News Chronicle* was loud in opposing Henderson's and Chamberlain's line of appeasing Hitler.

The Germans are convinced that Beneš is merely throwing dust in our eyes and he believes that Germany won't dare take action. The worst is that the Germans are losing or have lost faith in the efficacy of our intervention . . . If the Czechoslovak Government gets its Parliament to put through a Nationality Law, regardless of Sudeten agreement, there is bound to be trouble. If on top of it, they pass a three-year Military Service Law, it will be worse.

In other words, if Beneš ceded all the "valid" claims of national equality to the Sudetens, the ground would be cut from under Hitler's raison d'être for intervention. Henderson continued, betraying his pro-German bias, *The moment has come for Prague to get a real twist of the screw."* After the jolt the Germans had gotten on May 21st, now Henderson thought "it is Prague's turn." He felt "it is better to have the French do it, but Britain must act in French default . . . I do not feel that we can afford to wait much longer. I wish we had an independent mediator on the spot . . . We did not begin our intervention at Prague to be agreeable to the Czechs, but to help them out of an intolerable situation." [10]

On July 21st, the manager of the Witkowitz Coal, Iron, and Steel Works in Moravska Ostrava, I. Federer, propositioned the British Foreign Office via Sir Alexander Cadogan to buy a majority or at the least a 25 percent interest in the works, chiefly to prevent its acquisition by the Germans, who

have been very anxious to buy control and have made several approaches offering large sums of money . . . Baron Louis Rothschild, presently still in prison in Vienna, owns 2-1/2% of the Co., with the likelihood it will be requisitioned by the Authorities. The remaining shares, held outside Austria, could be made available to 'friendly parties.' The British Government at present have an order of £1 million with the company . . . The Foreign Office is fully aware of all that is going on . . . It might be in the interests of all concerned if an English group of iron and steel manufacturers could be formed to buy a majority share in Witkowitz, which they would undertake not to part with, so that the control should always be in this country . . . The price would obviously have to be modest . . . The real snag is the foreign exchange difficulty . . . The Witkowitz output is only something like 5% munitions work, the other 95% being purely commercial. [11]

The proposed cession of lands to the Sudetens, or to Germany, and/or to Poland involved a serious diminution in coal, iron, and steel production for Czechoslovakia, amounting to about a third, provided that the Witkowitz works would remain in Czechoslovakia. "These works are situated in a predominantly Czech region . . . According to the 1930 Census, the population of 125,910 consisted of 21,914 Germans, 471 Poles, and all the rest Czechoslovaks . . . The coal supply," calculated the Witkowitz manager, "is critical." In 1937, "domestic consumption was 27 million tons. If one deducts a third within territories to be ceded, 18 million tons of coal are left for internal use. The country would lose to Germany, their lignite [brown coal] mines situated in Northwestern Bohemia." The manager's estimate is that "only about 4½ million tons would remain, leaving a shortage of 13½ million tons . . . The district proposed to be ceded to Poland, where the percentage of Poles is insignificant, included the mines in Freistadt, [which] produced 13 million tons last year." Again he cited census figures: "The entire population of this district was 85,726, of which 29,790 were Poles, 3,651 were Germans, the rest Czechs. Ceding this district of Freistadt to Poland would cripple Czechoslovakia, while Poland is a coal exporter with a large surplus of coal." The Witkowitz manager made a convincing case to the British against the cessions of land and vital resources demanded by Czechoslovakia's hostile neighbor. [12]

More political maneuvers by Poland ensued, generating pressures on Prague. Within the following week, a report was sent to the British Foreign Office from the British embassy in Warsaw, raising a hue and cry that the proposed cessions to Poland had been entirely ignored. The complaints cited in the report include "numerous arrests and dismissals." The government press blew these out of proportion, citing "depolonisation of Polish children in Czech schools and claiming that "the alleged concession made did not affect the fundamental desiderata of the minority." The report concluded "by emphasizing Polish desire for autonomy for the minority." Upon checking, the Foreign Office received a cool report from its unbiased investigator declaring that "the Poles now require a very sharp rap on their attitude in regard to Czechoslovakia." They should be told that "we take considerable offence at this consistently hostile attitude, which is not only *no contribution to European peace, but a contribution to the opposite . . . We should say the same thing to Colonel Beck as we are saying to Herr von Ribbentrop, and morally there is nothing to choose between the pair of them. We must check Colonel Beck's poisonous attitude, which . . . reacts on the Germans.*" [13]

The government at Prague had its hands tied; it could make no response on its own to deal effectively with these disruptions; it was forced to await the already appointed British mediating team.

NOTES

1. British Legation, Prague, June 9, 1938, FO 371/v. 21578, pp. 191-99.

2. Basil C. Newton, Prague, to Foreign Office, June 11, 1938, FO 371/v. 21578, p. 11.

3. British Military Attaché, Warsaw, FO 371/v. 21809, pp. 129-30.

4. British Embassy, Warsaw, June 14, 1938, FO 371/v. 21776, pp. 137-38.

5. Lord Halifax to Viscount Astor, June 23, 1938, FO 800/v. 309, pp. 197-98.

6. Nevile Henderson to Halifax, FO 800/v. 314, pp. 6-8.

7. Henderson, Berlin to Halifax, July 18, 1938, FO 800/v. 314, pp. 10-12.

8. Halifax conversation with Capt. Weidemann, report to House of Commons, June 20, 1938, report filed August 10, 1938, FO 371/v. 21771, pp. 38-44.

9. Henderson, Berlin, to Halifax, July 18, 1938, FO 800/v. 314, pp. 10-12.

10. Ibid. Italics added.

11. I. Federer, Manager of Witkowitz Mines, Steel & Ironworks Corp. Moravska Ostrava 10, Czechoslovakia, secret, July 21, 1938, FO 371/v. 21582, pp. 271-72.

12. Ibid., pp. 292-95.

13. Morton, Warsaw, July 27, 1938, FO 371/v. 21809, pp. 164-67.

10

The Runciman Mission (Summer 1938)

The Runciman Mission was Neville Chamberlain's instrument to stall on resolving the impasse at Prague between the government and its Sudeten German minority, which was directed and financed from abroad. When Hitler declared himself the virtual guarantor of Sudeten rights and claims, the controversy began to threaten the Prague government. The mission quickly gained the aspect of negotiator between aggressive Germany and hapless Czechoslovakia. The role of impartial mediator was assumed by the British leaders whose secret new policy was to give greedy Adolf Hitler "his bellyful of Europe." But this revised policy was kept secret and had to be rendered acceptable to public opinion wherever.

Viscount Walter Runciman had impeccable qualifications for the job. He could be counted on for loyalty to the Foreign Office and its objectives. As an ex-minister of wide and varied experience, he had an international reputation for integrity and impartiality. He was a man of wit and charm who was esteemed in aristocratic circles, as elsewhere. One of the British government insiders said of him: "Someone would have to accompany him and do most of the work, but he could be relied on to put results across."[1]

Sir Frank Ashton Gwatkin was appointed as that "someone," the "workhorse" deputy to Lord Runciman. Ashton Gwatkin was an internationalist of competence and experience, especially in the sphere of German relations. As high counselor of the Foreign Office, he had served as aide to Sir Horace Wilson, who later became Chamberlain's special envoy to Berlin.[2]

Arriving in Prague with his wife and staff on August 3rd, Runciman and his party were met at Wilson Station with full diplomatic panoply by the minister of the British legation, Basil C. Newton, and Deputy Troutbeck, who had made all the arrangements for their reception and installation. There was also an impressive deputation representing the Czechoslovak government.[3] The new arrivals settled directly into their rooms at the Alcron Hotel and promptly paid brief calls on President Eduard Beneš, Premier Milan Hodža, and Foreign Minister Kamil Krofta.

Runciman then listened attentively to the grievances presented by the Sudeten representatives currently negotiating with the government. At the outset, the "Sudetens . . . welcomed the Mission," expecting to soften "Czech obstinacy" via this channel. "Czech public opinion [however], including the Czech press," was on the whole, "hostile to the mission."[4]

Henderson had been instructed by Lord Halifax "to acquaint Lord Runciman with . . . the German view," which Henderson had more or less imbibed. "The Germans," he wrote, "have all along never believed that Beneš meant to go far enough . . . They are now anticipating . . . the tug of war for September. The fortifications of the Siegfried line and the military measures, calling up reservists in September are definite indications of this."[5]

Henderson was alarmed. "The omens of the storm are rolling up in Germany," he wrote Newton. "I still cling to my *belief that Hitler wants a peaceful solution, but* he will not wait indefinitely." Henderson saw "the whole problem . . . [as] a racial and a national one." His prescription to the mission was "home rule and a genuine state of Nationalities [as] the only solution."[6] Henderson's hostility toward Beneš for stalling on a settlement that would grant self-determination to the Sudetens increased a decibel daily. His advice fell on fertile soil at the Foreign Office, fortifying its tolerance of Hitler's escalating demands and impatient timetable. It is difficult to discern whether Henderson or Lord Halifax was acquainted at this juncture with Hitler's secret agenda for expansion which would backfire against Great Britain.

Henlein's deputy chief, Karl Frank, met with Lord Runciman at noon on August 18th at Schloss Rothenhaus, the home of pro-Nazi Prince Max von Hohenlohe, where Runciman was now installed. Frank told Runciman that the mission "was extraordinarily welcome" and "the delegation . . . was in full agreement" on the mission's line. Although he spoke pessimistically on the "possibilities of a settlement with the Czechoslovak Government," he hoped "with the assistance of the Runciman Mission, the Sudeten Germans would be accorded their just dues . . . making *their last attempt at a settlement within the frontiers* of Czechoslovakia." He saw the present situation as "acute and tense . . . with all communications between Czech officials in the area ruptured from the populace." [7]

Ashton Gwatkin met separately with Hohenlohe, who, although "not dissatisfied with the way things were going," told him: "The intentions of Henlein and the SdP leaders had been for him to ignore the Runciman Mission; to allow it four weeks . . . to waste time and to show that it could accomplish nothing; and then to come out with a demand for a plebiscite, which means in fact demand for Anschluss with Germany." Hohenlohe himself had seen Konrad Henlein at Zürich several days earlier, around August 9th, and deemed him "a dangerous, mischievous, and jealous man." Henlein, by his own account "impressed upon him his [Henlein's] foolishness of losing this opportunity to getting all or most of what he wants by peaceful means and without absorption by Germany, which seemed to summarize the goal of the Runciman Mission."

Hohenlohe said he had persuaded Henlein to see Lord Runciman at a lunch meeting at Schloss Rothenhaus, one and a half hours from Prague, to be followed by a "more detailed discussion." Hohenlohe told Ashton Gwatkin he believed "the [German] Army and von Ribbentrop and the Secret Service [Canaris] favor a peaceful settlement." Ashton Gwatkin observed that the people around Hohenlohe were pro-German and strong supporters of the SdP, who had approved of the Anschluss with Austria; they "think poorly and contemptuously of the Czechs who could never be gentlemen—never. They admire England and the English and think that friendship between England and Germany 'can save the world,' [but complained that] England was carrying off Germany's trade from Yugoslavia, which are vital for armaments." [8]

Henlein had his "long talk" with Lord Runciman following the luncheon, which included Frank and Hohenlohe's friends. The Sudeten leader expressed ardent opposition to the Prague government, which instead of giving the Sudetens protection against discrimination and persecution, carried on discrimination and persecution of its own; he called the government an "enemy of the people." The only remedy Frank saw was "the greatest possible separation of the Czech and German people." He proposed to Runciman alternatives of two policies: "(a) to negotiate a settlement or (b) to demand a plebiscite. He would greatly prefer the former, and he would continue the present negotiations so long as he could." He claimed "he had always urged moderation on his people . . . He had kept them in hand to a remarkable extent and under great provocation," according to Runciman, who was taken in. Henlein was worried "about the return of 10,000 men now finding temporary work in Germany, . . . soon to return to swell the ranks of the unemployed during the winter." He was affronted by Hodža's letter "offering seven [government] posts to Germans," which he deemed as "not much when they have taken 50,000 away from us." Runciman got him "to admit grudgingly that the offer had some value as a first step . . . also as a sign that the Government were prepared to take action as a sign of Good Will in Lord Runciman's Mission." Henlein gave him assurance that he had "no wish to break up the State frontiers of the Czechoslovak Republic; but rather to obtain a large degree of home rule within those frontiers." [9]

On August 22nd, Ashton Gwatkin had his meeting with Henlein at Marienbad, the details of which the Englishman conveyed home. Henlein said he preferred a solution based on a "grant of local autonomy," as he had proposed. A tentative agreement was worked out by the mission's "workhorse", Ashton Gwatkin, with President Beneš, who knew full well he had to make "satisfactory concessions." As outlined by Ashton Gwatkin, these consisted of the following seven points, which became Benes's Plan 3:

1. Three local autonomous districts in Sudeten German land.
2. Exchange of officials, i.e. Czech officials in German lands to be removed, German officials in Czech lands to be restored to German lands, to begin at once.
3. Independent budget for the three districts.
4. Loan from the central government to the three districts.
5. A constitutional commission to be set up to decide on wanted changes.
6. Propaganda and press armistice.
7. Withdrawal of state police from German districts.

Beneš had thus conceded the entire Karlovy Vary eight point program, which Henlein had pronounced on April 24th! Henlein queried whether this were not the president's effort to torpedo the Runciman Mission. Ashton Gwatkin replied, "If so, never [was] torpedo more welcome." He continued:

Henlein said he would be prepared to negotiate at once on this basis; *he did not think Berlin would make any difficulties* . . . He thought that Germany would move into Czechoslovakia if there were . . . disorders and bloodshed and Sudeten lives were lost. He was impressed by the growing fear of war in Germany . . . Henlein would be glad to have Lord Runciman verify these proposals with the President. His own suggestions ran along similar lines beginning with the withdrawal of Czech State police, the substitution of local communal police, and strict prohibition of persecution of Sudeten Germans by State authorities, and punishment of [official] excesses.

Henlein denied he was a dictator aiming at a totalitarian rule. He wanted to see a rapprochement between England and Germany and a restoration of friendly relations between Czechoslovakia and Germany. He would give England a week to comply to the agreed terms, *and then go to Hitler with them.* [10]

Frank, on the other hand, according to Ashton Gwatkin, seemed to be set "against a settlement and desires an Anschluss of the Sudeten-German areas to the Reich." Frank issued a manifesto that the Englishman thought "ill-timed if the SdP wish for a settlement. Czech circles have naturally reacted in a hostile manner towards the Manifesto." Ashton Gwatkin saw it as "the attempt of *extremists in the SdP* to undermine the prospects of a settlement." He then surprisingly, saw "*a favorable development [as] possible . . . [and] the Sudeten-Germans as showing signs of being conciliatory.*" [11]

Beneš had taken the precaution to discuss the terms of the possible settlement, based on his deep concessions, with his erstwhile adversaries, with whom he probed the problem on August 24th; they arrived at specifics the next day. Deputy Ernst Kundt summarized his understanding of the "domestic problem." He thought the nub was that "the President thinks that self-government in the degree which the Sudeten German Party demand is incompatible with the unity of the State . . . even if the proposal of the Sudeten German Party does not entail autonomy." The moderate Kundt saw the SdP's demands as paramount "for proportionality in regard to officials and budgetary allocations." [12]

Lord Runciman announced on August 27th that "negotiations will take place on Monday and Tuesday with a view to *putting [the terms] in writing in a definite form.*" Hohenlohe was sent by Henlein, who inquired whether a "settlement will be possible as to the working of the points." This confirmed Beneš's and Runciman's impressions that an agreement had been struck on the president's concessions. Beneš expressed pleasure that "Hohenlohe was very satisfied." [13]

All relevant parties in the negotiations soon realized that internal grievances were only one aspect of the Sudeten-Czech problem. Another, less obvious, aspect was Germany's objection to Czechoslovakia's foreign alignment. The British Foreign Office observed: "As long as Czechoslovakia remained in the orbit of Russia and France, particularly Russia, there could not be friendly relations between Czechoslovakia and Germany." And as for the loyalties of the nationalities:

The democratic Czechoslovak State recognized the right to owe allegiance to any nationality and any world outlook . . . The only real solution [of the dilemma] lay in the neutralization of Czechoslovakia . . . Both leaders agreed that national fears played a significant role in the impasse . . . [concluding] *Germany was afraid of Czechoslovakia's friendship with Russia and France, while Czechoslovakia was afraid of the presence of a much bigger and stronger country along so much of her frontier.* [14]

This grasp of the foreign policy aspect of the confrontation was aired in the conversation between Beneš and Kundt. Unfortunately, these realities of foreign relations did not filter either to Lord Runciman or to Hitler's tool, Henlein.

British considerations were analyzed for the Foreign Office in a secret memorandum by a member of the Runciman Mission, who wrote that a suggestion had been forwarded that the prime minister "should see Hitler and ask him to do nothing at Nuremberg" at the forthcoming Nazi Party Congress on September 6th "to wreck negotiations now proceeding here." The memo said that the terms of a general settlement that Henlein was to be asked to discuss with him "are not clear." It was argued that "Hitler will scarcely dare publicly to reject . . . an approach from an independent mediator who has achieved success here." If Hitler goes along with the negotiated terms in hand, "a general peace will follow," assuming Hitler's word could be trusted. If, however, "you (PM) go and do not succeed, a solution here will be impossible under any conditions and Hitler will be forced to take an actively hostile line toward Czechoslovakia." Further, "would it not morally commit Great Britain to support Czechoslovakia and [convert] the Sudetens into a mediator between Czechoslovakia and Germany," when at present "a settlement between Czechoslovakia and the Sudetens may be achieved?" If the settlement were reached "it would be extremely difficult for Hitler to take action . . . His claim to intervene in the Sudeten question would have disappeared in the eyes of the world . . . Moreover, the Czech Government would probably hold very strong views on your visit at this moment as taking matters out of their hands . . . [Moreover] will Hitler interpret it as a sign of weakness before Nuremberg?" [15]

Winston Churchill now intervened at the Foreign Office with ideas for action by Great Britain, which he had already tested on the Soviet ambassador to the Court of St. James, Ivan Maisky, with whom he dined on August 19th. Judging from Maisky's telegraphed report to Moscow, Churchill, in a state of high agitation, said, according to Robert Tucker:

If the Germans attack, he was sure the Czechs would fight and this would bring about a situation in the West, in which France would come to their aid, and even Britain, would come into motion although perhaps not from the start . . . Churchill's plan was as follows:

At the moment when the attempt to reach a compromise with Germany collapsed and Hitler started to brandish the sword, Britain, France, and the USSR would send him a collective note protesting German threats against Czechoslovakia. Less important than its exact content was the very fact of the three powers' collective action, which would frighten Hitler and might stop Halifax, who would take it up with Chamberlain . . . Churchill inquired about Soviet reaction to his plan. Maisky answered that he couldn't say anything on behalf of the Soviet Government and referred to Litvinov's public statement of March 17th. [16]

The British Foreign Office archive contains a letter on this subject directed by Churchill from his home, Chartwell, in Kent, to Lord Halifax, dated August 31, 1938. It read: "If Beneš' proposal, which Runciman thinks a 'fair offer,' is turned down in Berlin, there are two things which might be done to increase the deterrents against violent action by Hitler, neither of which would commit you to the dread guarantee." First, Churchill proposed "to frame a joint note between Britain, France, and Russia" stating:

a. their desire for peace and friendly relations;
b. their deep anxiety at the military preparations of Germany;
c. their joint interest in a peaceful solution of the Czechoslovak controversy;
d. that an invasion by Germany of Czechoslovakia would raise capital issues for all three powers.

The letter should be shown to Roosevelt by the ambassadors of the three powers,

and we should use every effort to induce him to do his utmost upon it . . . It seems to me not impossible that he would then address Hitler emphasizing the gravity of the situation . . . that a world war would inevitably follow from an invasion of Czechoslovakia, and that he earnestly counselled a friendly settlement . . . [this] would give the best chance to the peaceful elements in German circles to make a stand . . . The important thing is the Joint Note . . . The second step . . . to save the situation would be fleet movements . . . five or six flotillas . . . [To] make a great stir in the naval powers

. . . could only be beneficial as a deterrent and a timely precaution if the worst happened . . . It is clear that speed is vital. [17]

Churchill could hardly be charged with pro-Soviet bias, yet he was not averse to joint action with the USSR when British interests and security required it, especially to forestall a world war. This farsighted conservative leader was able, at the right moment, to devise the only course likely to avert disaster, for Czechoslovakia, Great Britain, and the world. The political leaders of the left in England and France, including the Communists and Socialists, were mired in a genuine popular aversion to war. The Communists, in particular, were unable to react flexibly in time to meet the new menace. The entire Western left and centrist liberal forces underestimated the brutal aggressiveness of Hitler and the agility of his diplomatic manipulations. The French and English Communists, to their credit, changed their stand from peace to rearming against Hitler and advocated collective defense of Czechoslovakia well before the Runciman Mission arrived in Prague.

Throughout the month of August, the French government continued to be passive. The Quai d'Orsay put off any public statements save "It is necessary to await the results of the Runciman Mission."[18] Its Ambassadors, François-Poncet in Berlin and Léopold Victor de Lacroix in Prague, were directed to "active vigilance" in monitoring events. The French foreign ministry obtained news from Lacroix following a meeting late in the month with Lord Runciman. The emissary saw Prime Minister Hodža and President Beneš regularly, when the latter updated him on developments. Instructions from Paris did not exceed the standard advice to the Czechoslovaks for "prudence and rapid concessions."[19] Beneš reproached Lacroix, complaining sadly that his friends "always wish to put me into a pessimistic mood, and then deceive me."[20]

François-Poncet, ever since June 22nd, when a decree by Hermann Göring instituting civil conscription alerted his government that the Germans were mobilizing without proclaiming it, expressed high skepticism of the Runciman Mission's accomplishing anything. The Germans recalled their reservists, completed their active units, and requisitioned workers, vehicles, and horses. Now, backed by his military attaché, Gen. Gaston Renondeau, François-Poncet thought the leading Nazis would not accept any compromise. He feared that France, even with British support, could not stop Hitler.[21] He was confirmed in this opinion after the visit to Berlin August 16-21 of Gen. Joseph Vuillemin, chief of France's air force, who was welcomed personally by Hitler and Göring. The latter artfully eulogized Edouard Daladier and gave his guest an impressive show of Luftwaffe strength, of remarkable factory production, and of the high quality of German equipment and morale. Vuillemin was deeply impressed, deciding that France could hardly dare to confront this redoubtable machine, and informed Daladier accordingly in mid-September.

Despite the pessimistic accounts from Lacroix and Vuillemin, on

September 2nd, French Foreign Minister Georges Bonnet received the German ambassador to Paris, Johannes von Welczeck, to tell him clearly and firmly "that France had decided to hold effectively to her commitments" [toward Czechoslovakia]. [22] Welczeck with equal clarity responded that "the autonomy of the Sudetenland and her re-attachment to Germany was the only satisfactory solution" to the impasse. [23]

President Beneš, taking into account the new Nazi escalation of terms, while not underestimating Hitler's aggressive intentions, reluctantly drafted his famous Plan 4. This yielded extreme concessions to the demand for total autonomy, to the extent of perhaps undermining the unitary democratic state. Beneš expressed reservations to the British and French ambassadors that he might even be impairing his country's national security. He took the precaution again to discuss his new terms with Sudeten deputies Kundt and Dr. Wilhelm Sebekowsky, envisaging "self-administration on a territorial basis . . . or a cantonal system . . . Language equality is recognized, for schools and administration . . . Herr Kundt has . . . indicated to Lord Runciman his belief that it would be impossible to reconcile the unity, sovereignty, and integrity of the State with the principles of the Karlsbad Eight points. Lord Runciman believes that the new Czech proposals are a genuine effort to meet this idea." [24]

Sir Ashton Gwatkin noted at the same time: "It is understood that Hitler approved . . . the direction" in which the negotiations were moving, that is, "toward autonomy *within the Czechoslovak State* . . . [and he] encouraged Herr Henlein to continue in this. If autonomy on terms to be negotiated failed, [there was] an alternative to a plebiscite."

Henlein talked twice with Runciman on September 1st and 2nd, then he hurried to Berlin, returning to Prague on the evening of September 3rd. He saw Ashton Gwatkin at 10:30 A.M. Saturday morning, the 4th. [25]

At news of the agreement to the Sudeten demands by the Prague government, the Sudeten leaders were elated and exclaimed incredulously: "By God! They have given us everything." It is mystifying in this light that the experienced diplomat Runciman did nothing to dissuade Henlein from returning to Berlin to obtain Hitler's assent to the latest draft which was acceptable to both parties at home. This move gave Hitler a veto over the Prague negotiations; the opportunity to explode the potential agreement so laboriously stitched together by the expert staff, so ably assisted by the malleability of Beneš and Hodža.

It is astonishing to note the extent to which Runciman, Halifax,

Henderson, and Henlein all trusted the sincerity of Hitler's avowals of peaceful means while rearming as rapidly and as publicly as possible. Not only did Runciman fail to do all possible to prevent Hitler from wrecking the accord he had in hand, that merely awaited specifics and initials, but Runciman went a step further to guarantee the blowup. He appended a "very private message" to Hitler with Henlein, saying among other things, "His Majesty's Government are *very anxious* to reach a settlement of both the Karlsbad Eight Points and of the new proposals of the Czech government." He thereby tossed Berlin his last bargaining chip. Less anxiety and a show of indifference might have vastly improved his bargaining posture.[26]

Issued on September 5th, Plan 4 had the diplomatic world electrified at the flexibility of the Prague government. In Berlin, it had the interesting effect of depriving Hitler of dealing with the subject in his speech to the annual Nazi Party Rally at Nuremberg on September 6th. It occasioned a spate of secret sessions to hatch schemes for renewed violence in the Sudeten area, this time featuring weapons imported from Germany.

Incidents that had erupted galore throughout Sudetenland ever since the advent of the Runciman Mission were now climaxing. It was realized by government people and members of the mission that the disorderly demonstrations had been organized as a form of pressure on Beneš and Runciman, to dramatize the agitated circumstances and provoke an excessive use of police repression that would merit a crackdown. One of the earlier incidents occurred at Gabersdorf late in August, which Maj. Sutton Pratt of the mission was asked to investigate. "His impression," as reported by Newton to London, "was that the incident was in fact a *put-up job by the Sudetens* and might well have turned into something very ugly." He strongly suspected that a report on the incident in an SdP newspaper was based on information received before the incident occurred.[27]

Riots occurred on September 7th at Mährisch Ostrau where a "Sudeten German deputy was insulted and beaten by a Czech police-man." Kundt, Frank, and the entire deputation in Prague demanded full punishment of the police on threat they would suspend negotiations. Following another personal investigation by Major Pratt, "it seemed clear that the Mährisch Ostrau incident was yet another put-up job, the culprits being not the police but Deputies May and Kollner."[28]

In Paris on September 8th, Daladier personally intervened in foreign policy. He talked at length with Sir Eric Phipps, who reported: "Daladier expressed his conviction that if Hitler could only be made to realize that German aggression on Czechoslovakia means a general war, he would abstain. Hitler firmly believed . . . that France would not march and that Great Britain would do nothing . . . M. Daladier declared positively that if German troops crossed the Czechoslovak frontier, the French would march to a man . . . [as] it is a question of their own skins." The French Ambassador in Berlin reported "a state of alert . . . [had been] declared in Berlin, which is nearly equivalent to mobilization." If confirmed, France would take similar measures. [29]

This conversation was shortly followed by another in London between Lord Halifax and Charles Corbin, who wanted to know precisely what the British intended regarding Czechoslovakia, "to remove any ambiguity . . . and as a clear warning to Hitler."

Lord Halifax said that he did not think public opinion in this country was at present willing to contemplate being involved in war on direct account of Czechoslovakia . . . Great Britain might feel obliged to support France in a conflict, because our interests were involved in any threat to French security; it did not mean that we should be willing automatically to find ourselves at war with Germany . . . France might get involved because of her treaty obligations, which Great Britain did not share, and which a large section of opinion in this country has always disliked. [30]

Corbin had gone to see Halifax on express orders from Bonnet, who had in hand Britain's clear commitment of May 22nd, saying that Britain willingly accepted the idea of a war over Czechoslovakia. [31] Corbin was told to say that "in the event of failure in Prague by Lord Runciman's Mission, the British should carefully formulate its own strong position . . . to forestall a proposal by Herr Hitler . . . for a plebiscite, which would be unacceptable to the Czechs and . . . create a very difficult position." Information had reached Bonnet privately "that Herr Hitler had decided to intervene by force in Czechoslovakia, counting upon what he judged to be the uncertainty of British policy and the hampering effect that this was exercising on the French." Bonnet thought it "urgent that we should do anything in our power to correct this impression." Corbin added that "if a German attack was made on Czechoslovakia, the French Government had no choice. They must mobilize and declare war . . . only in the case of a deliberate attack by Germany." [32]

Halifax replied that reports to the French government on Hitler's intentions for war corresponded with information received in London. Lord Halifax repeated what he had said before: *"He did not think that opinion in this country . . . would be prepared to enter upon hostilities with Germany on account of aggression by Germany on Czechoslovakia."* Further, in the event that Hitler demanded a plebiscite, "a great mass of opinion in all countries would most certainly think it was unreasonable to embark upon a European war to prevent people voting as to their future position." [33]

In France, the government, contemplating the possibility of war, requested the War Ministry for an appraisal of its war potential and the disposition of its troops. This was done under the supervision of Gen. Maurice Gamelin, the chief of general staff. Gamelin said that France "when fully mobilized could put 5½ million men into the field," excluding Air Force personnel or garrisons in the colonies, in the Levant, and elsewhere. He would concentrate his manpower in Germany, "60 divisions excluding troops occupying the Maginot Line . . . the equivalent of . . . four or five divisions . . . At the present time, France has about 1½ million men mobilized." Gamelin had no intention of sitting behind the Maginot Line and waiting for a German offensive. His plan called for an immediate advance into Germany "until he met really serious resistance. He would then, if necessary, withdraw to the protection of the Maginot Line, leaving it to the Germans to break through their strength against the permanent fortifications . . . *Immediate action would be to the advantage of France*," said the report, in view of the Germans having "only eight divisions on their western frontier." The French anticipated a hostile Italy and were not particularly frightened of this, but this prospect "involved the retention of troops which might be better employed elsewhere." [34]

Gamelin said that French intelligence sources indicated that the German general staff were averse to the war and that the intermediate commanders were weak. "The eight divisions opposite the French frontier were at present employed on building fortifications and [in] policing duties . . . The majority of German long-range bombers were disposed in a ring around the Czechoslovak frontier. There were also a few fighter squadrons, but the majority were situated opposite France."

Then Gamelin turned to his assessment of Czechoslovak military capabilities. He estimated that

Czechoslovakia could mobilize about 54 divisions. They would put up a good show, but it was impossible to say how long they could resist a German onslaught . . . Their intention . . . was to protect their flanks at all costs, to retreat from their western salients, abandon Prague if necessary, and take up strong defensive line from north to south across Moravia. The Russian Army could not intervene in Czechoslovakia since "neither Poland nor Romania would give them passage.[35]

Gamelin's calculation regarding English assistance was that "even a small contingent to start would have a tremendous moral effect on the French Army . . . [with] the prospect of considerable reinforcements at the end of . . . six months would be an enormous encouragement." French aircraft production at present was extremely low, but could be in full swing in a year. Gamelin and the French foreign ministry shared this significant secret document with the British government.[36]

The air attaché of the British legation in Prague filed a confidential report with the Foreign Office on August 30th, relaying news that the Czechoslovak chief of staff, Gen. Jaroslav Fajfr, "did not believe the Germans would go to war this year . . . [with] the opinion of the rest of the world . . . against them . . . A well-informed friend from Italy . . . had told him that public opinion there was crystallizing more and more against Germany . . . It was *a known fact that Germany was not yet ready to make war.*"[37] The Czechs were counting heavily initially on both France and Russia, especially for reinforcements of bombers. "Several nuclei of French and Russian-speaking personnel had already been assembled in various parts of the country in preparation for the arrival of aircraft." Although the Germans had made models of Czechoslovak factories, "this bombing would not dislocate supplies as much as they thought as the Czechs had already moved part of the essential factories to Moravia and Slovakia."[38]

The British military attaché in Prague, Col. H. C. T. Stronge, asked by Newton his opinion of the relative strength of the Czechoslovak and German armies, thought encouragingly:

The Czechoslovak Army will give a good account of itself against heavy odds, and that contrary to Herr Hitler's calculations, the War may drag on for months . . . The army is well equipped . . . Absence of anti-aircraft artillery and the comparative weaknesses of the Air Force should mean very heavy losses among civilians . . . In such a war, Czech morale is unlikely to crack . . . at the front or behind the lines.[39]

Also from Prague, Newton alerted the Foreign Office of the likelihood of incidents in the frontier areas being accompanied by acts of violence against state authorities. Karlsbad, Graslitz, Rumberg, and Liberec were mentioned. Maj. Sutton Pratt was already in Karlsbad, and another man was dispatched to Liberec and Rumburg.[40] Disturbances and riots, which were designed as a putsch, broke out simultaneously in some 60 localities in Bohemia and

Moravia but they were handled by the Czechoslovak police without bloodshed. Orders were issued from the capital to avoid shooting, and the police, with high discipline, followed them to the letter against all provocations. The so-called putsch failed again.

Göring's speech on September 10th contained blood and thunder threats "to frighten the world, and particularly this country [Germany]," reported Henderson from Berlin, who said it dangled "bribes to German public opinion of white bread and Most beer . . . to deal with the recent wave of anxiety and pessimism," [41]

Hitler's speech to a parade of armed forces at Nuremberg on September 12th was an unalloyed appeal to force and a negation of international cooperation. The threat of military action had the effect of splitting the French cabinet. Proponents of resistance took heart from Gamelin's prognosis, while the appeasers argued the case of French "unpreparedness" dictating taking no foreign risks.

On the same day, September 12th, Neville Chamberlain emerged from the shadows of Whitehall. He held a press conference, reported Corbin, saying that "England had no commitments in Central Europe vis-à-vis Czechoslovakia, but she could not remain aside from a general European conflict." [42] This statement sent Bonnet into a fury, although he thought it best to abstain from a war but desired joint public communiques. He felt the least his British ally could do was to maintain a public facade of strength in action to oppose Nazi aggression. [43] This apparent rupture compelled Daladier to intervene, again, to forestall disaster.

On September 13th, Daladier tried his last straw. Taking foreign policy again into his own hands, he proposed to Chamberlain to call an international conference of England, France, and Germany, to which proposal Chamberlain responded with lightning speed. Overnight, Phipps informed the French government, that Chamberlain had decided that he personally would visit Hitler in Berchtesgaden. Bonnet declared he was satisfied, and the Germans were even more so. Beneš disagreed vehemently, via Lacroix. Beneš was about to concede territories containing, 800,000 to 900,000 Germans to Germany. He sent his highly trusted Social Democratic minister of public health, Jaromír Nečas, a personal friend of Léon Blum, to Paris to talk with Daladier. Bonnet, however, insisted emphatically that Czechoslovakia refrain from military mobilization. [44] Although himself convinced that taking a firm stand for honoring the alliance with Czechoslovakia was the best course, as urged by Corbin at Whitehall, Daladier hesitated to go it alone. He finally deferred to Chamberlain to seek the best settlement possible in direct talks with the Führer.

The idea of issuing a joint communique to Hitler, as Churchill had proposed, was dropped at both Whitehall and the Quai d'Orsay, but not at Moscow. There, the French ambassador told Viscount Aretas Chilston, Britain's envoy, that the vice commissar for foreign affairs had responded to his question of Soviet intentions toward Czechoslovakia with "an emphatic affirmative [that] in the event of a conflict, the Soviet Government would intervene with all their resources," Ambassador Chilston believed Maxim Litvinov was working in Geneva toward some manifestation by the three Powers, "by means of a Joint Note to Berlin." [45]

Bonnet was most anxious to probe Soviet intentions before committing France firmly to honoring her treaty obligations. He went personally to Geneva on September 11th to put the question directly to Litvinov, who fired one back about French intentions, because "the Soviet obligation was dependent on the action of France." [46] Then, acknowledging the difficulties created by Poland and Romania over the right of passage, Litvinov said he thought that in the case of Romania "these differences could be overcome, especially if joint action went through the League of Nations." [47] Although Beneš's stratagem of concessions rallied democratic opinion in England around the leadership of Winston Churchill and of the Labour Party, and in France within Popular Front circles, these opposition forces were inadequate to halt the drift of appeasement or to pressure Hitler to accept reasonable terms for Prague at the negotiating table. For what they were worth, Beneš clung to his alliances with France and Russia, a foreign alignment that was totally anathema to Berlin. Topmost on Hitler's private agenda for Czechoslovakia was a repudiation of these alliances; secondarily, he would require Prague to outlaw the Communist Party and negotiate a trade pact with Germany. The situation had drastically deteriorated due to the violence of the incidents occurring throughout the Sudetenland, which Major Pratt had found to be "put-up jobs." Hitler's demand in the name of self-determination sounded democratic and justifiable, but it now escalated to calling for the still unacceptable plebiscite as the only solution of the impasse. [48]

There was no constitutional provision in Czechoslovakia for a plebiscite without the approval of the Council of Ministers, which could not be had. With the exception of Slovakia, throughout the entire country, save for three compactly German districts, the nationalities were too intermingled to be separated. Newton was persuaded by Beneš that it was "technically impossible because no compact and heterogeneous area adjacent to Germany existed." Severing the three distinctive German districts would amount to an amputation, leaving the country "at the mercy of Germany militarily and economically . . . The country's industries depended on the regular supply of raw materials from these sections." [49]

In arguing against the plebiscite with Halifax in London, Czechoslovakia's ambassador, Jan Masaryk, added the grounds "of the historical lands of Bohemia for a thousand years. If they by hook or crook were attached to Germany, nothing could stand in the way of German expansion through Eastern and South Eastern Europe." A plebiscite would, moreover, mean "shocking terror on one side," he continued, rendering "the free expression of the voters' will an impossibility." [50]

Next day, Masaryk in fury protested to Halifax that "France and England have squeezed us like a lemon." He took strong exception to "Newton's language to Beneš [which] was such as has never been employed by a Minister to a Head of State." Then he spoke heatedly:

> For some time past, the impression has been gaining ground in Czechoslovakia that you are going to sell us out . . . [He said he received] hundreds of hard spoken communications in this sense. I beg you not to underestimate this feeling of desperation in Czechoslovakia . . . We have done everything we could to give satisfaction to the Western Powers . . . If Hitler is determined to create incidents . . . to justify his marching in, it will be almost impossible to stop it. [51]

British Military Attaché Stronge in Prague wired home the warning that "acceptance by government of a plebiscite might lead to a military coup d'état" by the Czechoslovak military, who felt strong enough to fight in preference to capitulating to foreign domination by the Nazi regime. They thought a plebiscite "might easily precipitate widespread bloodshed . . . [prevention of which would require] an overwhelming international police force" to patrol such a plebiscite. [52]

According to Sir Nevile Henderson, it was Henlein who dreamt up the plebiscite idea, in full realization that this course provided no solution. Publicly, Henlein adhered to the terms of the Karlsbad Program, which he said Beneš would not accept, but to which in fact, Beneš did accede. Henlein succeeded, however, in convincing the British diplomats involved in the proceedings that Beneš was unreasonable, or at least, rigid and inflexible. In Berlin, Henderson had Göring's persistent assurances "that no aggression was contemplated." Henderson then tipped his hand in his report home: "*Versailles was the error* which has got to be corrected . . . that is the hard fact. It is *revision by peaceful negotiations*, which in fact *means compulsion at Prague and not Berlin.*" [53]

Reports had arrived in Prague that "attempts had been made in various places to seize railway stations, Post Offices, and [other] public buildings." Herr Frank himself telephoned from Karlsbad to ask when martial law would be proclaimed. Instead of rebuking him for having initiated the lawlessness, Hodža asked Frank and his cohorts to cooperate on "maintenance of order." Frank replied that he would have to call back. Hodža asked Runciman's staff to discuss a halt to the violence with the Sudetens to forestall the martial law which the government would feel obliged to impose. Newton thought that the SdP "were deliberately fomenting a revolution." [54]

Eight deaths had been reported, 5 Germans, a Czech policeman, one civilian, and a Slovak. "The police had orders not to shoot, but they protected the public buildings from seizure, and recaptured some," which Hodža thought "a tribute to their self-restraint and efficiency." [55]

Martial law was finally declared by the Czechoslovak National Council sitting in virtually perpetual session, at 7 P.M. on September 14th in 16 Sudeten districts, including Liberec, Rumburg, and Schluchenau, where the riots were the worst. Major Sutton Pratt made a two-day inspection tour of the area and recounted that "police and military had the situation well under control . . . The capture of party headquarters in Eger revealed an extensive organization." He also said that "both military and police are now behaving with restraint under great provocation." He added that "the more violent of the Sud-Deutsch elements were escaping across the frontier . . . [if they were] in any way compromised." [56]

At the same time, Newton told London authorities that he had it from "an absolutely reliable source", also informing the Prague government, that "Germany is not ready to march at present . . . that preparations have been made to call up 12 classes of German reservists between October 8th and October 16th, when military situation will become critical." Newton asked the Foreign Office to relay this information to the War Office. [57]

The Runciman Mission on September 14th received a delegation "representing Jewish Communities in Bohemia, Moravia, and Silesia," voicing a "plea for special consideration if a negotiated solution of the nationalities problem were achieved." They complained that in the German districts, they were being everywhere "boycotted and squeezed out of all societies and organizations, whether cultural, economic, or political." They would require "quite special protection if their life was to be at all tolerable." [58]

The Sudeten leaders now pulled a startling switch of position in their communique to Newton. They declared themselves willing to resume negotiations with the government, but that the "degree of autonomy represented by the Karlsbad programme . . . no longer satisfied [them] . . . *Self-determination within the present Czechoslovak State is at present no longer considered enough.*" [59] Hitler had clearly re-written the terms of the settlement two days following his September 12th speech at Nuremberg, where he still employed his camouflaging formula of "self-determination." Henderson relayed the news he received from Deputy Foreign Minister Weizsäcker that a plebiscite was now the only solution. There was nothing haphazard in the communications between Henlein and the German Foreign Ministry. At the same time on the 14th, both Newton and Runciman at Prague perceived that "Anschluss of the Sudeten districts with Germany [now] seemed like a foregone conclusion if peace was to be preserved." [60]

The British Foreign Office and its emissaries abroad coolly accepted the probability of Czechoslovakia's dismemberment as Hitler's price for peace now. At home, it turned to examining the "pros and cons of settling the question by means of a plebiscite rather than by direct annexation . . . It rests with Hitler rather than with us to decide in the last resort by what process the Sudeten territory is to be transferred from Czechoslovakia to Germany." [61]

The demands had escalated to accord with Hitler's own expansionist agenda, requiring the acquisition of Sudetenland, which included the formidable Czechoslovak military fortifications. Not only was dismemberment of the sovereign State of Czechoslovakia openly threatened now, but also indicated was the intention to deprive the rump State of its carefully wrought means of self-defense.

NOTES

1. Private Secretary of Secretary of State, 10 Downing Street, Whitehall, June 22, 1938, FO 800/v. 309, p. 194.

2. Foreign Office Memo, Campbell, Paris, to Speaight, August 5, 1938, FO 800/v. 301, p. 231.

3. Basil C. Newton, Prague, August 1, 1938, FO 371/v. 21782, p. 237.

4. Minutes of a conversation between Nevile Henderson and Ullrich, August 15, 1938, FO 800/v. 304, pp. 266-267.

5. Henderson to Newton, August 11, 1938, FO 800/v. 309, pp. 319-322.

6. Henderson to Lord Halifax, August 8, 1938, FO 800/v. 314, pp. 42-45. Italics added.

7. Minutes of a conversation between Lord Runciman and Karl Frank, FO 800/v. 304, pp. 255-56. Italics added.

8. Ashton Gwatkin, August 15, 1938, FO 800/v. 304, p. 208. Italics added.

9. Runciman Mission, August 19, 1938, FO 800/v. 304, pp. 141-42.

10. Ashton Gwatkin talk with Henlein, Marienbad, August 22, 1938, FO 800/v. 304, pp. 242-45.

11. Ashton Gwatkin, August 27, 1938, Confidential, FO 800/v. 304, p. 208. Italics added.

12. Kundt's Compromise, September 2, 1938, FO 800/v. 304, pp. 367-68.

13. Runciman Mission, August 27, 1938, FO 800/v. 304, p. 220. Italics added.

14. Beneš-Kundt conversation, FO 800/v. 304, pp. 223-226. Italics added.

15. Runciman Mission, August 26, 1938, FO 800/v. 304, pp. 223-24.

16. Quoted from letter of Robert Tucker to Sylvia E. Crane, comprising a digest from his manuscript, *Stalin's Revolution*, to be published by W.W. Norton.

17. Winston Churchill, Chartwell, to Lord Halifax, August 31, 1938, FO 800/v. 313, pp. 96-97.

18. J. B. Duroselle, *La Décadence, 1932-1939* (Paris: Imprimerie Nationale, 1979), p. 340.

19. Ibid.

20. Ibid., p. 342.

21. Ibid., p. 341.

22. Ibid., 343.

23. Ibid.

24. Runciman to Prime Minister (hereafter PM), September 7, 1938, Telegram, FO 371/v. 21771, pp. 79-80.

25. Runciman Mission, September 4, 1938, FO 800/v. 305, p. 35. Italics added.

26. Ibid. Italics added.

27. Newton Prague, August 31, 1938, to Foreign Office, repeated to Berlin, FO 371/v. 21774, p. 37. Italics added.

28. Newton telegram, September 10, 1938, FO 371/v. 21774.

29. Foreign Office to Commonwealth governments, for Prime Minister, September 10, 1938, FO 37l/v. 21771, pp. 94-96. Italics added.

30. Ibid.

31. Duroselle, *La Décadence*, p. 344.

32. Foreign Office to Commonsealth, September 10, 1938, FO 371/v. 21776, pp. 99-101.

33. Ibid. Italics added.

34. French War Potential, FO 371/v. 21782, pp. 418-422. Italics added.

35. Ibid.

36. Ibid.

37. A.H. McDonald, Air Attaché, August 30, 1938, Confidential, FO 371/v. 21770. Italics added.

38. Ibid.

39. Newton, Prague, September 3, 1938, copy sent to War Office, FO 371/v. 21770, p. 53.

40. Telegram, Newton, Prague, to Foreign Office, FO 371/v. 21774, p. 122.

41. Henderson, September 11, 1938, FO 371/v. 21760, p. 13.

42. Duroselle, *La Décadence*, p. 344.

43. Ibid.

44. Ibid., p. 345.

45. Chilston, Moscow, September 13, 1938, FO 371/v. 21776, p. 192.

46. Jiri Hochman, *The Soviet Union and the Failure of Collective Security* (Ithaca, N.Y.: Cornell University Press, 1984), p. 157.

47. Ibid.

48. Newton, September 13, 1938, Secret, FO 371/v. 21771, p. 113.

49. Newton telegram and letter, Prague, September 11, 1938, FO 371/v. 21782, pp. 270 and 276.

50. Jan Masaryk to Halifax, September 12, 1938, FO 371/v. 21782, p. 284.

51. Jan Masaryk to Halifax, September 14, 1938, FO 371/v. 21782, p. 282.

52. Stronge, British Military Attaché, Prague, telegram to Foreign Office, September 14, 1938, FO 371/v. 21782, p. 289.

53. Henderson to Foreign Office, Berlin, September 8, 1938, CAB/24v. 278, pp. 125-26. Italics added.

54. Newton, Prague, September 13, 1938, FO 371/v. 21774, pp. 133-34.

55. Ibid., FO 371/v. 21774, p. 28.

56. Newton, Prague, September 15, 1938, FO 371/v. 21774, p. 167; Foreign Office to Commonwealth, September 17, 1938, FO 371/v. 21771, p. 183.

57. Newton, Prague, September 13, 1938, FO 371/v. 21774, p. 28.

58. Runciman Mission, September 14, 1928, FO 800/v. 307, p. 41.

59. Newton, Prague, telegram, September 14, 1938, FO 371/v. 21782, p. 290. Italics added.

60. Ibid, pp. 290-291.

61. Orme Sargent, Foreign Office, in response to Newton, September 16, 1938, Repeated to Berchtesgaden for the Prime Minister, FO 371/v. 21782, p. 292.

1. Hradčany Castle, Prague, viewed from the Charles Bridge, October 1971. Courtesy Charles M. Crane.

2. Presidential country palace at Lany, 1977. Courtesy of Thomas S. Crane.

3. Gravestones of Charles, Tomáš, and Jan Masaryk at Lany. Courtesy of Thomas S. Crane, 1977.

4. Entrance gate to Hradčany Castle, Prague. Courtesy of Thomas S. Crane, 1977.

5. Jan Masaryk at the United Nations. Courtesy of the Library of Congress.

6. Bust of Tomáš G. Masaryk by Ivan Mestrovic. The Crane family archive.

7. Richard Crane, dean of the U.S. diplomatic corps, addressing President Tomáš Masaryk on Czechoslovak Independence Day, October 28, 1921, at Hradčany Castle. The Crane family archive.

8. Tomáš G. Masaryk. Courtesy of the Library of Congress.

9. At Lany in fall 1922. Left to right: Charles R. Crane, Tomáš G. Masaryk and Eduard Beneš. The Crane family archive.

10. Jan Masaryk in the 1920s. Courtesy of the Library of Congress.

11. Sylvia Crane, 1990.
Photo by Charmian Reading.

12. John O. Crane. Photo by
Pirie MacDonald.

13. Jirí Mucha, foreign minister in the Prague Spring Cabinet. Photo by Karen Hagen.

14. The Mucha residence on Hradčanské Nam, Prague, October 1971. Courtesy of Charles M. Crane.

11

Munich
(September 1938)

At this precarious turn of events in September, when Czechoslovakia was being threatened on all sides by dismemberment and a deprivation of her defenses, Eduard Beneš hoped that the alliances he had created would hold. French Premier Edouard Daladier repeatedly insisted through his foreign minister, Georges Bonnet, that France would comply with the defensive supports under her alliance with Czechoslovakia. Soviet Foreign Minister Maxim Litvinov in Moscow avowed his intention to honor his pledge to enter militarily if France met her obligations. He had continued to supply Czechoslovakia with bombers flown over hostile Poland and Romania, whose regimes had recently turned sharply to the right.

The Little Entente had admittedly become a "wasting asset," from Whitehall's perspective. Romania was now ruled by Ion Antonescu, fortified by his Iron Guards; Yugoslavia was under the thumb of Milan Stojadinović; and Hungary was in the grip of fascistic Adm. Miklos Horthy. A Polish foreign ministry official at Bucharest told the British minister, Fahrquahr, that "the Polish government would undoubtedly resist any attempt by the Soviet Government to come to the assistance of Czechoslovakia across Polish [land] . . . The Polish-Romanian Treaty, and more particularly *the secret military treaty*' was in effect directed against Russia." Fahrquahr told the Foreign Office that the country was

completely unprepared to undertake operations on a large scale . . . [hence] it would try to remain neutral as long as possible . . . [Moreover, he observed] the difficult nature of the ground [terrain] in Northern Romania would in all probability cause the Soviet Government to give up any attempt to come to Czechoslovakia's assistance by

land . . . As regards passage of Soviet aircraft over Romanian territory, he thought
Romania would turn a blind eye. [1]

Between September 9th and 13th, the new Romanian minister of
foreign affairs, Nicholas P. Comnène, had been negotiating with the
Russian envoy at Geneva the right of passage for Red Army troops
to march to the aid of Czechoslovakia, if called. But the Romanians
required explicit guarantees by the Russian government of Romania's
territorial integrity when time came for their withdrawal. The bone
of contention was Bessarabia, which had belonged to old Russia since
1812, despite its largely non-Slavic population. The province had
been taken from Russia following the 1917 Revolution, when it was
given to Romania. Now Romania wanted to keep it, and the Soviets
viewed it with irredentist eyes. No agreement on this point had been
reached in time to guarantee right of passage during the developing
Czechoslovak crisis of September 1938. Disbelief abounds regarding
the sincerity of Russia's vows to stand by Czechoslovakia if she were
invaded by Hitler's armies. [2]

This degree of skepticism would seem unwarranted in the light of
the barrage of Soviet press criticisms of the failure of the Western
Powers to confront Hitler with joint action. Litvinov returned to the
theme repeatedly. The reaction in the Soviet-controlled press was
"extremely unfavorable" following Neville Chamberlain's visit to
Hitler. One writer taunted sharply, as reported to the Foreign Office:

There can be no doubt that Mr. Chamberlain's purpose in visiting Herr Hitler was
to *conclude a deal at the expense of Czechoslovakia*. HM'sG have abandoned the
principle of collective security . . . It would now seem the intention of Mr. Neville
Chamberlain is to call a Conference at which Great Britain, France, Germany, and
possibly Italy . . . [would revive] the old plan of a four Power pact to deal with the
Czechoslovak-German crisis.

The Soviet press warned that "concessions to aggressors serve only to
increase the danger," and went so far as to charge Chamberlain with
an "attempt to deceive world opinion and to represent his efforts to
come to terms with aggressor as a peaceful gesture." [3] This mocking
attitude suggests that the government was serious in its insistence on
collective security and on its pledges to Czechoslovakia, if called upon
to fulfill them.

Poland, to Czechoslovakia's north, and now laboring under the
passionately anti-Soviet regime of Colonel Beck, stubbornly refused
the right of passage to Soviet troops and also objected to overflights
of Soviet planes, going to the extent of sending up fighter planes to

challenge the Soviet bombers. The Russian pilots got through by varying the times and destinations of their flights, before they turned to the longer but safer Romanian route.

Polish hostility was seen toward Czechoslovaks, both by the government and the people, wrote the British ambassador, who observed that "despite the historical Polish dislike of the Germans, the Poles did not share "the same horror of Nazism as is felt in democracies." [4] The pervasive Polish hostility toward Czechoslovakia rippled over to affect France, where the British ambassador, Sir Eric Phipps, reported that "M. Bonnet fears that Poland would also be on the wrong side in the event of war . . . [He was also] not much impressed by the perspective of late and limited Russian help." [5]

Czechoslovakia had tried earlier to cut the Gordian knot at Warsaw. On September 1st, Prague had negotiated a civil aviation accord, even though it meant the Poles got the better of the bargain. Prague was permitted to fly from Brno to Moravska Ostrava to Riga, and the Polish Airlines could fly over Czechoslovakia from Warsaw to Budapest, but no flights could be arranged to Moscow by either party. [6]

London's Foreign Office also probed Italy's intentions. It saw Mussolini as a "moderating influence . . . toward a solution by peaceful means." Moreover, her weak economy would not position her "to wage a long war." Britain was encouraged by signs that Mussolini was contemplating, as a prerequisite for an Anglo-Italian agreement, "a withdrawal of Italian infantry from Spain" (all six battalions) as a "settlement of the Spanish question." [7] These hopes were dashed [8] on the 18th of September, when Mussolini, in a speech at Trieste, declared: "The only solution was plebiscite for all nationalities which demanded them." The reporting British ambassador noted dryly, "Italy's place in war alignment has . . . been chosen." [9]

Nor were reports from Paris any more heartening in regard to withstanding Hitler. Phipps wrote privately on September 16th:

I feel pretty certain that the French will by no means resort automatically to arms, even if the German forces cross the Czechoslovak frontier . . . Bonnet said to the assembled journalists on September 13th that France rejected any solution by recourse to arms; but that she was ready to examine any proposal made . . . [for] peaceful settlement. [10]

From Berlin, Henderson reported that "public opinion, while extremely anxious for peace, is gradually being inflamed by propaganda against the Czechs." [11]

Karl Frank's new revolutionary policy was thought by Newton to be opposed by the majority in those districts because of advocating "treasonable manifestos . . . [which] would mean the destruction of their homes." [12]   There was no mass exodus of Nazi sympathizers from Sudetenland; only the leaders fled. Wenzel Jaksch, leader of the Sudeten Democratic Party, retaining loyalty to the state, inquired of Newton as to the probable fate of his 400,000 adherents, who would face persecution under a Hitlerite regime. [13]

On September 15th Chamberlain, without consulting his French ally but merely informing her via Phipps in Paris, [14] set out optimistically on his globally publicized peace mission.   Arriving at Berchtesgaden following his two-hour drive with the German ambassador to London, Herbert von Dircksen, he was immediately received by Hitler, and then he talked with Foreign Minister Joachim von Ribbentrop and his Deputy, Ernst von Weizsäcker. Sir Horace Wilson, who accompanied Chamberlain, reported to the cabinet next day that Adolf Hitler was "much impressed with Chamberlain" for his rapidity "at grasping the essentials of the situation . . . [and for] his statesmanship." [15]   Chamberlain pleaded with Hitler to compromise Germany's differences with Czechoslovakia on the basis of the 1925 Arbitration Accord. Hitler brushed aside this suggestion for international arbitration, to which Beneš was willing to submit his case. Hitler, moreover, objected to any intimation that the Sudetenland could remain within Czechoslovakia. He could not say explicitly that if an internal solution were struck, his justification for military advances would thereby disappear. He insisted upon the formula of "self-determination," as Henlein had last demanded, now signifying separation from Czechoslovakia. Self-determination sounded utterly democratic and equitable, as expressing the will of the people. Von Dircksen prophesied that "we might have a little trouble with the French . . . [but] they could not oppose the principle of self-determination." [16]   Chamberlain objected to Hitler's new terms, which signified the dismemberment of Czechoslovakia, declaring he had to consult his colleagues before accepting such a recommendation, which would inflame British and world opinion.

At the same time, Hitler's demand was imprecise as to the means of accomplishing the latest version of self-determination. Were the Sudeten provinces, once separated from Czechoslovakia, to become an independent state or enclave, or would separation indicate their Anschluss with Germany? Who would supervise the transition and how? Would there be resort to a plebiscite? Runciman suggested:

It would be possible to hand the area over now to the control of the Four Powers [Great Britain, France, Germany, and Italy] who would administer it temporarily on an international basis, pending a decision by a conference of the Four Powers . . . It might be easier for the Czechoslovak Government to hand over its authority . . . to the Four Powers than to Germany.[17]

The British cabinet meeting next day, again reviewing the Czechoslovak government's position, agreed to a separation from Czechoslovakia of these districts in the Sudetenland which contained 50 percent or more Germans. Ignoring President Beneš's generous proposals, this formula was adopted as the Anglo-French Plan and was elaborated on September 18th at a London meeting with the French ministers. Premier Daladier was badly demoralized by this radical turn of events. How could he tell a friend to amputate a leg? He knew Czechoslovakia would not survive the cession of Sudetenland. Nor could he so quickly formulate French reaction to ceding these areas to the Reich. He needed more time to think.[18] At the least, in view of Czechoslovakia's losing her fortifications, she would require security guarantees by England and France for her survival. Although the British were displeased at this prospect, they resigned themselves to the necessity.[19]

The diplomatic pattern established at Berchtesgaden was that of settling the fate of Czechoslovakia without her participation, a disconcerting twist for Prague, especially for President Beneš, who had so painstakingly built his alliances. Even more important, the Anglo-French Plan fortified Hitler's claim with the prestige of the British and French governments. Runciman was called to London to learn the new terms and readily agreed to the justice of self-determination.[20] The French cabinet was given a brief report on September 18th by Daladier, who said he had fought hard for the French position to oppose the terms, but that after the two-hour debate they had all agreed that France could not, in any case, intervene without Great Britain to save Czechoslovakia.[21] Bonnet was convinced that Russia, even if she could intervene, did not wish to do so.[22] Bonnet promptly sent for Czechoslovak Ambassador Štefan Osuský to explain, emphasizing the difficulty France had in obtaining a British guarantee for Czechoslovakia. The plan was presented in Prague on the 19th by Basil C. Newton and Léopold Victor Lacroix. The old system of alliances would be replaced by a Great Powers guarantee of Czechoslovakia's new, indefensible frontiers. The "ultimatum" mechanism was articulated over three days of successive threats.

Chamberlain blamed Beneš for his dilatory maneuvers. [23] If Prague rejected the terms, Germany's imminent invasion would no longer be ruled as provocative or aggressive, thus freeing France from coming to her aid. By September 19th, both Runciman and the Foreign Office became convinced that maintaining the chiefly German districts within bounds of the Czechoslovak state could not in fact continue without imperilling the interests of Czechoslovakia herself and European peace. [24]

There was a prolonged, nerve-wracking silence emanating from Prague to the British and French foreign ministries while the Czechoslovak leaders debated the heartrending ultimatum. A member of the French cabinet, Georges Mandel, a disciple of Georges Clemenceau, telephoned Beneš to implore him to reject the terms, emphasizing that international guarantees of the new boundaries of the truncated state would not necessarily protect it "against unprovoked aggression . . . in place of existing treaties." The memo stressed "the need of secrecy." [25] Ambassador Lacroix wired Paris on September 20th that "the Czechoslovak government were leaning in their deliberations toward a refusal and favoring international arbitration instead." [26]

On the same day in Prague, Newton relayed home news that his military attaché, Col. H. C. T. Stronge, had learned from a colonel on the Czech general staff "that in view of fact that Czechoslovakia was being betrayed by France and abandoned by Britain, it would be *suicidal* to fight Germany single-handed . . . It was [consequently] not proposed to resist." The top military officers in Prague estimated that the army, aided by the fortifications, could hold out against a massive German invasion perhaps two or three months, but they calculated that the fighting would reduce the country to ruins, to say nothing of the number of deaths. Prague would surely be blitzed, even if the Czechoslovak Air Force could retaliate against Dresden. Colonel Stronge credited opinions that "while the army would certainly have defended their country, with the Allies' decision not to do so,[the decision not to fight] alone has only been taken in the last few days . . . when [they] came to realize [the reality of their situation] for the first time." Stronge so informed his French colleagues in "strictest confidence." [27]

The favorable estimate of Czechoslovakia's military defensive capacity was confirmed by another British military emissary to Prague, Lt. Col. MacDowell, who had been invited by the Czech ministry of national defense to inspect and appraise the Czech military establishment. He assured London that the army "should be able to give a good account of itself." [28]   Czechoslovakia had a standing army of 200,000 men with a million in reserves, including 200,000 experienced Legionnaires, who had undergone a month's training annually. The population was intensely patriotic, yielding high morale. The armed forces had mechanized heavy artillery and a plethora of guns. Czechoslovakia had for years been a major exporter of arms fabricated in the Škoda and Brno iron, steel, and munitions works. Now their plants had been removed from the border or Sudeten areas and camouflaged. [29]

Beneš himself recorded his reasons for rejecting the fight-to-the-finish scenario, despite Russian assurances, in his memoir *Munich*, as follows:

1. Czechoslovakia would herself be destroyed.
2. She could never be reconstituted without the collaboration of the Western Powers whose friendship she would forever forfeit for causing war.
3. The difficulty of passage for the Red Army through either Poland or Romania.
4. The near certainty of civil war erupting behind the lines, provoked by the large, anti-Soviet Agrarian party and its Rightist partners. [30]

The British Foreign Office received a report of a conversation between Beneš and Lacroix, at 5:00 P.M. on September 21st, describing Beneš's sad acceptance, which was relayed to Henderson in Godesberg for the prime minister. Because the Prague government promised to treat its Polish and Hungarian minorities with equality under a plan of autonomy within the state, the French government was being asked to oppose Polish and Hungarian territorial adjustment claims and also to assure the transfer of Sudeten territory by the Czechoslovak government to an international commission. Beneš counted on France and Britain to ascertain that no German invasion occurred during negotiations. He complained that the sessions "took no account of vital necessities of [the] Czech State from [an] economic point of view . . . including communications" and transportation. [31]

The imposition of the Anglo-French plan and its acceptance under protracted agonizing duress on the night of September 20th–21 [32] had so inflamed the already tense public that popular clamor for resistance gave rise to demands for the resignation of the appeasing Prime Minister, Milan Hodža. The demonstrators insisted, literally from the streets, on the installation of a government of national emergency under Gen. Jan Syrový of Legion fame. The new cabinet, which took charge on the evening of September 22nd, was "to be one of national concentration with military participation. All representatives of the parties of the former Government are to remain members." [33]

With the Czechoslovak acceptance of the Anglo-French plan in hand, Chamberlain took off optimistically to meet Hitler in Godesberg. He justifiably looked ahead to the smooth implementation with his host. After relating all he had accomplished subsequent to the Berchtesgaden understanding, he was shocked when Hitler abruptly told him that the plan was no longer adequate. Hitler informed him that he now intended to take the Sudetenland by force under the timetable of Operation Grün, signifying that the German troops would "occupy the Sudetenland" promptly "up to a final line of demarcation to be settled with an international commission." Chamberlain again demurred, saying that "British and French public opinion could not accept this solution." [34]

Chamberlain withdrew to his suite in the Hotel Petersburg thoroughly shaken. Occupation by German troops would be construed at home, in France, and throughout the world as an invasion, which would occasion French entry into the fray, followed by that of the Soviet Union. His hopes for peace dimmed considerably. He set about to ease the situation, and wrote two notes to dissuade the Führer. In the first, he stressed the futility of invading

areas which will become part of the Reich at once in principle, and very shortly afterwards by formal delimitation . . . [Invasion] would be condemned as an unnecessary display of force . . . The Czech Government would have no option but to order their forces to resist. [Hitler's revision accomplished] the destruction . . . of an orderly settlement . . .

The maintenance of law and order could be . . . entrusted to the Sudeten Germans themselves [or by other means] . . . The Czech Government cannot . . . withdraw their forces nor can they be expected to withdraw the State Police so long as they are faced with the prospect of forcible invasion. [35]

This firmer tone was then moderated by a second note to Hitler later that evening. Chamberlain said modestly that he was acting merely in "capacity of intermediary" and as such would "at once forward [your memorandum] to Prague and request a reply of the Czechoslovak Government at the earliest possible moment." Meanwhile "no action should be taken . . . by the forces of the Reich to prejudice any further mediation." [36] Chamberlain's sharper tone prodded Hitler into reality. By morning, he produced a detailed memorandum, his Godesberg Memorandum, "with a view to bringing about an immediate and final solution of the Sudeten German problem." He presented his conditions to deferring his invasion to October 1st, as follows:

1. Withdrawal of the whole Czech armed forces, the police, the gendarmerie, the customs officials, and the frontier guards from the areas to be evacuated.
2. The evacuated territory is to be handed over in its present condition.
3. The Czech Government discharges at once all Sudeten Germans serving in the armed forces or the police anywhere in Czech State territory . . . to return home.
4. The Czech Government liberates all political prisoners of German race.
5. The German Government agrees to permit a plebiscite to take place in those areas [to be] more definitely defined, before at latest, the 25th November . . . The plebiscite . . . [to be] carried out under . . . an international commission.

An appendix emphasized a prohibition against "destroying or rendering unusable . . . military, commercial or traffic establishments . . . air services and all wireless stations . . . rolling stock of the railway system. . . . undamaged . . . utility services (gas works, power stations, etc.) . . . Finally, no foodstuffs, goods, cattle, raw materials are to be removed." [37] In other words, the evacuees, who would become refugees, were to depart their homes carrying nothing more than their clothes and a few personal possessions, and go without food or livestock.

This latest plan would render over a million Czechs homeless and hungry. The numbers were supplied by Jan Masaryk in London: "In the territory stipulated in the Anglo-French Plan there would be 382,000 Czechs to be handed over to Germany, whereas in the territory to be ceded by October 1st . . . 836,000 Czechs are to be handed over to Germany . . . Further, in the area which is shaded green in the Herr Hitler map, there are 1,116,000 Czechs and only 144,000 Germans." [38] These figures demonstrate dramatically just how intermingled were the two peoples in the so-called German districts. The refugees were to abandon their homes, property, farms, and livestock and leave without food. The stipulation of "no compensation" would mean "immediate pauperization, first for the evacuees, but also for the State in the loss of ceded properties"; and then the British government was given the burden of providing for the care and transition of these people elsewhere. [39]

A private memorandum in the Foreign Office archive explained: "The Germans are so insistent on the occupation of the whole Sudeten territory by the 1st October [because they] fear that the

Czech Government, at the instigation [perhaps] of the French, have decided, if they are given time, [they could] blow up the whole of their fortifications . . . [so as not to] give the Germans useful and dangerous information as to the construction of the Maginot Line."[40]

The major portion of the border fortifications would now fall on the German side of the frontier, and the land corridor connecting Bohemia and Moravia was reduced to a width of 50 miles. The two rail trunk lines running into Slovakia were severed east of Brno, capital of Moravia.

Chamberlain departed Godesberg in a rage. Lord Runciman, then in London, was equally indignant. He wrote Halifax:

I am getting more and more unhappy about the maintenance of our veto on Czech mobilization . . . This veto should not be maintained one hour after lunchtime today . . . We have got a bad enough name over this whole business . . . The Czechs are going to fight if pushed too hard or attacked . . . It is *we* who have prevented them from defending themselves effectively . . . So may we please remove a ban . . . so unfair as to be iniquitous . . . It is also universal opinion . . . [that we are] being duped. [41]

Almost simultaneously, Phipps wired from Paris that "owing to German aggressive movements, the Czechoslovak Republic is determined to defend itself by force . . . The Czechoslovak Government shall be told that our [and French] advice not to mobilize is withdrawn."[42]

The Czechoslovak government reacted swiftly. Mobilization was proclaimed at 10:15 P.M. on September 23rd. It "commenced officially at midnight on September 24-25th. By the 28th, mobilization was complete," giving them "something more than a million men . . . under arms." Newton reported that "confidence is felt that if French take the offensive reasonably early, [the] German army cannot overrun Bohemia and Moravia." The Czech general staff estimated that they had "technical parity" with the Germans.[43]

In France, Gen. Maurice Gamelin, prodded by an aroused public opinion, thought that "the only way to save peace now was to demonstrate that France was prepared to fight."[44] On the 24th, a partial mobilization was ordered; 753,000 reservists were directed toward the North East frontier[45] and the foreign ministry issued a press release saying that "if Czechoslovakia were the object of a German attack, France would be obliged to go to her aid and that Great Britain and Russia would certainly stand at their side."[46] A message was delivered to Voroshilov alerting him to French military preparations. The prompt Soviet response advised that "the Soviet High Command was readying 30 infantry divisions, motorized divisions, and air forces along the western borders of the Soviet Union." [47] At this juncture, the Soviet government had a Romanian note granting them explicitly "consent . . . to the passage of Soviet troops and to massive overflights of Romanian territory en route to Czechoslovakia." [48]

Jan Masaryk in London was requested to respond for his government to the Godesberg proposals. He wrote an indignant rejection to Lord Halifax on September 25th:

My government wish me to declare in all solemnity that Herr Hitler's demands in the present form are absolutely and unconditionally unacceptable to my government . . . a de facto ultimatum of the sort usually presented to a vanquished nation and not a proposition to a sovereign State . . . Our national and economic independence would disappear with [our] acceptance . . . The nation of St. Wenceslas, Jan Hus, and Thomas Masaryk will not be a nation of slaves. [49]

On the morning of the same day, Chamberlain, flanked by Lord Halifax, Sir John Simon, and Sir Samuel Hoare, consulted with Premier Daladier, who had come to London with Bonnet and several other government luminaries, and accompanied by Corbin. Daladier argued with all his force against accepting such dishonorable terms, that "France will never accept such concessions." [50] Chamberlain reiterated that the British would not go to war over the Sudetens. [51] The meeting ended in a stand-off.

At 5:30 P.M. on the same day, Masaryk was invited to join Lord Halifax and Prime Minister Chamberlain for a brief conference, wherein Chamberlain asked whether on pain of facing Hitler's immediate invasion short of Czechoslovakia's acceptance of his terms, his government would consider participating in an international conference "to negotiate a settlement based on the Anglo-French Plan." The conference would include Germany and Czechoslovakia and perhaps other powers, "to arrive at methods of carrying out the proposals. [52] Masaryk responded that he would inquire. Next day, he wrote an affirming note:

The Czechoslovak Government would be ready to take part in an international conference where Germany and Czechoslovakia, among other nations, would be represented to find a different method of settling the Sudeten German question . . . possibl[y] reverting to the . . . Anglo-French Plan . . . [He requested] definite and binding guarantees . . . that no unexpected . . . [aggression] would take place during the negotiations, and that the Czechoslovak defence system would remain intact during that period. [53]

Chamberlain told Daladier the next day, September 26th, that he was sending Sir Horace Wilson to Berlin with a message for Hitler, saying: "The French Government have informed us that, if the Czechs reject the Memorandum [Godesberg] and Germany attacks Czechoslovakia, they will fulfill their obligations to Czechoslovakia. Should the forces of France in consequence become engaged in active hostilities against Germany, we shall feel obliged to support them."[54]   Further, Wilson was to ask Hitler to substitute the methods of negotiation for military action.[55] The French reservists marched resolutely toward the frontier on the 26th. General Gamelin was asked to join the deliberations in London, arriving with Admiral Jean Darlan, who shared Gamelin's optimism, although the air force chief, Gen. Vuillemin, remained pessimistic. Daladier was asked by Chamberlain to approve the message; he declared himself "absolutely in accord" without further comment. He had become determined now to oppose his own foreign minister, Bonnet, and not abandon his Czechoslovak ally, "even if only the Communist Party declared positively for military resistance in the face of the strong pacifism of his country. Absolute secrecy was agreed to."[56]

In his note, Chamberlain summarized for Hitler the arguments he had employed during their Godesberg talk about public opinion reacting negatively to the "excessive use of force by Germany." He detailed Czechoslovakia's objections to the new onerous terms, whereunder "her national and economic independence would automatically disappear." He felt that Czechoslovakia's adherence to the Anglo-French Plan rendered "a settlement by negotiation possible." Hence, he proposed a great-power conference as a means of implementation. In a personal plea aside, which proved counter-productive, Chamberlain wrote: "The situation is very serious . . . the terms of your memorandum have profoundly shocked public opinion."[57] He virtually begged Hitler privately to bail him out, giving Hitler the edge in their negotiation.

Chamberlain presented to the cabinet Czechoslovakia's acceptance of a conference on September 26th, and he declared his readiness to journey to Berlin the following day with a Czechoslovak representative to negotiate the Sudeten transfer. He requested Hitler to postpone military action awaiting the outcome of further negotiations.

Hitler received Wilson, accompanied by Henderson, immediately upon their arrival, but their critical meeting occurred the next day. The threatened general mobilization had not materialized. Wilson made a second effort to persuade Hitler of the gravity of the British and French response should Germany advance across Czechoslovakia's frontier. Hitler broke into a rage, proclaiming his indifference to the warning, and insisted that his military timetable was unalterable. Wilson wired the negative response to Chamberlain, who instantly relayed it to Beneš in Prague. Hitler's army, he warned, would cross the frontier on September 28th (the next day). He said:

Bohemia would be overrun by the German army and nothing which another Power or Powers could do would be able to save your country and your people from such a fate. This remains true whatever the result of a world war might be . . . His Majesty's Government cannot assume the responsibility of advising you. [58]

Chamberlain, in his radio appeal to his nation on September 27th, recounted his efforts to stave off the "horrible war" looming out of a distant quarrel that had already been settled in principle. He tipped his hand, saying: "However much we may sympathize with a small nation confronted by a big and powerful neighbor, we cannot in all circumstances *undertake to involve the whole British Empire in a war on her account.*" [59]

Prior to his speech to Parliament next day, Chamberlain had received a shrewd appeal from Hitler, reversing his rude, unpremeditated dismissal of special envoy Wilson during an uncontrolled tantrum. In a show of conciliation, Hitler pleaded with the prime minister not to abandon his good offices to persuade the Czechoslovaks to accede to the German demands.

Five reasons converged at this point to prod the Führer to comply with Chamberlain's appeal. Foremost among these was the reluctance of the German general staff, headed by General von Halder, to face war at this time, as it advised Hitler. Although Hitler said he was responding to the plea of Benito Mussolini for a 24-hour delay, mobilization was in any case a few days behind schedule. [60]

President Franklin D. Roosevelt sent an urgent second message in response to an appeal from Daladier to do all he could in the interest of peace. [61] Roosevelt recommended calling a conference of all involved parties.

On September 28th, Hitler received the anticipated reply from Chamberlain, who declared his readiness to journey to Berlin with a Czechoslovak representative to negotiate the Sudeten transfer. Chamberlain added gratuitously: "I feel certain you can get all essentials without delay and without war." [62] At the same time, the prime minister wrote to Mussolini, urging his attendance at the forthcoming conference.

Early the afternoon of the 28th, as Chamberlain was concluding his report to Parliament on his peacekeeping endeavors, a telegram arrived from Hitler inviting him "with M. Daladier and Sig. Mussolini" to an international conference next morning in Munich. Omitted was mention of a representative from Czechoslovakia. Chamberlain indicated his acceptance "amid general acclamation." [63]

Jan Masaryk, who sat listening in the Diplomat's Gallery, was aghast at Chamberlain's reply and the strong applause it elicited. Was Czechoslovakia, queried Masaryk silently, after all British commitments, to be cast aside in the hysteria of the last moment? As soon as he grasped the grim reality of being excluded, he said with intense calm to two Englishmen adjacent, "If you have sacrificed my nation to preserve the peace of the world, I will be the first to applaud you, but if not, gentlemen, God help your souls." [64] The die was cast when it came to light that Hitler had agreed to the conference on condition that Russia and Czechoslovakia be shut out.

President Beneš on September 27th had objected that the British-German negotiations "looked like bilateral negotiations . . . We had in mind negotiations between Czechoslovak and German Governments in which His Majesty's Government would willingly be associated." [65] With the Munich conference in the offing, he and his premier, General Syrový, summoned their military commanders to Prague. The officers reportedly spoke with great emotion. It was their considered conviction that regardless of the outcome of the Four Power conference, the Allies were bound to come to the side of Czechoslovakia if she were attacked. In any event, these military leaders opposed abandoning their fortifications without a fight. "Our nation would never forgive us," they said, "for the army has the duty of defending the territory of the Republic." [66]

After tense moments of reflection, Beneš decided that the military men were carried away emotionally with notions of their duty to the nation. Beneš thought their earlier decision to yield the single-handed clash with the German Wehrmacht more rational. His appraisal was that under no circumstances would France or Britain now fight a war on account of the Sudeten Germans or the remains of Czechoslovakia. He had received no response to his last-minute appeal on the 27th to the Soviets for "an immediate Soviet Air Supply." Discounting renewed Soviet pledges of help in any case due to inaccessability, and uninformed of the latest Romanian concession, [67] Beneš rejected his military's advice as "a fatal and unpardonable error . . . [which would] allow the massacre of our nation in a local war against Germany." He saw it as his duty to preserve the republic from destruction "so that it may take part in a future war that might be waged under more favorable circumstances."[68] He bowed before the Big Four decision to appease Hitler at the expense of his country and dispatched Hubert Masarik of the Foreign Ministry to join his ambassador to Berlin, Vojtech Mastný, to attend the conference at Munich.

The two envoys arrived at the Munich airport at 3 P.M. on the 29th, three hours after the Conference had commenced. They were awaited by a "large detachment of police . . . accompanied by members of the Gestapo" and driven in a police car to Hotel Regina Palace, head-quarters also for the British delegation. They could find no one to inform them about the Conference proceedings until 7 P.M., when Sir Frank Ashton Gwatkin came. He "could not then communicate" what was already completed. The Czechoslovak envoys' attempts to explain their country's "really vital interests . . . [and] the consequences . . . from the internal politics, economic and financial points of view" were ignored.   Nothing seemed to register; all their points seemed foreclosed. Ashton Gwatkin returned to the conference.

At 10 P.M. he returned and led the envoys to Sir Horace Wilson, who paid "no attention" to their protestations about "Czechoslovak strategic places." Wilson left, and they had only Ashton Gwatkin to explain to them the proposed revisions of frontiers. They were told bluntly that the "English delegation favoured the new German plan," and Ashton Gwatkin concluded frostily, "If you do not accept, you will have to settle your affairs alone with Germany. Perhaps the French will say this to you more kindly, but believe me, they share our wish . . . They are disinteresting themselves."[69]

Not until 1:30 A.M. in the morning of September 30th did they meet the British and French conferees in the otherwise vacated negotiating hall. Chamberlain said the agreement was about to be concluded and handed the text to Mastný to read aloud. Horrified at the devastating new terms, Mastný asked only "whether the Czechoslovak members of the international commission would have the same voting rights as the other members." The answer was yes. Chamberlain yawned with fatigue and want of sleep, but Daladier was agitated. No further answer was required of Czechoslovakia, whose representative on the commission "must be in Berlin at the latest at 5 P.M. that day . . . [to reach agreement immediately] on the details of the evacuation of the first zone." Hubert Masarik, reporting, added that the French foreign ministry's officer, Alexis Léger, said "The atmosphere was beginning to be dangerous for the whole world." There was to be no "right of appeal or possibility of revision." Masarik concluded his report, saying: "The Czechoslovak Republic as constituted within the frontiers of 1918 had ceased to exist." He foresaw "the most unpleasant [and eventually, the most serious internal] consequences."[70]

The evacuation of the designated territories in Sudetenland was to commence on October 1st and be completed in stages by the 10th. The terms were as harsh as previously described for the Godesberg Memorandum. It was left to the international commission, composed of the secretary of state in Germany and the British, French, and Italian ambassadors in Berlin, plus a Czechoslovak representative, to determine in which territories a plebiscite would be held and the dates, not later than the end of November. The commission would delineate the precise new frontier. It would also undertake revisions in "cases of minor modifications," based on "strictly ethnographical" considerations. People had the right of option of where to live within six months hence, to be supervised by a German-Czechoslovak commission. Within four weeks, a mutual exchange of political prisoners was to be completed.

In an annex to the treaty, the British and French governments, in accord with the Anglo-French proposals of September 19th, provided an "international guarantee of the new boundaries of the Czech State against unprovoked aggression." Germany and Italy would join in this guarantee only after the Czechoslovak government settled the claims of the Polish and Hungarian minorities, for which both Hitler and Mussolini had separately pledged their support. It was given three months to comply with this point. [71] Although Czechoslovakia was a full member, Lord Halifax later admitted that every point of contention before the commission was decided in Germany's favor. The full arrangements of the dismemberment were finalized in the Vienna Accord in December, which also confirmed the Polish occupation of Teschen and the alienation of the Hungarian districts in south Slovakia. Beneš had attempted to forestall these additional losses "by initiating talks with Warsaw immediately after Godesberg . . . to settle the Teschen problem before Germany would strike." [72]

At 7:30 A.M. September 30th, the day after Munich and one day before the German Army was scheduled to march, Beneš called Alexandrovsky, the Soviet Ambassador in Prague, to ask, "Is the Soviet Union willing to grant full military assistance to Czechoslovakia, independent of France and of the League of Nations, if Prague would refuse the Munich Diktat and defend itself?" He requested the answer before noon. For no discernible reason except perhaps a feeling of futility, Alexandrovsky delayed until 11:30 A.M. that morning to send his cable. The Soviet answer arrived with a hearty affirmative on October 2nd, a day after the Wehrmacht had marched into Sudetenland. [73]

In a broadcast appeal to the nation at 5 P.M. on September 30th,

General Syrový, the president of the National Council, announced the government's decision "to accept the terms of the Munich Agreement," as it had been told "that in the event of a refusal, they could expect no assistance. To stand up against overpowering forces . . . would have meant the death of millions." The army commander-in-chief, Gen. Ludvik Krejči, joined in the appeal. "The evacuation would start on the morrow." [74]

In London, Jan Masaryk wrote Halifax about some consequences to be faced on economic and human grounds. He wrote:

> We expect about one million people escaping from the ceded territories, to arrive in new Czechoslovakia within the next few days. We must find employment, shelter, and refuge for these victims . . . Our industrial coherence is being thoroughly cut to pieces . . . Most of the industries remaining . . . will be cut off from their . . . raw materials [and] their exclusive markets in the ceded territories.

He said that the figure of "£30 million sterling is my conservative estimate" for economic reordering "to enable us to live at all . . . It is plainly impossible to obtain a loan in the open market, hence His Majesty's Government guarantee for such a loan is essential." He asked Halifax to instruct Ashton Gwatkin and Sir F. Leith Ross to deal with Czechoslovakia in these problems. [75]

Czechoslovakia's economy was indeed grievously undercut. Her staggering economic losses, in addition to "dislocating completely the whole system of railway communication . . . deprived her" of the following resources:

> 66% of her coal and 80% of her lignite. Her industrial losses, according to German statistics, amount to 70% of her iron & steel, 80% of her textiles, 75% of her railway carriage works, 80% of her cement, 90% of her porcelain, 86% of her glass, 86% of her chemicals, 90% of her news type, 40% of her timber, and 70% of her electric power supplies. [76]

These abundant resources would eventually be employed by Hitler's war machine against the Allies. Czechoslovakia was reduced to an agricultural state. As for direct military supplies, Germany obtained more than 1,500 modern aircraft left intact on the airfields, along with vast supplies of guns and munitions. Regarding the fortifications, after the war Field Marshal Wilhelm Keitel and Marshal Fritz von Mannstein candidly admitted at the Nuremberg military trials that they did not believe Germany then had the power to break through the barrier. As Hitler had whispered to *Il Duce* at the conclusion of the Munich conference, the settlement would immediately release 30 divisions for deployment elsewhere.

In Sudetenland there were also impending political ravages. Konrad Henlein, newly appointed commissar for the area, announced that "he would imprison all political opponents until they turn black."[77]

Churchill pronounced the obituary for Czechoslovakia. Speaking in the House of Commons, he said, "All is over. Silent, mournful, abandoned, broken. Czechoslovakia recedes into darkness . . . It is a tragedy which has occurred—the story is over and told."[78] Churchill, returning to the subject later, blamed Beneš for capitulating. He wrote with hindsight: "He was wrong to yield. He should have defended his fortress line. Once fighting had begun . . . France would have moved to his aid in a surge of national passion, and Britain would have rallied to France almost immediately."[79] Had Churchill held the reins of power in London instead of Chamberlain, in all likelihood Beneš would indeed have stood ground and permitted his military leaders to make their stand at the fortifications.

Chamberlain was acclaimed on his second return to London, declaring he had achieved "peace with honor. I believe it is peace in our time." There were also massive protest meetings in London, voicing vast popular disapproval. At the Nuremberg war trials, when Marshal Keitel was asked by Czechoslovak Colonel Eger: "Would the Reich have attacked Czechoslovakia if the Western Powers had stood by Prague?" Keitel answered: "Certainly not. We were not strong enough militarily. The object of Munich . . . was to get Russia out of Europe, to gain time, and to complete the German armaments."[80]

In Paris before the Chamber of Deputies on October 2nd, Daladier received a long ovation. Daladier's defense rested on his having obtained Britain's assent to frontier guarantees for Czechoslovakia, and he proclaimed "the necessity to fight for peace."[81] His policy was approved by 515 votes against 75, 73 of whom were Communists, one Socialist, and one moderate centrist."[82] General French public sentiment was that "Munich is a catastrophe."[83] Daladier judged Munich as "an immense diplomatic default for France and England."[84] The Munich supporters on both sides of the channel acknowledged the truth of this judgment but preferred it to a Soviet victory; anti-Communism coincided with "peace in our time," the stand taken by the right. The fight against fascism became the message of the left. The only saving grace of the Munich capitulation was that Tomáš Masaryk had died on December 14, 1937, thereby escaping the pain of the sellout by his friends and supporters.

Beneš, under pressure from Berlin, resigned on October 5th. Before his departure, he made an appeal to his countrymen to "remain united, brave, and faithful to their national ideals and principles." Once again, on October 22nd, he went into exile to work for his country's liberation and restoration. He soon issued an organizing proclamation for the future: "Before the conscience of the world and before history, I . . . proclaim that the Czechs and Slovaks will never accept this unbearable imposition on their sacred rights . . . They will never cease their struggles until these rights are reinstated for this beloved country." [85]

NOTES

1. Fahrquahr, Bucharest, September 9, 1938, repeated to Paris, Berlin, Warsaw, Moscow, and Prague, FO 371/v. 21776, p. 160.

2. Jiri Hochman, *The Soviet Union and the Failure of Collective Security* (Ithaca, N.Y.: Cornell University Press. 1984), pp. 75-77.

3. Viscount Chilston, Moscow, September 17, 1938, FO 371/v. 21776, pp. 252-53. Italics added.

4. Kennard, British Ambassador, Warsaw, to Foreign Office, September 10, 1938, FO 371/v. 21776, pp. 175-77.

5. Phipps, Paris, to Foreign Office, September 23, 1938, FO 371/v. 21777, p. 62.

6. British Embassy, Warsaw, September 1, 1938, FO 371/v. 21809, p. 203.

7. A. Noble at Foreign Office, September 13, 1938, FO 371/v. 22353, p. 1.

8. Strang, Foreign Office Minute, September 15, 1938, FO 371/v. 21777, p. 17.

9. N. Charles, Rome, September 18, 1938, FO 371/v. 21782, p. 302.

10. Phipps, Paris, September 16, 1938, FO 800/v. 311, pp. 77-80.

11. Foreign Office to Commonwealth, September 17, 1938, secret, FO 371/v. 21777, p. 183.

12. Basil Newton, Prague, September 16, 1938, FO 371/v. 21774.

13. Newton, September 12, 1938, FO 371/v. 21740.

14. Duroselle, *La Décadence* (Paris: Imprimerie Nationale, 1979), p. 345.

15. Report on PM's visit to Germany, Cabinet Minutes, CAB 24, pp. 6-9.

16. Ibid.

17. Lord Runciman, FO 800/305, p. 61.

18. Duroselle, *La Décadence*, p. 346.

19. Ibid.

20. Ibid.

21. Ibid., p. 348.

22. Ibid.

23. Ibid., p. 346.

24. Foreign Office to Delegation to Geneva, September 19, 1938, secret, FO 371/v. 21777.

25. Duroselle, *La Décadence*, p. 346.

26. Ibid., p. 349.

27. Newton, Prague, September 19, 1938, confidential, FO 371/v. 21770, p. 84.

28. Lt. Col. MacDowell, British Military Attaché, Prague, FO 371/v. 21578, p. 16.

29. *"Czech Army Defences and Armament Factories,"* FO 371/v. 21578, pp. 20-25.

30. Eduard Beneš, *Munich* (Paris: Stock, 1969), pp. 224-33; Wheeler-Bennett, *Munich: Prologue to Tragedy* (New York: Duell, Sloan, & Pearce, 1948), p. 175.

31. Foreign Office to Henderson at Godesberg, September 22, 1938, FO 371/v. 21740.

32. Newton, Prague, September 26, 1938, FO 371/v. 21770, p. 125.

33. Telegram; Foreign Office to Commonwealth, Secret, September 22, 1938, 7:30 P.M., FO 371/v. 21771, p. 230.

34. Phipps in Paris talked with the Prime Minister at Godesberg, September 23, 1938, 10:30 P.M., FO 371/v. 21740.

35. First Letter of Prime Minister to Reichskanzler, September 23, 1938, FO 371/v. 21747, p. 55.

36. Second letter from Prime Minister to Reichskanzler, September 23, 1938, FO 371/v. 21747, p. 64.

37. British Delegate at Godesberg, September 24, 1938, CAB 24/v. 279, p. 94; also FO 371/v. 21740, pp. 112-14.

38. Jan Masaryk to Lord Halifax, Czechoslovak Legation, London, September 28, 1938, FO 371/v. 21786, p. 195.

39. Jan Masaryk to Lord Halifax, Czechoslovak Legation, London, FO 371/v. 21786, p. 202.

40. Orme Sargent, Foreign Office, September 27, 1938, FO 371/v. 21770, p. 133.

41. Lord Runciman to Lord Halifax, FO 371/v. 21770, pp. 100-101.

42. Phipps, Paris, September 22, 1938, FO 371/v. 21770, p. 90.

43. Newton, Prague, September 28, 1938, FO 371/v. 21770, p. 97.

44. Phipps, Paris, September 24, 1938, FO 371/v. 21770, p. 127.

45. Duroselle, *La Décadence*, p. 351.

46. Ibid.

47. Hochman, *Soviet Union*, p. 164.

48. Ibid.

49. Masaryk to Halifax, FO 371/v. 21747, pp. 69-71, quoted also in Wheeler-Bennett, *Munich*, p. 471; also in *British White Paper*, No. 5847.

50. Duroselle, *La Décadence*, p. 353.

51. Ibid.

52. Notes by Halifax of an interview. Present: Halifax, the PM & Mr. Masaryk, September 25, 1938, at 5:30 P.M., FO 371/v. 21743, p. 8.

53. Masaryk to Halifax, FO 371/v. 21747, pp. 76-77.

54. "The International Situation" FO 371/v. 21742, p. 111.

55. Duroselle, *La Décadence*, p. 353.

56. "The International Situation," FO 371/v. 21742, p. 111.

57. Chamberlain to Hitler, response to Godesberg, FO 371/v. 21772, pp. 19-21; also CAB 24/v. 279, pp. 112A-113.

58. Wheeler-Bennett, *Munich*, p. 152, based on. Czechoslovak archives

59. *London Times*, September 27, 1938, quoted in Wheeler-Bennett, *Munich*, p. 138; Beneš, *Munich*, p. 237. Italics added.

60. September 28, 1938, FO 371/v. 21744, pp. 5A-C.

61. Duroselle, *La Décadence*, p. 354.

62. Documents re Czechoslovakia, No. 1, September 28, 1938, ZHC I/8717.

63. Foreign Office to Commonwealth, September 28, 1938, FO 371/v. 21771, p. 142.

64. Wheeler-Bennett, *Munich*, p. 171.

65. Newton, Prague, September 27, 1938, FO 371/v. 21742, p. 153.

66. Beneš, *Munich* (Paris: Stock) p. 239.

67. Hochman, *Soviet Union*, p. 164, 165.

68. Beneš, *Munich*, p. 240.

69. Masarik report of Munich Conference, September 30, 1938, 6:30 P.M., FO 371/v. 21772, p. 133.

70. Ibid., pp 122-24. Attendees at the Munich Conference on September 29th were: Germany: Hitler, von Ribbentrop, and Weizsäcker; France: Daladier and Léger; Great Britain: Chamberlain, Sir Horace Wilson, Nevile Henderson, William Malkin, and Ashton Gwatkin; Italy: Mussolini, Ciano; Czechoslovakia: Mastný and Masařik, who were present at Munich but excluded from the conference.

71. Annex to the treaty; FO 371/v. 21772, pp. 122-24.

72. Hochman, *Soviet Union*, p. 165.

73. Ibid., p. 166.

74. Newton, Prague, September 30, 1938, FO 371/v. 21744, p. 92.

75. Masaryk to Halifax, Czechoslovak Legation, London, CAB 24/v. 279, pp. 98-99.

76. Wheeler-Bennett, *Munich*, p. 195, Hubert Ripka, *Munich: Before and After* (London: 1939), p. 492.

77. Wheeler-Bennett, *Munich*, p. 198.

78. Vera Olivova, *The Doomed Democracy: Czechoslovakia in a Disrupted Europe-1914-1938*, (London: Sidgwick & Jackson, 1972), p. 263.

79. Winston Churchill, *The Gathering Storm* (Boston: Houghton, Mifflin, 1948), p. 302.

80. Nuremberg trial documents, quoted in Churchill, *The Gathering Storm*, p. 319.

81. Duroselle, *La Décadence*, p. 356.

82. Ibid.

83. Ibid., p. 357.

84. Ibid., p. 356.

85. Beneš speech to his nation, Prem. 1, p. 249.

12

Aftermath of Munich
(1938-41)

The dismembered Czechoslovak state was further disrupted on October 6, 1938, upon Eduard Beneš's resignation, when at a rally in Zilina the Slovak People's Party proclaimed Slovakia's autonomy, flouting Beneš's appeal for state unity. Following the death of Father Andrej Hlinka, Father Josef Tiso succeeded to leadership of the Slovak National Party, which became "the only party in Slovakia by elimination of and union with other parties" on November 8, 1938.[1]

Eduard Beneš's resignation catapulted Gen. Jan Syrový temporarily into the Hrad as head of state. Syrový was replaced on November 30th by the National Assembly, which designated Emil Hácha, retired chief justice of the Supreme Administrative Court, as president and head of state. Rudolf Beran, the Agrarian rightist, succeeded as prime minister. This right-wing pair proved willing collaborators of the dominant power. All routine decisions in foreign affairs were referred to Berlin for approval. The new government forthwith annulled the Soviet alliance, banned the Communist Party, and curbed the trade unions and the press. It accepted the resignation of Ludvik Krejčí as chief of general staff on February 19th.

Notably cooperative with the new, pro-Nazi Czechoslovak government were business and financial circles, eager to take advantage of German trade and investment. On September 30, 1938, the day following the Munich accord, Jaroslav Preiss, chairman of the national Živnostenská Bank, accompanied by the new foreign minister,

František Chvalkovský[*] from the Agrarian Party, paid a visit to Berlin. Chvalkovský stayed on as ambassador, where he was forced to await reception by Hitler and von Ribbentrop until January 21, 1939.[2]

In Washington, President Franklin D. Roosevelt commented presciently on some consequences of the occupation of the Sudeten territory. He said pensively on October 26th, "It is becoming increasingly clear that peace of fear has no higher or more enduring quality than peace of the sword . . . if the reign of law is . . . to be replaced by a recurrent sanctification of sheer force."[3] Roosevelt little realized how prophetic his reaction was, as only five days earlier, on October 21, 1938, Hitler had already issued his general directive to Marshal Wilhelm Keitel for a surprise attack on Czechoslovakia. Two weeks later, on November 9th, a Jewish pogrom of unprecedented severity erupted in Germany, followed by sparse protests of a few resolute Jewish leaders in the West, while official communications of condemnation, or at the least disapproval, were noticeably lacking. Hitler gained in confidence and had definitively made up his mind to "crush Prague" by early December.[4] Czechoslovak intelligence obtained this information on March 10th and gave it to the general staff on the 15th. Beneš undoubtedly was informed by Gen. František Moravec.

Eduard and Hana Beneš installed themselves in Putney, outside London, that fall of 1938. In a nearby cottage lived Jan and Alice Masaryk, whom they saw daily until Jan departed for a lecture tour in the States. Under his pledge to abstain from political activity, Beneš maintained a low profile, seeing only trusted friends. The lack of action put him into a depression which was deepened by his physical and psychological exhaustion.

In December, the Reichsführer made his first visit to Sudetenland and discovered the beauty of the country. He keenly inventoried his gains of the country's rich resources.

Meanwhile, Beneš had received an invitation from President Robert Hutchins of the University of Chicago to give a graduate

---

[*]František Chvalkovský, while serving earlier in Rome as Czechoslovak minister, had voiced enthusiastic admiration for Italian fascism and for Il Duce personally. He made remarks critical of Beneš's pro-French foreign policy to these authors.

course. Beneš accepted with alacrity the professorship of political science under the Walgreen Foundation of American Institutions and designated as his theme "The Sociology of Democracy." He departed for the United States on January 27, 1939, and arrived in New York on February 10th, where he was given the customary official reception by Mayor Fiorello La Guardia, followed by many banquets in his honor, notably one by Nicholas Murray Butler, the president of Columbia University. His reception in the United States by notables and the public generally indicated "a strong sympathy and admiration" there, in contrast with his declining political stock elsewhere, especially in Western Europe, where it was at an all-time low. He was persona non grata in Daladier's France, where Milan Hodža organized anti-Beneš sentiment among the émigrés. Beneš continued on to Chicago, where he took up residence with his wife in the Windemere Hotel, practically next door to Jan Masaryk, who had preceded him to America, and to his nephew, Bohuš Beneš. [5]

On January 27, 1939, the governments of Great Britain and France advanced the truncated state of Czechoslovakia £10 million sterling, although £30 million had been estimated as required. The British and French governments guaranteed a loan by the democratic Czechoslovaks in exile for £8 million, to be raised by their followers in London. The British government granted £4 million outright, while the French undertook to service the loan, pay the interest, and repay the 5 percent bonds of the Czechoslovak republic. These emergency sums were deemed vital for the maintenance and resettlement of the vast number of displaced persons. [6]

Internal tensions between Czechs and Slovaks soon gave Hitler a handle for further manipulation. The first meeting of the Slovak parliament was convened on January 18, 1939, simultaneously with the adoption of a new constitution by the autonomous Slovak government. [7] Intrigues were hatched in Slovakia. Slovak populist leaders, encouraged by the Nazis, concocted maneuvers in concert with the Sudetens. On March 14th, the Slovak diet in Bratislava proclaimed Slovakia an independent state. Slovakia was recognized the next day by the satellite government in Hungary and the following day by a compliant Poland, which was happy to preserve her occupation of Teschen and further dismember Czechoslovakia. Throughout the spring and summer, Western countries followed with recognition of independent Slovakia. The Kremlin eventually followed suit as well. It took the Slovak legislature three ballots to arrive at a vote for separation, the third ballot succeeding only after Premier Tiso announced a military threat to Bratislava from the south.

Ordering Czech troops into Slovakia on a disciplinary mission, President Hácha on March 14th sought clarification in Berlin. There, to his consternation, he learned that German divisions were already poised along the frontier "to restore order." While he was still on his way at 10 P.M., and before he could sign the document creating the German protectorate of Bohemia and Moravia, the German military forces marched, took possession of Moravska Ostrava, the salient industrial center and military point on the Czechoslovak-Polish-German frontier, and continued northward through the night. The advanced motorized units arrived in Prague in the morning of March 15. The "invitation" to them took the form of a state treaty, signed that day by German Foreign Minister Joachim von Ribbentrop and by President Hácha and his docile foreign minister. The Nazi dictator entered the "golden" capital city of Prague that same evening and discovered its spectacular beauty at first hand.

Hungary annexed the self-proclaimed independent province of Carpatho-Ukraine. The formerly democratic republic of Czechoslovakia was turned into a territorially mutilated, indefensible, and economic and political fascist corporate state. On March 23rd, German troops continued northward to occupy Memel.

A chastened Neville Chamberlain announced the German invasion of Czechoslovakia in the House of Commons on the same day it happened. He noted that "the Czech people have been ordered by their government not to offer resistance." He then formally abrogated the Munich Agreement, declaring it null and void because the guarantees given Czechoslovakia of its territorial integrity "no longer had any validity," having been cancelled by Hitler himself in this act of "unprovoked aggression." He further cited the "declaration of independence of the Slovak Diet" as evidence of "internal disruption of the frontiers Britain was pledged to guarantee." Chamberlain said of this development, much to Winston Churchill's surprise: "I . . . bitterly regret what has now occurred." Churchill observed that Hitler had mistaken Chamberlain's accommodation at Munich as stemming from weakness, rather than from "his passionate desire for peace." Churchill went on to note that the Führer "did not realize that Neville Chamberlain had a very hard core and that he did not like being cheated." Chamberlain "reproached Hitler with flagrant personal breach of faith about the Munich Agreement," an anathema to old-school conservatives. [8]

From Chicago, on March 16th, Beneš promptly denounced the German incursion as a violation of the Munich accord, which Beneš nullified outright while proclaiming the legal continuity of the First

Republic. Believing that neither Britain nor France had shown any disposition to make an issue of Germany's violation of the Munich Agreement, Beneš addressed diplomatic notes to the signatory powers, as well as to the United States and Soviet Russia, asking "all Four Powers not to give recognition to Germany's occupation of Czechoslovakia." [9] After Hácha next day yielded state sovereignty, Beneš sent a message to the general secretary of the League of Nations at Geneva requesting him to "invoke Article 10 of the Covenant and such other pertinent articles." [10]   The principal Czechoslovak legations and consulates were not surrendered by the republic's emissaries in spite of orders from the protectorate regime. Col. Vladimír Hurban on that day refused the demand of a representative from the German chargé d'affaires, Hans Thomsen, to take over the Czechoslovak legation, and he reported his resistance to the U.S. State Department. [11]

On March 19, 1939, Beneš broadcast an appeal to the American people on the public affairs program of Chicago University, presenting his plans to set up a resistance organization modeled, as he knew so well, on the lines of Tomáš Masaryk's successful one in 1915-1918. Jan Masaryk addressed the crowd of 10,000 at the Pilsen Park Pavilion in Chicago and all Czechs and Slovaks everywhere, urging them to renew the struggle for Czechoslovak independence. Beneš then set out on an intensified lecture program to other university campuses and Czech and Slovak communities through the midwest.

Chamberlain's horror of war did not impel his return to a foreign policy of collective security, either through or outside the League of Nations. Eventually there came to light a clue to the conundrum in a letter written by Chamberlain privately to a friend on March 26th: "I must confess to the most profound distrust of Russia. I have no belief whatever in her ability to maintain an effective offensive . . . [and] I distrust her motives." [12]   This antipathy goes far to explain Chamberlain's lack of response to Soviet overtures for a Three-Power alliance with Great Britain and France, first on March 21st and then on April 16th. The British silence, in Churchill's later reflection, undoubtedly propelled the Soviets to pursue a normalization of relations with Germany for the sake of their own security. [13]

Chamberlain turned around on March 31, 1939, to pledge all support of the power of the United Kingdom, with France in accord, should Germany attack the next target on Hitler's military agenda, Poland. Perhaps it was easier for conservative Chamberlain to stake British lives and fortunes for the rightist Polish government than for the moderate social democracy of Czechoslovakia, despite the manifest advantages of the latter's formidable fortifications, backed by 35 armed divisions and its Škoda and Brno munitions works. Britain and France made the strategic declaration to offer Poland, Romania, Greece, and Turkey pacts of guarantees similar to the one they had just chosen to ignore with rump Czechoslovakia. These security pledges could not conceivably be effective in time to impede Hitler's armies from marching, but they would insure that Hitler would face a war on two fronts if he proceeded against any of these others. The guarantees were given none too soon. On April 3rd, Hitler's chief of staff, Wilhelm Keitel, issued a directive for the armed forces named Case White, the code name for preparations to invade Poland, to be carried out at any time from September 1 onwards. [14]

The Western Allies were wary about making any arrangement with the Soviet Union, which seemed to them militarily enfeebled by the purge trials of 1937. In any case, the Soviets went further than matching the British and French notes of remonstrance to Hitler's invasion of Czechoslovakia. On March 21st, they proposed convoking a Six-Power conference, to include Great Britain, France, the USSR, Poland, Romania, and Turkey, to deal with possible further aggression. On April 19th, Maxim Litvinov outlined to the British and French ambassadors in Moscow the objectives of his government in his proposal for a Three-Power collective security alliance, as follows:

1. Pact of mutual assistance against any aggression in Europe,

2. Extension of this commitment to cover all states bordering on the Soviet Union, and

3. Specific agreements with regard to military cooperation. [15]

These terms amply demonstrated Soviet Russia's preference for strategic protection under a defensive West European alliance. Against the advice of Churchill favoring a pact with the USSR, Chamberlain disregarded the suggestion as "premature." This proved the last straw for Litvinov's pro-Western policy. He was replaced on May 3rd by hard-line Vyacheslav Molotov, who heralded Stalin's definitive change of policy to one of striking the best deal possible with Hitler for Russia's own security. Intuiting this shift in Moscow, Hitler switched Joseph Goebbels' propaganda line from anti-Bolshevism to reviling the "pluto-democracies."

In America, Beneš and Jan Masaryk continued their rounds of speeches. Beneš gave a number of addresses at universities, several of which awarded him an honorary degree to signal their sympathy. The three major Czechoslovak national organizations in the United States met in Chicago over the weekend of April 18–20 to endorse and finance Beneš's program of national liberation. A delegation of 20 leaders conferred with Beneš and asked him to head the liberation movement. They claimed to have 300,000 supporting members. Only a minority of Slovak Americans, however, rallied to the common cause as they had done earlier for the republic's founding. The majority of Slovak Americans remained hostile or indifferent this time around. [16]

On May 28th, before departing from the United States, Beneš spent an informal day at Hyde Park. President Roosevelt greeted him cordially as an opposite number. Roosevelt had already responded on March 17th to Beneš's telegraphed appeal from Chicago, asking him to join the British, French, and Russian protests to Berlin at the German military occupation of Czechoslovakia, which these Allies condemned as "wanton lawlessness" and "arbitrary force . . . threatening world peace and the very structure of modern civilization." Accordingly, this statement had been enclosed with a note to Berlin from Acting Secretary of State Sumner Welles on March 20, 1939, in which "the Government of the U.S. refused to recognize the March 16th decree of the German Government announcing its protectorate over Bohemia and Moravia." At the same time, Welles ordered "the closing of the American Legation at Praha, the turning over of Government property and archives to the Consulate General and the departure from Praha of the American Minister." To Beneš, FDR had wired his "deep concern" over the German military seizure of his country. [17]

Roosevelt had to balance the friendly accounts of the Red Army's fighting capacity with the strong negative estimates he had received from his two proappeasement ambassadors in Western Europe, Joseph P. Kennedy in London and William C. Bullitt, now in Paris but formerly in Moscow, who were seconded by the U.S. counsellor of embassy in Moscow, Loy Henderson. Beneš concluded the interview with an urgent request for U.S. assistance on the long road to retrieval of Czechoslovak independence, and he outlined his plans to contribute to winning the war.

Beneš returned to London in mid-July an acclaimed public figure in America. Arrangements to have London serve as his operational base were eased by his friend Hamilton Fish Armstrong, editor of *Foreign Affairs*. Beneš then resettled in Putney, where a clerical staff was set up in a house across the street from his to aid his work of propagandizing for the liberation and reconstitution of Czechoslovakia.

At this stage, when Europe hung on the brink of war, it was useful that, before escaping from Prague, Colonel Moravec had underpinned and extended his intelligence network so that he would be able to provide private reports from his well secreted sources in Germany proper, as well as in the Czechoslovak provinces. Beneš would transmit these intelligence bulletins to 10 Downing Street, although he still lacked official relations with the British Government. Jan Masaryk's contacts over his 15 years in London proved useful as well.

The day following Beneš's arrival, he had received Colonel Moravec, who had reported to him that Berlin and Moscow were already in private contact. It had started with Soviet Foreign Minister Litvinov, with a view to sounding out possibilities for expanding trade between the two countries. On April 17th, Litvinov had specifically instructed his Berlin ambassador, Alexei Merekalov, to inquire about the fulfillment of important Russian contracts negotiated with Škoda and other armaments firms. He soon received the reply that the relevant deliveries could proceed after the occupation authorities had taken a plant inventory.

Another communication link that Beneš had with Prague over the next two years was with various resistance groups, which ultimately set up a loose central organization known as the UVOD. Prominent in one of these groups was Gen. Sergej Ingr, who had escaped to London in June 1939. Upon becoming Beneš's aide-de-camp, Ingr by prearrangements had established channels for Beneš to exchange instructions and information by radio, courier, and other means. Some 14,000 messages were claimed to have passed between London and Prague in this period.

The key liaison between the Beneš organization and the UVOD was none other than the new Czech prime minister, Gen. Alois Eliáš. Soon after Ambassador Konstantin von Neurath assumed supreme authority in Prague as Protector, President Hácha persuaded him to assent to Eliáš's appointment, supplanting the unpopular Beran. Eliáš had served Beneš as military aide when the latter was foreign minister and later Eliáš had served as minister of transport under Beran. More importantly, in Geneva he had come to know Neurath, the chief German delegate. In some instances, Eliáš was able to carry out Beneš's instructions from London while feigning support of the Nazi line. Sudeten leader Frank, who had been named state secretary in charge of domestic affairs, was often thwarted by Eliáš when the Nazis were beginning the "final solution" roundup in Bohemia, and Eliáš succeeded in deftly curbing anti-Jewish activities conducted by Fascist leader Gen. Rudolph Gajda.

Repression at home focused on the destruction of the intellectual class, including university students, and on isolating these elements from significant contact with workers and peasants. Although reduced to a subordinate position, business and finance found it profitable to collaborate with the Nazi-imposed regime. The economy generally was reshaped with some success, to cater to the needs of the new master.

The first act of expropriation embraced the entire inventory of military equipment and stocks found intact, which were instantly subjected to selective removal to Germany. The developed Czechoslovak productive plant was refocused to feed the German war machine. In accordance with the expanded trade agreement with Moscow, Czechoslovak industries were also encouraged to seek new markets, not only in Germany, but in Soviet Russia herself. With German consent, Vilém Hromádko, the general manager of Škoda, formed a syndicate of the nine largest arms producing companies in November, and business delegations were again exchanged and new contracts negotiated. A by-product of Škoda activity was regular reports that Beneš received, which went beyond the warning of the pending Nazi invasion of Soviet Russia.

Molotov's first countermove regarding Berlin on taking office May 3rd was to inform the German Government that before trade talks could proceed, proper political foundations must be laid. The German ambassador in Moscow, in turn, now advised his government to advance political proposals of the widest scope.

Feeling slighted when it observed the arrival in Moscow of second-rank representatives from the West, with powers merely to negotiate, not to conclude a pact, the Kremlin chose to exploit the delaying tactics to probe, as Britain was doing, alternate avenues to security. William Strang sensed this dangerous drift directly upon his arrival, when he reported to Halifax: "It's we, not the Russians who have taken the initiative . . . *Our need for an agreement is more pressing than theirs* . . . They have at least two alternative policies; isolation and an agreement with Germany."[18]   On June 29th, a blistering article appeared in the official Soviet party newspaper, *Pravda*, declaring: "The French and British governments want no part of a pact concluded on an equal footing with the USSR . . . The negotiations have already gone on for seventy-five days, fifty-nine of which have been spent in excuses on the part of the French."[19]

Halifax finally decided on July 20th to move off dead center. He instructed his ambassador in Moscow to inform Molotov of his "readiness to enter military negotiations immediately." Molotov invited him to send representatives straightaway. To persuade the

British to take the negotiations seriously, Molotov declared in a speech at this time that the "anti-Comintern Pact [was nothing but] camouflage for an alliance aimed at the Western democracies." [20]

Meanwhile, on July 25th, both Daladier and Chamberlain received intelligence reports that Hitler's deadline for action against Poland was September 1st. The reports cited as evidence the fact that harvesting in Poland had been speeded up. Notwithstanding the warning of the dire necessity for speed, Britain and France failed to send qualified negotiators to Moscow.

Even less than Czechoslovakia did Poland look forward to Soviet occupation during a devastating war. In these mid-August exchanges, the Soviets gained the conviction that all that the Western powers offered, possibly due to Polish opposition, was a symbolic Soviet accession to the Anglo-French pact of guarantees to Poland and Romania.

Daladier and Bonnet, at virtually the last moment, decided to act without the Poles. They telegraphed Gen. Joseph Doumenc, their negotiator in Moscow, "authorizing him to sign the military convention forthwith in the best common interest." [21] The next day, August 23rd, Colonel Beck consented to allow his general staff to study the best means of protecting Poland from Hitler's anticipated onslaught.

The tardy reversal by Chamberlain and Daladier to authorize their envoys to conclude a military convention with the Soviets arrived too late in Moscow to alter the Soviet decision. Although Marshal Klementy Voroshilov was paying close attention to his negotiations with the British and French delegations, on August 14th he received an offer from Berlin to send the German foreign minister to Moscow. The foreign minister certainly outranked any representative from the Western Powers. Molotov immediately agreed in principle. He quickly outlined to Stalin on August 20th a plan for a nonaggression pact with Germany, which Hitler had agreed to accept. Foreign Minister Joachim von Ribbentrop arrived in Moscow on August 23rd, prepared to sign the proposed non-aggression pact. Further negotiations with the Western representatives were terminated abruptly by Voroshilov on August 24th.

While the rival delegations were sitting in adjoining rooms in the Kremlin, Stalin did not hesitate to make his most controversial and startling realpolitik decision. The Nazi offer promised immediate strategic advantages, chiefly that the Soviet frontier would be pushed westward some 200 miles, roughly to the Curzon line, from which it had been displaced by the Brest-Litovsk treaty. In the end, the Soviet leader did not buy as much time as he had bargained for, but the 22 months he obtained proved crucial to Soviet survival.

The pact had far-reaching political repercussions. In the West, disorientation and confusion disrupted the ranks of the collective opposition to Nazi aggressions. In September, the Kremlin recognized the puppet state of Slovakia, and three months later, in mid-December, the Czechoslovak ambassador in Moscow, Zdeněk Fierlinger, was suddenly expelled from his post. The fall of Prague had driven thousands of officers and men of the Czechoslovak armed forces into exile. One group joined the fighting in Poland and ultimately congregated in Russia, while others escaped to the West to serve in the British and French armies and air forces. France welcomed Czechoslovak volunteers into its army, but would not countenance independent political activity that called into question its persistent policy of appeasing the Nazis.

Among the factions in Paris with access into government circles, the Czechoslovak intermediary was Monsignor Jan Šramek. He mediated to unify Hodža's chiefly Slovak anti-Beneš faction among the émigrés with the pro-Beneš group. Beneš was now invited to Paris, where he strengthened the unified committee and signed a treaty with the French government on October 2, 1939, permitting the Czechoslovak Army to operate in France. On November 14,1939, a Czechoslovak National Committee was again set up in Paris and was recognized immediately, on the 17th, by the French Government.[22] The Czechoslovak-French treaty was terminated on June 22, 1940 when the Nazis overran France and imposed an armistice.

By mid-December 1939, a National Committee was formed in London, resembling the National Committee of two decades earlier. The committee would transform itself early in July 1940 into a provisional government-in-exile seeking international recognition. Beneš was designated president and Šramek prime minister.[23] The National Committee functioned as a "shadow cabinet," including moderate socialist and Catholic leaders. They attracted to their banner outstanding liberal English friends and the conservative Churchill. Beneš consented to help by accepting a testimonial dinner in his honor, reminiscent of the London tribute to Masaryk in 1915.

On December 20, 1939, Beneš communicated news of the formation of the committee to Foreign Minister Halifax, to whom he also sent the list of members. These were Beneš, General Ingr, Štefan Osuský, Hubert Ripka, Juraj Slávik, Šramek, and Gen. Rudolf Viest, all quite well known to the Foreign Office. In addition to desiring regular communication with His Majesty's Government, they wanted assistance to reconstitute the Czechoslovak Army in France.

Halifax responded promptly, recognizing that the "committee is qualified to represent the Czechoslovak peoples . . . and to make such arrangements as may be necessary . . . in connection with the reconstitution of the Czechoslovak Army in France . . . The competent departments of His Majesty's Government . . . [would] afford it requisite support." [24]   Recognition would be given to the Czechoslovak provisional government-in-exile by the British Government on July 21, 1941, a month following the Nazi attack on Soviet Russia, which was quickly welcomed into the Allied camp by Prime Minister Churchill.

On February 14th, 1940, the Czechoslovak minister in Washington, Hurban, handed the State Department a memorandum composed by Beneš, stating the Czechoslovak peace aims. It was summarized in part as follows: "Not only must the Czechoslovak State be reunited, the frontiers with Hungary be revised in favor of Czechoslovakia, but the Sudetenland, with its German population, must be returned, with possible minor corrections of boundaries." [25]

A year later, on March 14th, 1941, Hurban returned to press the State Department for recognition. It could have been easy, as the United States had never recognized the Munich Agreement. [26] The State Department saw the situation quite differently and rejected the request for the while. Its analysis of the question is illuminating. In a memorandum especially prepared on February 5, 1941, it argued that Beneš had effectively resigned the presidency on October 5, 1938, and that Hácha's government had been accorded recognition. [27]

At that time, George Kennan was first secretary of the U.S. embassy in Berlin, where he saw a good deal of Chvalkovský, the collaborationist Czechoslovak ambassador in Berlin and was undoubtedly much influenced by him. Kennan, whom the State Department saw as "extremely well informed on Czechoslovak subjects" rendered the opinion upon request that "the Government in London is viewed in Czechoslovakia as an expression of the personal ambition of Dr. Beneš to re-establish his prestige . . . The publicity given to Dr. Beneš and M. Jan Masaryk adversely affects the Czechoslovak people . . . Recognition of the Provisional Government in London would cause great embarrassment to the Government in Prague of President Hácha," and he argued that Beneš and his group were greatly disfavored at home. Kennan recommended as the ultimate solution to the complicated postwar arrangements "a federation that may embrace Austria, Hungary, Bohemia, Moravia, and Slovakia with the establishment of a monarchy." The State Department reporter noted that this coincided with certain proposals made that past spring by the Archduke Otto, the pretender to the Austro-Hungarian throne. [28]

Last, but hardly least, the reporter argued, manifestly in concert with Kennan, that "consideration must be given to the fact that Dr. Beneš and his group have approved the policies of the Soviet Government. Should the United States Government recognize the Czechoslovak Provisional Government, it would amount to an endorsement of its policies regarding Russia, and this would be a cause of real embarrassment to the United States Government in the future." [29]   On February 7, 1941, the American press reported that the Secretary of State said "that technical questions were being studied concerning the recognition of the Czechoslovak Government." [30]

John Winant, the U.S. ambassador in London, filed a contrary opinion to Kennan's on April 2, 1941, regarding recognition of the provisional Czechoslovak government, followed by another reinforcing one on May 7th. Addressed to the Secretary of State, Winant wrote as follows:

Beneš is frankly troubled about the continued omission of our government to recognize . . . the Czechoslovak Government-in-exile as he thought you were very sympathetic with his plans as he explained them to you in Hyde Park in the summer of 1939 before he left for Europe . . . [Regarding] complaints that Beneš' Government does not include representatives of all political groups in Czechoslovakia, . . . the reasons for the exclusion of the Extreme Right and the Extreme Left are not difficult to understand. As far as I can discover, the Beneš Government, whatever its imperfections, is as democratic as any other government-in-exile and has as much, if not greater influence and contact with the democratic groups in its homeland and it is . . . pledged to the restoration of democratic government.

Being sympathetic with Beneš' desire for recognition and fearing that our failure to recognize his Government is being exploited by the Nazis, I should like very much to be helpful in clearing up the difficulties . . . which may stand in the way of some form of recognition.

Most important, Winant wrote that British Foreign Minister Anthony Eden "has expressed the hope that our two countries might go along together on the matter of Czechoslovak recognition." [31]

On July 1, 1941, the Foreign Office sent a confidential memorandum to the U.S. embassy, to be forwarded to Washington, favoring recognition. The chief reason it advanced was "to give further encouragement to the Czechoslovak population at home and to show them that their leaders in London are regarded as being on the same level with the other exiled national leaders now here." This was followed on July 18th by an accord signed by Soviet Ambassador Ivan

Maisky and by Jan Masaryk for Czechoslovakia to exchange diplomatic representatives and mutual assistance, military and otherwise, in the war against Germany. The formation of a Czechoslovak fighting force under Soviet command was sanctioned. [32]

The United States clearly felt too far out of line with its Allies. On July 30, 1941, it announced its recognition to the press "in furtherance of its support of the national aspirations of the people of Czechoslovakia under the Presidency of Dr. Beneš . . . While continuing its relations with the Czechoslovak Legation at Washington, the U.S. would accredit to the provisional Government . . . [an] Envoy Extra-ordinary and Minister Plenipotentiary, to reside in London." [33] This note was dispatched to the U.S. ambassador in London with instructions to deliver it to the foreign minister of the provisional government of Czechoslovakia in Great Britain, Jan Masaryk, as coming from the U.S. Secretary of State.

NOTES

1. National Archives, Washington, D.C., 1218, Reel 29.

2. Radomír Luža: *The Transfer of the Sudeten Germans, A Study in Czech-German Relations, 1933-1962* (New York: New York University Press, 1964), p. 171.

3. National Archives, 1218, Reel 30.

4. Luža, *Transfer*, pp. 168-69.

5. National Archives, 1218, Reel 29.

6. Ibid.

7. Ibid.

8. Winston Churchill, *The Gathering Storm* (Boston: Houghton, Mifflin, 1948), pp. 343-45.

9. National Archives, 1218, Reel 29.

10. Ibid.

11. National Archives, 1218, Reel 30.

12. Keith Feiling, *The Life of Neville Chamberlain* (London: Macmillan, 1946), p. 403; quoted in André Fontaine, *History of the Cold War, vol. 1* (New York: Random House, 1967), p. 106; also quoted in Churchill, *The Gathering Storm*, p. 349.

13. Churchill, *The Gathering Storm*, pp. 364-65.

14. Ibid., p. 350.

15. Fontaine, *History of the Cold War*, vol. 1, pp. 106-7.

16. National Archives, 1218, Reel 29.

17. National Archives, 1218, Reel 30.

18. William Strang, Letter to Lord Halifax, June 20, quoted in Fontaine, *History of the Cold War*, vol. 1, p. 111. Italics added.

19. Ibid., p. 109. Italics added.

20. Ibid., p. 110.

21. Georges Bonnet, *Memoirs*, p. 280, quoted in Fontaine, *History of the Cold War*, vol. 1, p. 115.

22. National Archives, 1218, Reel 30.

23. Ibid.

24. Ibid.

25. Ibid.

26. Division of European Affairs, U.S. State Dept., "The Czechoslovak Government," 3-page memo, February 5, 1941, National Archives, 1218, reel 30.

27. Ibid.

28. Ibid.

29. Ibid.

30. Ibid.

31. Letter of John Winant, London, to Secretary of State, May 7, 1941, National Archives, 1218, Reel 30.

32. Ibid.

33. Ibid.

13

War on Two Fronts
(1941)

The lightning Nazi invasion of Soviet Russia on June 22, 1941, altered the course of the war and transformed its character. Overnight, Britain gained a vital partner in arms. Winston Churchill, who had become prime minister on May 10th, reacted on the very afternoon of the unprovoked aggression. He publicly accepted the challenge of a wartime collaboration against the Axis powers and wholeheartedly offered the latest victim all available aid. Churchill's lead in the West to form an alliance with the Soviets at this point unquestionably changed the course of history, heralding Hitler's eventual defeat by the triumph of Allied arms. On July 12, 1941, Great Britain and the Soviet Union signed a pact of nonaggression and mutual assistance, each pledging not to make a separate peace.

The Allied governments-in-exile in London, in particular those of Czechoslovakia and Yugoslavia, soberly understood the parallel commitments of military cooperation and assistance. The Soviets resumed diplomatic relations with the Czechoslovak government-in-exile on July 18th and renewed the suspended treaty of alliance. Now vindicated with the Allied leaders, the Czechoslovak national cause gained significantly in prestige also from British recognition. The British Foreign Office declared that among its war aims were "the restoration of the independence of the Czechs and Slovaks." The Czechoslovak National Committee now became "an organ which handles the affairs of the Czechoslovak refugees and . . . the Czechoslovak arms . . . from among the refugees."[1]

The British had opened their doors to Czechoslovak refugees directly following the Munich Accord, when they had advanced some monies and established the Czechoslovak Refugee Institute in Prague to handle the evacuation of refugees. After Hitler's invasion of the country, this committee was disbanded and a British Committee for Refugees from Czechoslovakia was set up. The secretary was Margaret Layton, daughter of Sir Walter Layton, chairman of the *News Chronicle*, who had become involved earlier during the Munich crisis. Immediately after Munich, Layton had organized a fund for contributions to assist Czechoslovak refugees.

The British committee focused on rescuing people who had opposed the Nazi regime, including those from Germany and Austria who had fled to Czechoslovakia. Help was given as well to Sudetens who had opposed the Nazis. The admission of German and Austrian communists was permitted at the request of Ellen Wilkinson, a member of Parliament, supported by members of the British Labour Party and the Trade Union Council, who were also interested in saving the numerous Social Democrats caught in the Nazi net. By March 15, 1939, the Home Office had granted entry permits to about 2,000 Czechoslovak refugees. These were welcome provided they would not become state wards.

The British government's award of £4 million was supplemented by an official Czechoslovak Refugee Trust, which inherited the unexpended portion of the government money, amounting to about $13 million. By September 1, 1941, a special census found the Czechoslovak colony in England numbered over 10,000 civilians, armed forces having been excluded. [2]

On March 23, 1940, the former counsellor of the Czechoslovak legation in Budapest filed an intelligence-based report requesting urgent attention:

The police terror is stronger than ever in Bohemia and Moravia. The surveillance and interferences of the Gestapo to prevent a subversive movement are intense and cruel . . . The Czechoslovaks, hopeful of an Allied victory. . . remain passive. Rationing is less strict and the cost of living is cheaper than in Germany. No Czech has been enrolled in the German Army, even as a laborer behind the lines . . . All production not necessary for military ends has been stopped. [3]

The Communist Central Party Committee in Prague, on July 23, 1941, passed a turnabout resolution regarding the war. It annulled its December 15, 1938, line condemning the war and Beneš as bourgeois-imperialist and "now pledged unreserved resistance to Nazi aggression in conformity with the changed war situation." Irving Linnell, chargé d'affaires of the U.S. legation in Prague, reported "some murders of German police and reprisals thereto consisting of many arrests of former Czechoslovak officers, churchmen, and students" in November 1939. [4] Beneš's stock now rose in London and elsewhere, reflecting his unity with his home front. His broadcast to his nation on July 24th renewed his old theme of unity and cooperation in the anti-Fascist struggle for national liberation.

Western anti-Soviet behavior was moderated when President Franklin D. Roosevelt sent a prompt message of encouragement to Stalin, offering lend-lease assistance. Harry Hopkins, FDR's most trusted counsellor, was forthwith dispatched to Moscow to work out arrangements. Hopkins arrived in Moscow at the end of July for his first meeting with Stalin and Molotov, who presented him with a detailed list of Russian requirements. By October 30th, Roosevelt had pledged $1 million in lend-lease aid.

The stupendous challenge of waging war against the Soviet Union required the Nazi government to tighten its economic and political grip in the Czechoslovak Protectorate, where production had been successfully integrated into the German war machine. The compliant president, Emil Hácha, broke entirely with the Czechoslovak government-in-exile in June 1941 and issued fervent public appeals for support of the Nazi war effort which was dedicated to extinguishing Bolshevism. After the invasion of the Slav motherland, the communist underground turned to cooperation with the liberal UVOD groups, and the population shifted markedly in favor of the Soviets. The joint actions of the underground groups gave rise to noticeably increased acts of military and industrial sabotage.

Although the von Neurath administration was relatively indulgent of the workers for the sake of greater productivity, this largess did not extend to the farmers, who were repeatedly harassed and ill-treated. A press release in New York by the American Friends of Czechoslovakia on February 1, 1941, revealed:

Hitler's New Year gift to Moravia . . . [was an] order for all Czechoslovak families in the most fertile area north and northeast of Brno . . . to vacate their farms and homes by March 1, 1941 . . . Some 80,000 families in 36 purely Czech towns. Also the whole Czech population of 20 towns in the Elbe Valley . . . in central Bohemia were to be vacated.

They were to make way for Germans who were being removed from Bessarabia and Bukovina, which Russia took from Romania before the German occupation of that unfortunate country.

The dispossessed . . . families have been denied the right to buy farms elsewhere. The official notice limits the amount of baggage the families may take, which means that all farm tools, livestock, furniture, must be left behind . . . This is the fourth large area from which the Nazis are forcibly removing all Czechoslovaks . . ."The Bohemian-Moravian basin will be colonized with German peasants". . . The Czechs must be got out of Central Europe. [5]

Irving Linnell, chargé d'affaires of the U. S. embassy in Prague observed that "the Germans . . . maintain a firm hand on the economic, cultural, and even social life of the Czech people . . . [The regime's oppressive rule had forfeited its] last opportunity to rule the people except by force." [6] Facts such as these were frequently cited in Linnell's reports. The State Department had also received another information bulletin on the Czech situation on March 27, 1940, from the U.S. legation in Belgrade, extending the litany of constraints to the world of culture:

Strict control over Czech education . . . [as well as] the press, theaters, and radio . . . [Even history] books have been revamped to place emphasis on the fact that Bohemia and Moravia are a natural unit of the Reich . . . deletions [were] . . . made from the textbooks . . . relating to Czechoslovakia as an independent nation, and those referring to Beneš and Masaryk. [7]

Redoubled repression was now deemed necessary. The escalated acts of sabotage were to be met with sterner treatment. On September 28, 1941, the ruthless Number 3 Nazi henchman, Reinhard Heydrich, called "the most Satanic of all the top Nazi leaders," took office as Reich Protector in Czechoslovakia, replacing the diplomat von Neurath. As Gestapo chief in Berlin, Heydrich had built a record as a tough policeman, the mastermind of the Nazi death camps. He was a brilliant organizer especially suited to the task of absorbing the rich lands of Czechoslovakia. He instantly proclaimed a state of civil emergency in the districts of Prague, Brno, Moravska Ostrava, Kladno, Kralove, and Olomouc and ordered the arrest of Premier Alois Eliáš on the charge of preparation for treason. [8]

German sources reported on October 1st that "death sentences by the emergency Courts in Prague and Brno [were given] against the former Czech Generals Josef Bílý and Hugo Vojta" and 13 others charged with organizing resistance. Next day, 39 more death sentences in Bohemia and Moravia were reported from Berlin and "the arrest of 228 more persons by the Gestapo, on charges of high treason and economic sabotage." Heydrich set up "economic supervisory boards to overcome the sabotage of the food supply" and then, with supreme irony, he placed the blame for the German food shortages in the industrial areas on these "subversives." In any case, a new rationing system was announced on October 2nd. [9]

It took Heydrich only one day to have Premier Eliáš sentenced to "death, permanent disgrace, and confiscation of his property for aid to the enemy and preparation for high treason" by the German People's Court in a special session in Prague. Eliáš's execution was postponed in hopes that his testimony would implicate others acting with him. It was said he had confessed everything, but this was contradicted by an anonymous Czech newsman covering the proceeding, who relayed a secret message from Eliáš saying that "he hoped his conviction would help the Czech people at least to free itself of errors and illusions and choose the right path." [10]

Official German sources admitted in Berlin on October 4th:

During the past week . . . a total of 136 executions, many hundreds of arrests by the Gestapo in Bohemia and Moravia . . . [and] very many former high Czech army officers and a number of Czech officials and a few Jews . . . The Jews in particular are accused of being the "intellectual authors" of the sabotage and . . . subversive propaganda and they are also made responsible for the chronic food shortage.

Official announcements "confirmed the suspicion" that the Jews were "outstanding in inciting the population and in organizing active resistance." New drastic anti-Jewish measures were imposed by Heydrich, including closing all synagogues and forbidding any non-Jews to "converse with them in public places." The German reports insist that "the entire subversive organization . . . [is] being systematically eradicated." [11]

It was also observed in the regular reports from the U.S. embassy in Berlin that "the peace-loving Germans" of a year earlier, in October 1940, had vandalized the Museum of the Czechoslovak Revolution in Prague and "carted away the complete historical archive to no one knows where." The reports mentioned especially the names of "outstanding high officials in the Republic, such as Dr. Soukup, Václav Klofáč, and Petr Zenkl among those imprisoned. Soukup was severely tortured and Zenkl was sent to heavy labor on a new super highway out of a concentration camp." [12] On October 7th, it was learned in Berlin that the puppet mayor of Prague gave testimony against Eliáš as the "secret chief of the whole organization." [13]

President Beneš from his London exile hailed the accelerated resistance at home as demonstrating that the Czechoslovak people were pulling their weight in the Allied war effort. As the Heydrich-directed repression mounted at home, Beneš took steps to bolster the UVOD structure and accelerate its activity. He increased the training in Britain of professional organizers and saboteurs at the renowned

Special Operations Executive. His most audacious move was the preparation of two saboteurs to undertake the assassination of Heydrich himself.

Josef Gabčik and Jan Kubiš were air dropped 20 miles from Prague on the night of December 28-29, 1941, and after making their way to Prague they merely participated in the counsels of the resistance organization. The specially trained assassination team then spent the winter studying and plotting with others the work habits and movements of their quarry. The systematic decimation of resistance ranks continued, and Heydrich was preparing to wind up his tour of duty, his mission accomplished. Against strong reservations expressed within the resistance organization in fear of brutal reprisals, Beneš decided that Gabčik and Kubiš must strike.

On the morning of May 27th, 1942, five months after the pair's arrival in Prague, Heydrich was driving to his office seated next to his chauffeur when the car slowed to take a sharp turn outside the city. Two bombs were thrown against the car, demolishing it and severely wounding the Protector, who died several weeks later on June 4th. He was buried with high Nazi ceremony in Berlin on June 9th. The two assassins escaped to various resistance "safe houses" and eventually hid in the Karel Boromejsky Orthodox Church in the center of Prague, where the priest, with his bishop's assent, hid them in its deep recesses. Despite a massive manhunt, they lived there in safety for a short while until they were betrayed by a colleague.

Hitler had at once telephoned Vice-Protector Karl Frank ordering swift and onerous reprisals threatening to engulf 10,000 hostages. This was the same Sudeten leader who was described by a Foreign Service officer in Belgrade as "of a vindictive nature and probably responsible for most of the oppressive measures taken against the Czechs."[14] Through the happenstance of uncovering a radio transmitter in the neighborhood, the village of Lidiče was selected to be razed to the ground, its 193 male inhabitants executed, and its women and children deported to extermination camps. The same liquidation measures were meted out to the tiny village of Lazaky in Eastern Bohemia, a minor resistance center. Massive reprisals and numerous executions continued throughout the summer.[15]

The Nazis admitted to the execution of 1,331 people in direct reprisal, in addition to a special shipment of 1,000 Jews who were sent to Majdenek in Poland, of whom not one survived the war. Estimates ran to 30,000 women being sent into concentration camps. Although even Frank advocated ameliorating the brutalities, the uprooting of the resistance centers continued after Heydrich's death. The execution of Eliáš took place on June 19th. The two assassins and their protector priest, after battling fierce SS attackers three days, committed suicide. The bloody reprisals following the assassination of Heydrich resulted in the murder of 30,000 persons, according to the protectorate's own ministry of interior.[16] The Germans "had apprehended and executed all . . . key figures in occupied Czechoslovakia, who had been in touch with the government-in-exile."[17]

The Czechoslovak minister in Washington, Vladimír Hurban, told Acting Secretary of State Sumner Welles on March 8, 1943:

for a period of some six weeks, all communications had been cut off between the Czechoslovak Government-in-exile and the homeland . . . The situation has now been corrected . . . The appalling bout of persecution . . . led to a great depression . . . nervous exhaustion from the autumn of 1942 onwards . . . The German authority state[s] . . . that they will fight to the last man to retain their hold on the Czech territories and if they were compelled to leave the Protectorate, they would wipe out the Czech population.[18]

By May 1944, a year later, "the sum total of the Czechoslovak casualties," in Beneš's estimation, amounted to "half a million killed, imprisoned, (or) deported," while "property damages suffered by the nation (were) incalculable."[19] In reaction, the people reaffirmed their loyalty to the status quo ante:

Their sentiments for the President of the Republic are particularly enthusiastic . . . People who previously were not particularly fond of President Beneš now refer to him always as 'our President' . . . and take it as a matter of course that he will continue to be head of State after war . . . As for the Germans living in Czechoslovakia . . . [public opinion] is quite unanimous . . . that expelling 'one and all' of them was the popular state of mind.

According to his report to Welles, Hurban's intention was to put Welles on notice at this time for the forthcoming demands of Beneš when peace terms would be discussed.[20]

Exacerbating the situation was the influx into Czech territories of bombed-out German refugees, including some Jews from Carpatho-Russia, who had poured into Czech territories since the beginning of 1943. Although they built their own camps for shelter, they inevitably created a shortage of food, which had been strictly allocated and rationed for the existing population, with nothing to spare. These refugees worsened living conditions for an already alienated population.

Adding salt to the wounds, the German authorities decreed a

forced mobilization of 19-year old Czech youths, including girls, for labor in Germany. Many of these, who sought the help of family physicians through certificates of their inability to perform hard labor, were caught and put to death along with the obliging doctors. Czechs were systematically evacuated from many areas to make way for SS barracks, camps, and warehouses for the increased German presence in the country and for emergency aerodromes built by the government to help German pilots making forced landings at night.

Support of President Beneš overseas was to be found "thoroughly organized in the Czechoslovak National Council of America and its four large root organizations: the Czech-American National Alliance, the Federation of American Slovaks in Texas, the National Alliance of Czech Catholics, and the Slovak National Alliance." The Czech National Council claimed a total supporting membership of 300,000. "The Czech Americans, numbering roughly half a million, will be solidly behind President Beneš and his Government-in-exile," prophesied the head of the Nationalities Branch of the wartime Office of Strategic Services (OSS), in response to a query from the State Department."[21]

The expert went on to analyze the complicated factions among the Slovak-American groups, which were creating disunity in the U.S.-based Czechoslovak camp. The American Slovaks, whose numerical strength approximated that of the American Czechs, were reported on May 5 to be: "split into three tendencies . . . The largest group, demonstrat[ing] . . . hostility toward President Beneš . . . were embodied in the Slovak League," which claimed a membership of some 180,000 and stood for "far-reaching autonomy for Slovakia." The Slovak League, headed by Josef Hušek, was said to be "still carrying out . . . a slightly camouflaged propaganda for a permanent Czech and Slovak divorce." It favored "a federation of Eastern European States calculated to act as a bulwark against Russia, mak[ing] the rebirth of a Czechoslovak state unnecessary and even harmful."[22] These views accorded with those of Archduke Otto of Habsburg, which Beneš naturally opposed as a scheme for Eastern Europe.[23]

As for the Austrian monarchists, the nationalities chief attributed to them "deep-rooted hostility [to] Czechoslovakia . . . The independent Austrians led by Count Ferdinand Czernin and the small wing of Social Democrats share with Rustem Vambery, of the liberal Hungarians and Charles A. Davila of the liberal Romanians a friendly disposition toward the Czechoslovak President . . . As for the attitude of the 3 million Polish Americans," their press has launched "violent attacks on Dr. Beneš and his Government-in-exile." [24]

Milan Hodža was apparently brought to the United States (in 1941) by at least a part of the State Department to solidify American Slovaks behind its policies, which at the time stood for Slovakia's independence from the Czechs. [25] A year later, on June 12, 1942, Hodža talked with Cordell Hull, Welles, and Adolf A. Berle at a meeting in the State Department about Slovakia. He declared that "he had been in touch with various Slovak groups in this country and felt he had made progress in his efforts to convince them that Slovakia should work out its problem *within the framework of the present republic, not as a small independent state.*" This moderation of Hodža's stand might be ascribed to the prevailing views among these top leaders of the State Department, who wanted unity against the Nazi onslaught. Except for the two extremes on the right and the left, including the Communists, who opposed Beneš, Hodža felt that the bulk of the Slovak Americans favored the Czechoslovak government-in-exile. [26] A State Department memorandum acknowledged that

Milan Hodža, Prime Minister at the time of Munich has never collaborated with Dr. Beneš in exile, though he is a member of the State Council. A resident of the U.S. since the fall of 1941, Dr. Hodža has raised the issue of greater autonomy for Slovakia after the war . . . Osuský [in Paris] has begun a pamphleteering campaign against Pres. Beneš . . . [charging him] as a 'tool of Moscow.' [27]

Despite Hodža's optimism about his ability to swing Slovak-American support to Beneš and his government in London, Beneš early in 1943 wrote to Hodža saying that "his current political activities were not in the best interests of the common Czechoslovak cause." [28] What had Beneš been told, to arouse his mistrust of Hodža? He was not privy to the State Department's confidential memorandum. A Beneš-Hodža meeting was palpably indicated soon.

On the occasion of the State Department meeting with Hodža on June 12th, Berle had emphasized that the primary interest of the U.S. government lay in seeing that "our domestic unity was not disturbed by conflicts among the American citizens of different foreign descents regarding Old World problems." This attitude also reflected opinions among Carpatho-Russians in the United States, whose Communists preferred to have the province stay in the Soviet Union. [29] Berle repeated the message to DeWitt C. Poole on September 17th that the "State Department is not at present interested in the merits of the controversy, but it has a distinct interest in preserving that harmony and unity with the best contribution towards winning the war." [30]

A declassified letter two months later reported a Slovak meeting in Pittsburgh to found a new organization called the Slovak Council of Organizations and Newspapers. This signified a break with the Slovak National Alliance which Jan Papánek backed. Poole said that

The mood now . . . is divided . . . Fourteen or fifteen organizations . . . back the new Council . . . The Slovak League was not itself included in the new organization, but some of the League's subsidiaries are . . . The plain fact seems to be that we are confronting a Czechoslovak schism . . . and the new organization may represent a majority of the Slovaks. [31]

The State Department had been reviewing for years its position on recognition of the Czechoslovak government-in-exile. The subject was first broached by Hurban in Washington in October 1939, preceding the formation of any provisional government. Beneš in London, acting as president of the overrun republic, had formally joined the Grand Alliance by declaring war on Germany on September 4, 1939. Coincidentally, Osuský in Paris approached the French government and Beneš talked about it with U.S. Ambassador William C. Bullitt. [32] On February 6, 1941, President Roosevelt submitted to the U.S. Senate for confirmation as ambassador to the Czechoslovak government-in-exile the name of Anthony J. Drexel Biddle, Jr. of Pennsylvania, then also ambassador to Poland's exile committee as well as to the governments-in-exile of Norway, Belgium, and the Netherlands, all congregated in London. The next day, the U.S. Government told the press that it was studying the question of such recognition.

One suggestion advanced to ease this recognition was to declare the Munich Agreement invalid, which would facilitate a return to the status quo ante. Nothing more would be required. Roosevelt stalled for time. He was balancing forces, including the fact that the core of his political support came from the solid bloc of votes in the big industrial cities, which included the ethnic American workers. His path to recognition was eased by the Nazi military occupation of Czechoslovakia on March 15, 1939, which obliterated the accord in any case. The State Department was directed to probe the problem further, which led to the adverse advice by Kennan, quoted in Chapter 12. Meanwhile, Soviet Foreign Minister Molotov concluded a 20-year alliance with Britain's Anthony Eden which they signed on May 26th. This pact of alliance and mutual assistance failed to include recognition of Russia's postwar frontiers. A positive fallout of this treaty was a repudiation of Munich by the British government, news of which was conveyed to Czechoslovak Foreign Minister Masaryk on August 5, 1942. During his visit in London, Molotov assured Beneš "that the

Soviet Union had never had anything to do with Munich and would never recognize any of its consequences," especially respecting the separation and independence of Slovakia and the absorption by Russia of Carpatho-Ruthenia. The pre-Munich borders of Czechoslovakia were virtually underwritten at this time by Molotov. [33]

Ambassador Biddle wrote the State Department about a conversation he had had on June 19, 1942, with Beneš and Hubert Ripka, the Czechoslovak acting foreign minister (during Masaryk's absences), who "had just received word from the Soviet Government to the effect that it would formally recognize the restoration of independent Czechoslovakia within its pre-Munich frontiers." Beneš and his associates assumed this signified also the promise to restore the province of Carpatho-Russia. British recognition had withheld any commitment about frontiers. Now, although "neither President Beneš, nor he [Ripka] . . . was asking postwar territorial commitments," wrote Biddle, "what they earnestly hoped for was our recognition of the pre-Munich political and legal status of Czechoslovakia." Ripka modestly asked for a "favorable consideration" by the U.S. Government. [34]

This information about Soviet intentions was reinforced on August 10, 1942, when Ripka informed Biddle of definite "assurances given them by Molotov that the Soviet Government would formally recognize the restoration of independent Czechoslovakia within its pre-Munich frontiers." Ripka added that a "cardinal condition to a (possible) Czechoslovak-Polish federation was a friendly relationship between the Poles and the Soviet Union." Asked about Czechoslovak attitudes in this matter by Molotov, Ripka gave his return pledge that "Czechoslovakia would not side with Poland against Russia in any difference." [35]

Roosevelt decided affirmatively on October 24, 1942, about recognizing the Czechoslovak government-in-exile, probably in response to Eden's request. Days later, U.S. Secretary of State Hull authorized the "discontinuance by the United States Government of the term 'Provisional' as relating to the Czechoslovak Government established in London." Beneš thanked Roosevelt publicly on November 12th when he addressed the Czechoslovak National Council. Beneš voiced pleasure in underscoring that "Our legal and political relationship with the United States . . . is now . . . the same as with Great Britain." [36]

Hurban called on Welles in Washington early in March 1943, directly upon his return from London, bearing news of Beneš's desire to visit Washington before going to Moscow. Welles was sympathetic and felt certain that "the President would be happy to receive President Beneš, but that the President's engagements" would preclude such a visit before a delay of six weeks, "until some time in May." [37]   Beneš was determined to improve relations with the United States which he felt was required; toward this end, he wished to remove the stumbling blocks among his own peoples in exile there. He was also resolved that his forthcoming trip to Moscow not becloud his Western ties. He wanted Roosevelt's and the State Department's approval of the anticipated arrangements. High on his agenda for this trip was to clear away his misgivings about Hodža.

The State Department protocol office went into high gear to cover the panoply of arrangements required for a state visit. The chief of the nationalities branch of the OSS was directed to prepare a detailed confidential memorandum to brief the President on "Issues Related to the Visit of President Beneš," which was ready on May 5th, a full week before schedule. [38] The questions likely to come up for discussion were thus summarized: (1) Beneš's pro-Russian orientation and (2) His attitude on the postwar political organization of Eastern Europe. The memorandum noted that "the Czechoslovak President finds himself 'a particular target . . . of those who argue for a large Eastern European federation calculated to be strong enough to resist the pressure of either Russia or Germany." [39]

An American friend ascribed Beneš's Russian policy as "rest[ing] on security." He explained: "A small state always stands in need of a large friend, and Russia was that friend and was ready to prove it in 1938, when France and England sold her down the river." [40]

Immediately after the arrival in New York of Beneš and his entourage, which included Jaromír Smutný, the presidents's chef de cabinet, and Edward Táborský, Beneš's secretary, they were packed off in Papánek's car for a weekend in the country because no State Department representatives had come to greet them. The atmosphere changed upon their arrival in Washington on May 12th, when President Roosevelt tendered them a White House dinner, also attended by his military chiefs, political staff, and members of the cabinet and Congress. The political discussions between the two heads of state started over the dinner table and continued well into the night. Beneš was housed in the White House to ease the strain of the extended talk and to protect its privacy.

In the first conference with Roosevelt, Beneš announced his intention to proceed forthwith to Moscow, to conclude a treaty of alliance and cooperation. Beneš had in hand his draft treaty, approved in advance by Moscow, which he submitted for U.S. assent.

The Kremlin had acceded to his insistence that the treaty contain a firm commitment of noninterference in internal affairs. Having foreseen this sticky point in March 1942, discussions had been initiated in London, wherein Beneš, accompanied by Foreign Minister Masaryk and Deputy Foreign Minister Ripka, put precise policy queries to the Soviet ambassador, Alexander Bogomolov. A month later, assurances were forthcoming from Moscow. These were reaffirmed to Beneš before the end of his U.S. visit. A new, moderated orientation of the U.S. administration was mirrored to Beneš in his more detailed talks the following days with both Hopkins and Under-Secretary of State Welles.

Jan Masaryk, who stayed behind in charge in London, related Beneš's cabled reports to him of the talks in Washington: "In the very first long conversation between Dr. Beneš and President Roosevelt a complete agreement of views was reached on all questions affecting Czechoslovakia and her interests." Churchill by coincidence was present in Washington a day before Beneš's arrival. Churchill had come with 100 officials for the Trident Conference, when the Normandy Cross Channel invasion timetable was scheduled for May 1, 1944. Beneš's visit had been set before Churchill's journey had been considerably advanced by the swift development of events in North Africa. Beneš reported on a meeting with the two Allied chiefs on May 17th where the problems of "the future international organization and the guaranteeing of peace and security," as well as postwar Germany, dominated the talks. Although both Big Power leaders expressed an interest in breaking Germany into five or six component states, Beneš emphasized the need to purge Germany of its Nazi elements and to bring them to justice. Disarmament through economic decentralization was of paramount importance, to be followed by thorough democratization of German life and its social structures. [41]

Realizing that Roosevelt was struggling to stand firm for Allied cohesion against the importunities of the strong anti-Soviet faction in the State Department, Beneš urged that the Poles be persuaded to reach a political accommodation with the Kremlin before the Red Army should reach Polish soil and impose a military solution.

Exacerbating the anti-Soviet tensions within the Allied framework was the recent break between the London Poles and the Soviet Union, provoked by the discovery of the Katyn Forest massacre which was being attributed to the Soviets. Beneš was accordingly pleasantly surprised to learn the lengths to which Roosevelt had already moved to accept the Soviet demand for a westward revision of its frontier.

Before his departure from Washington, Beneš also had extended conversations with Hull and Welles to ascertain their "full understanding of Czechoslovak policy . . . and actions." He then conferred to the same end with "the leaders of both American parties in Congress and the Senate." Beneš found agreement within the Roosevelt Administration for "the existence of a strong and independent Czechoslovakia" which had echoes in "public opinion and the American people." [42] He talked also with Vice President Henry Wallace, Treasury Secretary Henry Morgenthau, Secretaries of War and Navy, [Henry] Stimson and [Philander] Knox," as well as various "military, economic, and financial personalities." [43]

Beneš's Washington stay concluded on May 19, 1943, when he entrained for Chicago via New York and Detroit, to revisit Czech and Slovak communities. Throughout the trip, he was sharply questioned about his position and his intentions toward the Soviet Union. Unabashedly, he spoke of his long-held stand advocating close collaboration between East and West, both to win the war and to secure the peace. As a neighbor of Soviet Russia, Czechoslovakia could not avoid adapting its internal and international policy to the overriding imperatives of maintaining friendly relations. He foresaw that the democratic structures of his nation, which had been severely impaired under the Nazi yoke, would require thorough socialization after liberation.

Beneš made a detour into Canada, where he was welcomed by Premier Mackenzie King, whose government had never broken relations with the duly constituted Czechoslovak government, having never recognized the Munich Accord or the succeeding puppet regime at Prague, or the Nazi takeover on March 15, 1939. [44]

While Beneš was on his mid-Western tour, Marshal Stalin announced on May 22nd the dissolution of the Comintern. From the outset, Roosevelt had assured Beneš of his willingness to take Stalin at his word, especially with regard to his new policy of noninterference. Moreover, it soon became clear that the Comintern move would clear the way for the preparation of the inter-allied summit conference, which was necessary to reestablish working confidence and goodwill.

During his visit, Beneš satisfied himself that his views concerning postwar Germany had found acceptance. The Nazi brutality and genocide in Poland and Czechoslovakia necessitated radical counter measures. Roosevelt and his advisers went along with Beneš's strong advocacy of the harsh transfer of German populations out of both East Prussia and Bohemia-Moravia. The Nazi plan to move the

"slave" people of these countries wholesale into the Ukraine demanded drastic revision. After a lifetime of dealings with the German
problem, which had eventually disrupted his country, Beneš was
wholly sympathetic to his people's insistence on expelling them once
and for all, out of their homeland. Beneš found an analogy between
his German problem and that of the Spanish Republic's Fifth Column.
He promoted this solution even at the sacrificial economic cost of
losing the skilled workers who dominated the famed glass-making
industry.

After a brief second round of Washington consultations, Beneš
went to New York to attend a public rally that the authors had
arranged in his honor on May 27th at Carnegie Hall, under the
auspices of the American Friends of Czechoslovakia. The veteran
liberal, William Jay Schieffelin, former chairman of the International
Red Cross, headed the organization. As a close friend of both Mayor
Fiorello La Guardia and President Roosevelt, Schieffelin had chaired
a sponsoring committee comprising anti-Fascist organizational leaders
and prominent opinion makers, and excluding those who had
espoused appeasement. The meeting provided a platform for Beneš's
pro-Soviet foreign policy. It closed with a dramatic script written by
Norman Corwin that memorialized the Czechoslovak resistance's
heroic sacrifices, including the Lidice tragedy, and paid tribute to
Beneš as a key figure in welding the Czechoslovak republic.

Schieffelin had requested his close political colleague, Mayor La
Guardia, to preside at the rally. Although the mayor himself had
welcomed Beneš with open arms at City Hall and again at Gracie
Mansion in the evening, he now courteously begged off and sent his
deputy mayor, Newbold Morris, in his place. It was an open secret in
City Hall circles that the Mayor would find it inopportune to appear
on the same public platform with Beneš, his widely admired friend,
who unfortunately symbolized pro-Soviet cooperation. Likewise, the
Roosevelt Administration dodged Schieffelin's invitation to send
either Secretary of State Hull or his right hand aide, Welles, to honor
Beneš publicly. Elmer Davis, chief of the Office of War Information,
quite far down the State Department's totem pole, a most independent public servant, filled the gap. It took another year of bloody
fighting by the Red Army to turn the tide of the war and, in turn, to
impel the U.S. secretary of state, Edward Stettinius Jr., to address a
great Madison Square celebration of American-Soviet amity.

The Carnegie Hall meeting was a sellout success, turning away a
thousand people for lack of space. With this solid manifestation of
support reported in front-page banner headlines next day, Beneš

returned for his concluding talk with Roosevelt at noon on June 7th. [45]

Beneš expressed satisfaction with his comprehensive review of policies and decisions with Roosevelt and his closest aides, and with congressional and cabinet members too. At the end, Roosevelt expressed pleasure that they had reached a meeting of minds and that he now understood and generally approved the Czechoslovak position, especially vis-à-vis Germany and the Soviet Union. To mark this understanding publicly, the status of representation between them was raised from that of minister of a legation to the rank of ambassador heading an embassy.

Before departing U.S. shores on June 9, 1943, in an Army Transport Command plane with Smutný and Táborský, Beneš penned a fond thank-you note to Roosevelt. He wrote: "I found in your government and in the public opinion, the warmest sympathy for the cause of the Czechoslovak people, and I consider it a great privilege to have been able to witness your great war effort." [46] Roosevelt was not to be outdone in graciousness. He wrote with equal warmth in his bon voyage message to Beneš, aptly reflecting lessons learned, in part: "It has been most useful for us to have been able to consult . . . [as to] the most efficacious means to attain [our] goal . . . the unconditional defeat of the Axis forces . . . My best wishes . . . in your courageous efforts to liberate Czechoslovakia and restore your country and people to freedom and peace." [47]

Beneš departed from the United States, as he reported in successive cables to Jan Masaryk, with the conviction that, short of an alliance and frontier guarantees, Czechoslovakia would be assisted in its reconstitution by the United States.

NOTES

1. National Archives, Washington, D.C., 1218, reel 29.

2. Ibid.

3. Ibid.

4. Ibid.

5. Herman Rauschning, *The Voice of Destruction* (New York: Putnam, 1940), p. 38; quoted in report dated February 1, 1941, National Archives, 1218, reel 29.

6. Irving Linnell, Chargé d'Affaires, U.S. Embassy in Prague, to Secretary of State, National Archives, 1218, reel 29.

7. U.S. Legation, Belgrade to Secretary of State, Washington, D.C., March 27, 1940, no. 927, National Archives, 1218, reel 29.

8. Report from U.S. Embassy, Berlin, September 28, 1941, National Archives, 1218, reel 29.

9. Telegram from U.S. Embassy, Berlin, to Secretary of State, October 2, 1941, National Archives 1218, reel 29.

10. Telegram from U.S. Embassy, Berlin, dated Oct. 1, 1941, National Archives 1218, reel 29.

11. U.S. Embassy, Berlin to Secretary of State, Oct. 4, 1941, National Archives, 1218, reel 29.

12. Report from U.S. Embassy, Berlin, October, 1941, National Archives, 1218, Reel 29.

13. Morris, U.S. Embassy, Berlin to Secretary of State, October 13, 1941, National Archives 1218, reel 29.

14. Dispatch, U.S. Legation, Belgrade, to Secretary of State, March 27, 1940, No. 927, National Archives 1218, reel 29.

15. Memorandum, "The Situation in Czechoslovakia," National Archives 1218, reel 29.

16. Callum MacDonald: *The Killing of SS Obergruppenfuhrer Reinhard Heydrich* (New York: Free Press, Macmillan, 1989).

17. State Dept. Document, re meeting of Ambassador Vladimir Hurban & Acting Secretary of State Sumner Welles, March 8, 1943, Washington, D.C., National Archives 1218, reel 29.

18. Ibid.

19. A.G. Weidenfeld interview with Eduard Benes, May 25, 1944, FO 371/38931-Xc111097.

20. State Dept. Document re meeting of Hurban & Acting Secy of States Welles, March 8, 1943, National Archives 1218, reel 29.

21. Office of Strategic Services (hereafter OSS) report on Czechoslovak National Council in America, National Archives, 1218, reel 29.

22. Memo, Chief Minorities Branch, OSS, May 5, 1943, National Archives 1218, reel 29.

23. Ibid.

24. Ibid.

25. Irving Pflaum, columnist, written during Beneš's visit to the United States in May 1943, National Archives 1218, reel 29.

26. State Dept. Memo re Slovakia, June 18, 1942, National Archives 1218, reel 29.

27. State Dept. memo re meeting of Cordell Hull, Welles, and Adolf Berle with Hodža on June 12, 1942, National Archives, 1218, reel 29.

28. Ibid.

29. State Dept. memo re Slovakia, June 18, 1942, National Archives 1218, reel 29.

30. Letter of Berle to DeWitt Poole, September 17, 1942, National Archives 1218, reel 29.

31.   Letter to Berle November 19, 1942, National Archives 1218, reel 29.

32.   State Dept., Division of European Affairs, "The Question of Recognition of the Czechoslovak Provisional Government in London," October 11, 1946, National Archives 1218, reel 30.

33.   Report of Benes to State Council, February 12, 1944, National Archives 1218, reel 29, p. 23.

34.   Legation of U.S.A. near Provisional Czechoslovak Government in London, June 19, 1942, National Archives 1218, reel 30.

35.   Berle, State Dept., August 10, 1942, National Archives 1218, reel 30.

36.   State Dept. memo re "Public reference to Discontinuance of term 'provisional' by U.S. relating to the Czechoslovak Government established in London," National Archives, 1218, reel 30.

37.   Meeting of Hurban and Welles, March 8, 1943, National Archives 1218, reel 29.

38.   Memo, Nationalities Chief, OSS, May 5, 1943, National Archives 1218, reel 29.

39.   Ibid.

40.   William Zabransky, Jr. letter in *Bergen Evening Record*, Hackensack, N.J., March 31, 1943, National Archives 1218, reel 29.

41.   Jan Masaryk report to the Czechoslovak State Council, May 19, 1943.

42.   Ibid.

43.   Beneš report to the Czechoslovak State Council, London, February 12, 1944, p.15, National Archives 1218, reel 29.

44.   Ibid.

45.   State Dept., Division of Protocol, May 26, 1943, Franklin Delano Roosevelt (hereafter FDR) Library, Hyde Park, N.Y.

46.   FDR Library.

47.   FDR Letter to Beneš, June 8, 1943, FDR Library.

14

Wartime Conferences and Treaties

President Eduard Beneš's original plan on returning from Washington to London in June 1943 had been to proceed directly to Moscow. Both Roosevelt and Churchill had unreservedly recognized that Czechoslovakia could not avoid having a special relationship with her large, powerful neighbor to the east. They had approved the terms of the projected alliance that Beneš had drawn, also with Soviet consent, in April 1943. It was, moreover, a natural concomitant of the Anglo-Russian accord. The terms included Moscow's guarantee of the full sovereignty and unqualified independence of Czechoslovakia, with a pledge of noninterference. The agreement was eased by the absence of any frontier dispute. Declaring itself content to stay on its side of the Carpathian Mountains, Moscow had apparently accepted the return of the Carpatho-Ukrainian province of Czechoslovakia called Ruthenia. Stalin had also complied with the strong desire of Beneš for the transfer of the Sudeten German population out of the country, and "like Britain and the U.S., has assented to the trials of the Nazi war criminals following the war."[1]

Beneš fashioned his policies on the premise that the Grand Alliance would continue to be operative into the postwar period. He hoped that his treaty with Moscow would serve as a model for other Soviet neighbors and constitute an anti-German bulwark against any recurrence of the irresistible *Drang Nach Osten*. He further hoped that Polish adherence to the Treaty with Russia would be possible and would complete the line of security against another German attempt at hegemony in the east.

During the intervening months, however, Beneš encountered

"objections in English circles" to his Moscow mission, necessitating "its postponement for the time being."[2] The objections, he discovered, emanated from the Foreign Office as well as the U.S. State Department, where potent factions in both cases disliked his policy of friendship toward the Soviet Union, as prejudicial to the Polish cause. Beneš thought he had dispelled this attitude during his talks in Washington, but the opposition persisted.

Beneš had cause for haste in his Moscow mission. He well realized that further delay would expose him to the peril of having a rival provisional government set up there around the Czechoslovak communist refugees in residence. Of this possibility, he had in fact fair warning from his vacillating ambassador, Zdeněk Fierlinger. Only a few months earlier, the Union of Polish Patriots had been transformed into the Lublin Committee, the communist government body that later moved intact into Poland.

At a meeting on September 24, 1943, the government took "cognizance of Jan Masaryk's report on the imminent Soviet-Czechoslovak treaty of alliance [and] of Beneš's projected official visit to Moscow," which was heralded as being "in the interests both of the United Nations and of the Czechoslovak Republic . . . and of its certain and rapid reconstruction after the war, as well as to insure future peace especially in Central Europe." The British government was pleased "with the amicable and sympathetic understanding of the two governments concerned." Approval of the proposed treaty by the British Government on July 16th was unanimous, followed by approval by the Czechoslovak state council on July 22, 1943. British Foreign Secretary Anthony Eden stated in the House of Commons on September 22nd that he hoped to discuss this subject with Molotov at the forthcoming Moscow conference of foreign ministers when it would convene in October.[3]

The Big Three ministers' conference, which met in Moscow on October 29, 1943, as a necessary prelude to the summit meeting soon to follow, marked the apogee of Soviet-Western collaboration. Stalin's suspicions of Western collusion against Soviet Russia were dispelled at Teheran, especially by Roosevelt, who chaired the sessions that commenced on November 23, 1943, and who steered decisions to maximize Allied unity. Roosevelt liked Stalin and told the American people so in his Christmas Eve broadcast, 1943, when he said, "I believe we are going to get along very well with him and the Russian people—very well indeed."[4] The official postconference declaration emphasized the unity theme: "We came here with hope and determination. We leave here friends in fact, in spirit and in purpose."[5] Stalin reciprocated with confidence in F. D. R.'s perspicacity and sincerity. No general plan emerged from the deliberations, however, for cooperative measures in Eastern Europe, except in the case of Yugoslavia, where Churchill had reinforced his liaison and parachute drops to Tito's communist partisans.

The timing of Beneš's official visit to Moscow could not have been more propitious. The prospects for Allied solidarity shone brightly on the eve of his arrival there, with the text of his approved treaty of alliance in hand. He intended to negotiate the terms of his country's liberation not only with Marshal Stalin, but also with the Czechoslovak Communist leaders, Klement Gottwald and Rudolf Slánský.

Beneš arrived with several other assets in hand. He was universally recognized as chief of state, with a broadly based functioning government-in-exile, the political composition of which was acceptable to all the Big Power leaders. He led an army and air force that had made significant if modest contributions to the common war effort. He was assured of Western political and financial backing for the reconstitution of the state, and Britain, since March 1939, had been sustaining his government-in-exile. Lastly, the United States and Britain had assented to his plan to expel the German minority from the Sudetenland and to bring the Nazi war criminals to trial and punishment after the war.

Deducing from his people's history and tradition justification of his negative attitude toward Germany in presenting his case, he declared persuasively that "his country for centuries had suffered from the Germans, had always fought them, and would always fight them to maintain their independence."[6] He ascribed his more recent hostility toward Germany to Hitler's atrocious extermination campaign against the Slavs, "second only to that of the Jews."[7] He thus rationalized the focus of his pro-Soviet foreign policy on reducing to "the greatest extent possible the German danger in the future," whether by "disarmament, by control of German heavy industry, or [even possibly] by partition." He had imparted these suggestions in Washington to both Roosevelt and Churchill, who had courted them and had listened sympathetically. But, after all, they were situated at some distance from Germany, in contrast to Czechoslovakia's proximity.[8]

Beneš's attitude toward Poland was friendlier than previously, despite the historic border dispute over Teschen. He thought the joint domination of Poland and Czechoslovakia by Germany adumbrated their differences. As he saw the future, both countries would be attacked in the event of another attempt by Germany. "If the

Bohemian bastion is supported by Poland and above all by Russia, Germany can never again make war in Europe." This threat was for him paramount to postwar security in Central Europe. He repeatedly expressed confidence subsequently that "Poland eventually [will] enter the Czechoslovak-Soviet Pact." [9]

In Stanislaw Mikolajczyk, premier of the Polish government-in-exile in London, Beneš saw "a man with whom they [all of the Allies] could do business." The Soviet government had made it clear that before treating with the Polish government, they expected it to be reconstituted without Gen. Sosnowski and the anti-Soviet elements supporting him.* Moreover, Beneš thought that "the Soviet Government would probably accept Mikolajczyk as head of the Government, but it would have to include representatives of elements in the USSR and from Poland itself." [10]

The twenty-year treaty of alliance and friendship between Czechoslovakia and the USSR was signed in the Kremlin on December 12, 1943, the day following Beneš's arrival in Moscow. No further negotiations were required, as all the provisions had been cleared in advance. At the official banquet tendered by Stalin, Czechoslovak leaders of every political stripe were included among the distinguished guests. Beneš told the British ambassador afterwards that he thought "the Moscow and Teheran Conferences had evidently had a profound influence on the outlook of the Soviet Government. He found the atmosphere in Moscow completely changed from . . . 1935." He detected a "spirit of confidence and national pride . . . free from any signs of revolutionary exclusiveness . . . or any wish to interfere with systems differing from their own." [11]

Beneš's first week in Moscow was spent in official talks with Stalin at which Foreign Minister Vyacheslav Molotov and Defense Minister Klementy Voroshilov were present. Beneš was always accompanied by Ambassador Fierlinger and the secretary general of his ministry, Jaromír Šmutny. After their first survey, Beneš emerged, sustained by a feeling of shared objectives. He was convinced of the sincerity of Stalin's pledge of autonomy and noninterference, not only for his country, but also for other peoples of Eastern Europe, especially for the Poles, Ukrainians, and Byelorussians and for all Slavic peoples, who had "for centuries suffered the threat of German Imperialism." [12] Beneš would explain later to Anthony Eden that his

---

*Sosnowski was relieved as successor-designate to the presidency of Poland in June 1944. He was dismissed as commander-in-chief of the Polish Army on Sept. 30, 1944. *Foreign Relations*, 4 (1944): 995.

"Slavonic Policy" had nothing to do with the prerevolutionary concept of pan-Slavism, but "only in future collaboration to prevent any renewal of aggression." [13]

Manifestly at the hub of all official talks was the problem of Germany and its border with Czechoslovakia. The matters for discussion included the postwar frontiers, the transfer of the Sudeten population, and the purging of Nazi elements. Radical decentralization in the state structures of Czechoslovakia would also be required to accommodate the minority national aspirations. Beneš would not brook a "repetition of the treachery of our Slovak Fascists, and of their treasonable separation of Slovakia from the Republic in the service of barbarous German violence." He envisaged a thorough democratization of the social structures and political institutions of his regime and projected changes "in our new State [to be] carried out very quickly . . . in accordance with a previously prepared programme of a systematic, well thought out and scientifically prepared first Five Year Plan." [14]

Later, during a two-hour luncheon in London with U.S. Ambassador Averell Harriman, Beneš expanded on the economic section of his summary. He depicted the postwar economy as being mixed, with state ownership of the large munitions industry, especially the Škoda works, which had been seized by the Nazis to nourish their war machine. Cooperative ownership of productive property would be combined with private ownership of consumer goods industries. "Large landed estates will be broken up and sold to peasants . . . Private ownership of farms will be recognized and no pressure will be exerted to collectivize . . . The National Front government [was slated] to last for the first election period of six years," and the government would take responsibility for "employment and other social reforms." [15]

In his broadcast to the homeland afterward, on December 21, 1943, Beneš trumpeted optimistically: "Czechoslovakia is on the right path and in the right camp . . . of military victory and victorious peace." He prodded his countrymen to "contribute as much as possible toward this victory . . . [to] reconquer our national and State freedom . . . in collaboration with the Soviet Union and with all the Allied nations." [16]

As he had done in the States, Beneš made a long tour outside the capital to survey the war-torn countryside and its exhausted people. He spent half of his two weeks in Moscow in six successive talks with the Czechoslovak Communists, particularly with Gottwald and Slánský, although all the others with any standing in the Communist camp outside the country were assembled there. The Communists at that time estimated "that the impact of the Nazi regime in Europe [had] set back by at least half a century the time [when] Communism would be generally accepted." They were reported as realizing "that for the time being, they had no chance of converting Socialists, Agrarians, and others to their point of view and they thought that the Czechs' need at this moment was for national consolidation." So thought a staff officer of the British embassy attached to the Czechoslovak government-in-exile, who added in his report to the Foreign Office: "They were prepared when the moment was ripe to enter the Government. Meanwhile, they would collaborate cordially with it from the outside." [17]

The negotiations concluded that the projected postwar cabinet would include the Communists, but this move was still premature within the Allied framework. Beneš reported this point explicitly later, saying that "amicable talks with the Czechoslovak Communist leaders in the Soviet Union . . . [about] their participation . . . should not take place until the war was nearing its end." [18] Beneš asserted "They clearly undertook to accept for its [postwar] policy and its economic life the system of planning, as certain of our economists endeavored to do before the present war." [19]

Beneš repeated his assurances to British Ambassador Philip Nichols "that during the whole of his 15 days in Moscow, the Russians had never once mentioned to him the question of the inclusion of Communists in his Government, or indeed, any other aspect of Czechoslovak internal affairs." [20]

Beneš underscored the same message to Eden, saying, "The Soviet Government had shown no interest . . . in the proposed inclusion of Communist representatives in the Czechoslovak Government . . . Never during the talks . . . had any Soviet personage shown the slightest wish to influence him regarding the future ordering of Czechoslovak internal affairs." In conclusion, he explained: "The Soviet Government understood that whilst Czechoslovakia had its Alliance with the USSR, it also had bonds with the United Kingdom and the United States, and so must look both ways." [21]

In a subsequent interview, Beneš affirmed: "As regards the future of Czechoslovakia . . . all major problems had already been settled in principle. The cornerstone of the future Czech policy was the treaty signed at Moscow, as the Soviets would no doubt be the principal factor in the new Europe." With the Soviets, he reported, "he had come already to an arrangement with [their representatives] on the basis of wide autonomy to be enjoyed by Slovaks within the boundaries of a common state." A self-styled Slovak leader living in Cairo revealed gratuitously "that a postwar Government had largely been designated . . . [to] take over immediately on the expulsion of the enemy from their country." The government designate, consisting of 15 members, would include only four cabinet ministers of the present government in London. It would also contain two members of the Czech Communist Party. [22]

The postwar party system would be overhauled and consolidated, made "more humane and democratic, and simple." They would "create a new party system consisting of only three parties: a party of the Left, [one] of the Centre, and a Conservative Party." [23] Beneš made no secret of the fact that "he did not share Communist ideas." He had frankly stated at an interview to the correspondent of *Pravda*, which was subsequently published, that he, Beneš, was not a Communist, but that he respected other people's ideas, and that in postwar Czechoslovakia, the Communists would enjoy the same facilities as other parties. [24]

As the discussions proceeded with his Communist compatriots, Beneš encountered increasingly sharp criticism of himself. They took him to task for his collaboration post-Munich with the Emil Hácha regime before the occupation of Prague, which in effect had split the Resistance movement. He was rebuked also for resigning office in 1938 and for capitulating to the Munich Diktat. They declared that he should have stood his ground and accepted the military assistance offered by the Soviet Union, and heeded its later invitation to create national headquarters in Moscow.

Beneš met the charges about the Munich capitulation squarely, arguing that he had done everything in his power in 1938 to rally the backing of England and France against the Nazi threat. He had twice mobilized the armed forces, but without the united support from both West and East, resisting German aggression would have brought national ruin. This course, he insisted, had prevented the destruction of the country and averted the civil war that was now wracking both Poland and Yugoslavia.

Both sides to the heated debate held firmly to their positions, and the Communists went further to observe that there was still no assurance that liberation might not preclude a civil war. Beneš would do everything possible to forestall such a development. He assured them "he had no intention of bringing" his present Government back to Czechoslovakia after the war. He amplified his report: "The Government would be reconstituted, two-thirds of its future members coming from the home population, and only one-third from the émigrés." Beneš told Nichols confidentially "that he intended to work towards bringing [the Communists] into the present Administration . . . The Socialists would very much prefer to see the Communists in than out of it; for inside they would have to take some responsibility for the unpopular measures which will have to be introduced, while outside they can always attack the Socialists, while disclaiming all responsibility." [25]

Beneš and Gottwald both foresaw the threat ahead of a social revolution. In the interim, they accorded on the formation of an anti-Fascist coalition government, a cooperative prospect that would be realized two years later. The Communists started with proposing that they be assigned the portfolio of prime minister. Beneš retorted that this would depend on whether they were the strongest party in a democratic election, and he added that "even if they were . . . he would still advise them not to ask" for the top post. Next day, they agreed to take his advice. [26]

In stark contrast to Beneš's satisfaction with the results at Moscow, the reaction in Washington was reported as "on the whole . . . very cool except among the liberals . . . The official attitude of the State Department [was] unenthusiastic but noncommittal . . . Their private opinion appears to be definitely hostile." A nit-picking objection to the Czechoslovak-Soviet treaty was detected at the British embassy in Washington, which mirrored State Department opinion against "a revival of old-fashioned power politics . . . in favor of some system of general security," as if the general security were thwarted by the treaty of alliance. The prestigious *New York Times* columnist Anne O'Hare McCormack, speaking generally as unofficial mouthpiece of the State Department, also criticized the treaty as a "return to a system that failed to work." She claimed "that it did not fit in with the aim of the United States Government to build up a peace structure founded on a 4-Power Pact . . . [rendering] bi-lateral arrangements . . . unnecessary."

Walter Lippmann, on the other hand, saw no incompatibility between the new pact and a security system. He defended the treaty, pointing out that "the United States have signed pacts of mutual assistance with Canada, Mexico, and other States . . . [even if] the State Department policy under Cordell Hull was seen to promote the creation of a system of general security." Although Lippmann conceded to the opposition the point that "the Treaty just signed fails to provide any article of reference . . . to general security or the United Nations," he approved of the treaty, according to a British embassy report in Washington. [27]   U.S. Ambassador Harriman in

Moscow extolled the "wise policy of the Soviet Government" for Allied cooperation. [28]

The British Foreign Office had "felt some doubts about the expediency of the treaty on the score that it might (a) contribute to divide Europe into Eastern and Western zones of influence and (b) isolate the Poles." However, in view of the draft treaty provision for eventual "Polish accession," their objections, undoubtedly tempered by Eden, were dropped. On December 15th, Eden had made a supportive speech in Parliament applauding "this agreement against German aggression between two of [our] Allies . . . particularly as it provided for the adherence of neighboring countries." [29]

On the home front in Czechoslovakia, it was reliably reported: "The signing of the Czechoslovak-Soviet Pact produced a most favourable impression, [and generated] no criticism whatever." Good results were anticipated, and Beneš's reputation "reached a high pitch." The pact was said to have wrought "still more consolidated cooperation among all political elements," and the chances accelerated for "a positive response to the call for revolt." The pro-German regime of Karl Frank made efforts to initiate an anti-Beneš smear campaign through the newly formed Anti-Bolshevik League, but the poisonous seeds failed to sprout in the arid atmosphere. [30]

While Beneš traveled east to sign his treaty with the Soviet Union, Jan Masaryk went west to Washington, where he had been summoned for two interviews with President Roosevelt. The President told Masaryk that at Teheran he had urged Stalin to "take some action which would make the acceptance of the frontiers . . . claimed by the Soviet Union more palatable to American public opinion." FDR thought that "'the Soviet Government's recent Constitutional reform [giving] the Constituent Republics . . . increased autonomy were at least partly designed with this end in view.' Masaryk made it plain that a number of Poles in the United States had been behaving very foolishly and making things more difficult for everybody." He thought that although "the British people were grateful to Russia . . . towards winning the war . . . they did not like the attitude the Russians were adopting towards Poland, [objecting] more, partly over the question of the composition of the Polish Government . . . [and] leading some people to question the validity of Russian pledges of non intervention in Czechoslovakia." Masaryk for his part, thought that "the Western Powers must now do something for Czechoslovakia to offset the influence the Russians might be expected to obtain." Masaryk returned to London on February 11, 1944, and reported these exchanges to Ambassador Nichols the following day. [31]

In Washington, DeWitt Poole wrote he had been informed that Jan Masaryk would "jump at a practical alternative to Beneš' Russian policy." When challenged by the press on a possible rupture with Beneš, Masaryk disclaimed any differences with Beneš on policy and explained that "Beneš and I simply work by different methods." [32]

In London, it was widely agreed that "without exception, Eastern Europe . . . from Poland to Greece . . . cannot plan their future in opposition to Russia. Each of them is thinking of the best way to create a basis for friendly relations." A British diplomat suggested, "It might be better, in view of the necessary reconstruction funds and increased postwar trade, had the pact also included England and America." A Czechoslovak official replied that they were ready to move that way, but "it is you [British] who are unwilling." At all events, they agreed that the "new Czechoslovakia is preeminently qualified to act as the economic bridge between the West and the East." [33]

Beneš, at a special meeting of his State Council convened on February 3, 1944, summarized his report on Moscow, saying in part:

The year of 1943 was a very successful one in our work of liberation. Internationally, we have attained our ends, or almost achieved them. At home, the nation . . . is united, firm, and brave, quite ready for a Republican Constitution . . . In all the chief political questions . . . there will be no great differences of opinion . . . regarding the future democratic organization of the Republic, or our future social and economic plans and aims, or the relations between Czechs or Slovaks, or any other fundamental problem of the future life of the Republic . . . [even if] conditions will be difficult. [34]

Beneš described his expectations for a secure Europe as requiring "four main pillars: Great Britain, the United States, the Soviet Union, and France. A full understanding [among] the Powers would make a third war with Germany impossible. The days of Soviet Russia's exclusion from European affairs," he said, "were over, and he hopes that they would never return." He reassured his listeners at a luncheon of the City of London Livery Club, held on February 19, 1944, that "the Czechoslovaks had not in the past been afraid of Russia, faced as they were, by the constant German menace, and they did not believe that the Soviet Union today had any designs on their territory or their democratic way of life. Nor, he was convinced, did Soviet Russia intend to dominate Europe." In fact, he saw Czechoslovakia as a "link between Western Europe and the East [which] could never be purely Western or purely Eastern in its outlook. "As to France, he placed his hopes on the Free French forces led by Gen. Charles DeGaulle. He believed "that the refusal to recognize the status of liberated France as a Great Power would be as dangerous as the past refusal to recognize the Soviet Union . . . A strong France was universally needed on the European Continent."[35]

Beneš took the occasion of being in transit after quitting Moscow to detour to Algiers for a day on January 1st, 1944, and pay a call on General DeGaulle and his Free French Committee. These politicians, despite their meager resources, "put themselves out considerably . . . to give him an impressive welcome." On their part, they had much to gain in befriending Beneš; they were said to be "also playing strongly for a resumption of the close tie-up with the Czechoslovaks."[36] Happily, the British Foreign Office was in full accord as to "the restoration of a strong France and of close ties between France and Czechoslovakia."[37]

The Free French, however, were still far off in North Africa, while the Red Army was steadily slogging its way westward and destined to approach Prague the soonest. Everyone, whether at home under the Nazi heel or keeping the vigil in London, took heart after the stunning defeat of the Germans at Stalingrad, believing that the Russian armies represented the best hope for liberation of Czechoslovakia.

Beneš left little to chance, or to the magnanimity of the hard-fighting Red Army. He did his best in the treaty of alliance to ascertain that his people would not trade another army of occupation for the brutish one on the threshold of eviction. He obtained assurances in advance from the potential liberators that the Czechoslovak provinces would be administered by locally designated units. His clarion call for revolt was calculated to demonstrate graphically to the world Czechoslovakia's right to be treated as an Allied nation.

NOTES

1. Rudolf Schoenfeld, Chargé d'Affaires, U.S. Embassy, London, to Secretary of State, January 13, 1944, *Foreign Relations* 1944, v. 4, p. 804.

2. Standley, Moscow, to Secretary of State, August 12, 1943, National Archives, Washington, D.C. 1218, reel 29.

3. British Government meeting, London, September 24, 1943, National Archives, 1218, Document 860F001/171, reel 29.

4. Robert E. Sherwood, *Roosevelt and Hopkins* (New York: Harpers, 1948), p. 804.

5. Ibid., p. 798.

6. Wilson, Algiers, to Secretary of State, January 4, 1944, National Archives, 1218, reel 29.

7. Eduard Beneš's conversation with Anthony Eden re Moscow visit, London, January 14, 1944, FO 371/v. 38920-Xc/111097.

8. Ibid.

9. Wilson, Algiers, to Secretary of State and Under-Secretary of State, January 3, 1944, National Archives, 1218, Reel 29.

10. Beneš's conversation with Eden, January 14, 1944, FO 371/v. 38920-Xc/111097. Also *Foreign Relations*, 1944, v. 4, p. 995, footnote.

11. Wilson, Algiers, to Secretary of State, January 15, 1944, National Archives, 1218 reel 29.

12. British Embassy to Czechoslovak Republic, London, January 11, 1944, FO 371/v. 38920-Xc/111097.

13. Beneš's conversation with Eden re his visit to Moscow, January 14, 1944, FO 371/v. 38920-Xc/111097.

14. Text of Beneš's speech broadcast from Moscow to Czechoslovakia, December 21, 1943, FO 371/v. 38920-Xc/111097.

15. Ibid.

16. Ibid.

17. Godfrey Lias to Philip Nichols and Frank Roberts, London, January 26, 1944, FO 371/v. 38931-Xc/111097.

18. Nichols to Frank Roberts, British Embassy to Czechoslovak Republic, January 27, 1944, FO 371/v. 38931-Xc/111097.

19. Memo prepared by Czechoslovak Ministry of Foreign Affairs for Beneš's speech to Czechoslovak State Council, February 12, 1944. Copy to U.S. Embassy, filed under Czechoslovak Series, No 92, National Archives 1218, reel 29.

20. Nichols to Frank Roberts, January 27, 1944, FO 371/v. 38931-Xc/111097.

21. Beneš's conversation re his visit to Moscow. Substance of agreement, summarized by Averell Harriman to Secretary of State, from Moscow, January 14, 1944, FO 371/v. 38920-Xc/111097; also National Archives 1218, reel 30, January 7, 1944.

22. British Embassy, Cairo, Interview of Beneš with Dr. Chok, self-styled leader of Slovaks in Venezia Giulia, January 19, 1944, FO 371/v. 38931-Xc/111097.

23. Beneš speech to State Council convened on February 3, 1944, p. 48 in report from U.S. Embassy, London, February 12, 1944, London Series, No. 92, National Archives 1218, reel 29.

24. Interview of Beneš with Dr. Chok, British Embassy, Cairo, January 19, 1944, FO 371/38932/Xc/111097.

25. Nichols to Roberts, February 27, 1944, FO 371/v. 38931, Xc/111097.

26. Ibid.

27. British Embassy, Washington, D.C., December 28, 1943, FO 371/v. 38920-Xc/111097.

28. Harriman, Moscow, to Secretary of State, December 20, 1943, National Archives, 1218, reel 29.

29. Foreign Office to Resident Minister, Algiers, December 30, 1943, FO 371/v. 38920-Xc/111097.

30. Report of effect of Czechoslovak-Soviet Pact at home, National Archives, 1218, reel 29.

31. Nichols to Roberts, February 14, 1944, FO 371/v. 38920-Xc/111097.

32. DeWitt Poole report on Jan Masaryk to State Dept., *Foreign Relations* 1944, v. 3, p. 1280, footnote 740.00119, European War, 1939/2659.

33. Notes of a conversation, Ladislav Feierabend and Henry Andrews, February 10, 1944, FO 371/v. 38920-Xc/111097.

34. Beneš speech to State Council, February 3, 1944, National Archives, 1218, reel 29, p. 52.

35. Schoenfeld, Chargé d'Affaires, U.S. Embassy, London, to Secretary of State, National Archives 1218, reel 29.

36. Wilson, Algiers, to Secretary of State, January 3, 1944, National Archives, 1218, reel 29.

37. Foreign Office to Resident Minister Wilson, Algiers, December 30, 1943, FO 371/v. 38920-Xc/111097.

15

The Slovak Uprising:
The Government's
Return Home

Eduard Beneš's call to arms for anti-German action at home, following the completion of his treaty of alliance and friendship with Soviet Russia, led promptly to sprucing up the resistance. The broadcast caused "much excitement and enthusiasm among the Slovak people," and according to reports from home became "the sole topic of conversation in Slovakia." It was deemed a matter of "historic significance for [the] country and brought a still more consolidated cooperation among all political elements." The "call for revolt will be fulfilled," prophesied an informant, especially when the "Second Front is opened [and] the Russians approach our frontiers."[1] Another intelligence source, "a prominent Czechoslovak politician" who "enjoys authority and confidence in all walks of public life . . . and belongs to the inner circle . . . cooperating with Pres. Beneš," said unmistakably that "all the leaders of the underground movement in the Czech territories and in Slovakia have mutually unified their present activities and their political programme."[2]

The immediate fruit of the reaction was the formation during Christmas week of 1943 of the Slovak National Council, which naturally gained Beneš's prompt endorsement upon his return to London. The council represented a rudimentary coalition of the Slovak Communist Party, still semiautonomous from the Klement Gottwald organization in Moscow, and a group of Masaryk-Beneš adherents, comprising all partisan leaders hostile to the Josef Tiso regime, who ultimately banded together as the Democratic Party. This promising embryo of a future provincial government soon polarized, however, into left and moderate segments.

The latest intelligence report from home informed the government that "the former political groupings have completely disappeared. The nation is not divided . . . according to parties and social classes," but according to patriots and "a handful of renegades." The report said further that "profound depression [resulted] in government circles," who wishfully posed a possibility of "a compromise peace," wherein "the Germans [could] retain their hold on Austria and Bohemia." Karl Frank was desperately seeking some acceptable formula to forestall hostile partisan activity.

Rudolf Beran, president of the Agrarian Party, was released from detainment along with some hundred other Agrarians, who had been sentenced to eight years or less, after negotiations by Frank with the Agrarian Party, which comprised the most conservative political elements in the country. Because Emil Hácha was "showing extreme symptoms of senile decay," unable to "sit down or stand up without physical support," Beran was offered a post in the projected "new edition of the Second Republic." He declined, and the others followed suit.

The remission of the sentences was conditioned upon the group's joining in the League Against Bolshevism.[3] This was an important center of the anti-Beneš front, launched at home "under the slogan of the struggle against Bolshevism." The League, beamed to attract the small farmers to membership, spearheaded "a whispering propaganda," which originated with the Germans, spreading "the rumor that those who refused to join will be punished by confiscation of their food ration card . . . Public employees [teachers, professors, and prominent civil servants] will probably join the League . . . and [were] counselled to occupy leading positions in it."[4] Private intelligence reports remarked that government circles "are convinced . . . that Germany's defeat is inevitable . . . Especially Catholic clericals . . . fear . . . that Russia may swallow up the Slovak Republic and incorporate it in the Soviet Union."[5]

The National Council positioned itself at secret headquarters, "well concealed from the Gestapo," at Banská Bystrica in central Slovakia. "This industrial town of 15,000 inhabitants, situated on the river Hron, is the geographical centre of Slovakia," which was probably "one of the chief reasons why it had become the headquarters of the National Council and the Patriotic Forces."[6] By general consent, a non-Communist former national army colonel, Ján Golián, took command of the new unified Slovak resistance force. The force grew quickly among patriots and even attracted defectors from the Hlinka Guards. By all accounts there was good reason for popular disaffection toward the Tiso government's military arrangements under the Germans.

Gen. Ferdinand Čatloš, the Slovak minister of war, complained to an acquaintance secretly in touch with the London-based government:

The Germans are treating the Slovak units in the Eastern Front badly . . . being sent to Russia . . . for garrison purposes, or for guarding the railways, and were . . . accordingly equipped only with rifles. Then, without any previous warning from the German commander to the Slovak commander, these units were sent to the front lines, where, of course, they were almost wiped out . . . This had a very bad effect on Slovak public opinion, and caused . . . the position of the government to deteriorate.

The general also thought "that Germany was unable to hold out on the Eastern Front, [a view that] was shared by other well-informed Slovak military quarters." [7]

On February 23, 1944, President Beneš proclaimed the Resistance forces under Colonel Golián as the First Czechoslovak Army. In his broadcast to the nation, he set forth guidelines for the Slovak National Council, stressing its unitary mission. On March 17th, Beneš addressed the Czechoslovak Brigade in Great Britain: "I expect that within the next few days, or possibly weeks, there will be very important developments at home . . . We have to accomplish an anti-German revolution at home . . . [in] the form of open revolt." [8]

During his talks in Moscow, Beneš had foreseen the need of effective coordination between his nationals and the Red Army, which would be liberating his homeland. He requested that the Czechoslovak units fighting with the Russians be integrated into the liberating force and be left behind to function as a domestic militia when the Russians advanced beyond. At the same time in London, Gen. Sergěj Ingr, commander-in-chief of the Czechoslovak forces, would soon beat at British doors, demanding that "the Czechoslovaks should be given an active employment" in anticipation of questions to be thrown at them about their fighting role "when the war was on and [they] entered Prague . . . if only to offset to some degree the victories of the Red Army and of the Czechoslovak troops accompanying them in the east." [9] Beneš thought a plan of "effective cooperation with the Allied Commander-in-Chief" could be achieved by appointing a Slovak delegate to headquarters. The self-constituted local administrative units would be directed to inform the army commanders of their desires and needs. He also devised an exchange of military missions between his own leaders and the Red Army's. On his return to London, Beneš requested permission for Czechoslovak aviators serving with the British Air Force to return to Czechoslovakia upon liberation to serve there with the army units in "necessary and valuable duties . . . assisting the legal authorities, the police and the gendarmerie." In the war zones, episodes could arise and develop into hostilities, which he was intent on avoiding. [10]

Beneš took advantage of the presence in London of Under-Secretary of State Edward Stettinius, Jr. late in April to send a message to President Roosevelt assuring him "that he had made no agreements or commitments when he was in Moscow and that the Czech situation is exactly as . . . when he was last in Washington." He anticipated that "our operations" during the summer "would be a brilliant success, and that the Russian moves would be in tune." He felt that the German Army "could not stop the invasion." Beneš confided that "he had told his wife the day before that they would be back in their country this coming September." Beneš's optimism patently outran reality. The intelligence reports may also have been inflated. [11]

Moscow newspapers for May 9th announced a formal agreement signed in London on the 8th by the Soviet ambassador to Czechoslovakia, Victor Lebedov, and the Czechoslovak acting foreign minister, Hubert Ripka, detailing relations between the Czechoslovak administration and the Soviet commander-in-chief after the entry of Soviet troops into Czechoslovak territory, but the draft agreement had already been announced by Andrei Vishinsky on April 30th. Both Jan Masaryk, speaking from Philadelphia, and Ripka in London assured London and the world of their confidence "with the attitude of the Soviet Government toward the wishes of the Czechs and toward Czech laws." [12] A lead article in *Izvestia* said that this agreement had been cleared with the British and U.S. governments, which had been consulted in advance. [13]

The Patriotic Forces in Czechoslovakia were readying themselves for action in response to Beneš's call for open revolt, taking note that the Red Army was "only" 120 miles away. On March 14th, the fifth anniversary of the German occupation of Prague, Beneš renewed his call for "armed groups to go over from passive to active resistance." [14] The Germans were likewise preparing to meet the threatening invasion of the advancing Red Army and ordered "a partial German occupation in Slovakia . . . [concentrated] in the eastern end of the country as far as Presov." The Germans took control of all transport facilities, but Slovak civil administration was untouched and liaison officers were appointed to it by the German military. "The Slovak Government recommended the evacuation of Bratislava, but the people would not move out, although they sent the children away." [15]

There was another crackdown in Northern Moravia, where "the Germans arrested about 2,500 persons suspected of being members of the underground movement." [16] That was June 1944, when news flashed to London that Kamil Krofta, the former foreign affairs minister in the republic had been "confined in Pankrac prison in March." [17] In September, a disturbing report informed London: "There are a number of Czech and Moravian areas from which the German occupation authorities have driven out the entire Czech population. All adult Germans are receiving firearms and 525 rounds of ammunition." [18]

A chance event that precipitated the completion of the German military occupation of Slovakia occurred on August 25, 1944. A partisan unit operating near Turčiansky Svätý Martin, 50 miles north of Banská Bystrica, intercepted a through train on the main line from the east. Passengers' papers were routinely checked, and their valuables were confiscated. Last to descend was a group of 28 German general staff officers being evacuated from Bucharest following its fall to the Red Army. Without awaiting instructions from headquarters in response to a wire, the local partisan leader ordered the arrest of the officers, confining them in the town barracks for the night. Upon their attempted escape, the German officers were rounded up and executed to the last man.

Hitler's reaction was swift and harsh. The next day, two German divisions descended on Slovakia to punish the partisans and occupy the puppet state, a military step he had delayed, largely due to more serious preoccupations elsewhere. At the time, the Soviet and German armies were still bogged down north of the Carpathians.

President Beneš in London took equally prompt action to mobilize support for his embattled Slovak resistance forces against this German reprisal. His chief of staff, Gen. Rudolf Viest, flew at once to Banská Bystrica to take over command from Golián, who became his principal aide. Foreign Minister Masaryk beseeched Allied representatives to furnish military units and supplies. Wishing to avoid military intervention in Eastern Europe, however, the U.S. high command declined armed action, but parachute drops of all kinds were flown in from Italian bases, including a mission from the Office of Strategic Services (OSS).

UTOK, the organ of the Slovak National Council, reported the arrival of Czech patriots to fight for the liberation of Slovakia. "The outbreak of anti-German fighting in Slovakia" was heralded in intelligence bulletins as "a powerful call to Czech patriots, including [Moravians who] came to join the partisan units." At the moment, "the Germans [were] strengthening their terror in industrial plants and reinforcing their frontier guards." The report stated: "In spite of all difficulties, Czechs are fighting with greater determination against German production, industry, and transport." In other words, they were effecting Schweik-style slowdowns in production. These accounts were highly credited in London for emanating from their "prominent Czechoslovak politician." The reports from Slovakia came from a "number of political groups," comprising all parties, but given equal credence. The report on September 25th from Banská Bystrica was graphic:

Banská Bystrica has now a martial appearance. The streets are crowded with military vehicles, regular troops, partisan detachments, and many civilians busy in their war effort. Here, as in most of the areas held by the patriots, telegraphs, telephones, and postal services are working almost normally, and the buses connecting the town with neighbouring districts are keeping to the time-tables laid down by the military authorities. Industrial enterprises are working at full speed . . . After five years of totalitarian newspapers, there is again a free press in Banská Bystrica and through free Slovakia. [19]

The Slovak insurgency also attracted an amazingly broad participation of international groups, including some escaped prisoners of war. When the uprising had erupted, a Slovak delegation was on its way to Moscow, led by the local Communist chief, Karol Šmidke, and ably assisted by a young lawyer named Gustav Husák. The Soviets had already sent in a sabotage expert to train the partisan cadres. Surprisingly, the delegation was treated at the Soviet capital with marked suspicion, and its non-Communist members subjected virtually to house arrest, but its earnest pleas obtained the dispatch of Soviet parachute drops, albeit haphazardly executed.

The National Council was forced to galvanize its own disparate forces without the anticipated help from the Red Army. German divisions moved out from their garrison post in western Slovakia to capture control of the eastern and central portions, including the connecting main rail line. In a giant pincer movement, Banská Bystrica was seized by the Germans on October 27th, along with the general staff and most of the foreign volunteers. Many partisan leaders, including the commanding generals, were taken off to Bratislava and then to Berlin for interrogation, and shortly afterwards executed at Camp Mauthausen. Surviving partisan groups in the central regions withdrew into the hills after sustaining heavy losses and regrouped under the stalwart direction of Vilem Žingor, who, with others, joined the Communist Party during the ensuing cruel winter months.

Through the next five months under brutal Nazi rule, Slovakia endured. The German occupation meant the end of authority for Father Tiso's government, with the result that the Gestapo-SS regime was now free of constraints to arrest and deport large numbers of Jews, whom Father Tiso and his colleagues had hitherto succeeded in protecting. A result of the German takeover of the state machinery was the dissolution of the local administrative units representing all unified elements of the governing coalition. Beneš's meticulous plan of self-government by local administrative units was thus destroyed. The arrival of the Red Army commanders in March 1945 at Svätý Martin threw control of most emerging national committees into Communist hands, although some Democrats were included. The British Foreign Office confirmed the impression that "the effect of the premature rising . . . has been to strengthen the position of the local Communists and to lead to an increase in the activities of Soviet partisans." [20] The self-governing units conducted civil administration under the Soviet military government. The purged security police was infiltrated by partisan units.

Although the leaders of the Slovak National Council went to London after the suppression of the uprising and "accepted the general authority of the Czechoslovak Government," Beneš was apprehensive that "the local Communists and autonomists may get out of hand unless he is in a position to control them on the spot." [21]

The Russians were now pressuring the Czechoslovak Government "to recognize the Lublin Committee in Poland at once." [22] These circumstances, added to Beneš's desire to obtain Moscow's sanction of the expulsion of the Sudetens, provided impetus for him to rush his return home for the anticipated liberation by the Red Army.

On the Polish issue, as with others, Beneš and Masaryk tried to straddle between East and West; they could ill afford to alienate either side of the Great Powers. A Czechoslovak Foreign Affairs Ministry newsletter in London declared on January 2, 1945: "Our aim . . . our strong and inviolable Alliance with the Soviet Union and our friendly relations with the Great Allied Powers of the West form a better safeguard of our security than it has ever had before . . . a magnificent unity at home and abroad . . . [Our Constitution acknowledges] the sovereignty of the people." [23]

In a conversation Philip Nichols had with Beneš in mid-January, the ambassador suggested "perhaps an advantage to waiting for the return home until Bratislava was liberated." Beneš responded in a flash that "Košice or Presov would fill the bill,"[24] although his preference was Banská Bystrica for its symbolism of the resistance. He definitely disliked Bratislava for its identification with the Tiso government. At this point, Beneš was in haste. His Council of Ministers had seconded him on January 12th by voting to "return to their native soil as soon as . . . possible."[25]

On January 18th, Nichols talked also with Jan Masaryk, who, like Beneš, promised not only to inform the British government of his dealings with Moscow and with the native political leaders on his return, but would go beyond reporting to "consult." It emerged secretly that "there was already tension . . . between themselves and Moscow." The Russians had some time ago requested that they send a representative to Lublin "as General de Gaulle had one." They had not complied, and "the Russians were now demanding immediate recognition."

In his separate talk with Nichols that day, Beneš complained openly about his problems with his ambassador to Moscow, Zdeněk Fierlinger, who had volunteered "to go direct to Lublin himself to discuss matters with the Committee, and had earned from Beneš a very severely worded telegram." Fierlinger apologized, but such differences between them persisted. The rift was open knowledge in Moscow government circles.[26]

Nichols informed his superiors at the Foreign Office that "the President then admitted that he was in fact making the settlement of the Teschen question to his satisfaction a condition of his recognition of the Lublin Committee." Nichols chided Beneš, reminding him that such a move would cast him in an unfavorable light in London, especially if he were the first to do so. "Beneš did not deny this," wrote Nichols, "but reverted to the necessity of safeguarding his own interests" when making compromises with Moscow. The West had, after all, offered him no commitment on pre-Munich boundaries, which the Soviets had pledged. Beneš then added bitterly that "he must rely on himself and not on the Western Allies, for . . . in the last resort, these Allies would have, if necessity arose, to abandon him, i.e. to the tender mercies of the Russians, though he did not say so. I replied that on certain matters, we should never abandon Czechoslovakia, and we left it at that." Nichols concluded his report, saying that Beneš "assumes that the Lublin Committee will give way over Teschen in a very near future."[27]

A week later, Beneš informed Anthony Eden of his imminent revisit to Moscow with Masaryk, possibly "in about six weeks," in accord with the definite decision taken by his government. They would not await "the liberation of Bratislava." Beneš confided to Eden that he had foreseen the "differences with Moscow . . . more than a year ago, producing his anxiety to conclude his treaty with the Russians in 1943." He told Eden of his plan to "reconstruct his government . . . to make it more acceptable to local Slovak opinion." Due to difficulties in communicating from Slovakia both with Western Europe and with Bohemia and Moravia, he had decided he would leave "some of his Government . . . in London . . . to avoid [his] isolation." [28]

In confidence to Philip Nichols, Jan Masaryk underscored his disturbance "in general and at the probable extent and direction of Russian policy in Central Europe . . . [and] continually harped on the necessity for close understanding between the three Great Powers and the need for an early meeting." From Masaryk's and Beneš's perspective, East-West collaboration would be Czechoslovakia's only salvation. At the same time, Masaryk "seemed to regard His Majesty's Government as the only Power likely to be able to keep Soviet influence within its proper bounds . . . [All of this] was of course, confidential, and in no sense an official expression of the views of the Czechoslovak minister of foreign affairs." [29]

Masaryk took strenuous objection to Czechoslovakia being viewed as a bridge between East and West. He declared emphatically: "We do not and never have offered ourselves as a bridge." People "walk over a bridge and this would not suit us at all." [30]

The Foreign Office concluded its lengthy message to its ambassador in Moscow, Viscount Chilston, on February 25th thus: "The Czechoslovak Government's apprehensions [have been] increased by the strong pressure . . . upon them by the Soviet Government in recent weeks to recognize the Lublin Committee in Poland . . . They are now demanding full recognition at once . . . this demand has led to tension." Beneš repeated to Nichols that "he is now seeking to strike a bargain whereby recognition would be accorded in return for Polish acquiescence to the Czechoslovak claim to Teschen." [31]

On February 23rd Eden invited Beneš and Masaryk for a talk prior to their departure for Moscow en route home. Straight off, Beneš questioned Eden about varying Allied attitudes at the Yalta summit conference. Eden replied that "both the Americans and ourselves had gained the impression that the Russians were anxious to work with us . . . that Stalin and Molotov had appeared cheerful and confident . . . [and that] both had really enjoyed the Conference." Beneš wanted to know what had been arranged respecting the subject "which clearly preoccupies him most . . . his programme for the transfer of the German minority from his country." He had written about it to all of the Allies and to the European Advisory Commission the previous November (1944), but reports of the Yalta meetings show that this subject was omitted from the agenda. Eden knew this as he had attended the conference, but he was not at liberty to divulge this information. Quite clearly President Roosevelt had other more pressing matters to settle, thinking this one could wait. Beneš could only have been resentful, especially in view of his warm, pro-American bent.

Nichols had told Beneš that this matter would be left to the Allied settlement for all of Germany. Beneš raised the subject again with Nichols on February 13th, anxious to be enabled to announce the expulsion of the hated Sudeten Germans upon his arrival home, to satisfy pressing public opinion. Beneš said he could not wait. Eden told him now that "it was obviously impossible for the three Great Powers to reach agreement on this difficult subject before he left next week." Eden then suggested that Beneš restrict his remarks at home to his own advocated proposals for expulsion. Palpably, Beneš would review the subject with the Russians in Moscow very soon. [32]

The next day, Prime Minister Winston Churchill reiterated the instruction at a farewell luncheon with Beneš and Masaryk at his country home Chequers. Churchill "informed the President" that the Foreign Office was anxious that "he should not make an announcement concerning his German minority programme until he has consulted the Great Powers." By way of balance, he added the tribute that he deemed Beneš "a wise man and [said] that his country was lucky to have him at their head at this juncture." [33]

The British Foreign Office was crystal clear about its policy objectives regarding Czechoslovakia. The ambassador to Czechoslovakia summarized his understanding of the major points involved prior to his following the Czechoslovak government to its home base:

a. to ensure that she does not fall completely within the Russian orbit;

b. that she continues to be dependent upon the Western Powers as well as the USSR;

c. that she follows the lead of the major United Nations in security and reconstruction policy generally;

d. we should attempt to improve . . . our commercial exchanges with Czechoslovakia;

e. we should attempt to assume . . . a preeminent position as cultural guide in Czechoslovakia . . . really means ousting France, who occupied this position between the wars. [34]

In order to insure Czechoslovakia's "partial dependence on the West, or at least partially facilitate this outcome," the British government decided to assist Czechoslovakia by giving her "a credit of £5 million." Canada and the United States "are also providing her with credit facilities, but this by itself will hardly be sufficient . . . Further commercial credits . . . would be desirable . . . Another way of helping her . . . is to assist her to re-arm." The latter part was relevant merely in the short run, until Czechoslovakia could get its "first-class armaments industry . . . going again." Ambassador Nichols suggested that "the British supply the Czechoslovak Air Force with British machines, i.e. fighters . . . one or two fighter squadrons. This would mean that we should have done something [visible] to maintain that remarkable good-will" initiated during the war, as well as "Czechoslovak dependence upon the West." The Czechoslovaks, for their part, have asked the British to "oust Germany from the top place in the list of countries with whom they do business . . . I hope we shall do all we can . . . to realize this desirable objective . . . We shall later recommend the grant of further commercial credits." Nichols looked forward to "an Anglo-Czechoslovak cultural agreement" for starters in displacing the French influence. [35]

Nichols estimated in his memorandum that President Beneš

in his oft-proclaimed policy of balance, is, of course, perfectly aware of his advantages of having two strings to his bow and the possible advantage . . . of being able to play off the Russians against ourselves and vice-versa. All this is true, but . . . generally agreed . . . that it is very much to *our* interest that Czechoslovakia, given her vital strategic position in Europe, should not become wholly dependent upon Russia. [36]

Within another week, Beneš and Masaryk were in Moscow, where they promptly told U.S. Ambassador Harriman that the "Soviets have agreed to continue to arm the Czechoslovak army . . . but that supplies requisitioned by the Red Army in Czechoslovakia would be offset against the military equipment furnished by the Russians." Beneš managed to conclude an agreement with the Soviets to obtain "some [economic] supplies such as seed, transport equipment . . . to start the wheels of economic life." These supplies were to be be paid for by Czechoslovakia depending upon how soon and in what condition her industries would be when liberated.

On the key point of transferring the Germans out of Czechoslovakia, Harriman relayed home Beneš's information that "Stalin . . . agreed with Beneš' proposal that about 2 million of the 3 million Germans within Czechoslovakian territory should be transferred to Germany, and similarly about 400,000 of the 600,000

Hungarians to Hungary." [37] Beneš further informed Harriman that the "Soviets had maintained the principles of their previous agreements . . . regarding returning Czechoslovakia to her pre-Munich boundaries, leaving to the peace settlement . . . relatively small territorial adjustments at the expense of Germany and Hungary." The question of Ruthenia would be deferred. Neither Molotov nor Beneš felt strongly about Ruthenia. Beneš "did not seem particularly exercised over the possibility of losing Ruthenia." [38]

Another report relating to Ruthenia revealed that

The Czechoslovak Government have been clearly impressed by recent evidence of the strength of Ukrainian nationalist feeling in Sub-Carpathian Ruthenia, [whose] recent resurgence seems . . . attributable to the Ukrainian units of the Red Army, who played a leading part in the liberation of the territory. [There was] open talk of . . . reunion of Ruthenia with the Ukraine . . . The Czechoslovak Government have the impression that these nationalist manifestations are causing the Soviet Government genuine embarrassment . . . [They could find] no evidence [of its being] deliberately fostered by the Soviet Government . . . which seemed likely in view of the adoption by the Ruthenian National Council and the Red Army Council in the province it had liberated of a resolution on Nov. 26, 1944 in favor of annexation with the Soviet Union.

George Kennan, now chargé d'affaires of the U.S. embassy in Moscow, saw "no manifestation on the official Soviet Government level of any desire to incorporate the province into the Soviet Union." [39] Vishinsky assured the Czechoslovak delegate to Ruthenia and Ambassador Fierlinger on December 26th that until the peace conference "the Czechoslovak Government should administer all territories within the pre-Munich frontier" as provided in their treaty of alliance in 1943. [40]

After his arrival in Moscow, Beneš confirmed this pledge with the Soviet government during his talks in January, that "they agreed to the integral restoration of Czechoslovakia's former boundaries . . . that they were not claiming sub-Carpathian Ruthenia for the present . . . [He was,] however, quite ready to reconsider this matter later on." He recalled now that in 1918 he had not asked for this province, but had been given it by President Wilson because of the large Ruthenian community in America.* He did not intend it to become a source of

---

*As incorporated in the Czechoslovak republic after World War I, this territory was called Sub-Carpathian Rus. As annexed by Hungary in 1939, it was called Ruthenia. After being ceded to the Soviet Union in 1945, it was called Transcarpathian Ukraine. It is also sometimes referred to as Carpatho-Ukraine. See: *Foreign Relations*, 1945, v. 4, p. 509.

trouble with the USSR, if the Soviet policy changed. [41]

It soon emerged that the reason for the delay in permitting the transfer of the diplomatic corps to join Beneš on his return home was "due to Soviet objections." Soviet military authorities found "difficulties in accommodation for a considerable number . . . of the Diplomatic Corps . . . considers it unavoidable to postpone [their] arrival . . . for some time . . . The transfers . . . will be realized not at once, but in parts . . . in minimal numbers in the beginning." [42]

In the afternoon of March 30th, Beneš had a relaxed and frank two-hour talk over tea with Ambassador Harriman at the U.S. embassy. Beneš recounted that he was satisfied with his discussions with Stalin and Molotov, having concluded a variety of arrangements, including details such as "air transports and radio communications" for their contact in Slovakia with the outside world. The Soviet leaders had been persuaded "to agree to the diplomatic corps being moved from London to the seat of the new Czechoslovak Government at Košice." But delays ensued and the Soviet Government stalled on "permission for the Corps to travel through [Red Army occupied] Rumania and Hungary to Czechoslovakia." Beneš said he was anxious to have these diplomatic representatives with him and confessed to being "disturbed by the delay." But he hoped to clear up the impediments shortly. [43]

Stalin gave a dinner in the Kremlin in honor of Beneš at which he accorded with his guest in disclaiming "the old [czarist] policy of Pan-Slavism" in interpreting their "historic common objective of security against German aggression," a matter of such special importance to Beneš and to Czechoslovakia. Perhaps even more significant was Stalin's second speech. He seemed at ease with Beneš when "he spoke of the fact that many people had been suspicious that the Soviet Union *wished to bolshevize Europe*." Turning to Beneš, he said in all candor: "You were *justified* in sharing this suspicion." But now he assured him, "there is no longer a justification for this fear as the Soviet Government's policy has been reoriented *to present conditions*." In the same vein, he explained: "The various Communist parties would become nationalist parties, interested in the national interests of their own countries." In private conversation later, Stalin elucidated, saying *"he knew the Czechoslovak Communist leaders,"* after their five-year residence in Moscow. He deemed them "good patriotic men, but *wore 'blinders',*" meaning that "they were concentrating too much on their own ideology" and he suggested that *"Beneš should undertake to broaden their outlook."* [44]

Although Beneš told Harriman that he was well satisfied with the composition of the new government to be announced after his arrival at Košice, he conceded that "it might have been worse" and maintained that "his difficulties were with the Czechoslovak parties and personalities and not because of interference on the part of the Soviets." He was especially annoyed by Social Democrat Fierlinger (once again), who was designated as the new prime minister. He said he felt he could control him on home ground, as he was a career diplomat, with "no political following in Czechoslovakia." Stalin had also told Beneš in confidence that "*he too was displeased with the selection of the new Cabinet as the Western powers would think incorrectly . . . that it was an indication of Soviet domination of Czechoslovak internal affairs . . .* [Stalin assured Beneš] he had no intention *of so doing and did not like the implication.*"[45] Stalin distinctly shared Beneš's disapproval of Fierlinger and called his appointment "a foolish act," but he would not interfere.[46]

It was widely acknowledged in the West that, after the Yalta Conference, Stalin favored the establishment of popular democracies in Eastern Europe, which struck Beneš as reconcilable with his own views. After all, the Soviets had of necessity also to depend on the West to provide his country with the sinews of postwar rehabilitation and reconstruction. Stalin may have been reassured by Churchill's barefaced bargain at Yalta regarding the demarcation between them of spheres of influence. Under these, there would be equal influence in Yugoslavia and Hungary. London would prevail in Greece, while Moscow would be the final arbiter in Romania and Bulgaria. Czechoslovakia inspired no contention among the Great Powers at Yalta, which had a common desire for her independence. Moreover, she looked both east and west for her foreign policy. Hapless Poland remained equally divided. These popular democracies would provide basic freedoms and would have coalition-led, anti-Fascist governments, friendly to the Soviet Union and favoring free elections.

A further consideration arose before Beneš left Moscow. He told the Russians of his plan to reorganize the Czechoslovak Army, aiming at ten divisions. Stalin, without being asked, "promised to supply equipment for all these divisions and for the first five, free of charge."[47]

Beneš and Masaryk prepared to leave Moscow "well satisfied" with their accomplishments with the Soviet Government. They reported that "no unpleasant surprises [had arisen] and the Soviet–Czech relations remained firmly based upon the Treaty of Alliance." The Russians sounded them out about including the Warsaw Poles in this treaty, but the Czechoslovak leaders resisted, saying "the time was not ripe for this." They were reassured of "Soviet agreement to the integral restoration of Czechoslovakia's pre-Munich frontiers, specifically cover[ing] Teschen ... The Russians [seemed] sympathetic to Dr. Beneš' proposal to advance the Czechoslovak frontier slightly to cover Moravska Ostrava ... at the expense of the Poles," who were being compensated with all of Silesia.[48]

Trouble with the Russians had arisen, however, in the field. Reports reached Beneš that "the Russians were dismantling factories in Slovakia and taking away equipment on the pretext that it had been supplied by the Germans. This and the behavior of some of the Soviet troops [were] causing great dissatisfaction in Slovakia and Ruthenia." Beneš naturally did not share the Red Army's interpretation of "booty."[49]

Setting aside this problem, for which there was no quick remedy, Beneš decided not to delay his return home over a discussion of it with the Soviet leaders. The time had come for his departure for Košice to reconstitute his independent government. He agreed that Masaryk should return to the United States via London to attend the organizing conference of the United Nations in San Francisco. President Beneš arrived in Košice on April 3, 1945, well before the liberation of all of Slovakia, not to mention the other Czechoslovak provinces. On home ground, on April 7th, he announced the formation of his new government, headed by Prime Minister Fierlinger.[50]

NOTES

1. Secret Information bulletin, Czechoslovak Information Section, London, to U.S. State Department, National Archives 1218, reel 29, Washington, D.C.

2. "Situation in Czechoslovakia", February 16, 1944, State Dept. "Czechoslovak Series", National Archives 1218, reel 29.

3. Ibid., p. 3 of report.

4. Ibid.

5. Private Czechoslovak intelligence report, National Archives, 1218, reel 29, undated.

6. U.S. Embassy in London, "Czechoslovak Series," September 25, 1944, National Archives 1218, reel 29.

7. General Čatloš report, National Archives, 1218, reel 29.

8. "Beneš's Address to the Czechoslovak Troops," March 17, 1944, filed April 12, 1944, National Archives 1218, reel 29.

9. British Embassy near Czechoslovakia to Anthony Eden, April 3, 1945, FO 371/v. 47139-110145.

10. Rudolf Schoenfeld, London, report on Czechoslovakia to Secretary of State, March 17, 1944, National Archives 1218, reel 30.

11. State Department memo of a conversation in London re Czechoslovakia, April 25, 1944, National Archives 1218, reel 29.

12. U.S. Embassy, Moscow to Secretary of State, May 9, 1944, Cited in *Izvestia*, National Archives 1218, reel 30.

13. Ibid.

14. Harriman, Moscow, to Secretary of State, March 13, 1944, National Archives 1218, reel 29.

15. Schoenfeld to Secretary of State, June 21, 1944, National Archives 1218, reel 29.

16. Ibid.

17. Ibid.

18. "Czechoslovak Series" No. 184, U.S. Embassy, London, September 25, 1944, National Archives 1218, reel 29.

19. Ibid.

20. Foreign Office to British Embassy, Moscow, January 25, 1945, Secret, Political, FO 371/v. 47120-111069.

21. Ibid.

22. Ibid.

23. *Newsletter*, Czechoslovak Ministry of Foreign Affairs, London, January 2, 1945, FO 371/v. 47085-110023.

24. British Embassy to Czechoslovakia, London to Foreign Office, January 18, 1945, FO 371/v. 47120-109003.

25. Philip Nichols to Foreign Office, February 1, 1945, FO 371/v. 47120-109003.

26. Ibid.

27. Nichols to Foreign Office, January 18, 1945, London, confidential, FO 371/v. 47085-110023.

28. Foreign Office to British Embassy, Moscow, January 25, 1945 FO 371/v. 47120-111069.

29. Ibid.

30. Ibid.

31. Ibid.

32. Eden to Nichols, February 23, 1945, Secret, FO 371/v. 47120-109003.

33. Nichols to Foreign Office, February 27, 1945, FO 371/v. 47085-110023.

34. British Embassy to Czechoslovakia, London, March 14, 1945, FO 371/v. 47107-108451.

35. Ibid.

36. Ibid.

37. Avrerell Harriman, Moscow to Secretary of State, March 22, 1945, *Foreign Relations* 1945, v. 4, pp. 427-29.

38. Ibid.

39. George Kennan, Chargé d'Affaires, Moscow, to Secretary of State, January 25, 1945, *Foreign Relations* 1945, v. 4, pp. 509-511

40. Foreign Office to British Embassy, Moscow, January 25, 1945, FO 371/v. 47120-111069.

41. Clark Kerr, Moscow, to Foreign Office, March 26, 1945, FO 371/v. 47085-110023.

42. Schoenfeld to Secretary of State, March 28, 1945, *Foreign Relations* 1945, v. 4, pp. 429-430.

43. Harriman, Moscow, to Secretary of State, March 31, 1945, *Foreign Relations* 1945, v. 4, pp. 430-33. Italics added.

44. Clark Kerr, Moscow to Foreign Office, March 30, 1945, Secret, FO 371/v. 47085-110023.

45. Ibid. March 26, 1945.

46. Kerr, Moscow, to Foreign Office, March 31, 1945; Secret, FO 371/v. 47085-110023.

47. Kerr, Moscow to Foreign Office, March 26, 1945; Secret, FO 371/v. 47085-110023.

48. Kerr to Foreign Office, March 31, 1945; Secret, FO 371/v. 47085-110023.

49. Kerr to Foreign Office; March 26, 1945; FO 371/47085-110023.

50. Nichols, London, to Foreign Office, April 9, 1945, confidential, FO 371/v. 47121-109007; also Harriman to Secretary of State, *Foreign Relations* 1945, v. 4, p. 431.

16

The Government Reconstituted on Home Ground (1945)

Eduard Beneš had given the Western Powers due notice of his intention to reorganize his government on home ground to conform to the reality of Communist hegemony in the local administrative committees emplaced by the liberating Red Army. Stalin himself had told Beneš he thought the Czechoslovak Communists tended to swing too far to the left, risking offense to sensibilities in Western chancelleries. The leftward pull was sugarcoated by the "provisional character" of the new administration, which was to govern until free elections would be held following liberation of the entire country. Throughout his extended deliberations with the Communist exiles in Moscow, they all understood that the first liberated government would contain representatives of the London government-in-exile, the Communists in Moscow, and representatives of the Slovak National Council.

The structure of the new government, announced by Beneš at Košice on April 7, 1945, manifested this "swing to the Left," according to British Ambassador Philip Nichols, who noted that the new "strong Communist elements" had been "wholly absent from the last administration." The conservative Agrarians were banned, as were the Rudolph Gajda-led Fascist groups, as all these leaders were "badly compromised by their [collaborationist] activities since 1938." Hubert Ripka reminded Nichols sharply in London, however, that the "drastic decision" to liquidate the Agrarian Party of the small peasants had been agreed to "by all the parties in the Cabinet. It was not an exclusive decision forced by the Communists."[1]

The government included five experts, ministers of no particular

party, such as Jan Masaryk for foreign affairs and Gen. Ludvík
Svoboda, commander of the Czechoslovak Brigades with the Red
Army, for national defense.

There were three representatives each of the four principal Czech
parties: Communist, Socialist, Social Democratic, and Catholic; and
four representatives each of the two Slovak parties: Communist-
Socialist and Democratic. Prominent among the leaders were Zdeněk
Fierlinger (S.D.), Prime Minister; Ripka (Soc.), Minister of Trade;
Monsignor Jan Šrámek (Cath.), Deputy Prime Minister; Vladimír
Clementis (Comm.), Secretary of State for Foreign Affairs; Vavro
Šrobár (Comm.), Minister of Finance; and a Slovak, Viliam Široký
(Comm.), Deputy Prime Minister. It was understood all around that
although Fierlinger was officially a Social Democrat, he was "thought
to be very amenable to Russian influence," due to his having been
ambassador to Moscow since 1937 except for 1939-1941, the years of
the Nazi-Soviet pact. Most threatening to the stability of the coalition
government was Václav Nosek (Comm.), Minister of Interior,
although Nichols saw him then as "the best of the Communists
available," whose residence in London during the war "may well prove
a restraining influence." Nichols also estimated that retaining
Masaryk at the head of the foreign ministry augured "a great
advantage to the Western Powers." The appointment of Jaroslav
Stránský, considered by the ambassador as "a Democrat in the
Masaryk-Beneš tradition" to head the ministry of justice, as he had
done in the London government during the war, pleased all political
elements. The British ambassador liked Stránský's "closely reasoned
and moderate speeches" and "restrained delivery," "laying his finger on
a sore point" when "making a plea for true democracy." [2]

It was inevitable that General Svoboda should become the minister
of defense, as he was universally popular, even beloved, to the end of
his life for having commanded "the Czechoslovak forces on the
Eastern front for the last few years." Those men were in the forefront
of liberating the country. Moreover, he was an avuncular figure.
Although Svoboda was generally seen as subject to Soviet influence,
Nichols judged him as "absolutely loyal to the President and can be
counted on to put Czechoslovak interests first." Nichols felt the
government was a compromise of forces, and "might have been more
pronouncedly Communist than it is." In any event, the Communists
proved themselves formidable negotiators, "well-disciplined and
knowing exactly what they wanted." [3]

When closely questioned by Nichols on the afternoon of April 9th,
Jan Masaryk said that "the elections to be held in a few months . . .

would be really free" and that neither Beneš nor he would "stand for any hanky-panky" in this regard. Questioned again, Masaryk said he accepted Beneš's estimate that in free elections the Communists "would not poll more than 25% to 30% of the total votes." Nevertheless, Masaryk "did not give me the impression that he was happy about the Government; nor, indeed, did Dr. Ripka . . . [and] the President himself is not altogether content at the turn events have taken." In any case, everyone felt sure Dr. Beneš, the supreme realist, "will tackle the new situation with his usual energy and determination." [4]

Despite the Czechoslovak government's close relations with the Soviet Union, in accord with their treaty of alliance, the British ambassador told his chief at the Foreign Office, Anthony Eden:

It would be a mistake if we were to jump to the conclusion at this stage that the Soviet orientation is total, definite, and final . . . The population of the Czech lands which has a far better knowledge of the West than have the Slovak people is still inarticulate . . . A firm indication of Czechoslovak intentions will only be available after the Provisional National Assembly has been convened and after general elections. [5]

Directly upon his arrival in Košice, Beneš administered the oath of office to his new cabinet. Then on April 5th, he proclaimed his program, underpinning the socialist welfare state. Speaking prudently of "state direction" rather than "nationalization," the Košice program embodied Beneš's carefully worked out plan for a mixed economy, marked by small-sized capitalist enterprises, small peasant farms bolstered by cooperatives, and state control of credit, under a democratic central plan. On the political side, the program pledged a united state of Czechs and Slovaks on an equal footing. This part was formalized in an agreement signed between the government and the Slovak National Council on March 27th. [6] The Slovak National Council became the constitutional representative of the Slovak people and the official organ of the State authority. The unified state meant expulsion of the German and Magyar minorities, whose Czechoslovak citizenship was revoked. The disloyalty of the Sudeten Germans was officially assumed, and Germans returning from abroad were forbidden to reenter national territory. [7] Exceptions would be made for those who had proved their loyalty by deeds. Large numbers of these minority peoples fled during the ensuing months, while the government labored to obtain Allied sanction for their expulsion, which in the case of the German minority was finally granted at the Potsdam Conference. Beneš had worked out a clever scheme of compensation for their abandoned properties, involving a good deal of retribution. He would give them scrip, which would have to be redeemed by the new German government. [8]

While Russian armies were rapidly advancing in the protectorate from the east and south, the Košice government did everything "to invigorate to the maximum the spirit of resistance" among their still-occupied compatriots. There was a call for "secret sabotage . . . to steal or otherwise procure arms" and hide everything of value, especially foodstuffs and seed likely to be conscripted by the Germans. Farmers must plan to feed themselves and the nation. The people were exhorted by radio that "if they remain passive, the Germans will be able to carry out the plans to leave once-prosperous Czechoslovakia a desert. In the Nazi plan, Bohemia and Moravia constitute one of the last bastions of Nazi resistance." [9] The more his own nationals did for the country, the less beholden they would be to the contending Big Powers. The British figured likewise. At this juncture, they urged people in their broadcasts "to do a little private demolition work of their own on factories, vehicles, railway engines, etc." during air raid blackouts. [10]

At the same time, the Foreign Office warned Washington that "the crossing of the Czechoslovak frontiers by American troops needs careful handling because the vast majority of the inhabitants are Sudetens . . . The Allied military authorities are differentiating between Sudetens and Czechoslovaks." [11]

Ripka, who had tarried in London to oversee the foreign affairs ministry during Masaryk's absence, had made a request on April 18th of Ambassador Nichols. He officially petitioned for the immediate transfer of the superbly equipped, British-trained Czechoslovak Armoured Brigades from the western front to Czechoslovak territory, to be accompanied by only "a few pilots" from the Czechoslovak squadrons flying with the British Air Force. Nichols was surprised but could detect political advantages to be gained by the government. He figured that their "arrival in Western Czechoslovakia . . . would counterbalance the arrival of the Czechoslovak troops with the Red Army on the Eastern Front." Nichols advised Ripka to repeat the request to Allied headquarters at SHAEF (Supreme Headquarters, Allied Expeditionary Forces) and to the American embassy. [12] Whether this consideration had indeed prompted the government's request is not known, but subsequently it was repeatedly made.

The winter offensive on the eastern front now obliged the German high command to draw on its western forces and shift them to the defense of Berlin. This transfer facilitated the breakthrough of the

Anglo-American armies to the Rhine, where on March 21st they effected a crossing at the unarmed Remagen bridgehead. The U.S. Sixth Army under Gen. George S. Patton's command pressed its sensational march through Bavaria, to reach the frontiers of Austria and Bohemia within a month.

Establishing headquarters at Pilsen, 50 miles inside the Czech border, Patton sent scouts up the Prague highway, several of whom, in civilian garb, actually entered the capital. Encouraged by their enthusiastic welcome on all sides, Patton sent word to the underground organization in the capital to inquire whether it would not be advisable to move his forces into the city. Young Communist Josef Smrkovský, who had emerged as the local resistance leader, sent a negative reply. Simultaneously, Patton in Pilsen declined to receive a Prague delegation led by a Socialist.

Patton then telegraphed to Soviet General Ivan S. Konev, whose detachments were now approaching Prague from the northwest, to suggest that they proceed jointly into the capital. Patton received a sharp rebuke to his wire from Acting Chief of Staff Alexei I. Antonov in Moscow, instructing him to regroup his forces on the preestablished Karlovy Vary–Pilsen–Sudjeovice line. Commander-in-Chief Dwight D. Eisenhower, following government directives, assented to permitting Marshal Stalin the credit of participating in the liberation of the Slavic capital at Prague.

The subject of contention was examined by Gen. Hastings Ismay on behalf of the Chief of Staff Committee, who informed Sir Orme Sargent at the Foreign Office that in reviewing the matter with Eisenhower on the morning of April 24th, the U.S. commander had said that "he never had any plan or idea of going into Czechoslovakia. He seemed under the impression, though perhaps he is wrong, that this had already been assigned to the Russian Zone." He had never conceived of Prague as "a military still less a political objective." Eisenhower told Ismay further that "there were two or three really good German divisions in the Western tip of Czechoslovakia and that it would be a considerable operation to overcome them." [13]

Winston Churchill himself intervened at this point. He instructed Lord Cadogan "to write to John Winant," the U.S. ambassador and U.S. representative on the European Advisory Commission, "pointing out the political advantages which could result if the Americans could press forward into Czechoslovakia and liberate Prague" and asking whether the U.S. government agreed with the Secretary of State's views. Apparently, Winant passed Churchill's troublemaking challenge to the U.S. State Department, which evaded a reply.

Churchill pressed his argument: "In my view, the liberation of Prague, and as much as possible of the territory of Western Czechoslovakia by the Americans, might make the whole difference to the postwar situation in Czechoslovakia and might well influence that in nearby countries. On the other hand, if the Western Allies play no significant part in Czechoslovakia's liberation, that country may go the way of Yugoslavia." Point 4 of his memorandum, which he had crossed through, amplified the message explicitly: "I think the political issues at stake so important that it should be considered most seriously whether they should not prevail, even if the purely military considerations would not justify pushing as far as possible into Bohemia." Churchill substituted the following passage for the crossed out Point 4: "I have spoken to Eisenhower and his main effort is against Redoubt, of course. But I think he should be told to push into Czechoslovakia as only he can spare the troops." [14] The Americans stood firm, however, on the lines designated at Yalta at the insistence of President Roosevelt.

In the first days of May, the Resistance organization in Prague, reflecting wartime unity, had perfected its guerrilla plans to expel the enemy. The Czechoslovak National Council issued an urgent call to all to "come as quickly as you can to the help of Prague . . . to expel the Nazi hordes . . . With your arms, you will save Prague and its population . . . Glory to the heroic Red Army . . . Glory to President Beneš . . . Glory to the great Stalin . . . Death to the German invaders." [15]   Under the coordination of Smrkovský, the popular rising broke out on May 5th. [16]

From an eye-witness account in the city, we are told that upon hearing rumors of Americans having reached the vicinity of the airport, within an hour that Saturday morning, "a remarkable spontaneous demonstration" occurred and "all the houses were decked with flags . . . Demonstrations took place in the streets." People talked the German security police into surrendering themselves with their arms. There was "fighting . . . for possession of the Prague Radio Station." But the "American help failed to materialize"; instead, there came low-flying German planes, "machine-gunning inhabitants." A longtime American businessman residing in Prague said that "the rising in any case, started prematurely . . . that the Resistance . . . had planned a rising for two days later and had not had time to carry out the distribution of arms from hidden stores." The informant reported that "the failure of the Americans to reach Prague before the Russians had been a tremendous disappointment to almost the whole of the population." He averred that "the situation was only saved by the intervention of Gen. Andrei Vlasov's liberation army."[17] This informant, who had resided in Prague comfortably through the Nazi occupation, and who was subsequently flown out to London in a special plane provided by General Patton, supplied one side of the narrative. On the other side, the Resistance forces asserted they had declined the offer of General Vlasov to help expel the Nazis from the city, and they claimed the victory for themselves.

The next day, the formerly pro-Nazi brigade of General Vlasov, which was stationed at a training station in Bohemia some distance from Prague, began to move into the city, in a switch, to assist in ousting its former masters. The Vlasov forces, composed primarily of Ukrainian war prisoners and deserters, had been organized by Gen. Reinhard Gehlen, founder of the remarkable German spy network known as Foreign Forces East.[18] After Vlasov's offer of help was declined, thinking to save his skin, Vlasov marched his troops down the Pilsen highway, preferring to surrender to General Patton rather than to the Russians. The U.S. commander, however, following the agreement with the Russians, routinely turned them over to Konev's headquarters. Vlasov and his officers and men were subsequently transported to Moscow, where they were all hanged as traitors.

The German garrison, pressured by the partisans, withdrew its occupation troops from Prague in a well-coordinated move that was completed on May 8th, the very day Berlin's resistance collapsed. The Czech resistance, minimizing street fighting, gave the retreating enemy little opportunity to destroy their beautiful capital city, as it had done to historic Warsaw.

General Konev had diverted part of his forces toward Prague. Accompanied by Czech partisan detachments, the next day, May 9th, the two Slavic allies shared a triumphal entry into the capital. "President Beneš and his Cabinet transferred the seat of government home at last to Prague, the Cabinet arriving by plane on May 10th, Beneš following by train on May 16th. The President delivered his first address directly upon arrival to the unified and liberated nation."[19]

Even before its shift from Košice, the government requested the Foreign Office in London to return the three Czechoslovak fighter squadrons that had been flying with the Royal Air Force during the war. The Foreign Office received a message from the Czechoslovak minister of defense, General Svoboda, urging that "President Beneš wants the Czech Fighter Wing to come to Prague immediately." Commander Karel Janoušek was sent to Air Marshal Robb of SHAEF, who agreed immediately to return one fighter wing, which would fly over SHAEF-controlled territory. Robb delayed, feeling it was wise to alert the Russians and gain their permission. "There was an exchange of messages between General Eisenhower and the Russian General Antonov," which "resulted in SHAEF agreeing to keep out of Prague and to leave it a Russian area."[20] Upon resuming life as a sovereign power, "the foremost task of the Czechoslovak Government was . . . to ensure the safety of the State with [its] own forces, and to attain a speedy return to normal life." Almost at once, it declared a partial mobilization of the Czechoslovak armed forces. "An immediate difficulty arose from the fact that Czechoslovak territory is practically divided into two areas, American and Soviet," often "guided by different points of view."[21]

The Soviet forces were themselves divided into three military zones under separate commands. Negotiations by the Czechoslovak government with the Soviet government at Moscow, and directly with the armed forces, placed Marshal Konev in charge, who directed that local governments would remain "in the hands of Czechoslovak authorities." The Prague spokesmen argued abroad that their government wanted its frontiers to be "occupied entirely by Czechoslovak troops," as was appropriate to "the sovereignty of the State."[22]

To complicate matters, "the conduct of [some] Russian troops . . . [was] undisciplined," meaning misbehaved. These forces required prompt removal and repatriation. When Marshal Konev visited Prague on June 10th, President Beneš asked when the withdrawal would take place; Konev replied "immediately." Konev "had already said a final good-bye to Marshal Rodion Malinovsky."[23] The Prague government made clear that foreign troops were not required "by internal conditions or by . . . military security."

The government declared that the continued presence of the Soviet and U.S. armies has impeded the efforts of the Czechoslovak people to recreate their own independent national life and was "retarding Czechoslovak economic recovery and rehabilitation . . . The American Embassy in Prague cautioned the Secretary of State that the withdrawal of American and Russian armies should take place as soon as possible . . . and should be simultaneous and complete. The simultaneous withdrawal is necessary to prevent Czechoslovakia from coming under apparent control of any one Allied power."[24]

Officials were dispatched to Moscow immediately to conduct negotiations connected with "Poland's refusal to acknowledge Czech claim to Teschen District." Although Teschen was occupied by Czechoslovak troops following liberation, the Czechs subsequently withdrew and the Poles occupied the city on July 2, 1945, awaiting later international adjudication. [25]   Border incidents followed. Beneš felt he stood on high ground, insofar as the Soviets had for several years recognized the country's pre-Munich frontiers. The delegation, headed by Fierlinger, requested the withdrawal of Soviet troops from Czechoslovak territory. A note to the U.S. authorities on June 23rd asked for a similar phased withdrawal by the United States, emphasizing that "a separate withdrawal of the American Army would have a disastrous effect on public opinion and would inflict irreparable damage on the prestige of the Western Powers." [26] In response, that same day, the U.S. State Department declared itself in "favor of the restoration of the frontiers of Czechoslovakia as they [had] existed in 1937 and [it] does not recognize any territorial change made in the Munich Agreement and Vienna Award of 1938, or changes as a result of the annexation of Bohemia and Moravia in 1939." [27]

At the end of June, amidst much back and forth haggling between the Czechoslovak government and the British, the Czechoslovak Armoured Brigade was permitted to return home for obvious national security functions. As a consolation to the snail-paced British bureaucracy, an Anglophile, Maj. Richard Pollak, formed the Association of Czechoslovak-British Soldiers, initially counting 400-500 members, to enhance British prestige in Czechoslovakia. Beneš received the returning soldiers himself and told Ambassador Nichols of his plan to have General Svoboda "use the Czech Brigade as cadre formations on which the future Czechoslovak army might be built." [28]

Bruce Lockhart, working in London as a Czechoslovakia expert, sent a brief note to the Allied Expeditionary Force Supreme Headquarters, Psychological Warfare Division, that was possibly inspired by his friend Jan Masaryk. Bruce Lockhart suggested "that a clear policy of Britain as regards the restoration of pre-Munich frontiers of Czechoslovakia should be proclaimed . . . to counter the Communist propaganda in Sudetenland" and that for "the restoration of pre-Munich frontiers, they [Czechoslovaks] can only look to Russian help." [29]   It was already late in the day for this public relations ploy. The Russians had recognized pre-Munich frontiers a year earlier, and the U.S. State Department had just matched them.

The Foreign Office, spurred by its psychological warfare division, also played with several other proposals to improve its image among the Czechoslovak people. On May 13th, it circulated a memorandum asking "what we might do to put guts into the Anti-Communists [to counter the] Communist hold on several Ministries, such as Interior, Information, and National Defense, [who] were not likely to be evicted." It observed that other parties "have little intention of submitting to a Communist dictatorship."[30] The Foreign Office inquired of its Prague embassy, whether the old bromide of a series of lectures by prominent English scholars could spruce up relations counterbalancing the Russians.

On June 29th, another treaty was signed in Moscow between Czechoslovakia and the Soviet Union, incorporating sub-Carpathian Ruthenia into the Soviet Socialist Ukrainian Republic. This treaty raised no eyebrows abroad. The U.S. government had already, a week prior to the signing, expressed its readiness to accept the cession. A State Department memorandum "favor[ed] a direct settlement of the question of Ruthenia by Czechoslovakia and the Soviet Union."[31]

Within a week, both Fierlinger and Beneš approached Ambassador Nichols at a diplomatic reception in Prague to tell him that they "specifically requested His Majesty's Government to transfer the [Czechoslovak] squadrons without delay . . . The squadrons are wanted as soon as possible." Nichols urged prompt compliance in his report home. [32]

The pressure worked. Several days later, British Air Chief Marshal Arthur W. Tedder signed the necessary order. The Air Ministry specified that the squadrons fly direct to Prague via the U.S. zone, landing only at a British airfield for refueling. The planes were to come "wholly under Czechoslovak Government control, although they will be linked with the RAF for material purposes." The Foreign Office liked the arrangement, which accorded with its desire to have Czechoslovakia dependent upon Britain for spare parts, fuel, and so on. The "Czech personnel in this country are impatient at delays attending their squadron's repatriation and their morale is suffering."[33] Good will would be generated.

An unidentified newspaper clipping in English found in the Foreign Office files and dated July 17, 1945, said that "general disappointment [in Prague was felt] when the Czechoslovak Squadron of the RAF failed to arrive in time for the fifth anniversary of their formation, causing cancellation of plans for a parade last week." The delay of more than two months in the homecoming of the airmen gave proof to the "reluctance of the British Air Ministry to sanction the departure of the aeroplanes without a Russian guarantee of the necessary landing facilities." The Czechoslovak government kept insisting that "the Russians neither expect nor desire to be asked to approve of measures that concern the Czechoslovaks' own affairs." The withdrawal of two-thirds of the Red Army forces from Czechoslovakia may perhaps have impelled the Air Ministry to "reconsider the position . . . [and provide for the] speedy return of the Czechoslovak Air Force." [34]

Air Marshal Janoušek, commander of the squadron, who was soon to be elevated to assistant chief of staff, and the pilots of the fighters were officially welcomed on August 13th in Prague by Gen. Bohumil Boček, chief of the General Staff, who read a short message from Prime Minister Fierlinger soon after the fighters landed. Ambassador Nichols, unable to attend personally, sent his chargé d'affaires, John Taylor, to the rainy airport ceremony in his place. Nichols later reported he had "no doubt that the return of the Czechoslovak Squadron from the United Kingdom had aroused very great interest and . . . turned the thoughts of the people towards Great Britain." Within the week of August 21st, President Beneš took the salute at the ceremonial march of the Czechoslovak Air Force through Prague. [35]

The startling political overturn in Great Britain on June 20th, which unseated Churchill's conservative government in a stunning victory of the Labour Party, came as a "great surprise in Prague as everywhere else . . . General gratification was expressed at the swing to the left, which was interpreted as the final defeat of the Munich Men, [although] there was genuine regret at the elimination of Mr. Churchill, who is regarded as a true friend of this country, [and who] will forever remain to the Czechs the great statesman." It was generally deemed "that there will be no change in Great Britain's foreign policy." [36]

NOTES

1. Philip Nichols to Anthony Eden, April 20, 1945, FO 371/v. 47121-109007.

2. John Taylor, British Chargé d'Affaires, Prague, to Ernest Bevin, September 6, 1945, FO 371/v. 47093-111988.

3. Nichols to Foreign Office, April 9, 1945, confidential, FO 371/v. 47121-109006.

4. Ibid.

5. Nichols to Eden, April 20, 1945, FO 371/v. 47121-109007.

6. Agreement between Czechoslovak government and Slovak Council, March 27, 1945, FO 371/v. 47121.

7. Government edict re nationalities, April 20, 1945, FO 371/v. 47154/110023.

8. U.S. State Department memorandum of a conversation, London, Eduard Beneš and Edward R. Stettinius, Jr., Secretary of State, Subject: Czechoslovakia, April 25, 1945, National Archives 1218, reel 29.

9. Radio appeal to Czechoslovak people, Foreign Office to Washington, April 13, 1945, FO 371/v. 47100-09377.

10. Foreign Office repeat, Nichols to Washington, FO 371/v. 47100-09377.

11. Ibid.

12. Nichols to Eden, London, April 15, 1945, FO 371/v. 47139-109402.

13. Hastings Ismay, Whitehall, to Orme Sargent, April 25, 1945, FO 371/v. 47121-109007.

14. PM Winston Churchill to Secretary of State, April 23, 1945, FO 371/v. 47121.

15. Czechoslovak National Council, enclosed with May 11, 1945, FO 371/v. 47101-109377.

16. Nichols, Prague, Annual report to PM Atlee, November 16, 1946, FO 371/v. 56085-109377.

17. D. Allen, British Embassy, May 18, 1945, FO 371/v. 47159-12005.

18. Reinhard Gehlen, *The Service; The Memoirs of General Reinhard Gehlen* (New York: World, 1972)

19. Government return to Prague, November 16, 1946, FO 371/v. 56085-109377.

20. "The Return of the Czechoslovak Air Force," May 14, 1945, FO 371/v. 47139-109407.

21. Jaroslav Stránský, Acting Minister of Foreign Affairs to Klieforth, U.S. Chargé d'Affaires, June 21, 1945, *Foreign Relations* 1945, v. 4, p. 461.

22. Ibid.

23. Nichols, June ll, 1945, FO 371/v. 47140-109402.

24. Klieforth, Prague, to Secretary of State, June 19, 1945, *Foreign Relations* 1945, v. 4, p. 515.

25. Czechoslovak Note to U.S. authorities, Prague, July 2, 1945, *Foreign Relations* 1945, v. 4, p. 515, footnote.

26. Klieforth to Secretary of State, June 24, 1945, *Foreign Relations* 1945, v. 4, p. 464.

27. "Czechoslovak Boundary Changes," State Dept. Memo, June 23, 1945, *Foreign Relations* 1945, v. 4, pp. 515-516.

28. Nichols to Foreign Office, June 11, 1945, FO 371/v. 47140-109402.

29. Supreme Headquarters, Allied Expeditionary Force (hereafter AEF) Psychological Warfare Division, June 25, 1945, FO 371/v. 47129.

30. Allen, May 13, 1945, FO 371/v. 56008-112415.

31. State Department, "The Czechoslovak Boundary Changes," June 23, 1945; *Foreign Relations* 1945, v. 4, p. 516.

32. Nichols to Foreign Office, July 6, 1945, FO 371/v. 47140-109402.

33. From Air Ministry, Whitehall, to Headquarters in Frankfurt, Secret, FO 371/v. 47140-109402.

34. Newspaper clipping, Prague, July 17, 1945, in English, FO 371/v. 47140-109402.

35. Nichols to Bevin, September 4, 1945, FO 371/v. 47141-109402.

36. Nichols to Bevin, July 29, 1945, FO 371/v. 47108-108962.

17

Nationalities Transfers and Allied Army Withdrawals (1945)

Three issues of primary importance faced the Prague government during the summer of 1945: (1) transfers out of the country of the German and Hungarian minorities; (2) simultaneous withdrawal of occupation armies; and (3) nationalization decrees, their application, and their enforcement.

Klieforth, the U.S. chargé d'affaires in Prague, reported on June 28, 1945 to his chief, James Francis Byrnes, at the State Department:

The outstanding issue on which . . . reconstruction depends is solution of the minority problem, involving transfers to Germany and Hungary of about three million Czechs . . . who constitute 20% of the country's population . . . [This] must be undertaken in agreement with the Allied governments . . . All reconstruction is halted until the transfer problem is solved. This problem unsolved presents the greatest danger to President Beneš' prestige [presenting opportunities] for more radical leaders to arouse the people and seek a solution by force. [1]

The vast dimensions of the problem loomed at Washington and Whitehall as staggering, but they responded with delay. The Foreign Office had already advised the Czechoslovak representative in London that final authorization for the transfers would have to be made by the Great Powers at the forthcoming summit meeting scheduled to convene in mid-July. The determination of the method and timing of the transfers would be given to the Allied Control Commission set up for Germany and for Hungary.

Acting Foreign Minister Vladimír Clementis, acknowledging the Allied request for a plan, wrote to Klieforth on July 3rd advising that "the Czechoslovak Government was preparing a plan for the transfer" of between "2 and 2½ million Germans and approximately 200,000 Magyars." He petitioned the United States to help and said he was repeating the request to Great Britain and the USSR. [2]

The State Department responded on July 13th via its chargé d'affaires in Prague. It said that the U.S. government had made its views on this subject known on January 31, 1945. "While it fully appreciated the injuries inflicted by the German minority on Czechoslovakia over a decade . . . [and is] *prepared to examine the problem* . . . the solution will have to take into account the needs of Czechoslovakia . . . and broader aspects of the problem [related to the] peace and security of Europe."[3] The U.S. government agreed with the Czechoslovak authorities that the transfers should be gradual, consonant with facilities for the orderly settlement of transferred persons.

The transfers of these populations were duly authorized by the Potsdam summit meeting of the Great Powers, which convened on July 17th and met through August 2nd. President Harry S. Truman replaced the late President Franklin D. Roosevelt, and the new British prime minister, Clement Atlee, attended instead of the experienced Winston Churchill. Stalin had already given his assent for the transfers of the minority peoples out of Czechoslovakia. The Anglo-Americans could do no less, if they wanted to retain any prestige in Czechoslovakia. At a press conference with a BBC correspondent on July 26th, Beneš conceded the "serious consequences" of the manpower loss but insisted, "It is absolutely necessary." Beneš explained that "those allowed to remain in the country would be decided on a basis of political reliability . . . The guilty must go . . . The people who stay will have no rights as a German minority, but full human rights as Czechoslovak citizens."[4]

Although of smaller dimension, an analogous situation obtained for the Magyars destined for removal, chiefly from Slovakia. The population exchange with Hungary, numbering 200,000 in the original plan, included some 160,000 Magyars who were to be removed into Hungary, while many of those remaining resettled into land evacuated by the Germans leaving Sudetenland. At the same time, many Slovaks returned from Hungary. The 1946 census showed almost the same number of Magyars living in Czechoslovakia as before the war, numbering 700,000.

A further complication derived from the need of facilities to be arranged somewhere within occupied Germany to receive and relocate these people. The German workers to be expelled comprised the skilled work force of the great exporting industries of glass, textiles, and porcelain, the lifeblood of the country's economy for hard-currency exports.

In the Sudetenland, there had perforce been a good deal of fraternization between the U.S. occupation forces and the local, mostly German, people, chiefly due to the language barrier between Americans and Czechs. Even where the occasions for fraternization had largely been "boy meets girl" social occasions, these troops soon adopted the attitude of the locals antipathetic to the government's plan to ship them out. Ambassador Laurence Steinhardt, when asked about this development, reported to Secretary of State Byrnes that "the large number of American troops now occupying a relatively small area in Czechoslovakia are *in excess of the numbers required* and tend to emphasize the undeniable feeling of Czechoslovaks that *Americans are too friendly with Sudeten Germans in occupied area.*"[5]

In a vain effort to extirpate residual German cultural influences in Czechoslovakia, President Beneš, on October 18th, signed a decree abolishing the German University in Prague, one of the oldest and most revered in Europe, dating from the fourteenth century, and also the German Polytechnic Institutes in Prague and Brno. If asked, Beneš would have justified the closures in the national interest, as national sentiment against anything German had grown to fever pitch everywhere in Czechoslovakia. A Students' British Association was launched in Prague on October 19th with "tremendous enthusiasm," and cultural relations were resumed officially with France.[6]

After the return from England of the Czechoslovak Armoured Brigades, the government in Prague had no further need of the Allied occupation forces. Their withdrawal was in everyone's interest. The United States had pressing need of its troops elsewhere, chiefly in the Pacific war against the Japanese and to occupy former enemy countries. The Czechoslovaks were counseled early on to be patient. Still, in view of their reconstruction and rehabilitation requirements, feeding these Allied armies was a strain.

The Prague government made its first official request for removal on June 21st, after its fighting men returned from England, which Washington acknowledged on July 6th. The State Department said it "would deeply regret if presence of two Allied armies and divisions of the Republic into two zones, hindered the reconstruction of the country." The United States viewed this problem "with sympathetic interest." It revealed that further "orders have been issued to Commanding General U.S. Force European Theater to begin immediately a reduction in U.S. forces in Czechoslovakia."[7]

Difficulties ensued promptly. On the same day, Klieforth sent

Byrnes some prudent advice about reversing this policy: "I regard the Czechs' request for the complete withdrawal of the American troops from Zecho [sic] in advance of the complete withdrawal of the Russian troops, which . . . *was demanded by Moscow,* as a serious and most irreparable loss to American reputation and 'Western' prestige. . . this view is shared fully by President Beneš . . . [and all] except a small group of 'eastern' Communists, led by Deputy President [Klement] Gottwald." Thus, army withdrawals became a bargaining chip in Cold War bargaining. Klieforth expanded on complaints abounding in Prague regarding the "failure of American troops to liberate Prague when they were 20 minutes distant." These, the attaché reported, emanated from Moscow "orders." Actually, the Soviet troops were over 100 miles distant, thereby delaying the city's liberation by many days. There seems to be no limit to the exaggerations of rumors! Klieforth argued: "Zecho resistance to Soviet pressures, now on the increase in all reports," will be "greatly weakened by American unilateral withdrawal from serious decline of Western influence . . . The 'eastern Communists' . . . [he declared] will profit by it at the expense of Beneš' authority and the non-Communist parties." He concluded that "the problem is an important issue . . . [settlement of which is] awaited with impatience." [8]

The report drew an instantaneous reaction from Washington. Three days later, on July 9th, Acting Secretary of State Joseph Grew wired Klieforth his thanks for "your secret information," reporting at the same time that the State and War Departments approved his suggestion. "U.S. forces will remain in Zecho until further instructions after token withdrawals proportionate to Soviets," as reported on June 29th, wrote Grew. SHAEF had instructed the Twelfth Army Group to maintain existing lines of demarcation with Soviet forces. "U.S. has no intention of making complete unilateral withdrawal at this time . . . *If request for withdrawal of both armies should come from Zecho Government,* U.S. will probably propose withdrawal be complete and simultaneous." [9]

On August 23rd, Secretary of State Byrnes bluntly admitted to Ambassador Steinhardt that "continued *retention of U.S. forces Zecho is political matter.*" He added with equal candor: "US forces will be withdrawn simultaneously with and in proportion to Soviet withdrawal . . . Simultaneous withdrawal was the US objective for the near future." [10]

Steinhardt was "entirely in accord with policy that US forces should not be withdrawn . . . other than simultaneously with and in proportion to Soviet withdrawal." This policy, assured Steinhardt, "reflect[s] the desire of Beneš, Masaryk, and most of members of Government other than extreme radicals." Steinhardt reported having had a private lunch with Masaryk a day earlier, when he learned that 320,000 Soviet troops were still distributed throughout the country, notwithstanding Stalin's "personal assurance that all Soviet forces would be withdrawn by July 20th, other than 8 or 9 divisions along the Czechoslovak-German frontier." [11]

Acknowledging the "War Department's desire to withdraw all US forces from Czechoslovakia" in the near future and keeping in mind "the political advantages of retaining American forces," Steinhardt suggested that "two divisions about to be withdrawn not be replaced . . . [and] that the 3rd division not be withdrawn . . . One division would have advantages and no foreseeable disadvantages." The U.S. maneuver might strengthen the Czechoslovak Government vis-à-vis the Russians and might induce the Russians to reduce their forces. "The withdrawal of all American forces," he cautioned, "might have serious internal consequences such as: Russian infiltration into the evacuated American zone in Czechoslovakia, with the resultant wholesale 'requisitioning' by individual Russian troops of cattle and food, seizure of machinery, equipment, household and personal effects as 'war booty' . . . and various other depredations such as are all too common in the present Russian occupied zone." Complete withdrawal would also lead to the widespread feeling among the Czechoslovaks of being abandoned. Steinhardt argued for the retention of one full division. [12]

In Washington, pressures from Congress mounted for troop withdrawals. The War Department decided that one division could not perform efficiently over the lengthy border between Czechoslovakia and Germany. It was recognized that the problem required a decision "at a very high level," as Acting Secretary of State Robert Murphy wrote Steinhardt on September 11th. Murphy wrote to Secretary of War Robert Patterson, "urging him on political grounds to allow the retention of two divisions in Zecho" until explorations could be made more fully on simultaneous withdrawal. Murphy advised a "direct approach by this Government to the Soviet Government . . . for agreement on simultaneous withdrawal of forces on the ground that the . . . Allied armies . . . [were] no longer necessary." He pointed out, moreover, that Czechoslovakia was a member of the United Nations, and fully capable of maintaining order within its national frontiers. Murphy observed that "Our troops occupy friendly country without invitation . . . or agreement . . . It would be *difficult and undesirable to attempt to justify the deployment of US forces in a friendly power for the protection of the German minority.*" He continued: "If the question should be raised in Congress . . . regarding the necessity of US forces in Czechoslovakia, what reasons could be advanced in favor of it, [he] would hardly say, [he speculated], that we consider them necessary to offset the political effect of the USSR and its forces of occupation." On balance, Murphy found "small profit, if any, to retention of our forces in Czechoslovakia." He proposed instead waging a high-flown publicity campaign stressing "our friendly cooperation with Czechoslovakia and the contribution we've made to its liberation and welfare." [13]

The problem of troop withdrawals from Czechoslovakia was intrinsically related to the expulsion of the unwanted minorities. War Department pressures for alternate uses of the manpower escalated. In mid-October, General Eisenhower restudied alternatives. On October 14th, he sent Murphy and General Bull to Czechoslovakia to review the questions with government officials. Eisenhower submitted his recommendations forthwith on October 17th to the War Department:

[Our] two-divisional strength of about 30,000 is now spread over a 266-mile front engaged in blocking the movement of Soviet troops into the US section . . . and is protecting the German minority against Czech aggression . . . All missions assigned to our forces . . . have been substantially completed. These . . . included: the establishment of law and order, the defeat and disarmament of the enemy, the repatriation of United Nations displaced persons, and the disposal of captured enemy material.

Eisenhower recommended that two divisions be retained until "an orderly evacuation of Sudeten Germans was completed [and] that if possible, an agreement be reached with the Soviets on a schedule of withdrawal." In any case, "we should withdraw within two weeks, [following] the orderly evacuation of the Sudeten Germans." Like Murphy at State, he argued for a publicity campaign about U. S. benefits to Czechoslovakia. [14]

On October 29th, Eisenhower estimated that "a minimum of four months will be required" for the transfer and "that the Czechoslovak Government is . . . capable of effecting the orderly evacuation" once an inter-Allied agreement could be reached in accord with the Potsdam Conference decision. Secretary of War Robert Patterson affirmed to Secretary of State Byrnes that "there is *no military necessity for the retention of our troops* in Czechoslovakia after the target date of 15th November." Any retention beyond that date "must be justified by *non-military considerations*." Patterson requested a decision from the State Department by November 1st, "as Eisenhower's present instructions lapse on the 15th." [15]

The situation occasioned a meeting in Washington of the secretaries of state, war, and navy on October 30th, after which Secretary Byrnes gave instructions to proceed with a message to Stalin, proposing simultaneous withdrawals of Soviet and American troops, to be requested by President Truman. Byrnes further suggested, in view of the delays, a "fortnightly extension of the deadline for the beginning of mutual withdrawals to December 1st," as the troops were no longer needed and were a drain on Czechoslovak economy. [16]

Within Czechoslovakia, the response was instantaneous. Beneš was immensely pleased. He invited Ambassador Steinhardt alone to lunch on October 31st for an updated briefing and took the occasion to complain of a political snag. He had hoped to revamp his cabinet by eliminating some of the Communists, in view of their being overrepresented in the present cabinet, but the Party had balked. Changes in the cabinet labored under a unanimous rule, necessitating a compromise. The cabinet was enlarged by three posts until the elections, and these posts would go to the resistance groups, which, combined with the London forces, gave Beneš a majority. The three new members would be moderates.

Beneš took special exception to Václav Kopecký, Communist minister of information, whom he replaced, followed by a thorough purge of the entire ministry, a change that he communicated privately also to Nichols. The British envoy reported home that "the [ad]ministration of information is a great difficulty." [17]   The Czech Press Bureau, controlled by the minister, had produced a diet "monotonously eastern in flavor," according to Nichols.

> The radio was firmly in Communist hands. The Ministry responsible for the allocation of paper for books and periodicals, licenses to publish, and for the entire film industry . . . refused paper for the publication of a book of Britain's war effort because a similar account of Russia's contribution has not yet been published . . . Three-fourths of the books published here since May have been translations from the Russian or volumes about the Soviet Union.

Other examples of anti-Western bias of the ministry were abundantly cited by the ambassador. [18]

Steinhardt returned Beneš to his negotiations with the Soviets on troop withdrawals without any visible reductions thus far. Beneš estimated that the Soviet troops numbered some 300,000, the number for which food was requisitioned—fairly close to Jan Masaryk's off-the-cuff guess. The cost to the Czechoslovak government of feeding the

Soviet Army was 850 million crowns a month; for the U.S. Army, the sum was 120 million crowns monthly. No one accounted for the discrepancy.

Now, late in October, Beneš was decidedly set back to have a Communist, Clementis, the deputy foreign minister, confirm, after a personal check in Bratislava, the presence of Marshal Rodion Malinovsky's misbehaved Mongolian troops, after Stalin's "definite assurance" that these would all be withdrawn "before the end of July."

The Provisional Assembly "now afforded [Beneš] an opportunity to air the prevalent discontent at the presence of the Soviet Army in Zecho aside from its drain on State finances." He explained to Steinhardt that politics drove him repeatedly to protest against "both armies" and to say he desired simultaneous withdrawal. He told Steinhardt of his plan "to station Czechoslovak garrisons, comprising its reorganized Czechoslovak Army, near the large Red Army concentrations, [so as to encourage the local population] to refuse supplies to the Soviet forces [and to encourage] greater popular resistance to seizures of food and livestock [by Soviet troops], which were extensive." [19]

Stalin did not hesitate in replying to President Truman's delayed letter of November 2, 1945, regarding troop withdrawals. His response on November 9th was crisp and pointed:

Your proposal concerning the withdrawal of the armies during November can only be welcomed, particularly since it fully accords with the Soviet plans for demobilization and withdrawal of armies. Consequently, it may be considered that the withdrawal of the Soviet and American armies from Czechoslovakia will be completed by the first of December. [20]

Secretary Byrnes wired the news to Steinhardt on November 9th, adding "You may communicate substance of this message to President Beneš. Dept. is releasing statement to press," agreeing on that date also for withdrawal of American forces. [21]

By coincidence, Beneš had learned of the Soviet planned withdrawal a day earlier when he received General Ludvík Svoboda, who informed him that the Russian commander, Gen. Andrei Zhdanov, wanted to call on him in farewell, having received orders to "the withdrawal of his forces from Czechoslovakia immediately and to complete the same within 3 weeks." General Zhdanov also requested transportation for 40,000 troops eastward. [22] Ambassador Philip Nichols relayed the news to London on the 9th. [23]

On November 20th, Czechoslovak government representatives attended a farewell ceremony with the U.S. Army in Pilsen. The U.S.

commanding officer averred "that the American army would be out by December 1st." The Czechoslovaks were told that the Russians had given them permission to arrest Russian stragglers in the country after the first week of December. [24] Owing to the inability of the government to provide sufficient transportation, the Red Army was forced to abandon a large quantity of stores with a "sufficient number of troops to guard and maintain them." [25]

The British ambassador was also closely monitoring the reorganization of the Czechoslovak Army for omens of the political drift. The abysmal news for Whitehall was that "it looks as if the Second Intelligence Bureau . . . might now be entirely controlled by the Russian Military Intelligence" with its name changed to OBZ. The good news was that Gen. Heliodor Pika, "formerly Chief of Military Mission in Russia," who "sympathizes with Britain," had been appointed deputy chief of staff. Another item of good news was that Air Marshal Janoušek, "a sincere friend of ours," was made deputy chief of air staff. General Zeman, who had been second in command of the British-trained Armoured Brigade Group, was now commander of the tank corps. Nichols firmly believed that Beneš "will eventually do what he can to see that military and air officers conversant with our ways do come to the fore." [26]

NOTES

1. Klieforth, U.S. Chargé d'Affaires, Prague, to Secretary of State, June 28, 1945, *Foreign Relations* 1945, v. 2, p. 1260.

2. Vladimír Clementis to Klieforth, July 3, 1945, *Foreign Relations* 1945, v. 2, p. 1263.

3. Ibid., pp. 647-49. Italics added.

4. Beneš Press Conference, Prague, July 26, 1945, FO 371/v. 47154-110023.

5. Laurence Steinhardt to Secretary of State, Prague, September 4, 1945, *Foreign Relations* 1945, v. 4, p. 488. Italics added.

6. Nichols to Foreign Office, October 29, 1945, FO 371/v. 47094-107985.

7. U.S. State Department to Czechoslovak government, July 6, 1945, *Foreign Relations* 1945, v. 4, pp. 472-73.

8. Klieforth to Secretary of State, July 6, 1945, *Foreign Relations* 1945, v. 3, pp. 473-744. Italics added.

9. Joseph Grew to Klieforth, July 9, 1945, *Foreign Relations* 1945, v. 4, p. 474. Italics added.

10. James Francis Byrnes to Steinhardt, August 23, 1945, *Foreign Relations* 1945, v. 4, p. 484. Italics added.

11. Steinhardt to Secretary of State, August 25, 1945, *Foreign Relations* 1945, v. 4, p. 485.

12. Steinhardt to Secretary of State, September 4, 1945, *Foreign Relations* 1945, v. 4, p. 488. Italics added.

13. Robert Murphy, Acting Secretary of State, to Steinhardt, September 11, 1945, *Foreign Relations* 1945, v. 4, pp. 499-502. Italics added.

14. Secretary of War Patterson to Secretary of State, Washington, D.C., October 26, 1945, *Foreign Relations* 1945, v. 4, pp. 502-3.

15. Ibid. Italics added.

16. Ibid, footnote.

17. Telegram, Philip Nichols to Foreign Office, December 12, 1945, FO 371/v. 16129-207/12.

18. Nichols to Ernest Bevin, January 5, 1946, confidential, FO 371/v. 56006-112415.

19. Steinhardt to Secretary of State, October 31, 1945, *Foreign Relations* 1945, v. 4, pp. 503-6.

20. Byrnes to Steinhardt, November 9, 1945, *Foreign Relations* 1945, v. 4, p. 508.

21. Ibid.

22. Steinhardt to Secretary of State, November 8, 1945, *Foreign Relations* 1945, v. 4, pp. 507-508.

23. Telegram, Nichols to Foreign Office after a private tea with Beneš and wife, November 7, 1945, No. 744-747; N5337/207/12.

24. Telegram, Nichols to Warner, Foreign Office, No. 824, November 20, 1945, Repeated to Moscow and Washington, FO 371/v. 16021/207/12.

25. Nichols to Foreign Office, December 2, 1945, FO 371/v. 16021/207/12.

26. Telegram, Nichols to Warner, Foreign Office, November 5, 1945, FO 371/v. 10621. The fullest account of the transfer of the minorities is to be found in Radomír Luža: *The Transfer of the Sudeten Germans, A Study in Czech-German Relations, 1933-1962* (New York: New York University Press, 1964).

18

Democratic Socialization
(1945-46)

The Košice program of the first postwar coalition government contained a third objective beyond the expulsion of the hostile minorities and Allied Army withdrawals. It called for nationalization of heavy industries, insurance, and the banks; in short, of the large-scale enterprises that had been expropriated without compensation by the Reich or by the puppet governments following the 1939 Nazi occupation. Government ownership and operation seemed the most expedient means of restoring the country from its wartime disruptions and expropriations. The countryside lay near ruin as a consequence of the wholesale deportations of loyal Czechs to Germany, either for slave labor or merely to free the land for displaced Germans, who were moved in. "State administration" was the euphemism employed to render nationalization more palatable, especially to the British and American interests involved. Compensation invariably accompanied the program to ease its acceptance, at a fair value to be negotiated.

At the turn of the year 1946, conditions still bordered on hunger. Food supplies were observed by British Ambassador Philip Nichols to be "a matter of serious concern" even if "the rations of the Czech people . . . though fairly well distributed and adequate to maintain life [were] far from lavish. They [were] particularly short in fats." Meat was also in short supply, and "due partly to Russian requisitioning, vegetables were scarce." There was "plenty of flour and potatoes, and an exportable surplus of sugar," but "the food situation during the winter present[ed] serious problems." [1]

"A majority of the population remains always near the edge of hunger," continued Nichols. In the winter cold, "any slight cut of supply" was "keenly felt." "Without UNRRA's help, the situation would have been very serious," "serious" being a British understatement meaning critical. The delivery of UNRRA supplies was impeded, however. They were initially shipped to the Romanian seaport of Costanza, where vexatious delays and pilfering occurred before their dispatch overland to Czechoslovakia. The agency switched the sea route to Hamburg and Bremen and then on to Czechoslovakia through the somewhat more secure British and U.S. zones of occupation. Nichols calculated that the departure of the Russian Army would help. Meanwhile, he wrote, "symptoms of debility and undernourishment are serious in many parts of the country." [2]

The food crisis was exacerbated not only by delays in the army withdrawals, but also by a postponement of the expulsion of the Sudetens, "owing to the inability of the occupation authorities in Germany to cope with large-scale immigration in the winter, [even though] 700,000 to 800,000 had left by the end of 1945 for the Soviet zone . . . None of the 1,750,000 Germans to be transferred to the American zone had yet been moved." [3] Beneš explained in an interview with a Reuters special correspondent that he "avoided the term 'expulsion' of the Germans, substituting 'transfers' [which connoted] that the movement was to be carried out in a humane and civilized fashion," although he admitted that "in the beginning, many Germans were removed . . . in harsh conditions." [4]

Despite the good will, Ambassador Nichols was skeptical of early results. He confided to the Foreign Office his judgment that "transfers on a serious scale to the American zone are not likely to begin until the winter is well over," though a start would be made by the end of January. He also foresaw the "economic difficulties which these transfers will entail for the Czechoslovaks, loom[ing] larger and larger as the transfers get closer." In view of the hardships for the industries employing this highly skilled workforce, he predicted that the Czechs would be forced to "make every effort [to allow] . . . these workers [to remain], who will be most useful to them." [5]

As for industry, it had come to a "virtual standstill . . . during the first weeks after liberation." Initial coal shortages halted factory operations. Nichols ascribed the main problem to "a very large number of industries . . . [being] German owned." When the Germans withdrew, "National Administrators were put in charge and Workers Councils were set up." The first act of these authorities was "to eject German key-men and technical staff, often with stultifying results on the industry." These removals, combined with the lack of raw materials due to the chaotic state of European transport, had "the effect of depressing production to a new low level." Nichols found "widespread disorganization of this kind [for which there was] no quick remedy."

"The lack of transportation," he reported, "is, in fact, the major obstacle to economic development. Many more trains" had appeared by the end of 1945, but railroad transportation was "still far behind prewar standards . . . The railways are still very disorganized." Czechoslovakia "had only 25% of [its] prewar equipment." [6] By December 1945 he reported that the "Ministries of Commerce and Trade are beginning to obtain a grip of the situation." [7] At the turn of the new year, the Czech Press Bureau announced "a general improvement in the coal transport situation and that chemical and mining works, and cellulose and paper plants in Slovakia had resumed production after 11 months of inactivity and are now providing work for 1,000 employees." [8]

Shortages other than food contributed to the disarray. For example, there was a dearth of "soda ash and salt for the glass and chemical industries." Efforts were made to obtain these vital supplies from Austria in exchange for window glass. "The Russians supplied a small proportion of the iron ore required." Czechoslovakia then turned to "ask large credits in Sweden for iron-ore purchases." Conferences were held in London to explore how these problems could be alleviated. Housing in Prague was particularly tight, especially for Czech families returning from wartime exile in Britain. "The government evacuated all Germans from Prague to ease the scarcity but it was insufficient." [9]

On the whole at this stage, thanks to the food, medicines, and such supplies provided by UNRRA, the American Red Cross, American Relief for Czechoslovakia, and the Unitarian Service Committee, Czechoslovakia pulled through the first postwar winter in better shape than her neighbors. The distribution of seed grains and fertilizers gave the country a near-normal harvest in 1946. The Unitarian Service Committee and the Red Cross concentrated on sending medicines and equipment for hospitals and private clinics. UNRRA, plus the other agencies, contributed over $200 million in economic assistance, not including an Export-Import Bank credit of $20 million for raw cotton, which was permitted by Secretary of State Byrnes on October 31, 1945. Americans of Czechoslovak origin sent in a flood of "Care" packages to friends and relatives well into the 1950s, and the U.S. Information Service provided postwar books and technical literature. [10] These funds, as estimated by Ambassador Steinhardt, were the "equivalent of Zecho imports from the U.S. for nearly 10 years," which he later revised to "7 years normal peacetime imports."[11]

Among the early nationalization decrees was one signed on June 21, 1945, that "provided for a far-reaching land reform, whereby the landholdings of Germans and Magyars" and of "Czechoslovak collaborators were confiscated and redistributed on easy terms of repayment to Czech and Slovak peasants and small farmers." Ambassador Nichols observed the consequences. "Large estates virtually disappeared; there was a land-rush to the frontier areas, and the Communist Minister of Agriculture [Julius Duriš], largely responsible for the measure, won considerable support for his Party among the beneficiaries."[12]

On October 24, 1945, President Beneš signed a number of nationalization decrees, extending them to the food industry. These impinged heavily on British interests, in particular those of Lever Brothers and of Unilever, a subsidiary button and thread combine. Although Western diplomats thought Beneš's pace in these matters had accelerated, it was pointed out that he had "refused to sign some 20 decrees which the provisional government had tried to slip through during the last days before the Provisional Assembly met" at the end of October. Beneš wanted the admittedly Communist-dominated cabinet to take the responsibility, a maneuver that evoked heavy "criticism . . . at the first meetings of the Assembly." He told Ambassador Nichols he thought that the government had turned a significant "corner" in its political jockeying and he was now, for all practical purposes, "certain that the country would develop along democratic, parliamentary lines." Nichols decided that "despite his recent apparent surrenders on . . . the nationalization decrees, he [Beneš] will be proved in the long run to have played a skillful and successful hand against extremism and communism."[13] Nichols, in short, saw Beneš "as one safeguard" against "a Communist stranglehold which would disable the government from staging free elections . . . especially in the . . . absence of much resistance from non-Communist minority."[14]

Beneš also explained his strategy patiently to Ambassador Laurence Steinhardt, remarking "that the decrees were much more sweeping than he had desired . . . [that] he has done everything within his power to restrict their scope, but had been unable to restrain the radicals, without precipitating an open break." He anticipated "that there will be *considerable modification of the progress of nationalization as it is put into effect.*" Steinhardt was persuaded, like Nichols, that

Beneš felt "a major concession had to be made to the radicals to avoid communism." [15]

The Provisional Assembly convened for the first time on October 28th, the Czechoslovak Independence Day. Although during the next two months "it served rather as a debating chamber than a legislative body, it was of great value as a forum for criticism of the Administration, and for the ventilation of grievances." The Communists, seconded by the Social Democrats, "maintained their dominance," according to the observant Nichols. [16]

Beneš delivered a special broadcast to the United States on November 9, 1945, the second anniversary of the founding of UNRRA. Beneš "wished to assure the U.S. public opinion concerning [the] nationalization policy at a moment when Czechoslovakia is seeking large credits from U.S. sources." [17] American and British anxiety on this score needed to be allayed, especially as the UNRRA aid packages arrived in red, white, and blue wrappings and were labeled with the Stars and Stripes, which redounded to the prestige of the United States, much to the chagrin of Alexeev, the Russian UNRRA chief, and of the British and Canadian diplomats.

Beneš elucidated the four reasons for the nationalization policy, thinking it might be made more acceptable if it were demonstrated as a reasonable procedure. He argued:

1. Czechoslovak industry and banks had been appropriated by the Germans, who "plundered them into ruin," rendering them impossible "to return to individual Czech owners without considerable State support." As the government could not afford to subsidize these establishments "at the expense of the rest of the population, . . . the best course would . . . be to leave the property in the hands of the State."

2. "German industry and banks had been confiscated as the property of Germans." Debate ensued over their distribution among Czechoslovak capitalists as "compensation . . . for losses caused by the Germans."

3. "The whole of Europe was moving from pure liberalism towards Socialism . . . Czechoslovakia was in the van . . . [with these] progressive social measures."

4. It was natural for the great Slavic power adjacent to Czechoslovakia to "influence this country." [18]

Beneš perceived the nationalization program as appropriate to the economy, which was faced with a severe stringency of private capital and a reluctance to invite foreign investments. The program was reasonable, he thought, especially in view of his plan for "fair compensation" to British and American claimants, as well as to citizens. Nevertheless, here lay the snag of endless negotiations and repeated recriminations that provoked a heating of the Cold War caldrons. On November 23rd, Nichols detected that the speeches of government officials "did not lead us to believe that these proposals were likely to prove adequate," chiefly because "the Czechoslovak Government did not . . . command the necessary resources." Masaryk, with whom he was discussing the matter, blandly commented "that he was not at all surprised that HM'sG took this view." Masaryk, moreover, acknowledged that "it was inevitable that . . . if British interests were taken over, this was bound to weaken the commercial and industrial relations between our two countries" and in turn would "weaken our political relations." He regretted deeply that this was happening at "this moment when we . . . particularly wished these relations to remain close and intimate." Masaryk and Nichols agreed that they should "press [for] commercial and industrial contacts . . . [to] be maintained and not abruptly severed." Nichols then cagily suggested that the nationalization program "should start with domestic concerns first and . . . leave all foreign concerns until later . . . [hoping] that a free Parliament [would request] . . .that these concerns should be exempted from the scope of the nationalization decrees." [19]

A fair evaluation of these nationalized properties arrived at London's Foreign Office early in January 1946 in the form of a letter from Tomáš J. Báta of the famous shoe-making enterprise at Zlin, who was now located in Ottawa, Ontario. Báta stated that he owned at least "40% of the shares" of Báta Co. at Zlin, which in addition owed him "the amount of $1,122,826 on a loan account," for which he had obtained a writ through the Ontario courts. The value of his interest alone was $52 million. Báta requested the British government to present this claim as coming from a British-held interest, not a Czechoslovak one. Báta complained further of egregious mismanagement of his plant by the state administrators, for which he would demand additional compensation. [20]

Trouble for pro-Western leaders was foreshadowed in the newspapers at home on December 8th. Ferdinand Peroutka, editor of an independent, pro-Beneš weekly, wrote an editorial "attacking the British and American policy toward Germany." He reported that "in British and American zones of occupation influential Nazis were not being ejected." [21] To make matters worse, word got out about the secret flight arranged in August 1945 by Gen. Walter Bedell

Smith, in violation of Eisenhower's directive forbidding fraternizing with the enemy, which carried Reinhard Gehlen, chief of Nazi East European intelligence operations, to Washington with six of his officers. All had been provided with U.S. passports. Gehlen was to return in July 1946, following almost a year of briefing sessions with U.S. Army Intelligence in Washington. Significantly for Czechoslovakia, Gehlen would carry a special mandate from the War Department, with U.S. financing, to organize his autonomous intelligence network, ORG, which would extend through Czechoslovakia and into Poland and Hungary. Gehlen would conclude an agreement in July 1949 to share his material with the CIA, which was set up in 1947 to replace the wartime OSS. In his article in December 1945, Peroutka charged further that "Britain was grossly violating the Potsdam Agreement by maintaining large German military and air formations in her zone."[22] Such flouting of wartime unity by the Western Powers could only reverberate in Czechoslovakia to the advantage of the pro-Russian Communists.

Another important problem for the Prague government derived from efforts to rehabilite Jewish properties. Under the Germans, some confiscated Jewish property had been given to Czechs, who were now reluctant to hand these possessions back, despite a presidential decree. Immediate reparations had been proposed, but "amazingly little has been done so far," according to a visiting member of the British parliament.[23]

On January 15, 1946, a westward-looking Socialist deputy announced in the National Assembly "that an invitation to visit Czechoslovakia had been extended to Mrs. [Eleanor] Roosevelt." Two days later, it was unanimously agreed that the general elections to the Constitutional National Assembly should be held on the 26th of May.[24]

The National Court opened in Prague at the same time, on the 15th, for the start of treason trials. The Ministry of Justice had stated on the 13th that "70 or 80 persons in all, including members of the former Protectorate Government, would come before the National Court." Justice Minister Petr Drtina told the press that "24 People's Courts have been set up in Bohemia-Moravia" and that all were functioning. "So far," he reported, "1,650 verdicts have been returned by these courts," 150 of them being death sentences or life imprisonment.[25] Father Josef Tiso, notorious chief of the independent puppet Slovak state would come up soon for trial in a Slovak national court on charges of treason. A Czechoslovak delegation headed by the minister of justice, accompanied by five newspaper editors, was appointed to go to Nuremberg early in February to represent the country when "the Soviet team present their case."[26]

Steinhardt now perceived that "the chasm between the moderates, including Masaryk, [Hubert] Ripka, Drtina, [Petr] Zenkl, [Jaroslav] Stránský, on the one hand and the radicals, such as [Zdeněk] Fierlinger, [Klement] Gottwald, [Bohumil] Laušman, [Václav] Nosek . . . [Václav] Kopecký, [Julius] Duriš . . . on the other hand, has perceptibly widened . . . Every effort by [Vladimír] Clementis, [Ludvík] Svoboda, and [Václav] Majer to shift from radicalism to a more moderate course is bitterly resented by the radicals . . . who pursue aggressive tactics." He attributed the leftward drift to a timidity stemming from "a fear complex" of the moderates. "Seven years of Gestapo operations" in their country apparently left a mark, inducing "fears of personal reprisals for political obstinacy," which must be coupled with "Communist control [of] the press . . . radio, and the police."[27]

On January 20th, other apprehensions arose in Prague for the British and United States diplomats from a speech of the minister of information on January 20th, in which he "referred to a scheme brought home from Moscow by the Minister of Industry [Bohmil Laušman] under which Czechoslovakia was to be included in the Soviet 5-Year economic Plan." Details of the Moscow arrangement were not forthcoming from either Laušman's office or the Foreign Trade Ministry. The Western diplomats assumed that "the Russians appeared to desire a monopoly of trade with Czechoslovakia." It turned out, according to a respected foreign journalist, that Laušman had demurred to Anastas Mikoyan, claiming that his country needed various finished products and machinery from the West and that he had been told bluntly that "Czechoslovakia could very well do without these articles." Appeals to Masaryk or Ripka were foreclosed, as they had left for London before Laušman's return from Moscow.

Nichols reasoned: "On the other hand, Russians, being realists, must realize that if Czechoslovakia is to provide goods which they themselves want, she must obtain equipment, etc. from the West. The agreement might well recognize this necessity and yet ensure production is first offered to Russia."[28]

On February 7, 1946, U.S. Secretary of State James Francis Byrnes telegraphed Steinhardt a secret-urgent message of signal importance. "For your confidential information, National Advisory Council on International Monetary and Financial Programs has approved at meeting January 29th, negotiation of an Eximbank reconstruction loan to Czecho of approximately $50 million, with the understanding that loan negotiations may result in data showing need for larger credit." Byrnes said this decision resulted from the official application for $300 million filed on September 1st by the Czechoslovak ambassador. Also approved was "the $25 million cotton credit." These reconstruction loans merely required statements documenting the need. The Czechs "have not submitted" these. "Czecho explanation for delay is that special mission from Praha possibly headed by Masaryk, would arrive in Washington to negotiate loan. No information available to Dept. on possible arrival of Mission." The embassy had not heard anything or "received sufficient instructions of even authority to submit statements of requirements prepared by them."

Byrnes continued his noteworthy directive: "Pending receipt of definite information concerning engagements assumed by Laušman in Moscow, Dept. considers that negotiations for Exim loan should proceed." The Secretary of State went on to advocate "economic assistance to Czecho [as] necessary if Czecho Govt. *resists inclusion in any Soviet economic plan.*"

His other prerequisite for loans was that the Czechs would compensate Americans for nationalized properties at fair value as promised. He authorized Steinhardt to explore the ground for further accommodations "informally and unofficially with Czecho For. Min. and other appropriate key officials . . . [and] report to Dept." [29] He clearly respected Steinhardt's advice and sought it. Steinhardt failed to take note of "widespread flooding in various parts of Bohemia-Moravia." Nichols, on the other hand, informed the Foreign Office that he had learned "many road and rail bridges have been destroyed," as if the paucity of railroad rolling stock were not enough of a plague. [30]

Meanwhile, Czechoslovak-Hungarian talks were held in Prague from February 6th to 10th regarding population exchanges of their respective nationals, especially of Hungarians living in Slovakia, involving about 120,000 people on each side. Although of smaller dimension than the removal of the Sudetens, these exchanges involved shunting a considerable number of people about due to popular resentment against wartime collaborators, a sentiment diligently stroked by the Communists. Two months later, on April 24th, Jan Masaryk declared it a "matter of decisive importance that . . . the Conference of Foreign Ministers in Paris" should discuss the Czechoslovak desire to have an additional 200,000 Hungarians transferred out. [31]

He was given assurances by the spokesman for the Foreign Ministers Council that the Czechs "would be given an opportunity to present their case regarding the Hungarians."[32] Direct negotiations for these exchanges dragged on interminably within the commission set up by the Foreign Ministers Council, and at the end of June, they were inexplicably and abruptly terminated by the Hungarian Government.[33] An office for the assistance of Magyar "repatriates" was opened, however, in Bratislava by a Magyar named Ferenc Wagner.[34]

President Beneš in mid-February received a delegation from the glass-making factories in Sudetenland informing him "that the complete transfer of the Germans would make it impossible to produce glass for export." Because Beneš had foreseen the problem, it was not difficult for him to respond considerately that "a certain number of Germans would be retained." He thought then that "the National character of the State need not be affected if 200,000 or 300,000 Germans remain with us."[35] Weeks later, in March, the Economic Council convened a meeting of ministers to consider its proposal to retain "17,000 qualified German employees in the mining industry, 43,000 German specialists in other . . . industries, and from 20,000 to 60,000 in agriculture . . . [in addition to] 7,500 German china workers, the government consented altogether to exempt some 400,000 persons, which figure included the workers' families"[36] At all events, by early April, the Colonization Office announced to a Parliamentary Committee that "during the past 8 months, 1,800,000 Czechs settled in the former Sudetenland."[37]

A high-level Polish delegation, including several ministers of state, also arrived in Prague in mid-February accompanied by a "large number of experts for negotiations," which eventually deadlocked by the end of the month. Some progress was reported, however, on "cultural and transport questions," but the top officials departed "to report home." Several of the experts stayed on to hammer out differences, and the legations were elevated in status to embassies.[38]

Marshal Tito of Yugoslavia stopped off in Prague on his way home from Poland in March. Each side avoided concluding a treaty at the time. A month later, however, it was announced that the disagreements had been composed and a treaty of alliance would be signed in Belgrade on May 9th. For the occasion, the top Czech officials who would accompany the Prime Minister were the heads of the ministries of foreign affairs, trade, justice, defense, and the secretary-general of the economic council.

A potentially shattering incident occurred in mid-February that might have ruptured Czechoslovak-American relations had not cooler heads in Prague prevailed. On February 11-12, 1946, a "group of 13

American non-commissioned officers and men, furnished with American Army papers, arrived in Prague" and went to the village of Stěchovice, 15 miles south of the capital. They were guided by a German prisoner of war to a spot where they proceeded to dig for 38 hours, protected by their own sentries, who shot at government security guards attempting to approach.

They departed with several filled chests, loaded them into their cars, and headed toward Prague. Three of these men were later detained briefly in the Alcron Hotel by security police. This proved to be a U.S. Intelligence operation. Government officials protested the incursion of their sovereignty. Jan Masaryk was quoted in the *New York Times* as saying: "Some folks don't seem to know that we are an Allied country and that the war is over."

The next day's *Times* revealed what had been taken from the cache:

In addition to Czech State documents of the highest importance, the cache included the following: complete files kept by the 'protectorate' between 1940 and 1945 with evidence more damning than has hitherto come to light on German occupation methods; Élite Guard records for Bohemia and Moravia; top secret daily Gestapo reports from 1940 to 1945; long lists of Czech collaborationists, including "honorary espionage leaders"' directions for the secrecy of all German research projects; files of Gestapo leaders, including the infamous Reinhard Heydrich . . . and inventories of treasures, including the crown jewels, stolen from Bohemian castles. [39]

The plans for the secret mission had been known only to a few U.S. and French intelligence officers. No Czechoslovaks were informed, nor had state officials been asked for entry permission. The U.S. leader lied on this point to the border guards. After powerful protest, deep apologies were extended by Ambassador Steinhardt and the materials were turned over to the Czechoslovak authorities. Beneš declared he was "extremely glad to get back his own official and personal papers, which formed part of the cache." [40]

At this juncture, Secretary of State Byrnes clarified his position to Steinhardt regarding the extended negotiations for a sizable U.S. loan. He told his emissary on February 19th that "the Eximbank reconstruction loan is not likely to exceed approximately $50 million," plus a cotton credit of about $25 million more. He wrote:

Department understands that Czecho Government considers a [reconstruction] loan of only about $30 million would be considered a failure of Masaryk's mission and would result in unfavorable political repercussions . . . [He suggested that Steinhardt counsel Masaryk to] reconsider the advisability of coming here and [to] entrust loan negotiations to other officials. *Department wishes to avoid situation which would result in lessening Masaryk's prestige and thus weakening of democratic forces in Czecho Government.*

Byrnes thought that Czechoslovak credit needs would probably have to come from the International Bank for Reconstruction and Development after it begins operations. This bank was eventually set up under the U.N. Development Plan. [41] In other words, Byrnes did appreciate the potential counterproductivity of a hard line, but he apparently underestimated the negative consequences of Masaryk's delay.

The next week, on February 26th, Steinhardt defended at length his rigid, hostile stand toward Czechoslovakia, writing candidly to Byrnes:

I have been given to understand that in some circles in the U.S., it is being argued that "American loans to foreign countries tend to deter the spread of Communism." To my mind, this argument fails to take into consideration the fact that *Communists are already so strongly entrenched* within the Governments of many European countries that *large American loans to such countries are more likely to help them than to harm the Communist cause.* It is my considered judgment that *a large American loan to any foreign Government in which the Communist Party is strongly represented* will be availed by them indirectly *to entrench their position and extend their grip.*

While I favor the cotton credit as a routine commercial transaction, which is as much in our interest i.e. disposing of surplus cotton as it is in the interest of Czecho to resume manufacture of textiles on a large scale, I *do not favor a large loan for reconstruction purposes at this time* and certainly not unless the elections in May evidence the desire of the people to rid themselves of the very real threat that now exists of virtually complete Communist domination, not until tangible evidence exists that American properties . . . nationalized will be paid for in dollars or exportable merchandise as distinguished from the vague promises of Laušman.

Steinhardt vetoed the approved reconstruction loan to Czechoslovakia of "more than 30 million dollars, [which he calculated as] sufficient for the Government's present needs." He then tossed a sop to the Czechoslovaks: "If later in the year, or next year, it is deemed necessary or desirable to loan an additional 20 million dollars," that would be all right. He would not now "mortgage our future decision"; he thought we should wait and see what happens with regard to communism within the country and to compensation for American claims. He told Byrnes that he had informed Masaryk "who fully understands the situation" and had postponed his trip to Washington. Instead, Masaryk authorized Mladek to "make soundings" in Washington on the loan situation. [42]

In relaying Byrnes's advice to Masaryk not to go to Washington at this time, it is not clear whether Steinhardt knew that the Export-Import Bank had already approved a $50 million reconstruction loan and was simply awaiting information on its planned uses from the Czechoslovak government. Nor is it clear whether he communicated to Masaryk his private advice to his government to stall. reduce, and cut off funds for this "Communist dominated" country. On the latter point, he probably withheld the news.

On March 5th, in remarkable coincidence with Churchill's "iron curtain" speech at Fulton, Missouri, Steinhardt reverted strongly to his hard-line stand, when he disapproved "the Czechoslovak request for surplus property be increased from $10 million to $50 million." Washington corrected his confusion on the 15th, informing him that the Foreign Liquidation Commission had increased the credit to $50 million for "surplus property," which was "in no way related to the contemplated Export-Import Bank [reconstruction] loan to Czechoslovakia." The State Department "did not regard the request excessive in view of similar credits to other countries and the desire of the Foreign Liquidation Commission to dispose of the maximum amount of surplus property." [43]

In mid-March Byrnes directed Steinhardt to communicate to the Czechoslovak foreign ministry news that the "U.S. Government [is] ready [to] enter negotiations [on compensations] with Czecho Government," as proposed by Foreign Minister Masaryk on January 25th. It appreciated the Czechoslovak foreign ministry's assurance that "Czecho does not intend seclude herself from economic cooperation with other countries." Byrnes then added significantly, "Solution depends on facilities granted Czecho export trade . . . Department desires to start as soon as practicable in Prague with American Embassy." The bottom line in the Byrnes directive on the negotiations, which he was delegating to Steinhardt, was, "where original investment was in dols., compensation should be in dols or currencies freely convertible into dols." [44] Byrnes was fully apprised that the Czechoslovak credit for surplus property purchases would be paid a modest interest of 2.375 percent annually, and that the first $10 million would be repaid in crowns. [45] Steinhardt had also assured Byrnes that "the Czech Gov't desires economic development." [46]

The amounts involved for Americans were relatively modest in comparison with those of the British compensation claims or the values of properties confiscated from nationals of enemy countries, such as the Germans, Italians, Austrians, or Hungarians. The figures, as published in a Prague periodical, *Czechoslovak Industry*, for percentages of foreign participation in Czechoslovak industry as of May 1st, 1945, were: Great Britain, 19.7 percent; United States, 3.6 percent; Germany (including Austria), 61.6 percent; Italy, 4 percent.

The British were mainly involved in mining, iron manufacturing, and chemicals. U.S. citizens had invested in trade of mineral oils. As former enemy investments were to go without compensation, sufficient funds were manifestly available as reimbursements to the British and Americans. [47]

Steinhardt remained "disturbed at the prospect of our last trump, the $50 million reconstruction loan being played before we have a definite commitment from the Czechs that adequate and effective compensation" for American claims would be forthcoming. He also opposed signing an interim commercial arrangement "two or three weeks before the general elections as against a very great political advantage to the Communist Party." He favored "the conclusion of an interim commercial arrangement immediately following the general elections . . . prior to or simultaneously with an Exim Bank loan. I would not sign before May 27," he insisted. [48]

On a different tack, the British Foreign Office concurred with Ambassador Nichols' sophisticated line that its best course was to bolster the moderates politically by generating a friendly atmosphere toward their country's culture and war and peace accomplishments for popular consumption. They established a British Institute at Bratislava and sent an important British art exhibit to Prague, which would eventually also be shown at the Institute. They prodded British wives residing in the country to a more energetic effort at pro-British propaganda by various devices, promoting exhibits of British art, peacetime industries, textiles, and fashions and by participating in the Anglo-Czech Club, the English-Speaking Students Club, the Women's Council, and so on. [49] The British dispatched some of their best-known scholars to give lectures, as well. Inspired competitively, Ambassador Steinhardt gave a lecture at Charles University on "American Democracy," which was attended by top officials of the government.

The Communists, on their side, played their part to popularize the Russian cause. One event they staged was a celebration of the 28th anniversary of the founding of the Red Army, at which Gottwald's address attributed "Czechs ability to get rid of the Germans . . . to the assistance of the Red Army and to Stalin." One-sided as it was, this view was readily swallowed at the time. The USSR sent a fully equipped Russian secondary school to Prague on March 4th, which it undertook to maintain. [50]

NOTES

1. Philip Nichols to Foreign Office, November 6 and 8, 1945, FO 371/v. 47094-107985.

2. Ibid.

3. Nichols to Warner, Foreign Office, January 12, 1945, FO 371/v. 56003-112415.

4. Guy Bettany, Reuters Special Correspondent, Prague, January 11, 1946, FO 371/v. 56006-112415.

5. Nichols to Warner, January 12, 1946, FO 371/v. 56006-112415.

6. Nichols to Foreign Office, October 26, 1945, secret, FO 371/v. 47094.

7. Ibid.

8. Czechoslovak Press Bureau, January 4, 1946, FO 371/56003/Xc 110148.

9. Nichols to Foreign Office, November 6, 1945, FO 371/v. 46094-107985.

10. Laurence Steinhardt to James Francis Byrnes, February 26, 1946, *Foreign Relations* 1946, v. 6, pp. 185-87.

11. Byrnes to Steinhardt, February 7, 1946, *Foreign Relations* 1946, v. 6, p. 182.

12. Nichols to Ernest Bevin, "Annual Political Review," November 20, 1945, confidential, FO 371/v. 56085-109377.

13. Nichols to Bevin, November 12, 1945, FO 371/v. 47045-108440.

14. Nichols to Bevin, December 15, 1945, confidential, FO 371/v. 47096-108451.

15. Steinhardt to Byrnes, October 31, 1945, *Foreign Relations* 1945, v. 6, p. 555. Italics added.

16. Nichols to Bevin, December 15, 1945, FO 371/v. 47096-108451.

17. Nichols to Bevin, November 17, 1945, secret, FO 371/v. 47045-108440.

18. Ibid.

19. Nichols to Foreign Office, November 14, 1945, FO 371/v. 47114.

20. Tomáš Báta to Foreign Office, January 4, 1946, FO 371/v. 56021-114167.

21. Nichols to Foreign Office, December 14, 1945, FO 371/v. 47096-108451.

22. Ibid.

23. V. Morris to Foreign Office, December 15, 1945, FO 371/v. 47046-108451.

24. Nichols to Bevin, January 18, 1946, FO 371/v. 56003-110148.

25. Nichols to Foreign Office, January 18, 1946, FO 371/v. 56006-112415.

26. Ibid.

27. Steinhardt to Secretary of State, January 25, 1946, *Foreign Relations* 1946, v. 6, pp. 178-80.

28. Nichols to Foreign Office, January 22, 1946, FO 371/v. 56014-110132.

29. Byrnes to Steinhardt, February 7, 1946, *Foreign Relations* 1946, v. 6, p. 182. Italics added.

30. Attaché Schuckburgh to Bevin, February 15, 1946, FO 371/v. 56003-110148.

31. Steinhardt to Secretary of State, April 26, 1946, *Foreign Relations* 1946, v. 6, pp. 190-91.

32. Steinhardt to Secretary of State, May 8, 1946, *Foreign Relations* 1946, v. 6, pp. 194-95.

33. Nichols to Bevin, June 28, 1946, confidential, FO 371/v. 56004-Xc/110148.

34. Jan Masaryk from Foreign Office, June 30, 1946, FO 371/v. 56048-Xc/114443.

35. Ibid.

36. Nichols to Bevin, March 22, 1946, FO 371/v. 56003-Xc/110148.

37. Nichols to Bevin, April 6, 1946, FO 371/v. 56003-Xc/110148.

38. Ibid.

39. *New York Times*, February 24 and 25. 1946, FO 371/v. 56045-114224.

40. Nichols to Foreign Office, March 14, 1946, FO 371/v. 56045-114224.

41. Byrnes to Steinhardt, February 19, 1946, *Foreign Relations* 1946, v. 6, pp. 184-85. Italics added.

42. Steinhardt to Byrnes, February 26, 1946 *Foreign Relations* 1946, v. 6, pp. 185-188. Italics added.

43. State Department to Steinhardt, February 7, 1946, *Foreign Relations* 1946, v. 6, p. 182.

44. Byrnes to Steinhardt, March 14, 1946, *Foreign Relations* 1946, v. 6, pp. 188-89.

45. Steinhardt to Byrnes, January 31, 1946, *Foreign Relations* 1946, v. 6, p. 181.

46. Steinhardt to Secretary of State, January 30, 1946, *Foreign Relations* 1946, v. 6, pp. 180-181.

47. Nichols to Bevin, "Weekly Information Bulletin," March 4, 1946, FO 371/v. 56003-Xc/110148.

48. Steinhardt to Secretary of State, July 30, 1946, *Foreign Relations* 1946, v. 6, pp. 209-10.

49. Foreign Office to Prague, March 14, 1946, FO 371/v. 56063-114792.

50. Nichols to Foreign Office, March 11, 1946, FO 371/v. 56003-Xc/110148.

19

Cold War Beginnings (1946)

During June 1946, British notables arrived in numbers, fulfilling the Foreign Office's design to generate favorable publicity for Western concepts in Czechoslovakia. Values such as liberty, justice, and democracy were featured. British Attorney-General Elwyn Jones came for a two-day visit on June 17th, the first to Czechoslovakia by a British official since liberation. Jones performed his public relations tasks superbly. During his visit, he mentioned that his government offered "to extend the Anglo-Soviet Treaty of friendship to a period of 50 years." He also catered to public taste by acknowledging "the necessity of close association between the Soviet Union and Czechoslovakia."[1]

The British lord chief justice followed Jones to Prague, as did Prof. Robert William Seton-Watson of Oxford on June 19th, at the invitation of his friend Jan Masaryk. This British specialist on Eastern Europe was soon joined by A. J. P. Taylor, the celebrated historian from Magdalen College in Oxford, for two weeks of lectures in Prague, Bratislava, and Moravska Ostrava. A broad parliamentary delegation, including five Labour members, was expected in July for two weeks for a full program of visits, to be shepherded by the embassy's commercial attaché, who would take them to Slovakia and the industrial regions of Moravia and Western Bohemia. Also in June, Ambassador Philip Nichols took the time officially to inaugurate his British Institute in Bratislava.[2] In the fall, the left-wing Labour member of Parliament, Konni Zilliacus, came to support his government's policy and was acrimonious in his criticism of U.S. Secretary of State James Francis Byrnes's Cold War speech at Stuttgart.[3]

No official U.S. delegations matched the British effort, but a party of 13 doctors, led by Dr. Erwin Kole, arrived on June 27th to contribute a series of lectures on their specialties. [4]

In response to these libertarian voices from abroad, in June President Beneš delivered an important address to the Writers Union, declaring "that freedom of literary and cultural expression should not be interfered with by party or class, by politics or the State, or by any non-literary [read political] influences." [5] Beneš undoubtedly meant his official pledges of freedom, prizing them himself as a fundamental principle of government.

Reactions in Prague to Winston Churchill's Cold War speech at Fulton, Missouri were temperate in tone while opposing its essence. In the judgment of the pro-Western, democratic leaders, such East-West discord would extinguish democracy in Czechoslovakia. Masaryk personally shared this estimate with Orme Sargent at the Foreign Office during his visit in London in June. He explained: "The fate of Czechoslovakia . . . depended on whether or not the Western Powers were able to come to an agreement with the Soviet Union. If there were no agreement, Czechoslovakia would inevitably be sucked into the Soviet orbit." [6] The U.S. embassy in Prague claimed to understand the attitude of the moderates generally, who "appreciated that their position would be greatly weakened if Western Powers were to . . . [become] indifferent and non-cooperative." [7]

Only three members of the government mentioned Churchill's speech publicly. Masaryk, feeling that a response was required of him, said a fortnight later in a speech on March 16th simply "that he fundamentally disagreed with it." He would not enlarge upon his differences. Vice Premier Jaroslav Stránský declared the speech stemmed from a "misunderstanding." He expanded: "Churchill saw the only guarantee of world peace [in] a British Alliance, which would impose peace on other nations. [His] mistake lay in the fact [that] even if Britain joined America, they would not have sufficient power to enforce legal order on the rest of the world . . . There was another Power, Soviet Russia" in Europe. [8]

The Communist education minister, Zdeněk Nejedlý, dealt with the subject in his distinctive, scholarly style. In a broadcast on March 17th, he said, "It was clear that Stalin attached great importance to Churchill's speech . . . It was worth a reply . . . Churchill was renewing Hitler's ideology in regard to the antagonism between the Anglo-Saxon and Slavonic worlds." On behalf of Stalin he charged Churchill with not understanding "socialism and socialization as manifested in Europe after the war. His antiquated and erroneous notion that freedom was incompatible with socialism made him unable to comprehend developments in Central and Eastern Europe." Nejedlý accused Churchill of launching a self-fulfilling prophecy, and he cited Churchill's prewar record of denouncing communism rather than fascism. These public statements guided Prague's perception of postwar Stalin in 1946. Stalin's reply was widely circulated in the press. The die was cast on Cold War attitudes, and the Czechoslovak democratic leaders grimly did their best for their own political survival, to bridge the gap and to stem its widening.[9]

Beneš was quoted in a *New York Times* interview on March 10th as saying, "I don't believe . . . that it will come to a conflict between England and the U.S. on one side and Russia on the other." He added that he was, however, disillusioned with the West over Munich, when "assurances of security had come from the East." But he acknowledged that "Western influence is still strong in Czechoslovakia, despite the Teheran Conference consigning Czechoslovakia to the Soviet sphere of influence."[10]

Meanwhile, British diplomats wrestled with more tangible matters to strengthen their country's trade position with the beleaguered country. They weighed their course prudently and took cognizance that:

Russia is at present moment the sole supplier of the bulk of the raw materials . . . iron and manganese ore for the iron and steel industry and raw cotton for the textile industry . . . It must now be expected that Czechoslovakia's trade will be pretty closely integrated with the Russian Five-Year Plan . . . Are we then in our trade with Czechoslovakia to have only the Russian leavings?[11]

They noted that "Czechoslovakia had commercial treaties with a dozen countries, half outside the Russian orbit. These would compete with Russia for her export products." This "should have some effect in offsetting any tendency toward a monopoly of Czechoslovak trade by Russia." The British position was aided by Russia's "inability to supply all the raw materials needed by Czechoslovakia." The Foreign Office asserted its having "no objection at all to Czechoslovak trade with the West." A drawback existed insofar as "most of the goods needed by Czechoslovakia cannot be supplied from the West at present." And judging from the items offered for sale to the Board of Trade in London, they had not "much to spare . . . A further limiting factor in Anglo-Czechoslovak trade is credit." The British lacked the resources for an effort to "capture the former German export trade to Czechoslovakia," due to their inability to extend substantial credits. The Board of Trade had no plan to overcome this deficiency, but hoped trade would grow between them in time. [12]

These practical considerations impelled British Foreign Secretary Ernest Bevin's definite support "on political grounds" for an application from the Unitarian Service Committee for the government to finance 50 percent of the cost of a home in Prague for displaced people. Hana Beneš gave her name to sanctify the project. The cost would be £3,000 for this "piece of reconstruction work . . . It is the policy of HM'sG to strengthen such [pro-Western] elements wherever possible." The institution would redound to British prestige and Ambassador Philip Nichols favored this "supplementary project to UNRRA's operations." [13]

The Foreign Office took note concurrently that the Czechoslovak minister of foreign trade was scheduled to lead a top-level delegation to Moscow on March 18th to negotiate a trade agreement for 1946, comprising representatives from several ministries as well as the Czechoslovak National Bank. It was patently a serious mission. [14]

It was not until April 12th that Hubert Ripka, the minister of foreign trade, signed a trade agreement in Moscow. Because the terms would soon become known, he previewed them for the U.S. ambassador "in strict confidence." Ripka reported that the Russians showed "little interest in consumer goods." Their principal concern was to obtain "machinery with which to manufacture their own consumer goods." "They could provide the Czechoslovaks iron ore, manganese, aluminum, lead, zinc, salt, and cotton—although not more than one-third of Czechs' requirements of cotton." Transportation was the "principal obstacle to a substantial expansion in their trade relations," requiring joint effort. "No reference was made . . . to inclusion of Zecho in the Soviet Government's new 5-Year Plan." Ripka was happy to observe that "Commodities Zecho is to receive from the Soviet Union could not . . . readily be imported from the U.S. and that Zecho's prospective exports to the Soviet Union were not readily salable to the U.S." U.S. ambassador Laurence Steinhardt rated Ripka as a moderate who was "inclined to attach considerable importance to his [grudging] optimism as to the prospects of satisfactory trade relations between Zecho and the U.S." [15]

A few days later, Steinhardt owned that he had been approached by a Czech trade official to explore a trade agreement. His reaction, diametrically opposed to that of the British, was hostile, as he attributed any improvement to a "political motive." He vetoed "an interim commercial arrangement [as] both undesirable and unsatisfactory, particularly as most-favored-nation treatment is now in effect." If such negotiations were to be pursued, however, the ambassador preferred that they take place in Washington, because experts were on hand there to help with the "highly technical nature" of the negotiations. [16]

Domestic attention in Czechoslovakia was riveted that spring of 1946 on the elections to the National Constituent Assembly, set for May 26th by a voting list of 7.5 million people under universal and compulsory suffrage from age eighteen. Four Czech and four Slovak parties were contending. Although Beneš had anticipated a smaller vote for the Communists than their strength presently registered in the cabinet, the Communists were anticipating 35 percent of the vote in Bohemia and Moravia and a smaller proportion in Slovakia. They had justification for this high expectation. They enjoyed a special relationship with the great Russian ally, whose political and economic support was manifest and whose "influence in the country has been exercised with discretion." In the context of the severe economic disruptions wrought by the German occupation, it was widely accepted that nationalization and economic planning were indispensable. The outburst of nationalism following liberation was equally understandable, underpinning the expulsion of the hostile minorities and punishment of collaborators. Ranged against the Communists were peasants and Catholics, as well as Western-oriented libertarian intellectuals steeped in their centuries-old historic traditions. It was generally conceded that "in no other country of Eastern Europe is there a stronger tradition of Western ideas." [17]

A week before Election Day, the press reported "Moves of Soviet Troops." Ambassador Nichols checked and learned that an "arrangement was . . . reached between Russian and Czechoslovak military authorities . . . on May 18th." Masaryk confirmed that the initiative had come from General Konev's emissary. The prime minister had given his permission for Soviet troop entries, but had failed to notify either Beneš or Masaryk, who "went through the roof" when they learned of the arrangement. Klement Gottwald was also kept in the dark. Ludvik Svoboda sent a messenger to Konev to countermand the orders, and the Russian ambassador, Valerian Zorin, was asked to enforce the cancellation. Four army corps, totaling some 100,000 troops, were involved. Their movement through Czechoslovakia, now postponed until after the election, was confined to nighttime and took three weeks to complete. Masaryk did his best now "to damp down as far as possible repercussions of the affair and to save Soviet face." [18]

At the same time, on May 21st, the old pro-Nazi collaborator and harsh wartime administrator, Sudeten Karl Frank, was sentenced to death by the National Court sitting in Prague. Ambassador Nichols reported that "some 5,500 people bought tickets to witness his hanging the following day in the courtyard of Pankrac Prison." [19]

Ambassadors Nichols and Steinhardt recounted that the elections were "free and . . . conducted with order and decency." They received "no reports of disorderly conduct or intimidation of the voters at the polls." Nichols was surprised at "the result [being] unexpectedly favorable to the Communists." They won 114 seats in the assembly of 300. He took comfort that the Communists could not obtain a majority vote without the Social Democrats. [20] Steinhardt concurred with satisfaction that "the Communist Party failed to achieve its objective of a majority in the new Assembly in spite of the unexpectedly large vote." [21]

Nichols foresaw that the vote on the new constitution which would require a three-fifths vote, "would be very close and might depend on . . . two or three members in the Constituent Assembly." The left bloc would require some support from the moderates. Nichols, in accounting for the Communist victory, saw "a very large vested interest," consisting of "jobs and influence in the large nationalized industries and firms of greater Prague," to which he added "that of the peasants, formerly voting conservatively Agrarian, who now received farms from the land nationalization program." He attributed another factor as well to the Communist success, namely "the work of the Communist dominated works councils and national committees." They campaigned cleverly, "emphasizing nationalism and their loyalty to Beneš and the Masaryk tradition." [22]

Altogether, the Communists polled 42 percent of the vote in Bohemia and Moravia, but much less in Slovakia, averaging 38 percent overall. The Social Democrats were reduced to 16 percent of the vote. In Slovakia, the right wing Democrats scored over 61 percent against the Communists' 30 percent. Nichols thought this disparity might foreshadow increased difficulties for Czecho-Slovak relations. [23] Steinhardt also prophesied a "struggle for control of the Social Democratic Party in which there is a strong difference of opinion between the left wing and the right." He predicted that "the Government of the National Front," comprising all parties, "will continue." [24] As leader of the largest party, Gottwald would be called to form a new cabinet. There was no question that Beneš would be overwhelmingly reelected. Nichols found him in high spirits on his 62nd birthday on May 28th.

In conclusion, Nichols decided that although the Communists were the strong party, feeding "the view that Czechoslovakia is within the

Soviet sphere of influence and should be written off accordingly," he thought this reading "a mistaken view." He insisted "*Prague is not behind the 'iron curtain'* . . . I am convinced that this country is not Communistically inclined. The character of the people is basically individualistic," analyzed Nichols, and the process of return to the Masaryk tradition might take considerable time. He counselled that "the Czechs will need all the help they can get from the West. I much hope that His Majesty's Government will . . . support her in every way possible." [25] Nichols "thought it right" to inform President Beneš that "Czechoslovakia could rely in the future as in the past upon the continued support of HM'sG," and he reported home with manifest pleasure: "There is no danger, I believe, of changes in the Ministry of Foreign Affairs for Mr. Masaryk." [26]

Nichols worked earnestly to contest Russian hegemony. He briefed the Foreign Office before Masaryk's visit to talk about Hungarian expulsions, to support the Czechoslovak claims on border adjustments against Germany and Poland before the Council of Foreign Ministers. To fail in this support, he said, "will play into the Russian hands." Moreover, "We British should sell [the Czechs] training equipment for the Army and aircraft supplies for the Air Force, otherwise they will buy them from the Russians." [27] Nonetheless, behind the scenes, Nichols fretted that "the non-Communist parties are showing a deplorable lack of guts in handling the Communists." He particularly lamented the permission granted to Soviet forces to cross the country at election time, and the Communist control of important ministries, such as interior, information, propaganda, and the police. [28]

Happier news was conveyed by Masaryk when he got to London's Foreign Office in June for his talk about Hungarian expulsions. He assured Sargent that "Dr. Beneš' position was extremely strong and the Communists would not dare to challenge it." He added in all modesty that "he himself was extremely popular throughout the country." [29]

In June Nichols repeated his caution to the Foreign Office about not writing off Czechoslovakia for allegedly being firmly implanted within the Soviet orbit, as producing "a bad effect." He alerted the Foreign Office to expect that "the new government will pay more lip service [now] . . . to Marxian theory and practice . . . but with *increasing* momentum oppose openly the more Communist aspects of the new Government's policy." Moreover, the Social Democrats, on whose support the Communists will have to rely, will resist any tendency toward totalitarianism. In foreign policy, as long as Masaryk remains, there will be no startling change. [30]

Immediately following the elections, Gottwald announced that the Communist victory would "entail no restriction of political or individual liberties . . . or academic liberties . . . that there would be no change in foreign policy, that shopkeepers need have no fears" of nationalization. "Nationalization, " he announced, "had now gone far enough." [31] In the interparty bargaining over cabinet posts, Nichols found Gottwald "a shrewd, hard, patient, and successful negotiator . . . Every Department in the Administration . . . of real importance, with the notable exception of Education," he observed "is subject to the control of the Communist Party . . . The Communists were, of course, deeply entrenched in the key positions." As a lifelong Communist trained in Moscow, "Gottwald's main purpose is to make of Czechoslovakia a Communist State." But Nichols saw Gottwald also dedicated to the "prosperity and independence" of his country. "The decisive question . . . is whether he . . . [and others in the government] in their reinforced positions of power will allow . . . parliamentary democracy to survive." [32]

Another agreement was signed by the Prague government with the Soviets confirming that "a full quota of 650,000 Germans" would be moved out by river and rail to the Soviet occupation zone. This order applied equally to the Sudetens and to German refugees from Silesia, Poland, and the Soviet zone of Germany. On June 5th, the Czechoslovak-Hungary Transfer Commission agreed that "transfers of Slovaks from Hungary to Czechoslovakia should begin on June 11th." [33]

The newly elected National Constituent Assembly convoked its first meeting on June 18th. Next day, Beneš was unanimously reelected as president. The old Zdeněk Fierlinger Government formally resigned and Gottwald was entrusted with forming a new Cabinet. Although endorsing the Košice nationalization program, a resolution was passed opposing further nationalization at this time and giving the private sector "legal security." The Trade Union Council supported the transfer to private hands of "certain categories . . . of confiscated industrial properties of traitors and collaborators." [34]

Goods news during the summer was that "the meat ration in Bohemia and Moravia will be increased by 100 grams per person in the next ration period." [35] It was surpassed on July 22nd by an agreement signed between the United States and Czechoslovakia, granting the latter a credit of $20 million at 2.5 percent interest for the purchase of raw cotton. [36] Beneš made an extensive tour of Moravia's towns and townships to spur industrial production in this time of crisis. [37]

The next great success for the government was scored by Jan Masaryk in his mission to Moscow on July 20th, for six days of grueling negotiations. His principal victory with Stalin was to obtain the return to Czechoslovakia of a synthetic petrochemical plant at Most, "which the Germans had greatly expanded" and the Russians took as "war booty" from their zone. The Czechoslovaks were negotiating for its repurchase. They bargained the price down from an assessed valuation of £39 million to a low of £12 million, still a burden on their pinched economy. In the end, Stalin said to Masaryk, "Do you want these works?" Masaryk nodded in affirmation and Stalin replied: "Well, you shall keep them—in spite of the experts." It was known to cognoscenti at the time that Stalin took keen pleasure in extending his generosity to Russia's friends.

Masaryk was "gratified" that the Russians "agreed with their plan to transfer 200,000 Magyars from Slovakia to Hungary," after the head-to-head exchange was already arranged. On Teschen, Stalin preferred that the Czechs and Poles negotiate directly, but he agreed to prod the Poles to get them started. They also explored terms for a permanent trade treaty to succeed the temporary one in existence. Masaryk's triumph was hailed at home in heroic fashion.

In his expansive mood, Stalin also took this occasion to confide "privately" to Masaryk an important policy decision of world significance, to wit: that "*the Russians definitely had no intention whatever of attacking Turkey.*" In view of Stalin's policy shift to accommodations with the Western Powers, Stalin took this occasion to back down on his claims in Turkey. According to Nikita Krushchev's memoirs, Vyacheslav Molotov, first in June 1945, then at the Potsdam conference in July, claimed three Turkish provinces in eastern Anatolia: Kars, Ardelian, and Artvin. These were populated by Armenians, and before the war had belonged to the Soviet Republic of Georgia.

This must surely have been communicated to the State Department in Washington, as Stalin undoubtedly assumed would happen, a year before the announcement of the Truman Doctrine, which included $150 million to Turkey for a defense buildup. This claim was certainly the basis of the United States' inclusion of Turkey in the Truman Doctrine, the opening of the United States' hard-line Cold War response.[*]

In his public report on the Moscow negotiations, Masaryk added that the Soviets undertook to supply the Czechoslovak army on a

---

[*]Eventually, in June 1953, following Stalin's death, the USSR offered to drop this claim on Turkey.

credit basis. He told Steinhardt when asked "that the Soviet Government had offered . . . equipment for 10 divisions" out of 16 the government intended to form. Pressed further, Masaryk said that his government did not intend to equip the Czech army exclusively with Soviet equipment, that they were buying aircraft from England and would build their own trucks and tractors. "No," replied Masaryk to more questioning, "they did not . . . intend to redevelop an armaments industry, as they considered that production capacity can be put to better use." Masaryk concluded ruefully that "it was inevitable for them to have close association with the Soviet Union, but the Czechs did not . . . intend to 'sell their souls', nor turn their backs on the West." [38]

The Russians also agreed to recognize, as Czechoslovak property, that of individuals and of corporations owned by Czechoslovak citizens in the Soviet zone of occupation. Masaryk reported that to date almost 750,000 Germans had been transferred to the U.S. zone and over 250,000 to the Soviet zone. He anticipated that the movements would be concluded by the fall for both sectors. [39]

The U.S. occupation army forces on July 25th handed over to the government in Prague a group of Germans, including their commander, SS general Hermann Höfle, who had suppressed the Slovak rising. [40]

In September, Steinhardt complained that the Communists, backed by the left-wing press, were giving exclusive credit to the Russians for complying with the Potsdam agreement for expulsion of Sudetens, while none of the moderates had the courage to credit the United States, despite "America's acceptance of 70% of expellees into the American zone in Germany." It took little to provoke Steinhardt against the Communists, in contrast to Nichols' "cool." In any case, the bulk of the transfers into the U.S. zone was completed by October. There was a temporary halt called in December due to inclement weather, leaving until spring the cleanup of the stragglers. Steinhardt announced a conference to be held "not later than Feb. 15, 1947 to decide upon technicalities for handling special cases of the infirm and insane, and orphans and derelict children." This compact was signed in Prague on November 12th by the Czechoslovak government and the U.S. military command. [41]

The figures mentioned in the assembly debate on September 11th revealed that "400,000 Germans still remained to be transferred out . . . and that 311,000 would be left" who were deemed essential to the country's "economic life." As it turned out, the last transport of Germans to the Soviet zone departed on October 27th; the last to the U.S. zone, on October 29th. [42]

The British chargé d'affaires in mid-September reported "a good deal of criticism amongst Socialist and People's Party personalities appear[ing] in the press against Jan Masaryk's performance at the Paris Peace Conference," although they conceded the continued high value of his name. They tore into him for "weakness in standing up to the Communists," ignoring Masaryk's demonstrable policy of avoiding clashes except on crucial points. They attributed this "weakness" to his having "no party behind him . . . [leaving him in] too defenseless a position."[43] Perhaps so, but these critics overlooked Masaryk's having always evaded party affiliations, preferring to keep his head above the "kuh-handlung" of party politics, as Masaryk often expressed it, to speak abroad only for the country as a whole. Perhaps these critics were frustrated because Masaryk refused to take up their partisan cudgels for them.

At the same time, Prime Minister Gottwald declared his *"gratification that Czech relations with the Western Allies are developing quite favourably"* and he deplored *"the loose talk about the 'iron curtain' and lack of freedom . . . in some quarters in the West."* He was happy to have read in the *News Chronicle* in London the "progressive and reasonably hopeful view" of Czechoslovakia as "a dynamo in Central Europe." He said "it would be a tragedy if the false ideas about England were to gain currency among the important sections of the populations." He himself made much of their wartime alliance.[44]

The British continued their efforts to overcome their negative image in the Czechoslovak Communist press. In September, Ellen Wilkinson, the British minister of education, lent her presence in Prague, which was "greatly appreciated by Czech officials." She attended the opening of a film festival on the 27th with Lawrence Olivier's magnificent portrayal of *Henry V*, which President Beneš attended with his minister of information and others. Nichols felt it all combined "to create an exceptionally pro-British atmosphere," to which was added a delegation from the Fabian Society, who made the rounds of interviews with officials.[45] The film festival traveled to Bratislava in mid-October.[46]

In late fall, Sir John Boyd Orr, director general of the United Nations Food and Agriculture Committee, was invited to Prague by the government. He held discussions with the Ministers of Food and Agriculture and gave "high praise to Czechoslovak economic recovery and intelligent outlook." In the press, he assured the country that "Czechoslovakia would not be made to suffer as regards food allocation because of her [excellent] efforts toward recovery."[47] Boyd Orr's favorable estimate overlooked strong criticism by Social Democrats in the Czechoslovak National Assembly against the minister of agriculture "for conditions in the frontier areas where . . . neglect by the authorities had caused grain to be left rotting in the fields and widespread sickness and mortality among cattle." [48]

The U.S. government agreed to pay the Czechoslovaks $400,000 in compensation for damage done by U.S. troops when occupying West Bohemia, and for reconstruction loans. The Czechoslovaks were making fine progress up to a certain point. The Canadians extended credits of $19 million against purchases; the British £5 million, plus £2.5 million for surplus stores; the Swedes, 24 million crowns; Brazil, $20 million for purchases; and the Export-Import Bank, $20 million to buy cotton and $2 million more for tobacco. The government planned to request "a further credit of $350 million from the International Bank," of "$20 million to buy cotton and $2 million more for tobacco." A trade union mission was dispatched to Egypt "to discuss a trade agreement and a cotton credit of 208 million crowns." [49]

Chief credit for the excellent results in the economy was due to the collaboration between Ludwik Frejka, head of the president's economic office, and Josef Goldman, director of the Charles University Institute of Social and Economic Studies. They advised the State Planning Office, which in turn developed close working ties with the trade unions, factory councils, and industrial management. But the government saw the need to acquire industrial equipment to round out UNRRA's assistance program for development. [50] On October 1st, the Ministry of Industry informed the National Assembly "that 19.3% of the factories. . . . affecting 61% of all industrial workers, were now nationalized. In the glass, electrical, and chemical industries, production has already surpassed the 1937 level, but the tanning industry was lagging far behind." [51] [52]

Vladimír Clementis, deputy foreign minister, addressed the assembly early in October to inform it that "the economic situation is improving . . . owing to the sensible policy of our government . . . the understanding attitude of our population, and their thriftiness and industry." [53] The minister of finance estimated that a profit would be made during 1947 "in all the nationalized industries except coal mines, power plants, mining, metal and engineering industries, and sugar refineries and life insurance." [54]

Suddenly, in the midst of the rising tide of understanding in the West about Czechoslovakia's special relationship with the Soviet Union and her economic strides forward, a most "unwelcome episode" occurred to upset Czechoslovakia's pursuit of "a policy of friendship toward the U.S. and Great Britain." Without any warning, the U.S.

State Department abruptly, on September 14, 1946, stopped all "further purchases of surplus war material from credit already granted, and so informed Masaryk." They also suspended "negotiations for a credit of $50 million, which was granted . . . by the Export-Import Bank for the purchase of machinery and raw material in America . . . an unusual act in the history of the relations of Czechoslovakia with a friendly State." On September 28th, the Czechoslovak chargé d'affaires in Washington was handed "a memo at the State Department on the suspension of negotiations with the Export-Import Bank," although the negotiations for a trade agreement continued. [55]

He was told that a memo was in process of preparation "in respect of the liquidation of an effective compensation for nationalized and confiscated properties of American citizens." The chargé d'affaires was officially and orally informed further that "the reasons for the stopping of purchases of surplus war materials is . . . [that the Czechoslovaks] have an erroneous conception of the nature of this credit and of American policy altogether." The Czechoslovaks had "presented a note of protest against the discrimination shown by American military authorities [re] war surplus purchases." This note had been presented on August 3, 1946, regarding "difficulties our Mission encounters in making its purchases." Clementis said, "The note is couched in mild terms, except where it twice uses the expression 'discrimination.' " [56] Ambassador Steinhardt on August 28th had protested "the charge of any discriminatory procedure." The head of the Czechoslovak Economics Department "had tendered both an oral and written apology for the use of the term discrimination."

Clementis speculated further in his attempted explanation to the National Assembly in November. He said that on September 14th, the government had concluded an agreement with Romania to repurchase some of the surplus materials they were purchasing from the United States. Czechoslovakia was now being accused by the Americans of profiting from these purchases. Clementis declared that this reason could not be accurate with respect to the shift of September 14th because the dates were exactly the same. The United States could not have known of the Romanian agreement in time to change its policy. Clementis continued his speculation. He said that people in the State Department delegation at the Paris Peace Conference had taken exception to the Hungarian reparations agreement and requested a one-third reduction on behalf of the Hungarians. They had also objected to Czechoslovak claims for a return of their Danubian shipping, which had been "detained [inexplicably] by the American Military Administration." The Czechoslovaks had fortified their claim as "part of their vital interests." The world press attributed the rupture to the "procedure of the Czechoslovak delegation" as one of "the foremost reasons." Clementis felt that it was due to "no agreement . . . [having] yet been reached . . . concerning compensation of nationalized property, nor any settlement of some questions of trading policy." Clementis argued in defense that the country had a history of paying off her loans and had never reneged. [57]

Clementis attributed the real difficulty "to the personal influence of Mr. Byrnes, owing to the attitude of the Czech Delegation in Paris." When he confided this opinion to Ambassador Nichols, the latter thought, on the contrary, "that the Americans had been much offended by the approval of the Czech Delegation to certain remarks made by Soviet spokesmen in Paris about their financial relations with Eastern Europe." Nichols suggested, "It might seem desirable for Dr. Clementis to put this right when he was in America." Clementis then informed Nichols, "he was much disturbed at [Britain's] suspending further progress with the projected British credit for £2½ million for purchasing stocks." Clementis asked whether Britain "intended to suspend this until all questions were settled between the Czechs and America?" Nichols replied, "It is our policy to cooperate closely with the U.S. Government in all economic and reconstruction matters—by consultations." [58] Another reason circulated that "Czechoslovakia had received far too much already" in comparison with other countries. None of these explanations sounded likely.

Masaryk told these authors he had observed "a distinct hostility in attitude within the U.S. delegation at the Paris Peace Conference," which had convened on July 29, 1946, following the Communist victory in the national elections held on May 26. He had run into flak for partially supporting Molotov's border revisions and for his protest on Western policies in Germany, while also responding sympathetically to the Hungarian request for a reparations abatement. These events may have reinforced Steinhardt's impression that Czechoslovakia was already deeply absorbed in the Soviet orbit and may have so induced Secretary Byrnes to make the sharp reversal. If these loans in hard currencies were thwarted, how could Czechoslovakia be expected to settle compensation of foreign claims as promised?

This potential breakdown of relations was countered by a joint U.S.-Czechoslovak declaration on November 14th on trade relations, which was not published in the Czechoslovak press until November 21st. The main points were "the joint agreement to remove all obstacles to mutual trade as soon as possible, and the guarantee of mutual fair treatment in trade matters and a guarantee of proper and effective compensation for the rights and properties . . . nationalized and confiscated." In addition, "Czechoslovakia undertook to furnish full information on her international economic relationships, similar to U.S. practice." Clearly, this alluded to Czechoslovakia's informing the United States on her trade commitments with the Soviet Union.[59]

By the end of 1946, U.S. and Czechoslovak relations had clearly moved to slippery ground. U.S. policy turned to a hard line on Czechoslovakia for her adherence to her close relations with the Soviet Union, and Washington took London with her. The breach portended ominously for the Czechoslovak moderates.

NOTES

1. Philip Nichols to Ernest Bevin, June 21, 1946, FO 371/v. 56030-114224.

2. Nichols to Foreign Office, July 19, 1946, FO 371/v. 56004-Xc/110148.

3. Konni Zilliacus speech, September 20, 1946, FO 371/v. 56005-Xc/110148.

4. Nichols to Foreign Office, July 19, 1946, FO 371/v. 56004-Xc/110148.

5. Nichols to Bevin, June 22, 1946, FO 371/v. 56004-Xc/110148.

6. Jan Masaryk to Orme Sargent, June 15, 1946, FO 371/v. 56015-Xc/110148.

7. Bruin to Secretary of State, June 10, 1946, *Foreign Relations* 1946, v. 6, p. 204.

8. Nichols to Bevin, March 22, 1946, FO 371/v. 56035-114224.

9. Ibid.

10. *New York Times*, March 10, 1946, FO 371/v. 56014-110137.

11. "Czechoslovak Trade with Russia and the United Kingdom," March 12, 1946, FO 371/v. 56014-110132.

12. Ibid.

13. Maurice Hankey to Lords Commissioners of Treasury, March 27, 1946, FO 371/v. 56035-114224.

14. "Czechoslovak Trade with Russia and the United Kingdom," March 12, 1946, FO 371/v. 56014-110132.

15. Steinhardt to Secretary of State, April 20, 1946, *Foreign Relations* 1946, v. 6, pp. 189-90.

16. Steinhardt to James Francis Byrnes, April 26, 1946, *Foreign Relations* 1946, v. 6. pp. 190-91.

17. *New York Times*, March 25, 1946, FO 371/v. 56008-112415.

18. Nichols to Bevin, May 24, 1946, FO 371/v. 56004-Xc/110148.

19. Ibid.

20. Nichols to Bevin, May 31, 1936, FO 371/v. 56009-112415.

21. Steinhardt to Secretary of State, May 27, 1946, *Foreign Relations* 1946, v. 6, p. 199.

22. Nichols to Bevin. May 31, 1946, FO 371/v. 56009-112415.

23. Nichols to Foreign Office, May 31, 1946, FO 371/v. 56004-Xc/110148.

24. Steinhardt to Secretary of State, May 27, 1946, *Foreign Relations* 1946, v. 6, p. 200.

25. Nichols report, May 31, 1946, FO 371/v. 56009-112415. Italics added.

26. Nichols report, May 28, 1946, FO 371/v. 56009-112415.

27. Nichols to Foreign Office, June 13, 1946, FO 371/v. 56036-114224.

28. Nichols to Foreign Office, May 27, 1946, FO 371/v. 56008-112415.

29. Orme Sargent, Foreign Office to Nichols, June 15, 1946, FO 371/v. 56015-110148.

30. Telegram, Nichols to Bevin, June 4, 1946, secret, FO 371/v. 56008-112415.

31. Nichols to Foreign Office, June 7, 1946, confidential, FO 371/v. 56004-110148.

32. Nichols to Foreign Office, July 5, 1946, FO 371/v. 56010-112415.

33. Ibid.

34. Ibid.

35. Nichols to Foreign Office, July 26, 1946, FO 371/v. 56004-110148.

36. Ibid.

37. Nichols to Bevin, July 19, 1946, FO 371/v. 56004-Xc/110148.

38. Walter Bedell Smith, U.S. Ambassador to USSR, Moscow to Secretary of State, July 26, 1946, *Foreign Relations* 1946, v. 6, pp. 208-9.

39. Nichols to Foreign Office, August 2, 1946, FO 371/v. 56004-Xc/110148.

40. Ibid.

41. Text of Agreement, *Foreign Relations* 1946, v. 5, p. 188.

42. Nichols to Foreign Office, September 20, 1946, Received October 25, 1946, FO 371/v. 56005-Xc/110148.

43. Shuckburgh to Hankey, September 13, 1946, FO 371/v. 56011-112415.

44. Shuckburgh to Foreign Office, August 27, 1946, FO 371/v. 56037-114224. Italics added.

45. Shuckburgh to Bevin, October 4, 1946, FO 371/v. 56005/Xc/110148.

46. Shuckburgh to Bevin, October 25, 1946, FO 371/v. 56005-110148.

47. Nichols to Bevin, November 30, 1946, FO 371/v. 56098-110148.

48. Minister of Agriculture to National Assembly, Nichols to Foreign Office, October 4, 1946, FO 371/v. 56005-Xc/110148.

49. Nichols to Bevin, November 30, 1946, FO 371/v. 56098-110148.

50. Nichols to Bevin, October 4, 1946, FO 371/v. 56005-Xc/110148.

51. Ibid.

52. Nichols to Bevin, November 22, 1946, FO 371/v. 56005-Xc/110148. Although UNRRA was phased out by the end of 1946, the mission in Prague denied rumors of its premature end and announced that "UNRRA will continue to operate in Czechoslovakia until 31st March 1947 to ensure the delivery of the agreed quota of supplies."

53. Nichols to Bevin, October, 1946, re Clementis speech, FO 371/v. 56098-114809.

54. Nichols to Bevin, November 10, 1946, FO 371/v. 56005-Xc/110148.

55. Foreign Office to Nichols, November 9, 1946, FO 371/v. 56098-114809.

56. Ibid.

57. Ibid.

58. Ibid.

59. Nichols to Foreign Office, November 23, 1946, FO 371/v. 56005-Xc/110148.

20

Storm Signals
(1947)

The winter of 1946-1947 saw mounting tensions on both sides of Churchill's Iron Curtain. On January 17th, John Foster Dulles, Republican adviser to the U.S. State Department, made an inflammatory speech advocating a Western buildup of Germany's coal and iron power as a bulwark against Soviet Russia.[1] In a follow-up speech a week later, he warned of "dire consequences" if "Soviet dynamism continued to be appeased." Dulles was reported to have cleared both speeches with U.S. Republican leaders, especially senators Arthur Vandenberg and Robert Taft and with Gov. Thomas E. Dewey of New York.[2]

On January 20th, the Polish elections established Communist control, evoking an acidulous reaction from Senator Vandenberg, who charged Russia with responsibility. East-West differences were exacerbated by Secretary of State George C. Marshall's announcement later in February that he was taking Dulles to the approaching Moscow conference of foreign ministers, as his adviser on Germany.[3] In Washington these strident voices of the widening East-West rift systematically depicted the Soviet Union as aggressive and expansionist.

On February 24, 1947, the British ambassador in Washington, Lord Reading, announced to U.S. under-secretary of state Dean Acheson that the British government would withdraw from Greece on March 31st, unable to continue its support of the corrupt Greek monarchy. On March 6, 1947 at Baylor College, President Harry S. Truman declared that an irreconcilable conflict existed between governments with planned economies and those of free enterprise democratic countries. Communism had to be countered and reversed if the democratic system were to prevail.

The U.S. response to the threat of "Communist" take-over in Greece was the Truman Doctrine, which the President read to Congress on March 12th. In response, Congress voted $400 million; $250 million to Greece and $150 million to bolster Turkey's military forces. "The U.S. would become the world's anti-Communist, anti-Russian policeman."[4] Since then, contemporary historians have found that no Communist threat existed in Turkey at the time; there was not even a Communist Party in existence there then. But Istanbul sat astride the Dardanelles, where Russian exits to the open sea in the West could be blocked. This was scarcely an innovative policy. The Russians had sought either control or assured passage through the straits for over a century. Turkey was brought securely into the Western bloc to thwart this purpose. The new U.S. policy represented a 180° switch from its wartime alliance.

East-West tensions gathered momentum chiefly over Allied policy toward Germany, which inevitably involved Czechoslovakia, situated as she was between Germany and Russia. After six years of brutal Nazi occupation there could be no choice of sides in Prague. President Beneš, whose pro-Western orientation was undisputed, had stated his position squarely in a speech while on tour of Moravia the previous summer. He declared: "If there should be a conflict, there is no doubt as to what we shall do. We shall go with our Ally," meaning Russia, with whom he had signed a mutual security and friendship treaty.[5]

Jan Masaryk reinforced this stand in his speech on foreign policy to the National Assembly on March 20, 1947. Focusing on U.S. policy in Germany, he said:

The Great Powers desired a rapid restoration of German economy [which was] not in conformity with a policy of demolishing German industry . . . The prospects of reparations in the future were not too inspiring . . . *Czechoslovakia's point of view was that compensation and economic restoration of Germany's victims should have precedence over the restoration of Germany herself.*[6]

Masaryk emphasized that "real peace could be assured only by agreements and cooperation among the Great Powers." His sole reference to the Truman Doctrine was his observation that "America was still a world which, in solving international questions, used its own standards . . . techniques . . . and methods of negotiation. It was from this angle . . . that we looked on President Truman's speech, offering help to Greece and Turkey." He concluded: "The whole world, particularly the small nations, was watching the development of their relations with interest, and sometimes with anxiety."[7] A frequent British visitor and observer of Czechoslovakia reported similarly to the Foreign office that "all political sections . . . are suspicious that the West is again building a strong Germany."[8]

Besides the settlement of claims for compensation of nationalized industries, which Masaryk and Eduard Beneš advocated for the speediest payment possible, even if the cost was greater than further bargaining might yield, there was another bothersome grievance. U.S. transit charges on Czechoslovak goods passing through their occupation zone in Germany were especially burdensome for coal shipped from German ports. The Americans were moreover demanding payment in dollars. Under-Secretary of State Acheson speculated to Robert Murphy, U.S. political adviser for Germany in Berlin, that this snag was "having serious repercussions" and would probably become a "political issue within Czecho between moderates and Communist elements." It was likely the greatest factor in turning the Prague government "to request a Czechoslovak-Polish Treaty of Alliance," which indeed it had just signed on March 10th.[9]

U.S. ambassador Laurence Steinhardt was assured by Jan Masaryk that "there has been no direct intervention by the Soviet Government in Czech affairs other than the Soviet request for a Czech-Polish Treaty." Actually, Steinhardt observed that even "indirect influence on Czech policies by the Soviet Government appears to be considerably less marked than heretofore." The U.S. ambassador calculated that "[Klement] Gottwald's leadership of the Czech Communist Party is in no immediate danger, but he is having increasing difficulty in controlling the 'younger extremists in the Party'."[10] Under Gottwald's leadership, Masaryk avowed that "people could say anything they liked." Although patently in reference to the Soviets, he added that "he did not believe in talking back too much . . . This freedom which we have is a very delicate flower."[11] A knowledgeable British observer agreed. "There is far greater freedom . . . of discussion than a year ago. Criticism of Communists both in the press and at public meetings is vigorous to a point of acrimony," he reported to the Foreign Office.[12]

Steinhardt fretted about Masaryk's perceived "weakness" of leadership. In a secret communication to Washington, he wrote: "The actual effect" of his accommodation, "however reasonable it may appear intellectually, has been to destroy his influence in Czechoslovak domestic politics" and "to deliver his Ministry into the hands of his Communist Under-Secretary [Vladimír] Clementis."

Steinhardt preferred what Petr Zenkl, Chairman of the National Socialist Party, advocated, to wit: "a firm resistance to the aggressive Soviet influence," meaning the Communists. The ambassador conceded that Masaryk's genial personality, "his predisposition to *laisser aller* and *dolce far niente*," and his great name made him very popular with the Czech public, but the ambassador found that "his effective political influence is negligible because the moderate party leaders . . . cannot count on him to stand up and fight on their side." The combination of his high reputation in the West with his pliability to Communist pressures made him "an almost ideal instrument from the Soviet viewpoint." Steinhardt documented his argument over Masaryk's stand by repeating the rumor that "the Soviets now seem to be pushing Masaryk forward as their candidate for strategic office in United Nations affairs." [13] Steinhardt's denigration of Masaryk was especially reprehensible in view of his continuous private assurances to him that he "would back him to the end," as Masaryk related to the authors personally in Prague later that summer and repeated again subsequently in a New York visit.

By the onset of summer, Steinhardt attested to the "relatively stable internal situation in Czechoslovakia." He cited "good food conditions and progressive economic recovery" as basic. He regarded it improbable that any such revolutionary events as had overtaken Hungary recently were likely to occur in Czechoslovakia in the near future. [14] "Fundamental differences in temperament and traditions," Steinhardt thought, would militate against a ripple effect. Moreover, he went on: "The continuous presence of the Soviet Army in Hungary as against the evacuation of Czechoslovakia more than 16 months ago" had brought revolutionary ferment to fever pitch there, while in Czechoslovakia, the withdrawal had dissipated any lingering apprehensions of Soviet intrusions. In Steinhardt's judgment, "it would seem hardly likely that Czechoslovakia would follow an Hungarian example in anything" in view of the traditional antipathy between them.

Encouraged by Steinhardt's assessment of political stability in Czechoslovakia, in April Acting Secretary of State Acheson announced to his Prague emissary: "This [is an] appropriate time to review policy with respect to credits to Czecho." As any change "would require the Secretary's approval," he solicited Steinhardt's guidance. He knew that $40 million of the $50 million credit for surplus property purchases was frozen and required thawing, especially in view of the U.S. need to dispose of "its surplus property overseas." The department's desire was to "review its position re credits motivated by improvement Czecho political situation since

Sept., 46 as reported by you." Polish credits had not been frozen despite the Communist takeover in Poland, unlike Czechoslovak credits. [15] It was noted that the "Communists are exploiting [the] issue to demonstrate indifference or hostility of West towards Czechoslovakia and necessity of Czechoslovakia to place sole reliance on Soviet Union and other Slav States." [16]

Steinhardt responded in June, seeing "improvement in general economic conditions continuing, but at a slower rate." He ascribed this to "difficulties which nationalized industries were encountering" deriving from "inadequate manpower and skilled labor." The expulsions of Sudetens had been especially onerous, as these skilled workers were replaced by "inexperienced, incompetent, and wasteful management, obsolescent machines, and shortage of raw materials . . . Low and irregular production of poor quality at high cost has been the result." [17]

British reports echoed news of "steady improvement" and then specified "especially in transportation conditions and in . . . basic industries—coal mining, heavy engineering," contradicting Steinhardt's negative account of national industrial production. The British ambassador Philip Nichols agreed, however, that "the general recovery was slow" because of shortage of labor and lack of capital . . . and the absence of substantial foreign credits." [18]

The recent cessation of UNRRA shipments had created an "imperative necessity [for Czechoslovakia] to obtain credits from the West." Steinhardt then assumed that these credits from the United States must be carefully measured, as the Communist-controlled "Czech Government would allocate these only to the nationalized industries under Communist direction." He suggested to the State Department "the advisability of encouraging extension of both private and public American credits for Czechs regarding the disposition of textiles produced from American cotton," as opposed to granting blanket credits directly to the government. [19]

The State Department did not object to the Export-Import Bank giving consideration to small credits to finance U.S. exports to Czechoslovakia, as such credits might accelerate the orientation to the West of Czechoslovak trade, and it requested Steinhardt's prompt response. On the 19th of June the ambassador replied that he agreed entirely with the plan to extend "small Export-Import Bank credits to finance Czechoslovak imports from the U.S." [20]

The new Czechoslovak ambassador to Washington, Juraj Slávik, had applied on February 19th to the Export-Import Bank for a $20 million cotton credit, as originally recommended by the State

Department. Slávik submitted a "comprehensive statement on Czechoslovakia's economic conditions" in support of the loan request. What would Steinhardt advise regarding the renewed request for a $50 million reconstruction loan, quizzed Washington? The department was doubtful "in view of their application to the International Bank for Reconstruction and Development on February 27th for $350 million long-term reconstruction loan over 3-year period." [21] No action had yet been taken by the U.S. National Advisory Council on International Monetary and Financial Problems. [22]

On May 9th, Steinhardt agreed that the time for review of the "severity of policy adopted by the U.S. in Sept. 1946" had arrived in principle. But, he requested, "not at the present moment," not before outstanding matters of contention were settled, such as compensation claims of American citizens for nationalized and confiscated property and payment of transit charges on Czechoslovak goods moving through the U.S. zone in Germany. Steinhardt noted the Czechoslovak "disposition to terminate protracted negotiations . . . [over a year] by agreeing to settlements satisfactory to U.S." The ambassador recommended that the State Department "induce the War Dept. to meet Czechoslovaks halfway and not insist on hard bargain, which it continues to strive for . . . to settle these matters in the near future." [23]

He said he would recommend the same reversal of policy to the Foreign Office. Following the settlements, he would advise $20 million in domestic surplus property credits and "unfreezing of unused portion FLC surplus property." Steinhardt did not favor "withholding credits until all American claims were disposed of." We should, however, "not commit ourselves to relaxing present position until we know a little more of disposition of Czechoslovak Government towards some of our larger claims." He was willing to open up, but slowly, or as he would defend it, prudently. He saw political advantage in "the promise of relaxation" for the moderates over the Communists. [24]

In reviewing matters to be squared away, the State Department at Washington cleared with Gen. Lucius Clay that of moving the last of the Sudeten expellees into the U.S. zone of occupation in Germany. General Clay on March 31st responded to the inquiry that all "transfers were completed," but this proved inaccurate at Prague. The Czechoslovak government was now requesting the additional transfer of 103,000 "stragglers" among the Sudetens, which, added to the millions of other refugees, totalled 3.5 million displaced persons in the U.S. zone, "who must find housing and employment" in defeated

Germany. Maj. Gen. Frank Keating, responding to the State Department's inquiry to Clay, wrote that the additional transfers "cannot be undertaken until conditions do permit." [25]   As seen from Prague, Germans were again being favored over the requirements of the Czechoslovak state, a victim of Nazi Germany's wartime oppression.

The overall friendly attitude of the State Department was put abruptly into reverse once again following Secretary of State Marshall's commencement address at Harvard University on June 5th. The new policy, to be known as the Marshall Plan, modified Truman's doctrine of military intervention against revolutionaries, or even leftists, the world over. The Western Powers would now deal with the economic and political crisis in Europe by means of extensive capital infusions to stimulate reconstruction via private enterprise. This was the successor approach to UNRRA's more even-handed practices. The British and French governments on July 4th issued invitations to 22 other countries to attend the forthcoming Paris Conference, scheduled to commence on July 12th. Czechoslovakia was included and accepted promptly on July 7th.

Two days later, on July 9th, Foreign Minister Masaryk went to Moscow with Gottwald to discuss the matter. Molotov indicated Soviet displeasure at the U.S. proposal, which the Soviet leaders saw as a means to bolster capitalism economically and politically in Europe at the expense of the Communists. The Soviets conveyed the sense that Czechoslovak participation in the international conference would be seen as "an act unfriendly to the Soviet Union . . . in disharmony with their Alliance," foreclosing any economic agreements. [26]   Stalin sent for Masaryk to probe his response to the banner headlines in American newspapers, clippings of which he had on his desk. "What," Masaryk demanded later of his British interlocutor, "could I do? I did the only thing I could do and said bluntly that I was not going to Paris." [27]

Just as the decision to attend had been made unanimously by the Czechoslovak Cabinet, its rejection of the invitation on July 12th had the same vote. Masaryk fumed privately to the authors in Prague a short while later, explaining that he had wished, at the least, to learn for himself at first hand the essence of the plan and to study its possible consequences for his country, adding that attending the Paris conference did not foreclose rejection of the terms. At the time, confusion reigned in Europe about the intent and means of the hastily devised Marshall Plan.

Ambassador Nichols concluded that the "withdrawal . . . cut the ground from under the feet of the non-Communists . . . [who were] genuinely disturbed at the possibility that under the Marshall Plan, German industrial potential will be restored to the detriment of Czechoslovakia." Nichols also observed a mood of "disillusionment and resignation" in the common people. He said, "They tend to blame the Western Powers, particularly America, for having put them in a position . . . of having to choose between the East and the West. Many speak of a second Munich." He reminded his superiors that "the position of M. Masaryk, who shared the responsibility for the decision and is known to be Western-minded, seems to be as yet unshaken." [28]

In the final analysis, however, Nichols later concluded that "Czechoslovakia could not accept the necessity of reviving German heavy industry" even if they reluctantly, under pressure, "accept an expansion of German light industry," which would "compete against Czech products." The Czechoslovak leaders thought "other industrialized countries of Europe could . . . replace Germany as the key to European recovery." [29]

The immediate effect of Czechoslovakia's early acceptance of the invitation to Paris was a letter from Marshall to the U.S. embassy in Paris canceling all credits and loans to her. Marshall declared that the State "Dept [was] not inclined [to] reconsider Czecho $50 million Eximbank credit," explaining that it "does not wish to [seem] to have secured Zecho participation by offer of prospects of U.S. aid." Moreover, "the $50 million Eximbank reconstruction loan, [suspended in September 1946], had not been reopened in Washington by Zech Emb, [who were instructed] rather to seek a $350 million, three-year loan from the International Bank of Reconstruction of the United Nations Development Plan." The board of directors of Eximbank decided on February 5th that this credit of $50 million would be considered as a new application, if the question were reopened. "In view present policies Eximbank, doubtful they would consider long-term reconstruction loan this amount." In any case, Marshall said, "the Amembassy Praha and Dept. under any circumstances, reluctant to reconsider Eximbank credit, pending settlement several important issues now being negotiated Praha, including compensation for nationalized American properties." These inside maneuvers document the fact that the Czechoslovaks in reality lost nothing for the present in rejecting the invitation to Paris, while retaining Soviet favors and security guarantees. Marshall continued his lengthy and explicit dispatch, saying that "Czechs are clearly eager to participate in Paris talks; their participation or absence will depend almost entirely on degree of Moscow pressure." [30]

Next day, July 10th, the State Department chairman of Central European Affairs disclaimed the assumption of Czechoslovak ambassador Slávik that negotiations on the Export-Import Bank long-term credit of $50 million would be reopened if Czechoslovaks participated at the Paris conference. [31]   Ambassador Steinhardt wrote several days later that the "prompt yielding of Czechoslovakia in connection with Paris Conference may or may not satisfy Soviets that they enjoy effective control over Czechoslovak foreign policy." But he went on to say "there are no visible signs as yet that they intend to tighten control over Czechoslovakia at this time." He recognized that "if harmonious relations existed between east and west, there would be no reason to fear reprisals against moderates within the country." [32]

At the risk of speaking after the fact, Vice-Premier Zdeněk Fierlinger gave a press interview to clarify the pullout from the Paris conference, in which he charged Western confusion about his country's behavior. He declared that Moscow's "friendly advice" was not to be confounded with "orders" not to attend. The crux of their "most difficult problem . . . was the inclusion of Germany" in "the reconstruction program for Europe."   Fierlinger insisted that Czechoslovakia would not have been able to go along with such a plan in any case. He affirmed: "We are not less independent, though, than Belgium, Holland, and Norway, which are looking West, yet [they] are never accused of being satellites . . . Czechoslovakia is interested in trade with the whole world." He took solace in "the economic cooperation offered by the Soviet Union and the consign-ment of raw materials [to] this country [that] will safeguard us against all possible adverse trends of foreign trade." [33]

The same newspaper carried a speech at Karlovy Vary some days later by Zenkl, chairman of the Czechoslovak National Socialist Party and deputy prime minister, headlined "Economic Iron Curtain Would Mean Catastrophic Reduction of Our Living Standards."   Zenkl declared that the decision to go to Paris "was right, [as] we are a country whose industrial production depends above all on foreign trade . . . It is . . . our duty to take advantage of every opportunity to improve our economic relations with the world by international economic cooperation." The reversal signified that "political viewpoint outweighed economic considerations." Czechoslovak participation was seen in Moscow as "threatening our Allied bonds with the Soviet Union, the only country able to provide us immediate and effective assistance. We would again be exposed to the German menace." It was therefore right for the government, he reasoned, to "revoke its participation at the Paris Conference . . . It would be irresponsible to foreign political security . . . [as] contained in our alliance with the Soviet Union for the mere possibility of economic advantage . . . The Czechoslovak-Soviet Treaty must remain a non-partisan issue above all parties." Zenkl protested that "it was vicious propaganda that only the Communist Party was a guardian of this Alliance." He concluded by appealing for unity among the Great Powers, saying, "We are also dependent on cooperation with Western Europe and America, on which in turn our standard of living depends . . . Just as we would not tolerate any political iron curtain, which would mean the end of our liberties, we equally refuse an economic iron curtain, which would inevitably mean a catastrophic reduction of our standard of living." [34] The following day the same newspaper carried a public statement of Petr Drtina, the minister of justice, explaining that "insurance against future German menace [was] more important than short-term economic needs, [but that] Czechoslovakia has not renounced cooperation with the West." [35]

On July 22nd, Steinhardt wrote to his superiors in Washington to justify his hard line in opposing economic credits to Czechoslovakia. He argued that "substantial loans or credits to Czechoslovakia would merely . . . assist in bolstering the weak spots in Czech economy." He thought the Soviet assistance on which the Czechoslovaks were relying would inevitably be inadequate without Western imports, threatening Czechoslovak industry with collapse. These shortcomings of the Communist-dominated government would be demonstrated and thus strengthen the moderates. On the other hand, he insisted, "loans would advance Communist claims of managing the economy well." In other words, a U.S. policy of virtual economic sanctions would provide pressure against Communist control. Steinhardt then turned to considering tactics in this strategy. He urged that "it would seem undesirable explicitly to refuse loans or credits. Such refusals would be played up by Communist press as indicating unfriendliness on part of U.S." He therefore recommended *"a disinclination to discuss"* loans or credits. If negotiations are forced, then "take matters under *advisement and postpone action indefinitely.*" On the other hand, he realized that U.S. policy "should not be exclusively negative." He counseled concluding a "cultural convention" similar to "the Anglo-Czech one . . . [which has] little practical significance [but] it would provide evidence that U.S. has not abandoned Czechoslovakia to the Soviet Union." This would have "an important psychological and perhaps even political effect." Another meaningless concession would be to "persuade the War Department, for political reasons, adoption of a conciliatory attitude in forthcoming negotiations [July 24, 1947] with Czechs on dollar charges for transit of Czech exports and imports across Anglo-US zones of Germany." Still pressing his hard line, Steinhardt further advocated that the State Department voice "vigorous protests in the UN Assembly against the Communist coup d'état in Hungary," as it would warn Czechoslovak Communists to proceed "with greater caution than they might otherwise . . . do." [36]

Almost immediately, on July 25th, U.S. and Czechoslovak representatives concluded an agreement to settle certain war accounts and claims incident to U.S. Army operations in Europe. [37]

The British Foreign Office was not exclusively guided by Ambassador Nichols, whose advice was occasionally supplemented by its research department, the reports of which it now forwarded to Nichols for comment. One of these estimated that in reaction to the Marshall Plan, "the Communist Party are probably not now losing ground . . . as it had done over the past year, since the elections of May 26th, 1946." It speculated that the Communists would take the line that the country "must now come to terms with [them as] potentially the greatest political power" because of the desertion of the West. It also agreed with the Communist affirmation that "Czechoslovakia is now primarily dependent upon Russia for its national security." Nichols challenged this assessment. He checked his opinion with President Beneš in early September during his interview. Beneš thought that the Marshall Plan, in splitting Europe, had also brought matters to a head internally in Czechoslovakia. The fragile accommodations of the Communists with the National Front began to unravel their political adhesions, which could only help the Communists, against the moderates. [38]

Nichols' appointment with Beneš was to have occurred late in July or early in August, but was postponed "owing to the President's illness. He had an attack of sunstroke as a result of a review he attended on a very hot day (July 4th) and he was allowed to do nothing, not even to read, for three weeks. He is better now and the doctors hope he will be back to normal health in another ten days, or a fortnight. I must say, however, I was shocked by his appearance and manner. He looks five years older . . . and by no means as vigorous . . . as usual." [39] The authors had the same experience. Following their arrival in Prague in early August, Jan Masaryk received them at lunch on August 6th in his apartment in the Czernin Palace. His explanation of Beneš's indisposition matched Nichols' account.

That very morning, Masaryk said, he had concluded an economic agreement with Bulgaria, following one earlier with Romania, to meet the country's grain deficit, which had been anticipated due to the 50 percent shortfall from the spring drought. Bursting into his top-floor flat Masaryk exclaimed in greeting the authors, "We'll eat like pigs this year, maybe like peasants, on black bread, but we'll eat this winter." Although Stalin had offered assistance following his virtual veto of Czechoslovakia's participation in the Marshall Plan conference, fulfillment was doubtful, as Steinhardt had observed, due to Soviet stringencies.

The disastrous harvest of 1947 dealt a severe blow to economic recovery, coming as it did on the heels of the UNRRA cessation. Masaryk told the authors he was counting heavily on concluding negotiations for the U.S. loan, which had already been requested. He would travel to New York in mid-September to preside at the opening of the UN General Assembly, and then go on to Washington. Masaryk begged them to wait around until Beneš's doctors would give him clearance to visit with them as he desired.

Beneš and his wife Hana received the authors affectionately on September 8th at their home at Sezimovo Ustí, the Beneš country house near the ancient Hussite capital of Tábor. Jan Masaryk, his left arm in a sling to protect his frequently dislocating shoulder, accompanied them. They found the president stricken, as Nichols had, but they remarked on his customary vitality and lucidity of mind, which lasted throughout the two-hour lunch and far beyond, through the afternoon, as he ignored the doctor's admonition to limit visits to an hour.

Beneš straightaway objected vehemently to the zealous U.S. reconstruction of Germany, which he saw as a menace to his country and to world peace. Beneš confided his chagrin that the Marshall Plan had forced Czechoslovakia to choose between East and West. In his mind, it split Europe into two blocs. As his Western allies were reluctant to guarantee Central European security against German "revanchism," he explained that he had no option but to choose the East. The fear of a resurgent Germany, not yet de-Nazified or entirely democratized, formed the core of Czechoslovakia's postwar foreign policy. "Didn't I warn your President Wilson after the first World War of the dangers of rebuilding Germany?" he asked. "He didn't listen then and we had a second World War . . . When will you Americans learn?" President Beneš spoke passionately and was forced to tone down, causing him to turn to other, equally interesting but less vexatious, questions and observations.

Nichols, in his September 6th interview, had asked Beneš's comment about rumors "current lately" that "Gottwald has been drinking far too much." Beneš confirmed that Gottwald was "indeed seriously ill from overdrinking about the same time as he [Beneš] was laid up." The doctors were pessimistic over Gottwald's chances "to cure himself of this habit." It looked as though "he might be eliminated," said Beneš. "His successor will almost certainly be Slánský . . . a fanatic . . . far more difficult to work with him . . . a change for the worse." [40]

Nichols reverted to the theme of Czechoslovak security later that month, declaring that Czechoslovakia's survival "does not really lie within the hands of the Czechs themselves, but is a function of the relations between the East and West." He continued to maintain that friendly relations and economic support from the West would bolster the moderate political elements in the country against Communist domination. He also feared that Slovak-Czech explosive tensions "must be to the advantage of the Communists." [41]

Rumors were afloat all summer and fall that the British and Americans had "sold the Czechs out to the Russians at Yalta." The British Foreign Office disclaimed them. It asserted that "no political agreement was made at Yalta which divided Czechoslovakia into a Soviet and an Anglo-American sphere of operations. Nor was any military agreement on this subject reached at Yalta." [42]

On October 6th, Jan Masaryk's private secretary, Mara, told a staffer at the British embassy that the political situation had seriously deteriorated owing to Fierlinger's wing of the Social Democratic Party having linked itself on a resolution three weeks earlier with the Communist Party. A split in the Social Democratic Party appeared imminent. At the same time, Mara recounted that "Mr. Masaryk and all non-Communist Czechs are nearly in despair at the tactics of the United States Government," by which "the State Department [is doing its best] to thrust Czechoslovakia for good and all into the Communist Camp by their failure to give any help to the non-Communists in the Czech Government." Mara said that "the policy of the British Government toward Czechoslovakia was far happier." He predicted that "it was most unlikely that the Czechoslovak delegation [to the United Nations] would be able to take a line differing from that of Moscow on any United Nations questions." Mara, reflecting Masaryk's sentiments, felt above all that the future of the Czech Communists "will depend to no small extent on American policy." [43]

This observation was borne out in Washington. Jacob Beam, chief of the State Department's Division of Central European Affairs, acknowledged that "the Czechs were in a most difficult position." He noted that "as Foreign Minister" Masaryk "had had to make speeches in the UN attacking U.S. policy, but he was always careful to observe proper forms." Masaryk had called on Beam to inquire about the possibility of Czechoslovakia "acquiring radio[active] isotopes for hospital use," a proposal that had been introduced at the UN Commission for Nuclear Energy by the Polish delegate, the only nuclear physicist member, who desired something positive to emerge, such as international medical uses of radioactive isotopes. These had no conceivable war potential. Beam took the request under advisement but could not go along. Masaryk's real mission was to "appeal for continued show of U.S. interest in Czechoslovakia." Beam, steered by Steinhardt's advice, advocated "cultural exchanges, but nothing more tangible such as Masaryk sought." [44]

The fall of 1947 witnessed "a degree of . . . party strife [that] considerably outstrips previous domestic agitation in Czechoslovakia since liberation." The friction was heightened by stepped-up "useless strikes in nationalized industry." Bohumil Laušman, the Social Democratic minister of industry, offered to resign, but his resignation was not accepted by the party presidium, according to the Chargé d'affaires of the U.S. embassy, Charles Yost. He wrote that "the vital question remains . . . whether political developments . . . will be held within bounds of normal party and Parliamentary activity." [45]

Steinhardt noted that the infirmity of President Beneš "prevents him from taking a continuing part in present political struggles . . . [depriving] the non-Communist leaders . . . [of] his invaluable guidance and support." The ambassador had private reports that "Communists have decided to make use of secret police to intimidate their political opponents, beginning with Slovak Democrats." He sounded an alarm to Byrnes:

I am of the opinion that Gottwald and other moderate Communists who had hoped and expected to gain an absolute majority at elections next May by relatively democratic means are now being forced to proceed more rapidly by undemocratic means if necessary to bring Czechoslovakia into line [with Moscow].

Steinhardt, reading the handwriting on the wall, predicted that within a period of months the "Czechoslovak Government will become a subservient tool of Kremlin," a self-fulfilling prophecy, considering his policy proposals. "It remains to be seen," he continued, "to what extent non-Communist party leaders will have courage to resist this trend and succeed in defeating or delaying a Communist program," [46] but Steinhardt did nothing to guide the State Department to formulate policies, such as the British Foreign Office were pursuing, that would bolster the moderates in their rear-guard stand.

To deal with the heating political climate, Beneš returned to Prague on September 15th. He castigated the Social Democrats for having signed a joint communiqué with the Communists, accusing them of fractious behavior in creating a "bloc within the National Front." He refused to accept the resignation of Food Minister Václav Majer, and he spoke to Gottwald in "strong terms," accusing him of wrecking the National Front and "subverting normal political life of [the] country." He told Gottwald that the "millionaires levy proposal" was a splitting tactic, which he would refuse to sign if it passed the National Assembly. The bill, he thought, would hinder industrial development, depriving it of potential private investment capital. In his anger, he told Gottwald that "in case of Putsch, he would not ease [the] Communist way by resigning or leaving the country . . . and that although he had been ill, he had no intention of dying for some time to come." [47]

In mid-October, the Czechoslovak Planning Commission, under the chairmanship of Gottwald, introduced a new five-year plan to take effect in 1948, when the current two-year plan expired. It envisaged "a switch of emphasis from consumer . . . to metal industries . . . proposed for expansion [to lead] Czechoslovakia [to] take Germany's place as a provider of capital equipment in Eastern Europe." As their famous textiles and glass products had to meet international competition, the Czechoslovaks had to keep costs of production low by trimming wages. They recognized their need to reorient "Czechoslovak trade so that more than half of it should be conducted with the USSR and other East European States," in contrast with the present situation in which "above 70% is with Western countries." Ambassador Steinhardt thought that in spite of extreme Soviet pressure for over two years, "nearly 80% of [the] country's total foreign trade is still with West." [48] The British embassy's impression of the new plan was "that the Communist elements seem to be getting their way in the formulation of economic plans." [49] Ludwik Frejka, an economic planner, said that the "reconstruction of Czechoslovakia's national economy . . . was rapidly progressing" and was "almost reaching its prewar target level." [50]

The new plan's aim was "the highest standard of living for the entire population." It would devote "no less than 33% of the national income . . . to scientific research . . . Industries in Bohemia and Moravia would receive an influx of 20% more workers, and those in Slovakia, 50% more." [51] "Women's work would be made easier by the construction of new laundries, canteens, and nurseries." By 1953, the number of nurseries was to be threefold that of 1948. Hospitals and other medical institutes were to be increased by 16 percent.

The planners, carried away by their vision of Utopia, observed that "the special Czechoslovak economy and political structure indicates that the Russian pattern" followed by other Slav countries "is unlikely to be the most advantageous one to us." The others were just beginning their process of industrialization, and moreover, the Czechoslovak "national economy is not Communist, but Liberal-Socialist . . . Our dependence on world economy is far greater than that of Soviet Russia or Slav countries with a substantially lower standard of living. This dependence dictates greater flexibility and adaptability."[52]

On the Czechoslovak independence day, October 28th, President Beneš reappeared at the Hradčany Castle for the celebrations there and then at the National Theater for at least the first act of Smetana's opera "Dalibor." Prime Minister Gottwald joined with other government officials in these festivities. The British Archbishop of York participated in special church services dedicated to peace. Beneš received the dean of the diplomatic corps, Ambassador Nichols, who was soon to leave, and they reviewed their six years of friendly relations. Beneš underlined his serious intent to settle British claims of compensation to her citizens for nationalized properties. He was zealous to preserve the country's reputation as an "honest commercial nation, who paid her debts promptly." Nichols feared, however, "that the President's will not be the last word on the subject."[53]

Within the week, Steinhardt reported the "Slovak political situation [as] increasingly serious," stemming from Communist official corruption and the "ineptitude [of] Democratic Party leadership." Deterioration was reported in the food supply. "Extensive black market activity" was alleged as the source of "financial support [of] subversive activity and general sabotage [of] Czech reconstruction program." Gustav Husák was directed to administer the cleanup. "Wheat lack [was] due to inefficient and corrupt distribution on top of drought and to some extent under-cultivation of about 30% of best Slovak land by Hungarians who feared removal." Alleviation from Prague was constrained by "food shortage in Bohemia and Moravia." Steinhardt concluded his dismal account that the "political situation in Slovakia was at [its] most serious point since liberation." He had "no doubt that with the Democrats on the run . . . [due to corruption], Communists will press for a rout."[54] He felt they had to clean up their act in a hurry and deliver efficient administration. In any case, his forebodings were ominous for an amicable resolution of the numerous staggering problems.

NOTES

1. *New York Times*, January 24, 1947, and January 29, 1947.

2. *New York Herald Tribune*, January 24, 1947.

3. *New York Times*, February 17, 1947, and February 27, 1947.

4. D.F. Fleming, *The Cold War and Its Origins*, (New York: Doubleday, 1961), Vol. 1, p. 446.

5. Philip Nichols to Ernest Bevin, July 11, 1946, FO 371/v. 56004-Xc/110148.

6. "Masaryk's Speech on Foreign Policy in National Assembly," Nichols to Bevin, March 29, 1947, FO 371/v. 65784. Italics added.

7. Ibid.

8. To Minister of State, Foreign Office, June 10, 1947, FO 371/v. 65785-115754.

9. Dean Acheson to Robert Murphy, March 25, 1947, *Foreign Relations* 1947, v. 4, p. 198.

10. Laurence Steinhardt to Secretary of State, April 3, 1947, *Foreign Relations* 1947, v. 4, pp. 200-3.

11. Ibid.

12. To Minister of State, June 10, 1947, FO 371/v. 65785-115754.

13. Steinhardt to Secretary of State, May 8, 1947, *Foreign Relations* 1947, v. 4, pp. 206-8.

14. Steinhardt to Secretary of State, June 12, 1947, *Foreign Relations* 1947, v. 4, p. 212.

15. Acheson to Steinhardt, April 24, 1947, *Foreign Relations* 1947, v. 4, pp. 203-4.

16. Ibid.

17. Steinhardt to Secretary of State, June 19, 1947, *Foreign Relations* 1947, v. 4, pp. 213-15.

18. "Annual Report on Czechoslovakia," Nichols to Bevin, June 25, 1947, FO 371/v. 65785-115754.

19. Steinhardt to Secretary of State, June 19, 1947, *Foreign Relations* 1947, v. 4, pp. 213-15.

20. Ibid., p. 215, footnote.

21. Acheson to Steinhardt, April 24, 1947, *Foreign Relations* 1947, v. 4, pp. 203-4.

22. Ibid., footnote, p. 204.

23. Steinhardt to Secretary of State, May 9, 1947, *Foreign Relations* 1947, v. 4, pp. 208-9.

24. Ibid.

25. Keating to Chief, Czechoslovak Military Mission to Allied Central Authorities for Germany, Dastich, Germany, May 1, 1947, *Foreign Relations* 1947, v. 4, p. 211.

26. Nichols to Bevin, July 12, 1947, FO 371/v. 65785-115754.

27. Political Division, British Element, Control Commission for Germany, Berlin, to Foreign Office, Northern Department, October 16, 1947, FO 371/v. 56802-115754.

28. Nichols to Bevin, July 12, 1947, FO 371/v. 65785-115754.

29. Nichols to Foreign Office, September 13, 1947, FO 371/v. 65786-115754

30. George C. Marshall to U.S. Embassy in France, July 9, 1947, *Foreign Relations* 1947, v. 4, pp. 218-19.

31. James Riddleburger-Memo of a conversation, July 10, 1947, *Foreign Relations* 1947, v. 4, pp. 219-21.

32. Steinhardt to Secretary of State, July 15, 1947, *Foreign Relations* 1947, v. 4, pp. 221-23.

33. "Fierlinger says Prague Followed Well-Meant Advice," *Daily Review*, London, July 19, 1947, FO 371/v. 65785-115754.

34. *Daily Review*, London, July 22, 1947, FO 371/v. 65785-115754.

35. *Daily Review*, London, July 23, 1947, FO 371/v. 65785-115754.

36. All quotations in this lengthy paragraph, Steinhardt to Secretary of State, July 22, 1947, *Foreign Relations* 1947, v. 4, pp. 223-26. Italics added.

37. Ibid, p. 226.

38. Nichols to Maurice Hankey, Foreign Office, September 6, 1947, FO 371/v. 65785-115754.

39. Ibid.

40. Nichols to Hankey, FO 371/65785-115754.

41. Nichols to Hankey, September 18, 1947, FO 371/v. 65786-115754.

42. Hankey to Rumbold, Prague, September 27, 1947, FO 371/v. 65786-115754..

43. Conversation with Mara, October 8, 1947, FO 371/v. 65786-115754.

44. Memo of a conversation: Jacob Beam, Robert Lovett, Acting Secretary of State, and Jan Masaryk, Washington, October 29, 1947, *Foreign Relations* 1947, v. 4, pp. 237-38.

45. Charles Yost, Chargé d'Affaires, Prague, to Secretary of State, September 9, 1947, *Foreign Relations* 1947, v. 4, pp. 229-31.

46. Steinhardt to Secretary of State, *Foreign Relations* 1947, v. 4, pp. 234-35.

47. Yost to Secretary of State, September 15, 1947, *Foreign Relations* 1947, v. 4, p. 231.

48. Steinhardt to Secretary of State, February 26, 1947, *Foreign Relations* 1948, v. 4, p. 739.

49. E. A. Nadice, Prague, to Foreign Office, October 16, 1947, FO 371/v. 65783-115754.

50. Nadice to Foreign Office, October 14, 1947, FO 371/v. 65783-115754.

51. Nadice to Foreign Office, October 21, 1947, FO 371/v. 65783-115754.

52. Nadice to Foreign Office, October 14, 1947, FO 371/v. 65783-115754.

53. Nichols to Bevin, October 29, 1947, FO 371/v. 65786, 115754.

54. Steinhardt to Secretary of State, *Foreign Relations* 1947, v. 4, pp. 239-41.

21

The Communist Coup
(1947-48)

A glimmer of some improvement in relations was announced to Washington, indecisively, by Ambassador Laurence Steinhardt on November 13, 1947, in his report of his conversation with Hubert Ripka, "moderate" Socialist minister of foreign trade. This reputable minister had "stated that if a $20 million cotton credit could be obtained from the U.S. in the near future, he was in a position to assure me that [the] Czechoslovak Government would promptly settle large American claims for nationalized property." Steinhardt speculated that otherwise "there was little hope for a settlement. I would not be averse to extension of cotton credit provided there is a really worthwhile quid pro quo." Ripka had told Steinhardt in confidence that the "Soviets had already informed him of a significant shortfall in their promise to deliver 20,000 tons," which would now be reduced to 14,000. [1]

Just at this time, Jan Masaryk was in Washington, accompanied by Ambassador Juraj Slávik, meeting with U.S. Secretary of State George C. Marshall and Jacob Beam, in charge of Central European Affairs. The department had that day received Steinhardt's telegram. On the table for discussion were the long deferred cotton credit and the retention by the Western Powers' Tripartite Control Commission of a gold pool in Germany, in which Czechoslovakia had a frozen $50 million claim.* The Czechoslovak application for the long-term loan

---

*This gold had been taken by Hitler from the Czechoslovak treasury after the occupation on March 15, 1939, and it subsequently was transferred to U.S. possession. The U.S. government retained the gold for use in compensating Czechoslovaks who became American citizens, whose enterprises were nationalized. (Told to Sylvia

at the International Bank was still "under advisement." Now the drought had depleted Czechoslovakia's wheat and potato crops, while 200,000 tons of Soviet wheat was slow in arriving.

Masaryk explained apologetically that his "country's contiguity to the Soviet Union forced their policy frequently . . . to cut across that of the U.S." At the same time, he would return to his country prepared "to do all he could for the survival of constitutional democracy."[2] No one present could foresee how desperate this struggle would be!

Masaryk had warnings and forebodings of closed doors at the State Department, against which he flung his entire weight. He could have had no idea whatever of the coincidental presentation that very day of a paper from the National Security Council to the State Department, which politely took all of Masaryk's requests "under advisement." The new policy paper was prepared in the State Department's East European Section on the "immediate U.S. Economic Policy Toward the Soviet Sphere" in response to the "fact of effective Soviet control, which is progressively tightening in those countries, where it is not already complete." This paper was adopted without opposition by the National Security Council a month later on December 17, 1947, confirming an earlier executive order to the same end, to take effect on December 1, 1947.[3] The paper declared:

U.S. National security required *immediate termination for an indefinite period* of shipments from the U.S. to the USSR and its satellites of all commodities which are critically short in the U.S. and which would contribute to the Soviet military potential. All exports to "recovery zones" would be controlled.[4]

In the name of national security and in the guise of controlling foreign trade, the United States hardened its policies toward "countries in the Soviet sphere," very likely in response to the organization of the Cominform, whose member countries, in the National Security Council's opinion, were "USSR, Yugoslavia, Albania, and Bulgaria." A second category, embracing "Czechoslovakia, Poland, Hungary, and the Soviet zone of Germany," were countries to be treated in the same manner, but whose people have an "ardent desire . . . for a Western orientation," indicating some small flexibility depending on their behavior. The policy "should not be publicized in any way," and the United States would request conformity by the "responsible Western Powers."[5] The door to U.S. loans and credits

---

Crane in Prague, November 5, 1989, by Jiří Hájek, foreign minister in the Prague Spring cabinet headed by Alexander Dubček).

had been definitely shut in Masaryk's face, but he had not been informed. He was allowed by his friend, Laurence Steinhardt, to stake his reputation and risk his position at home, along with those of his moderate political colleagues, on this foreclosed mission!

While in Washington, Masaryk had another inconclusive talk with Under-Secretary of State Robert Lovett, a friend of his and of Czechoslovakia, who was powerless to turn the administration around in their favor. The ultimate cruel blow was administered by the affable Democratic president, Harry Truman, who informed him coldly that in a crisis, Czechoslovakia could not count on more than the moral support of the United States.

As Masaryk recounted to these authors during their last visit with him on December 14, 1947, in his Carlyle Hotel suite in New York, he was aghast at the transformed political climate in Washington. The policy shift engendered by tough anti-Communism, and its predictable consequences, both for himself and for his country, were justifiably alarming. Beyond personal affronts by old friends, crossing the street to avoid greeting him, he was appalled at the rigidity of political thinking at Washington; it was all so senselessly arbitrary and counterproductive in his eyes. In response to his appeals for succor to bridge the gap between east and west in Central Europe, the typical phrase was: "Either all in or all out of the Marshall Plan." He commented bitterly with black Prague sarcasm: "Bridges were also made for armies to march over."

He was depressed and disconsolate over his inability to register in Washington the current reality of politics in Prague. He charged that even his closest friends had no idea of the gravity of the situation in his country, sandwiched in between the Soviet Union and Germany. He realized fully that his failure "to bring home the bacon," as he put it, would deprive him of his last trump card to forestall a Communist takeover. The Communists would tolerate his presence in the cabinet, along with that of other moderates, in the hope of attracting needed capitalist economic assistance. Without that assistance, they would necessarily go it alone; he would in any case return home disarmed and isolated. He declared with forced bravura that he would not tarry for stateside surgery on his dislocated shoulder, asserting that "our Czech doctors are every bit as good as yours." He was a Czechoslovak patriot, and Prague was his native home. Nor could he think to desert Beneš. And he was too angry at the betrayal by his friends in the West ever to think of trusting them again. Once more, he definitely rejected exile as an alternative for himself, and he said grimly, "You can go abroad to work *for* your country, not *against* it.

I won't be a puppet for others to pull my strings."

Dejectedly, he replied to our queries about his plans. Yes, he would go home to spend Christmas with his sister Alice in Prague. He would stop first in London to see his close friend, Robert Bruce Lockhart. While there, to the latter's astonishment, Masaryk declined a dinner engagement expressly arranged with Sir Orme Sargent, Under-Secretary of State for Foreign Affairs. Sargent had stood by faithfully ever since the bruising days of Munich. But Masaryk intuited that U.S. policy would require British compliance as before and that it would be futile to knock on doors at Whitehall.

Before his fateful return home via Geneva, where he saw another old friend, Pavel Eisler, Masaryk deposited with Bruce Lockhart a packet of his private papers Eisler confided to his wife that Masaryk was so low psychologically and physically that he could barely walk unaided back to his hotel.

The first and last success at home of the moderate parties in exploiting a swing from the left came on February 13, 1948. Suspicious of the official line about the numerous disturbances at Most during the previous summer, the National Socialist minister of justice, Petr Drtina, had ordered his department to undertake an independent investigation. In the cabinet meeting that day, Drtina revealed his discovery of complicity in the disorders of the security police, which functioned under the Communist-directed interior ministry. He then demanded the appointment of an all-party commission to probe the incidents and to recommend reforms of the police structure.

It was the department of the Communist interior minister, Václav Nosek, that had come under a cloud, charged with packing the police force with Communists. The non-Communists wanted the "packing" edict annulled. Prime Minister Klement Gottwaid, in the chair, attempted to rule the investigating motion out of order. The reoriented Social Democrats, sensing a crucial civil liberties issue, rallied to the side of the moderates, and for the first time, Gottwald found himself in the minority of a cabinet vote. British monitors of events at Prague recounted:

The crisis in Czechoslovakia came to a head on the 17th February, when Gottwald . . . suspended a meeting of the Coalition Government after certain non-Communist Ministers had complained that the Minister of Interior had failed to carry out the Cabinet decision annulling the appointments of Communists in the Police Force. [It was] being packed with Communist nominees. [6]

This was the last cabinet meeting of the Third Republic. The response of the National Socialists was to announce a boycott of any cabinet session that did not give priority to implementing the motion to annul the appointments.

The deepening deadlock assumed international dimension on February 19th with the simultaneous return to Prague of U.S. ambassador Steinhardt, who had taken leave on November 24th, and Soviet deputy foreign minister Valerian Zorin, former ambassador to Czechoslovakia. Steinhardt's popularity gave encouragement in liberal circles, but the indefinite promises of U.S. loans, now suspended for political reasons, and a cultural exchange agreement, were too vague and inadequate to defuse the crisis.

Zorin had been popular during his earlier tenure of office in Prague, and his return carried much weight. He arrived with two messages from Stalin, one to Beneš and the other to Gottwald. Stalin's message to the prime minister was delivered at the Soviet embassy, where Gottwald was in frequent contact with the current ambassador as well as with the intelligence services of both countries, which had collaborated during the war and were now integrated. By happenstance, Lavrenti Beria, the Soviet interior minister and chief of the KGB, had just sent an independent message to Gottwald, advising intensification of trade union activity.

In his letter to Gottwald, Stalin expressed satisfaction with the way the Czech party was handling the crisis and assured him that the Soviet Union stood ready to give a helping hand should the need arise. We have Ambassador Steinhardt's word that "the Soviet Government has been careful to keep well in the background of recent events in Czechoslovakia."[7] Weeks later, after further probing, Steinhardt concluded: "There was no evidence of any Soviet troop concentrations on the borders of Czechoslovakia."[8] There were, to be sure, Soviet troops in surrounding countries, notably in Hungary, but throughout the crisis they were never mobilized, or put on alert, or brought up to the borders.

The British Foreign Office likewise saw "absolutely no evidence of Soviet intervention, though the presence of M. Zorin in Prague at this very moment [February 25, 1948] is a clear indication that the Soviet Government have in fact rigged the crisis. Formally . . . the crisis appears as an internal Czech matter and its discussion by the United Nations would be debarred." It therefore concluded: "It is hardly feasible to take the Czech crisis to the United Nations."[9]

Stalin's message to Beneš was delivered during Zorin's talk with Masaryk that evening. The Soviet gvernment was gravely concerned, Zorin said, over the mounting crisis in Czechoslovakia, but expressed its confidence in a Slavic bloc of peace. The new Soviet line of Slav solidarity impelled the Kremlin to assure the president that Gottwald did not seek to expel non-Communists from the government; it wished to purge only those who were acting as Western agents.

In London, U.S. ambassador Lewis Douglas called on Foreign Minister Ernest Bevin to say "he was gravely concerned about the effect on Italy and the U.S. Government were considering the matter." [10] Secretary of State Marshall confirmed the State Department's apprehensions in a letter to his ambassador, Francis Caffrey, in Paris. He wrote: "We feel that there is a real possibility that [this coup in Czechoslovakia] would stimulate and encourage Communist action in Western European countries, particularly in Italy." [11]

The United States was indeed deeply involved in the tight election contest in Italy on April 18th, where they feared a Communist victory due to the general popularity of the Communist leaders, stemming from their bravery in the wartime resistance. It has since been revealed that the CIA was engrossed in the Italian election campaign, having spent between $1 million and $10 million to assist the Christian Democrats to defeat the Communists. The authors speculated in New York at the time that Zorin's visit to Prague might be motivated by Stalin's anxiety over the leftist tendencies of the Czechoslovak Communist leaders, about which he had warned Beneš in December 1943. Stalin might have felt concern about the timing of a Communist coup in Czechoslovakia, just two months prior to the Italian election. The secret purpose of Zorin's visit may well have been to persuade the Czechoslovak Communists to slow their timetable until after April 18th. Such speculations ran rife in UN circles in New York. Years later, Alexander Werth queried Zorin in Paris about his role in the Prague crisis; Zorin did not deny it. In any event, the separate intelligence advice to the trade union militants was producing the contrary effect of hastening the revolutionary process.

After refusing to attend the cabinet meeting called for February 20th, the National Socialist, People's Party, and Slovak Democratic ministers, numbering 12 altogether, tendered their resignations from the government to President Beneš. This ill-timed drastic move, designed to unhinge the Gottwald-led coalition cabinet, shocked Beneš, who had not been previously briefed. [12] The president concluded his interview with the recalcitrant ministers, promising not to register their resignations before and apart from forcing Gottwald to accept the proposed judicial investigation of the Interior Ministry scandal. The Communists alleged that the resigning ministers had put themselves into the position of a "subversive opposition." [13] In fact, the Communists suddenly "discovered a plot against the State."[14]

Realizing the fatal blunder of his liberal opponents, Gottwald now proceeded to implement the Central Committee's decision for full mobilization and direct action. Communist "action committees" that had been "formed all over the country" seized a number of ministries. Other public offices such as the Prague radio station, were also occupied, as well as the administration offices of a number of towns. "The Ministry of Food (Soc. Dem) & the Ministry of Posts (People's Party) were prevented from broadcasting by order of the Communist Minister of Information on February 21st in Slovakia, the non-Communist members of the Slovak Board of Trustees, and local Administrations, were arrested, and thus Slovakia also came under Communist control through a virtual coup d'état."[15] The fragile and vulnerable chief of state was now subjected to relentless pressures from both camps. Beneš found himself at the center of a storm, stripped of effective power. The action committees had moved beyond his control, leaving the outmaneuvered president exposed to the organized mobility of the left.

The Trade Union Congress of factory councils, which opened at noon on Sunday, February 22nd, in the great Obečni Dōm, was a true workers' soviet of 8,000 delegates from factory and farm. In his opening speech, Antonín Zápotocký proclaimed the way now open to socialism. Forthwith, the reform and nationalization measures, long sponsored by the Communist Party, were endorsed by acclamation. If there were any contrary voices among the 110 non-Communist delegates, they went unheard in the bedlam. The motion to organize action committees, some of which were already functioning, also carried. In Gottwald's closing address, he warned Beneš against trying to retrieve lost positions. The renewed National Front, radicalized by its new union members, was now a fact to be reckoned with.

The following day, the machinery of repression and purging went forward, affecting every ministry and institution. Opposition offices and newspapers were closed down, and they were denied access to the radio transmitters. An action committee entered the Ministry of Foreign Affairs. With Vice-Minister Vladimir Clementis at his side, Jan Masaryk was forced to demand the resignation of unacceptable envoys on foreign missions.

Also on February 23rd, the Czech Social Democratic Party decided to accept Gottwald's offer to them to join the Communists in forming the nucleus of a reconstituted coalition, which would not include the resigning ministers. This decision came after the police, headed by

Interior Minister Nosek, "had occupied the Social Democratic Party's premises and thrown out those leaders who did not wish to cooperate with the Communists." [16]

As directed by the congress, a general strike was called to persuade Beneš to accept the moderates' resignations. As he received the liberal delegations during the day, notably Social Democrat Bohumil Laušman, he was shaken but outwardly calm as he grimly reiterated his determination not to accept the resignations. He finally admitted the error of the tactic. At the organizing meeting of the overall action committee, Defense Minister Ludvík Svoboda declared that the army was "with the people."

On the morning of February 25th, President Beneš parried the requests of both Sokol and National Socialist leaders to call on them for action against the Communists, but instead he received Gottwald, accompanied by Nosek and, significantly, by Zápotocký, the trade union chief. The Communist chairman now presented his new cabinet list, composed half of Communists, five Social Democrats, Jan Masaryk, and Svoboda. Also included were a handful of liberal nonentities from three small parties. Gottwald clinched his case by presenting the names of 166 parliamentary deputies, a clear majority in the National Assembly, who agreed to support the new cabinet.

Beneš said that he would give his reply before evening, but the noon radio broadcast anticipated his consent. Gottwald routinely returned in the afternoon to pick up the signed decree. "It was officially announced that President Beneš had accepted the resignations of the non-Communist Ministers, and that he had approved a new Government under the leadership of M. Gottwald." The Communists had taken over all the remaining ministries necessary to make their control complete: Justice, Foreign Trade, and Education, in addition to Interior (police), Information, Social Welfare, Finance, Agriculture, and Internal Trade. Masaryk and General Svoboda remained as they were at Foreign Affairs and National Defense.

"A full-scale purge affecting every branch of Czechoslovak life is in progress," observed the British embassy. "President Beneš has resisted so far as he could, but has been powerless—little or no attempt [has been observed] by the population to resist . . . It would be difficult for President Beneš to exclude the Communists after the election of May 26, 1946 . . . The purges have been going too quickly and smoothly for the lists of victims not to have been already drawn up," [17] concluded the observant British embassy.

On February 24th, "the Communists have now virtually taken over control of the State . . . They have put their representatives in the

Government departments," reported the British embassy. "The Czech press offices and Czech airlines, and State travel agencies, were all taken over. All passports were revoked . . . Opposition newspapers were shut down." [18] Next morning the *London Times* correspondent announced: "There is still no censorship or interference with journalists, but no doubt this will come later." [19]

President Beneš on February 25th decreed the end of Czechoslovak democracy. His broadcast to the nation, scheduled for 6 P.M., was canceled. Throughout the crisis, he felt impotent and fearful to use his presidential powers to counter the Communist surge. "Pressures brought . . . by Gottwald and the Trade Union representatives and their adherents who marched on the Castle caused [him] to fear internal strife," [20] reported Steinhardt.

What stayed his hand from using the loyal Sokols and/or the Legionnaires in the army was not that he underrated the "mobilization on the streets." On the contrary, it was his fear, shared by Jan Masaryk, that riots and street fighting might precipitate Soviet intervention. President Truman had clearly told him that the Czechoslovaks could not count on the United States for anything beyond moral support. Both Beneš and Masaryk concluded that in this proletarian-led coup, a new generation of youthful idealists had entered stage center, and the Western oriented men, wedded to Jeffersonian notions of democracy, bowed before the popular tide. As Beneš viewed the situation, he made the decision, "a very difficult one for him personally," pragmatically. He declared: "The State had to be governed and the nation administered, and the new Government wished to do this by new methods, and by a new form of democracy." [21] The alternative might have culminated in general chaos. Two days later, "M. Gottwald and his new Government . . . took the oath [of office] before the President." Gottwald "complimented the President for heeding the voices of the people." He avowed: "Future developments would be strictly democratic, constitutional, and Parliamentary."

General Svoboda was delegated to call on President Beneš that day, accompanied by the chief of staff and his major military aide. The defense minister's mission was to dissuade Beneš, as he put it, from abandoning the nation. Beneš thanked them for their concern. The next day, Beneš withdrew to Sezimovo Usti; he returned to Prague only in March, to receive an honorary degree from Charles University on its 600th anniversary. What kept him from resigning his office until June 7th, 1948, was his futile effort to mitigate the blatant illegalities that had inaugurated the regime of "democratic centralism."

It was indeed "the supreme tragedy of Beneš's life that at every turn he had to make some awesome decisions." [23]

Masaryk stayed on awhile for similar reasons. On February 27th, he told Steinhardt "he had already saved about 250 people" from the purge and indicated that "his decision to remain in the Government [should] be labeled 'temporarily'." What he failed to communicate to Steinhardt was quite personal. It was a pledge to his father on his deathbed, known to his intimate friends, "never to desert Beneš."

Ambassador Steinhardt ruminated over the events and delivered his assessment to the State Department at length:

The little people, the Czechs, have always needed strong Allies for survival . . . It seems clear that the debacle which followed the resignations may be largely attributable to weakness on the part of the President, which is hardly excusable on the grounds of his sub-normal physical health.. . . The Czechs are firmly of the opinion that we [Americans] "wrote them off" or . . . consigned them to the Soviet sphere of influence in 1943 . . . Our later actions indicated the correctness of this belief in the eyes of the Czechs.

Steinhardt recapitulated some notable background events. "President Beneš [had] received a polite, but non-committal reception in Washington early in 1943." The Teheran, Yalta, and Potsdam conferences followed, without Czechoslovakia's presence.

The halting of our army in May, 1945, thus permitting Soviet forces to liberate Praha, confirmed our stand in the minds of the Czechs . . . Further attention by us to the political aspects of the war might have given us control of Central Europe at a nominal cost . . . *Since the Soviets in fact, continued to be aggressive, it was only a matter of time* before a crisis would be precipitated in Czechoslovakia . . . The resignation of 12 non-Communist Ministers created a vacuum and the Communists moved in. [24]

Secretary of State George Marshall, taking stock of the Communist seizure of power in Czechoslovakia, coolly decided that "the situation, which has existed in the last three years, would not materially alter in this respect. Czechoslovakia has faithfully followed the Soviet policy in the United Nations and elsewhere and the establishment of a Communist regime would merely crystallize and confirm for the future previous Czech policy . . . without challenge or compromise." [25]

The fate of Czechoslovakia's internal democracy was peripheral to the considerations of the Big Power leaders of either bloc in the Cold War lineup; it was her foreign policy and more specifically her votes on bloc issues within international bodies, such as the United Nations, that mattered.

The British took a more pragmatic reading of their tactics than did Washington.   Ambassador Nichols advised keeping the British embassy open in Prague with an "ominous silence." [26]   The Foreign Office adopted the sage advice of its emissary: "We will preserve 'frigid relations' with the Governments [of Eastern Europe] while endeavoring to maintain contact with as many people as possible." [27] Orme Sargent on February 26th wrote: "We ought at once to concert with the U.S. and French Governments as to the attitude we are going to adopt towards the new Czech Government. It is no use refusing to recognize it, and *we ought to discourage the Americans from taking this line, as they well might*. I submit a draft telegram." [28]

NOTES

1. Laurence Steinhardt to Secretary of State, November 13, 1947, *Foreign Relations* 1947, v. 4, p. 242.

2. Jan Masaryk to Jacob Beam, November 14, 1947, Washington, D.C., *Foreign Relations* 1947, v. 4, pp. 242-44.

3. "East-West Trade Policy," Washington, D.C., November 19, 1947, *Foreign Relations* 1947, v. 4, p. 500.

4. "Control of Exports to the USSR and Eastern Europe," November 14, 1947, *Foreign Relations* 1947, v. 4, pp. 506-7. Italics added.

5. "East-West Trade Policy," November 19, 1947, *Foreign Relations* 1947, v. 4, p. 500.

6. "The Czechoslovak Crisis," March 3, 1948, FO 371/v. 71786-115282.

7. Steinhardt to Secretary of State, February 26, 1948, *Foreign Relations* 1947, v. 4, p. 739.

8. Steinhardt to Secretary of State, April 30, 1948, *Foreign Relations* 1948, v. 4, pp. 747-54.

9. Maurice Hankey, Foreign Office, February 25, 1948, FO 371/v. 71284-115282.

10. Ernest Bevin, February 25, 1948, FO 371/v. 71284-115282.

11. George C. Marshall to Francis Caffrey, Paris, February 24, 1948, *Foreign Relations* 1948, v. 4, pp. 735-36.

12. Steinhardt, report of a conversation with Jan Masaryk, February 27, 1948, *Foreign Relations* 1948, v. 4, pp. 741-42.

13. "The Czechoslovak Crisis," February 26, 1948, FO 371/v. 71285-115282.

14. "The Czechoslovak Crisis," March 3, 1948, FO 371/v. 71786-115282.

15. "The Czechoslovak Crisis," February 26, 1948, FO 371/v, 71285-115282.

16. "The Czechoslovak Crisis," Page 2, March 3, 1948, FO 371/v. 71786-115282.

17. Ibid.

18. British Embassy, Prague, to Foreign Office, February 24, 1948, Secret, FO 371/v. 71284-115282.

19. British Embassy, Prague, to Foreign Office, February 25, 1948, FO 371/v. 71284-115282.

20. "The Czechoslovak Crisis," Steinhardt report, *Foreign Relations* 1948, v. 4, pp. 747-54.

21. Dixon, Prague, to Foreign Office, February 28, 1948, FO 371/v. 71284-115282.

22. Ibid.

23. Tad Szulc, *Czechoslovakia Since World War II* (New York: Viking, 1971), p. 26.

24. "The Czechoslovak Crisis," Steinhardt report, *Foreign Relations* 1948, v. 4, pp. 747-54. Italics added.

25. George C. Marshall to Caffrey, February 24, 1948, *Foreign Relations* 1948, v. 4, pp. 735-36.

26. "The Czechoslovak Crisis," Nichols to Foreign Office, March 3, 1948, FO 371/v. 71786-115282.

27. Dixon, Prague, to Foreign Office, February 25, 1948, FO 371/v. 71284-115282.

28. Dixon, Prague, to Foreign Office, February 26, 1948, FO 371/v. 71284-115282. Telegram text not in Foreign Office archive. Italics added.

22

The Death of Jan Masaryk
(1948)

In the morning twilight of Wednesday, March 10th, 1948, the limp body of Jan Garrigue Masaryk, Czechoslovakia's popular and charismatic foreign minister, was discovered in the courtyard of the seventeenth-century Czernin Palace. The body lay on the stone pavement some 50 feet below the bathroom window of his official apartment in the Foreign Office Building.

Six hours later, the Communist-dominated government of Klement Gottwald broadcast to the world that Masaryk's death had been an act of suicide. The tragic news was transmitted on New York's 7 A.M. news. After allowing Prague-based correspondents to file their dispatches, the Czechoslovak government severed all communications with the outside world.

Shortly thereafter, Jan Papánek, the Czechoslovak ambassador to the United Nations, leaked to some correspondents in his office his view that Masaryk had been murdered. Papánek later officially requested UN secretary-general Trygve Lie to call an emergency meeting of the Security Council. His note demanded a debate on his charges of a foreign-directed seizure of power in Prague, resulting in the destruction of Czechoslovakia's national independence and thereby creating a threat to world peace. At the accompanying press conference, he rehearsed his reading of the Czechoslovak crisis and, at the end, voiced disbelief of the suicide story.

Whatever the accuracy may be of the conflicting versions of his death, Masaryk must be perceived as a victim of the Cold War. His premature demise inflamed the intensity of the rival power polemics, as the murder charge was eagerly adopted and exploited by the Western governments and press.

An investigation of the murder charge is in order because its wide acceptance in the West served to escalate Cold War tensions. In addition, the great historical changes in East-West relations since 1989 present a unique opportunity for a more objective reconsideration of these events. Such a reconsideration was first attempted over 20 years ago by the Prague Spring cabinet, but was terminated abruptly following the Soviet–Warsaw Pact invasion of August 21, 1968.

The very manner in which we, the authors, came to learn of the two versions provides a vital clue to the mystery. At 9:30 A.M. Wednesday, March 10th, our telephone rang. On the line was the excited voice of Betka Papánek, wife of Jan Papánek, whom we had known well for years. "Hello! Is that you, Sylvia?" she blurted out. Both of us got on the line. "Have you heard the dreadful news? Jan committed suicide." We immediately knew that she was not referring to her husband, but to Jan Masaryk in Prague. "I heard it on the 7 o'clock news," she continued. We were shocked, but not surprised. We considered what we might do.

Our first impulse was to telephone John's sister, Frances, who had been married to Jan. But her line was tied up—for hours. We then placed a call to Jan's sister Alice in Prague, but we were informed that all communications with Prague had been cut. Not until four years later did we have an opportunity to discuss the tragedy with Alice, when she took refuge in the United States for the second time.

Later that morning, we finally broke through to Frances. John and his sister recalled Jan's past breakdowns and his depressions, especially those in 1912 and 1930. She reviewed her clamorous decision in 1930 to leave Jan for a private life at the family's summer base at Woods Hole, on Cape Cod, Massachusetts. John had been curious about this decision for years, as Frances had never concealed her ambition to succeed in her absorbing London social life as mistress of the Czechoslovak legation. She charged into John bitterly. "Why do you think I retired from my glamorous position? Through all these years of Jan's being foreign minister, I couldn't explain, even to my closest friends, or to you!" She confided that life with unstable Jan had become impossible for her to withstand.

That morning, we three Cranes, living in Woods Hole and New York, concluded that in all probability Jan had committed suicide. This decision seemed likely for several reasons. First, Jan had a long-standing history of emotional instability, which was known to our family. The instability in the Masaryk-Garrigue family had surfaced with Jan's mother, Charlotte Garrigue, whose balance had been crushed by the overwhelming burden of coordinating a branch of the wartime resistance movement following her husband's departure abroad.

The Crane family's familiarity with Jan's history of emotional problems dates back to 1912, when Jan worked at the personnel office of the Bridgeport plant of our family's Crane Company factory. Much later, in 1940, John and Frances took the opportunity to learn about Jan's treatment for his breakdown, when he spent almost two years at the Training School at Vineland, New Jersey.

In our search for the record of that confinement, we were fortunate to encounter Professor Johnstone, who had attended to Jan and was still heading the famous institution. Johnstone assured us that by the time Jan's mother had arrived in the late summer of 1913, Jan was already back on his feet and ready to resume his activities in the United States. Charlotte had reported on Jan's encouraging progress in Vineland in a lengthy letter to her husband in Prague.[1] She wrote that after Jan had completed his training, he would be ready to accept Alice's suggestion that he return to Prague for a family reunion and to attend the celebrations of the 500th anniversary of Jan Hus's martyrdom. Before taking the giant leap across the Atlantic, Jan returned briefly to his work at the Crane Company plant. The family reunion had trapped him in Prague at the outbreak of World War I.

Frances had witnessed a second breakdown in 1930 at close range, discouraging her from continuing her marriage. Jan had staggered into her room one evening inebriated, threatening, not for the first time, to kill her and then himself. These threats, uttered always under the influence of alcohol, had become frequent after Frances's miscarriage in 1925. In May 1930, Frances had called John, then living in Rome, from the Czechoslovak legation in London to consult. They decided something definite had to be done. Frances took Jan by train to Geneva to consult Dr. Henri Revillod, the psychiatrist husband of Jan's sister Olga. With his help, they located a good sanatorium for Jan's treatment.

In June, upon Frances's return to London, she had summoned John again from Rome to review her plans to separate from Jan. She had explained that they were very much in love, but she found life with Jan impossible. She never knew what to expect. Jan had agreed that Frances should join her three sons for the customary summer at home in Woods Hole. A month later, Jan's sister Alice arrived in London to accompany Jan to the Swiss sanatorium. Soon afterward, he moved to the Slovak watering place of Piešt'any "to dry himself out." He wrote John in the fall that undergoing the cure at Piešt'any and Karlovy Vary and giving up drinking enabled him to shed 30 pounds. But this time, the cure did not assuage the strained marriage relations, and Frances instituted divorce proceedings.

The subject of suicide was not foreign to Jan. He had repeatedly spoken of it in the family circle. He never looked upon the act of self-destruction with shame, only with deep sadness and sorrow. This view was not shared by his father, who had written a sociological treatise on the subject. [2] To the elder Masaryk, suicide was to be condemned as denoting the loss of religious faith. Jan was well aware, however, that the one exception that would justify suicide in his father's mind was as an act of self-sacrifice for a higher cause.

Our initial acceptance of Jan's suicide was based on two premises. Undoubtedly, Jan felt trapped by events, which he must have felt left him with no exit. Here was a Masaryk who was lending his name to a Communist government! But we knew that he had ruled out the possibility of leaving his country for London or the United States. We also thought that, whatever the Communists' ultimate plan may have been regarding Jan, it was implausible that they would murder him so quickly after gaining power. More likely, they needed Jan in their cabinet as foreign minister, to give them legitimacy at home after their illegal takeover. And that day at noon, he was to appear before the Chamber of Deputies in that role for the first time as part of the Communist cabinet. The Czechoslovak Communists, and certainly Klement Gottwald, had every reason to preserve Jan alive, at least for some transitional period. His death deprived them of an invaluable asset.

We soon learned that the source of the murder theory appeared to be Marcia Davenport, Jan's last companion, whom he had flown out of Prague the previous Sunday, March 7th. No clue to this source, however, was visible to us for some time. At the time of Jan's death we knew only what she reported in an interview, published in the *New York Times* the following morning. Her words were elusive: "No, no, there is more in this than meets the eye."

The first inkling of this source came to light one evening in mid-September 1948 when we were chatting in our New York apartment with a journalist friend, Frances McLarnen. While reviewing these events and the Communist coup in Prague, she stopped short and exclaimed: "You know, I also knew Jan well and loved him, so I tracked his death as closely as both of you. What I can't figure is how the report of suicide shifted so quickly to murder, when all telephone lines into and out of Prague were cut, eliminating Prague as the source of the revision."

We all stopped to reflect. McLarnen recalled the events of March 10th as clearly as we. Early that morning, her phone had rung at 7:30 A.M. Picking up the receiver, she heard the familiar voice of her close friend and UPI Moscow correspondent, Ira Shapiro, with whom she had spent the previous late evening. He hurriedly gave her the news of Jan's suicide. Dazed and shocked, she begged him to call her again later. "When Ira phoned back around eleven that morning," she continued, "he blandly spoke of Jan's murder . . . I reminded him of his previous talk of Jan's suicide," she went on, "and I demanded to know the basis of his changed story. He responded that he was now calling from Jan Papánek's office and that they had just talked with London." Thus, the origin clearly seemed to have come from London. Although we all suspected Davenport in London as the real source, we had no firm evidence yet.

Nineteen years after the tragedy, in 1967, Marcia Davenport published her sentimental memoir, *Too Strong for Fantasy*,[3] in which she dealt with her personal relationship with Jan. In particular, she reported that it was she who had told Papánek that Jan was murdered. This version was confirmed to John one fine day in spring 1970 when, for the first time, John had the occasion to talk with Papánek about Jan's death. John chanced to meet Papánek and his wife on the street in Rome. As they strolled together, John asked him simply where he had gleaned the startling news of Jan's murder in the late morning of March 10th. Papánek responded guilelessly: "As I could not get through to Prague, I had called Marcia in London, who informed me that on leaving Prague the previous Sunday, Jan had told her that if he failed to keep his promise to join her, he would only be prevented by the Communists, who might kill him."

Davenport's book stated four circumstances as the basis for the theory of murder. First, in the final week of his life, Masaryk had made firm plans to get Mrs. Davenport out to London "into the safety of Claridges'." She wrote that he feared tumultuous events in Prague. Second, she asserted that he was making plans to escape to London for the purpose of joining her in marriage. Third, he also contemplated leaving the country legally, perhaps on a pretext of attending some international conference. Fourth, she wrote that he had confided to her his apprehensions of the Communists.

Of course, none of these considerations can be absolutely refuted. The existence of some of this circumstantial evidence was confirmed by others, and we certainly do not know what Jan may have told Davenport. Unfortunately, the personal factors propelling the murder theory cannot be overlooked either. Jan had emphasized to us during our last talk in his Carlyle Hotel suite in December 1947 that the relationship was not at all as it appeared; Davenport was simply an attractive and interesting woman in whom he found companionship, as her apartment was next door to Alice's, across the Loretanska Square from his. He explained that he was not emotionally committed to her and had no intention to marry her. He subsequently repeated this statement to other close friends in Prague, such as Vladimír and Olga Hurban, who had served in numerous Foreign Office posts abroad and who were also good friends of ours. Whatever Jan may have told Davenport to persuade her to leave Prague, and whatever she actually believed, due to her own personal loss, it is of *critical* importance that her interpretation was taken at face value in high quarters throughout the West, despite the absence of factual proof. [4]

Rightly or wrongly, this was a period when the Western world would accept uncritically any version of events that portrayed those in power in the Eastern bloc as murderers. One popular view of the murder theory embroidered it into a case of defenestration, such as had been inflicted upon three imperial ministers at the Hradčany Castle in 1618, inciting the Battle of the White Mountain, outside Prague, which the Czechs had lost. These assertions took no account of the many historical differences, including the different palaces involved, the Hradčany and the Czernin, situated several squares apart.

Throughout the years, the sober assessments of family and friends reinforced our initial conclusion that Jan had taken his own life. Many of these conversations took place during two of our visits in Prague in 1966 and 1970, when we were able to probe the causes of Jan's death with several close friends and other family members.

On many occasions over the years we reviewed the events with Alice, who at the time of Jan's death lived in an apartment across the Loretanska Square from her brother. She was our frequent visitor in New York after she took refuge in the United States in 1950. Jan's two nieces, Ana and Herberta, took less interest in the subject, as their concerns were focused on the arts. They disclaimed any real knowledge of events and noted to us that they had not seen their celebrated uncle in quite a while. [5]

Many of Jan's close friends reinforced our view of his death. For example, Hana Beneš was totally convinced of suicide. Olga Hurban, who returned to live with her family in New York after her husband's death, agreed, as had her late husband, with our view of the death as a suicide; she expressed continued skepticism of the premise that Jan would move to London or ever marry Marcia Davenport. Others concurring with the suicide theory over the years included Prince Max Lobcovicz and his wife Gillian, long-standing fast family and personal friends, and writer Jiří Mucha, who was Jan's lifelong friend and who had seen Jan frequently in Prague during the last weeks of Jan's life.

An understanding of Jan's inextricable dilemma is central to dealing with this puzzle. Jan's overriding desire in life was to serve his people in the Masaryk-Beneš tradition of decency and democracy. Although he never sought power as a goal in and of itself, he looked upon any impediment to serving his country in this context as unsustainable. His rock-bottom determination was never to sully his family name. He was also surely driven by the solemn pledge to his father never to desert Eduard Beneš. It was particularly important, in view of Beneš's impaired health following his stroke, that he take some burdens off Beneš's shoulders.

Another critical factor in understanding Jan's dilemma was his having precluded the alternative route of exile. As he had confided to us and to other friends in New York and London, he looked forward with distaste to the prospect of earning his living abroad by resuming the lecture and social circuit, especially in his mother's homeland, which had accorded him such scant concern. Nor would he ever again become a "puppet for others to pull his strings." Despite his love of America, he had felt the sting of betrayal deeply when Secretary of State George C. Marshall had denied him the leverage to rescue his democratic government, and when friends had crossed the street to avoid a direct encounter. These rebuffs had hurt him to the quick.

He felt he could never go into private retirement abroad; he would inevitably become the cynosure of liberal groups escaping into exile. He had freely acknowledged to us that life in London would prove equally impossible. When his British confidant, Bruce Lockhart, finding him "depressed and terribly tired,"[6] pleaded with him in December to remain in London, he sadly and resignedly repeated substantially what he had already told us in New York: "You can leave your country twice or as many times as you have the strength to fight. You can't do it to fight your own countrymen."[7]

At the same time, staying at home, Masaryk would have had to face the harrowing prospect of isolation and perhaps harassment or even persecution. He would have been impotent to help his friends and could not bear to see them face the consequences. Finally, the notion of becoming embroiled in any plots to overthrow the government were rejected out of hand. He had told us plainly at lunch in his Czernin Palace apartment that the people's right to have any government of their choice ought to be preserved. If it were the Communists, they would soon learn their mistake and change it.

Despite his psychological barrier against exile, there were possible thoughts of leaving the country on a legitimate basis, to attend a conference or take a rest or cure. Since his recent chill verging on a bronchitis, his health had been deteriorating frighteningly, with complications from a longtime bursitis, which had worsened since our last meeting in New York, plaguing him incessantly. It was normal for him to plan a cure and rest at Grafenberg, Alice's favorite watering resort in Northeastern Bohemia. He discussed such a course openly, perhaps as a ploy. Plans of escape were rumored to be preying on his mind constantly. And at times his London flat undoubtedly seemed like a haven. Even though he had logically dismissed exile, such action was physically possible because, in view of his political status and position, he was able to keep his private plane at readiness at the airport at all times.

Three years after the tragedy, Bruce Lockhart, who had known Jan and understood him better than almost anyone else, published his touching and insightful *Personal Memoir*. If the Communists had ever had word of Masaryk's plan to leave the country, Bruce Lockhart thought that they would have had every justification for killing him. Abroad, he could not have avoided becoming the rallying point of hostile plots and propaganda. Bruce Lockhart said it for all of Jan's friends:

I do not doubt that he made his plans to escape. I also do not doubt that, when the time for action came, he preferred the simpler way out. He had come to the end of his physical and mental strength and my knowledge of him and my instinct tell me that, having lent his name to the new government in the hope of restraining it, he found collaboration impossible and gave his own life in protestation. [8]

Bruce Lockhart said that Czech friends of Jan saw him as having become "a great public figure on the international stage," who would be "unhappy to leave it." But Bruce Lockhart himself saw Jan simply as "an artist," who "belonged to the public, and whatever belongs to the public rarely leaves it willingly or with impunity." Almost the last words Jan spoke to his English friend in Prague were, "I wish to God I could be rid of it all." [9] This account squares with Jan's outburst to us in his apartment in response to our admiration of the painted ceilings. "Do you like this museum I'm forced to live in? I'd exchange it for your New York flat in a jiffy if I could."

It had seemed natural for the time being that non-party-aligned

Masaryk should remain in the cabinet as foreign minister. He had told several people this was only temporary. The government's pro-Moscow foreign policy did not face imminent change or challenge. It would continue anti-German; how otherwise following the Nazi occupation and the betrayal by their Fifth Column of Sudeten Germans? Beneš had specifically requested Jan to stay on. Beneš had told us previously that he wanted trustworthy "eyes and ears within the Cabinet." At the time this request accorded with Jan's own inclination as well as his promise to his father not to desert Beneš.

Beneš's own considerations in remaining at his post of president were similar to Jan's. Chiefly, by withholding his resignation, he might cushion the impact of Gottwald's inevitable purge campaign against their moderate followers in state ministries and in the bureaucracy. Indeed, Prime Minister Gottwald claimed to have given explicit instructions to check the pace of the militant action committees.

It seems likely that the rapidly changing events were causing Masaryk to reexamine his initial instinct to serve the new government. He was thoroughly shaken over the egregious blunder, as he saw it, of the liberals' resignations from the cabinet, and by Beneš's acceptance of them. Jan had seen the tactic as a boomerang, throwing Beneš and himself into an untenable position. Indeed, when the president was leaving Prague for Tabor, Gottwald had expressed gratitude at having been handed the reins of power.

Masaryk had personally pleaded with the once-friendly Gottwald to preserve intact the Foreign Ministry, the Ministry of Public Health, and the Institute of Public Health, the first of which was stocked with his personal friends and the other two with Alice's.* Although Jan had supplied Gottwald with an itemized list of outstanding experts specifically to be spared, in a few days time the Damocles sword had fallen on them. Jan was outraged and took it as a personal betrayal. He had fought with Gottwald over it, but the only concession he could obtain was a rescinding of the victims' banishment from Prague, not of their dismissal from their jobs. They could stay in town and work at whatever other labor they could find, without forfeiting their pension rights. Lacking the backing of a political party, Masaryk's power reposed only in his name and on his vast network of friends distributed throughout the ministries. Now, he was gradually being rendered impotent.

---

*The Institute of Public Health, under the directorship of the renowned Dr. Jan Krakes, had been founded and developed under the personal supervision of Alice Masaryk.

At this point, he seemed not to want any connection or post in a government headed by Gottwald, who had broken his word. Not only did Jan fear reprisal if he countered or obstructed Gottwald's will, but he himself wanted time to sort out his options. And his poor health surely dragged him into passivity and depression.

After February 25th, Masaryk felt himself to be a hunted man. He communicated this feeling to several intimates, who later told us. The following week, it was rumored that a bodyguard had been detailed to follow him closely and that gendarmes oversaw his movements. He assumed his rooms to be bugged and his phone tapped; he comported himself with caution, as he stood in mortal fear of becoming "a prisoner of Stalin." Perhaps he had a premonition of the Slánský-type purge trials that were destined to follow.

Throughout the crisis, Jan had kept in closest possible contact with Beneš, driving down to Sezimovo Usti almost every day and telephoning several times daily. On Saturday, March 6th, he undertook his most crucial mission there, to consult on their next move. Although he had seen Beneš only a few days earlier, he was shocked to find how rapidly his chief had declined in the week since he had left Prague; the slippage was manifest both physically and psychologically. After reporting on the Prague scene, Jan inquired about Beneš's plan for his own future. To his amazement, Beneš replied that he had none, and that Jan had better look out for himself. This is precisely what he intended to do, Jan replied according to Hana Beneš, who assured us that she was present during the entire conversation and that there was talk neither of suicide nor of escape. Jan took off with his customary hand-wave and "We'll see."

On Sunday, March 7th, in the late afternoon after seeing Davenport off to London, Jan drove out to Lany, where his father and mother were buried in the village cemetery, to mark his father's 98th birthday anniversary. There he met Alice and their nieces, Ana and Herberta. Jan remained alone at the green graves of his parents for some time in silent meditation. Now that Beneš had freed him to look out for himself, he probably was asking his father for absolution from his pledge to stick with Beneš to the end. It was probably here that he made his decision to withdraw his name from what he felt was an immoral and inhumane regime, a decision all his intimate friends later believed he had made.

Most of Monday, Masaryk spent quietly but busily in his room. He accomplished the significant act of destroying his private papers, but reserved in his bedroom chest his autobiographical materials, accumulated during his twice-weekly talks with his lifelong friend, the diplomat Vladimír Vaněk.

Tuesday morning, Masaryk drove down to Sezimovo Usti to be present when the new Polish ambassador presented his credentials to President Beneš. Other luncheon guests were Presidential Chancellor Jaromír Smutný and his wife. After the envoy left and the Smutnýs also retired, Jan stayed behind for a pleasant chat with Eduard and Hana Beneš. Contrary to other reports of this last meeting with the Benešes, Hana Beneš told us they talked themselves out, as they had done the previous Saturday, settling nothing.[10] Hana, who was present throughout the lunch that day, explained to us that they invariably raised their voices in making decisive points, especially when they talked agitatedly. But there was absolutely no inkling of a rift, she reassured us firmly. Nor was there any mention or intimation that Jan was making plans to leave the country.

Seemingly in a hurry to return to Prague, Jan departed in his normally cordial way, giving them no premonition. He returned to Prague on the afternoon of Tuesday, March 9th in a state of devastating depression, according to his secretary, Loumír Soukup.[11] Later that afternoon, Vladimír Houdek dropped into the apartment to say good-bye; he was returning to his post as secretary of the Czechoslovak embassy in Washington. Next day, after Masaryk's death, Houdek said in the *New York Times* he had found Masaryk nervous and disapproving of America's overly liberal policy toward Germany, but showing no particular signs of stress or depression.

His first secretary, Jiří Špaček, had been dismissed for the day; his old-time manservant Prihoda brought in his usual light supper and left him in an apparently relaxed mood. During the evening, he drafted a short greeting that he was to deliver next day to the Polish ambassador.

On his bedtable, Prihoda had left two bottles of mineral water and a bottle of beer. There were also the sleeping pills that Jan took for habitual insomnia, and in the dresser drawer lay a revolver.

It was reported that when the security police seized the apartment the next morning, the bottles of mineral water were empty and the room was in disarray, more chaotic than customary. In his bathroom, the contents of his medicine chest were scattered with broken bottles across the floor. There was a pillow soiled with excrement in the bathtub where Jan often lay when he was sleepless. It was cooler there than in bed.

A suspicious incident arose when the official autopsy was begun that day at noon in the military hospital, without awaiting the return of Jan's personal physician, Dr. Oscar Klinger. The doctor had gone to Sezimovo Usti with Smutný to inform the president and his wife of

Jan's death. When, toward the end of the autopsy, Dr. Klinger arrived at the hospital, he was not permitted to approach the body. Yet Alice, who related this episode, also told us long afterward, when affirming her belief in Jan's suicide, "Jan jumped like a true Sokol, feet first."

The autopsy report said that the legs and abdominal organs were rammed into his thoracic cavity. The fingerprints on the bathroom windowsill indicated that he had let himself go facing the wall. The scrapes of his stomach skin in that case would have been caused by his brushing against the ledge below the window as he dropped to the pavement. Had he been pushed, dead or alive, his body would have landed clear in a clump, sustaining other severe injuries.

It is our considered judgment and strong conviction that Jan Masaryk took his own life, not because he had another nervous breakdown, but as the most expeditious and honorable way out of the hopeless dilemma into which history had placed him. He had clung to his duties to the extent permitted by his physical and psychological endurance. He had rejected exile as too distasteful and humiliating. And he had remained true to his pledge to his father. When Beneš told Jan to look out for himself, it was a clear message that he had been released from any further obligations to his and his father's trusted colleague and friend.

Jan Masaryk also felt betrayed by the West as well as at home. During his 14 years as head of Czechoslovakia's London legation and his ten years working side-by-side with Beneš as foreign minister, Masaryk had given his utmost in skill and dedication to build Czechoslovak security and world peace on solid foundations. At the close of World War II, he had voiced his hope and worked diligently in the international arena to contribute his extraordinary prestige to this end.   At the United Nations, he had enjoyed an unrivalled position until it was undermined by Cold War distortions of the human values that he cherished. Masaryk saw his role on the world scene as that of mediator and moderator of the chauvinistic drives of the Great Powers. As international tensions mounted, he had sought nothing more than a stand-off truce to allow the forces of commerce and peace an opportunity to prevail.

But he also saw the superpower forces closing in on him and his country. His family heritage and training had led him to repose more faith in the leadership of his mother's native United States than in Soviet Russia. This preference was shattered by President Truman's rebuff and choice of Cold War instead. He knew that the United States could no longer be counted upon to aid his country.

At home, he was equally betrayed. His likely suicide was the ultimate protest against Gottwald and a regime so inhumane and contrary to everything that he, his father, and Beneš had stood for and worked for through all these years. He died spiritually, in the words Alice used with us so many times, when he saw his efforts so clearly failing. His chief raison d'être—to lead his people and to serve humanity—had been taken from him. He could no longer be loyal to his father's ideal of service. And he knew that a suicide in this context would not betray his father and the family name. So he chose to depart the scene at age 62 of his own volition, in his despairing but historically significant gesture of protest.

NOTES

1. Letter from Charlotte Garrigue Masaryk to Thomas Masaryk, dated September 1, 1913, 18 pages, handwritten (copy), Crane family archive.

2. Tomáš Masaryk, *Suicide and the Meaning of Civilization* (Chicago and London: University of Chicago Press, 1970), p. 7. Original publication in German, Vienna, 1881.

3. Marcia Davenport, *Too Strong for Fantasy* (New York: Scribner's, 1967).

4. To the best of our knowledge, Marcia Davenport first learned of Jan's death from Ambassador Steinhardt, who had been very friendly with Jan. He had talked with Davenport when she called him from London and he informed her of Jan's death, nothing more. Robert Bruce Lockhart, Masaryk's closest English friend, later wrote a memoir of Jan in which he spoke of Davenport and himself as having had no evidence of murder and said that he attempted to dissuade Davenport from charging that Jan had been murdered, as she lacked solid facts.

5. Ana and Herberta told the authors that they genuinely regretted having given one interview on this question to Claire Sterling, as they volunteered that they had no facts to go on. See Claire Sterling, *The Masaryk Case* (New York: Harper and Row, 1968).

6. Robert Bruce Lockhart, *Jan Masaryk: A Personal Memoir* (New York: Philosophical Library, 1951), p. 67.

7. Ibid., p. 68.

8. Ibid., pp. 78-9.

9. Ibid., p. 65.

10. Hana Beneš to authors. Sterling, *The Masaryk Case*.

11. Related to authors by Loumir Soukup in 1977 in London.

Abbreviations

AEF	Allied Expeditionary Force
Am.	American
Brit.	British
Cath.	Catholic
CIA	Central Intelligence Agency
Comm.	Communist
confid.	confidential
Czecho	Czechoslovak
Dept.	Department
dols	dollars
emb.	embassy
Exim.	Export-Import
FDR	F. D. Roosevelt
for.	foreign
FO	Foreign Office
HMG or HM'sG	His Majesty's Government
KGB	Russian Intelligence Agency
JOC	John O. Crane
M.	Monsieur
Mgr.	Monsignor
Min.	Minister or Ministry
NHT	*New York Herald Tribune*
NYT	*New York Times*
ORG.	Gehlen's Intelligence Agency
OSS	Office of Strategic Services
pg.	page
PM	Prime Minister
Pol.Bur.	Political Bureau
psych.	psychological
rel.	relations
Rept.	Report

Secy.	Secretary
SD	Social Democratic
SdP	Sudetendeutsche Partei
Sl.	Slovak
Soc.	Socialist
Tel or teleg.	Telegram
UN	United Nations
UNRRA	United Nations Relief and Rehabilitation Agency
v. or vol.	volume
WO	War Office
WW	Woodrow Wilson

Bibliography

PRIMARY SOURCES

This book is based chiefly on archival materials, in addition to John Crane's observations and researches during his several years in Prague. It also takes into account secondary sources.

The most important repository was the Public Record Office in London, containing the files of the Foreign Office and the War Office. These comprised:

Foreign Office: File numbers: 371, 382, 395, 608, ZHC, PREM;
War Office: File No. 106;
Cabinet Minutes (CAB): 21, 23, 24, 27, 28, 37.

These files contain over 50 volumes each for the 1918-1921 period and the Munich period 1937-1939. Foreign Office records for the World War II years, 1941-1945, and until 1948, were also searched.

The French Foreign Office records usually at the Quai d'Orsay for 1933-1939, including the Munich period, were destroyed in a wartime fire on May 16, 1940. Fortunately, numerous relevant documents or portions of them were preserved by the excellent scholar of French foreign relations at the Sorbonne, Jean-Baptiste Duroselle, in his bountiful volume, *La Décadence, 1932-1939* (Paris: Imprimerie Nationale, 1979).

The Czechoslovak Information Service published many important documents useful for this book:

Speeches of Jan Masaryk in America (New York: 1941);
President Beneš on War and Peace: Statements by Beneš during His Visit to the U.S. and Canada in May and June, 1943 (New York: 1943);
On the Reign of Terror in Bohemia and Moravia under the Reign of Reinhard Heydrich (London: 1942).

Publications of the Czechoslovak Ministry of Foreign Affairs in postwar Europe:

Czechoslovakia Fights Back (Washington, 1943);
Four Fighting Years (London, 1943);
Problems of Reconstruction (London, 1943).

Other Czechoslovak documents referred to were:

The Problems of Czechoslovakia;
Speeches of the President of the Republic;
Dr. Eduard Beneš in Northern Bohemia (Prague: 1936).

The Library of Congress collections that were examined were: Papers of Woodrow Wilson, of Richard Lansing, and of Newton D. Baker.

The National Archives yielded much pertinent material:

State Department records and correspondence, especially letters to and from its embassies in London, Paris, Moscow, Prague, Warsaw, Budapest, Belgrade, Cairo, and Algiers. Other internal memoranda and correspondence duplicated for me on microfilm under file number 1218, reels 29 and 30;
Records of the German Foreign Ministry: Container 2444, Frames E240: 630-31; 240: 665-66; 240: 721-22, 743-45; E240: 823-27; Container 2443: E240, 133-34, 136, 141-44, 239, 784-90;
Germany's Eastern Neighbors, Relating to the Oder-Neisse Line and the Czech Frontier Regions (London: 1938).

Princeton University has extensive material on Woodrow Wilson, including:

Arthur S. Link, ed., *Woodrow Wilson Papers and Letters*, 49 vols. (Princeton, N.J.: Princeton University Press).

The Franklin D. Roosevelt Library, Hyde Park, N.Y. has numerous works on FDR and World War II.

Georgetown University:

Papers of Richard Crane.

Crane family archive includes:

Charles R. Crane, letters to and from Woodrow Wilson;
One 13-page copy of letter from Charlotte Garrigue Masaryk to her husband reporting on Jan Masaryk's condition and treatment at Vineland, N.J;
John O. Crane, letters;
——Reports on Czechoslovakia prepared for the Institute of Current World Affairs;
——Diary for 1922.

Documents of U.S. Government Printing Office:

Documents on German Foreign Policy, 1918-1945, Series D, v. I, 1948;
U.S. Dept of State, Background Notes on Czechoslovakia, Bureau of Public Affairs, 1949;
Documents on British Foreign Policy, 1919-1939, Third Series, Foreign Relations of the U.S., 1955.

United Nations documents:

United Nations War Crimes Commission: *History of the UN War Crimes Commission and the Development of the Laws of War* (London: 1948).

UNRRA, European Regional Office:

Agriculture and Food in Czechoslovakia (London: 1946);
Foreign Trade in Czechoslovakia (London, 1947);
Industrial Rehabilitation in Czechoslovakia (London: 1947);
Transport Rehabilitation in Czechoslovakia (London, 1947).

SECONDARY SOURCES

Books (Selected List)

Armstrong, Hamilton Fish, *When There Was No Peace*. London: Macmillan, 1941.
Baerlein, Henry, *The March of the Seventy Thousand*. London: Leonard Parsons, 1926.
Beneš, Eduard, *Democracy Today and Tomorrow*. New York: Macmillan, 1939.
——*Munich*. French ed., Paris: Stock, 1969.
——*Memoirs, From Munich to New War and New Victory*. Boston: Houghton Mifflin, 1953.
——*My War Memoirs*. London: Allen & Unwin, 1928.
Betts, R. R., *Essays in Czech History*. London University: Athlone Press, 1969.
Black, C.E., Ed. *Challenge in Eastern Europe*. New Brunswick, N.J.: Rutgers University Press, 1954.
Bonnet, Georges, *Défense de la Paix*. Geneva: C. Bourquin, 1946; Paris: Plon, 1967.
——*Quai d'Orsay, Sous Trois Républiques, 1918-1938*. Paris: Fayard, 1961.
——*Vingt Ans de ma Vie Politique, de Clemençeau à Daladier*. Paris: Fayard, 1967.
Borkin, Joseph, and Charles A. Walsh, *Germany's Master Plan*. Toronto: Duell, 1943.
Bowman, Isaiah, *The New World*. New York: World Books, 1928.
Brady, Robert A., *Business As a System of Power*. New York: Columbia University Press, 1943.
Brown, Seyom, *The Faces of Power: Constancy and Change in U.S. Foreign Policy from Truman to Johnson*. New York: Columbia University Press, 1968.
Bruce Lockhart, Sir Robert, *Memoirs of a British Agent*. 1st Ed, 1932, Penguin, 1950.
——*Retreat From Glory*. London: Putnam, 1934.
——*Diaries, 1915-1918*. London: Macmillan, 1973.
——*Comes the Reckoning*. London: Putnam, 1947.
——*Jan Masaryk: A Personal Memoir*. New York: Philosophical Library, 1951.
Calic, Édouard, *Reinhard Heydrich*. New York: Military Heritage, 1982.
Čapek, Karel, *President Masaryk Tells His Story*. New York: Putnam, 1935.
Carr, Edward, H., *International Relations Between the Two World Wars*. London: Macmillan, 1961.
——*Twilight of the Comintern, 1930-1935*. New York: Pantheon, 1982.
Carsten, F. L., *Revolutions in Central Europe 1918-1919*. Berkeley: University of California Press, 1972.
Chmela, Leopold, *The Economic Aspect of the German Occupation of Czechoslovakia*. Prague: Orbis, 1948.
Churchill, Winston, *The Second World War: The Gathering Storm*. Boston: Houghton Mifflin, 1948.

Cisař, Jaroslav, and František Pokorný, *The Czechoslovak Republic*. London: T. Fisher Unwin, 1922.

Cowling, Maurice, *The Impact of Hitler—British Politics and British Policy, 1933-49*. Cambridge University Press, 1975.

Crane, John O., *The Little Entente*. New York: Macmillan, 1931

Crankshaw, Edward, *The Fall of the House of Habsburg*. New York: Popular Library, 1963.

Davenport, Marcia, *Too Strong for Fantasy*. New York: Scribner, 1967.

Davis, Forrest, and Ernest K. Lindley, *How The War Came: American White Paper from the fall of France to Pearl Harbor*. New York: Simon and Schuster, 1942.

Derend, Ivan and Györgyi, *Economic Development in East Central Europe in the 19th and 20th Centuries*. New York: Columbia University Press, 1974.

Dodd, William E., *Ambassador Dodd's Diary*, New York: Harcourt Brace, 1941.

Duroselle, Jean-Baptiste, *La Décadence, 1932-1939*. Paris: Imprimerie National, 1979.

Dvorník, Francis, *The Slavs in European History and Civilization*. New Brunswick, N.J.: Rutgers University Press, 1962.

Eden, Anthony, Earl of Avon, *Memoirs, Facing the Dictators*. London & New York: Houghton Mifflin, 1962.

Eisenmann, Louis, *La Tchechoslovakie*. Paris: F. Reider, 1921.

Feiling, Keith, *The Life of Neville Chamberlain*. New York: Macmillan, 1944.

Fleming, D. F., *The Cold War & Its Origins*. New York: Doubleday, 1961.

Fontaine, André, *History of the Cold War*. New York: Random House, 1969

Francis, David R., *Russia From the American Embassy, April 1916–November 1918* New York: Scribner, 1921.

Gaddis, John Lewis, *The United States and the Origins of the Cold War, 1941-1947*. New York: Columbia University Press, 1972.

Gehlen, General Reinhard, *The Service: The Memoirs of General Reinhard Gehlen*. New York: World Publishing, 1972

Geyde, G.E.R., *Heirs to the Habsburgs*. London: Arrowsmith, 1932.

——*Betrayal in Central Europe*. New York and London: Harper, 1939.

Gottwald, Klement, *Selected Speeches & Articles*. Prague: Orbis

Grant Duff, Sheila, *A German Protectorate; The Czechs Under Nazi Rule*. Toronto, Macmillan, 1942.

Graham, N.W., *New Governments of Central Europe*. New York: Putnam, 1924.

Graves, William S., *America's Siberian Adventure*. New York: Jonathan Cape, 1931.

Gruber, Joseph, *Czechoslovakia*. New York: Macmillan, 1924.

Hájek, Jiří, *Munich. Signal auf Krieg: München, 1938*. Berlin: Lötten & Loening, 1960.

Henderson, Sir Nevile, *Failure of a Mission*. New York: Putnam, 1940.

Herman, A.H., *A History of the Czechs*. London: Penguin, 1975.

Hexner, E., *The International Cartels*. Chapel Hill, N. C.: University of North Carolina Press, 1945.

Hines, Walter H., *Report on Danubian Navigation*. Geneva: League of Nations, 1925.

——*Hitler's Secret Conversations, 1941-1944*. New York: Farrar & Straus, 1953.

Hitler, Adolph, *Mein Kampf*. New York: Stackpole Sons, 1939 (first English edition).

Hochman, Jiri, *The Soviet Union & the Failure of Collective Security*. Ithaca, New York: Cornell University Press, 1984.

Hubback, David, *No Ordinary Press Baron: A Life of Walter Layton*. London: Weidenfeld & Nicholson, 1985.

Hunt, Richard McMasters, *Thomas Garrigue Masaryk.* Private printing. Pittsburgh: University of Pittsburgh Press, 1955.

Kann, Robert A., *A History of the Habsburg Empire. 1526-1918.* Berkeley: University of California Press, 1974.

Kennan, George, *Soviet-American Relations, 1917-1920.* Vol. I, *Russia Leaves the War.* Vol. II, *Decision to Intervene.* Princeton, N. J.: Princeton University Press, 1956, 1958.

——*From Prague After Munich, 1938-1940.* Diplomatic Papers, Princeton, N.J.: Princeton University Press, 1968.

——*Memoirs,* 2 vols., Boston: Little, Brown, 1967, 1972.

Kerner, Robert J., and Harry N. Howard, *The Balkan Conferences and the Balkan Entente, 1930-1935.* Berkeley: University of California Press, 1936.

Kettle, Michael, *The Road to Intervention in March-November 1918,* 5 volumes, V. II, *Russia and the Allies, 1917-1920.* London: Routledge, 1988.

Komjathy. Anthony and Rebecca Stockwell, *German Minorities & the Third Reich: Ethnic Germans of East Central Europe Between the Wars.* London: Holmes and Meier, 1980.

Korbel, Josef, *Twentieth Century Czechoslovakia, The Meaning of Its History.* New York: Columbia University Press, 1977.

Kovtun, George J., *Masaryk and America: Testimony of a Relationship.* Washington, D.C.: Library of Congress, 1988.

——*The Spirit of Thomas G. Masaryk, 1850-1937: An Anthology,* edited by George Kovtun. New York: Masaryk Publications Trust, 1990.

Krejčí, Jaroslav, *Social Changes & Stratification in Postwar Czechoslovakia.* London: Macmillan, 1972.

Laffan, R. G. D., *The Crisis Over Czechoslovakia.* Oxford University Press, 1951.

Lamont, Thomas, *Across World Frontiers.* New York: Harcourt Brace, 1961. (See pages 86-90.)

Lasch, Christopher, *The American Liberals and the Russian Revolution.* New York and London: Columbia University Press, 1962.

Lettrich, Jozef, *History of Modern Slovakia.* New York, Praeger, 1955.

Lichtheim, George, *Europe in the Twentieth Century.* New York: Praeger, 1972.

Link, Arthur S., *Woodrow Wilson and A Revolutionary World, 1913-1921.* Chapel Hill, N. C.: University of North Carolina Press, 1982.

——*Wilson, the Diplomatist.* Baltimore: Johns Hopkins, 1957

Lippmann, Walter, *U.S. Foreign Policy: Shield of the Republic.* Boston: Little Brown, 1943.

——*The Cold War: A Study in U.S. Foreign Policy.* New York: Harper, 1947.

Lowrie, Donald, *Masaryk: Nation Builder.* New York: YMCA, 1930.

Luckett, Richard, *The White Generals.* New York: Routledge, 1959.

Luža, Radomír, *The Transfer of the Sudeten Germans, A Study in Czech-German Relations, 1933.* New York: New York University Press, 1964

Mamatey, Victor and Luža, Radomír. *A History of the Czechoslovak Republic, 1918-1948.* Princeton, N. J.: Princeton University Press, 1973.

Masaryk, Thomas, *The Spirit of Russia.* 2 volumes, London, Allen & Unwin; New York: Macmillan, 1919; New York: Stokes, 1927; Volume 3, London: Allen & Unwin, 1967.

——*Suicide & the Meaning of Civilization.* Chicago: University of Chicago, 1970. Original in German, Vienna, 1881.

Mastný, Vojtech, *The Czechs Under Nazi Rule, The Failure of National Resistance*. New York & London: Columbia University Press, 1971.

May, Arthur J., *The Habsburg Monarchy, 1867-1914*. Cambridge, Mass.: Harvard University Press, 1951.

Mayer, Arno, *The Politics and Diplomacy of Peacemaking, 1918-1919*. New York: Knopf, 1967.

Miliukov, Paul, *Political Memoirs, 1915-1917*. Ann Arbor, Mich: University of Michigan Press, 1967.

Moravec, František, *Master of Spies, Memoirs*. London: Bodley Head, 1975.

Morton, Frederic, *A Nervous Splendor, Vienna*. London: Weidenfeld and Nicholson, 1979.

Namier, Louis B, *Europe in Decay*. London: Macmillan, 1950.

The National Bank of Czechoslovakia. Prague: Orbis, 1925.

Nicolson, Harold, *Peacemaking, 1919*. Boston: Harcourt Brace, 1939.

Nicolson, Nigel, ed., *Harold Nicolson, Diaries & Letters, 1930-1939*. New York: Athenaeum, 1966.

Olivova, Vera, *The Doomed Democracy, Czechoslovakia in a Disrupted Europe, 1914-1938*. London: Sidgwick & Jackson, 1972.

Papánek, Jan, *Czechoslovakia*, Introduction by Jan Masaryk. New York: International Universities, 1945.

Perman, Dagmar, *The Shaping of the Czechoslovak State, 1914-1920*. Leiden: E. J. Brill, 1962.

Pogue, Forrest C., *George C. Marshall, Statesman., 1945-1959*. New York: Viking, 1987.

Precon, Vilem, Ed., *T.G. Masaryk and our Times*. Published on the occasion of the International Conference: Thomas G. Masaryk 1850-1937, organized by School of Slavonic Studies, University of London, Dec. 11-16th, 1986.

Rašín, Alois, *The Financial Policy of Czechoslovakia*. Oxford: Clarendon Press, 1923.

Rauschning, Hermann, *The Voice of Destruction*. New York: Putnam, 1940.

Reynaud, Paul, *In the Thick of the Fight*. London: Cassell, 1955.

Rich, Norman, *Hitler's War Aims*, 2 vols. New York: W. W. Norton, 1974.

Ripka, Hubert, *Munich: Before and After*. London: Gollancz, 1939.

——*The Repudiation of Munich*. London: Czechoslovak Ministry of Foreign Affairs, 1943.

——*The Future of the Czechoslovak Germans*. London: Czechoslovak-British Friendship Club, 1944.

——*Czechoslovakia Enslaved, The Story of the Communist Coup d'État*. London: Gollancz, 1950.

Schuman, Frederick, *Soviet Politics: At Home and Abroad*. New York: Knopf, 1946.

Schorske, Carl, *Fin-de-Siècle Vienna: Politics and Culture*. New York: Vintage, 1981.

Seton-Watson, Hugh, *Eastern Europe Between the Wars, 1918-1941*. Cambridge: Cambridge University Press, 1944.

Seton-Watson, Hugh and Christopher, *The Making of a New Europe: R. W. Seton-Watson & the Last Years of Austria-Hungary*. London: Methuen, 1981.

Seton-Watson, R.W., *The Southern Slav Question & the Habsburg Monarchy*. London: Constable, 1911.

——*The New Slovakia*. Prague: Borovy, 1924.

——*Munich and the Dictators*. London: Methuen, 1939.

——*History of the Czechs and Slovaks*. London: Hutchinson, 1943.

Sforza, Count Carlo, *The Totalitarian War and After*. Chicago: University of Chicago Press, 1941.

Sherwood, Robert E., *Roosevelt and Hopkins*. New York: Harpers, 1948.

Skilling, Gordon, *Czechoslovakia's Interrupted Revolution*. Princeton, N. J.: Princeton University Press, 1976.

Smith, Howard K., *The State of Europe*. New York: Knopf, 1949.

Šmutný, Jaromír, *Germans in Czechoslovakia: Their Transfer from the Republic*. London: 1956.

Sterling, Claire, *The Masaryk Case*. New York: Harper & Row, 1968.

Strang, Lord William, *Home and Abroad*. London: A. Deutsch, 1958.

Street, C.J.C., *President Masaryk*. London: Geoffrey Bles, 1930.

Szulc, Tad, *Czechoslovakia Since World War II*. New York: Viking, 1971.

Táborský, Edward, *The Czechoslovak Cause; An Account of the problems of International Law in Relation to Czechoslovakia*. London: H. V. & G. Witherby, 1944.

——*Czechoslovak Democracy at Work*. London: Allen & Unwin, 1945.

——*President Beneš Between East and West, 1938-1948*. Chapel Hill, N.C.: University of North Carolina Press, 1982.

Taylor, A. J. P., *The Origins of the Second World War*. London: Hamish Hamilton, 1961.

Taylor, Telford, *Munich: The Price of Peace*. New York: Doubleday, 1979.

Teleki, Count Paul, *The Evolution of Hungary and Its Place in European History*. New York: Macmillan 1923.

Temperly, H. W. V., Ed., *A History of the Peace Conference of Paris*. Institute of International Affairs, Volume 4, London: Hodder & Frowdie & Stoughton, 1921

Textor, Lucy E., *Land Reform in Czechoslovakia*. London: Allen & Unwin, 1923.

Thompson, S. Harrison, *Czechoslovakia in European History*. Princeton, N.J.: Princeton University Press, 1953.

Turner, Henry Ashby, *German Big Business and The Rise of Hitler*. New York: Oxford University Press, 1985.

Ullman, Richard H., *Anglo-American Relations, 1917-1921*. Vol. I: *Intervention and the War;* Vol. II: *Britain and the Russian Civil War, Nov. 1918-Feb. 1920;* Vol. III: *The Anglo-Soviet Accord*. Princeton, N.J.: Princeton University Press, 1961, 1968, 1972.

Vondráček, Felix John, *The Foreign Policy of Czechoslovakia, 1918-1938*. New York: Columbia University Press, 1937.

Wandycz, Piotr, *Czechoslovak-Polish Coinfederation & the Great Powers, 1940-1943*. Bloomington: University of Indiana, 1956.

Wellek, René, *The Meaning of Czech History: Tomáš G. Masaryk*. Chapel Hill, N.C.: University of North Carolina Press, 1974.

Wheeler-Bennett, John W., *Munich: Prologue to Tragedy*. New York: Duell, Sloan & Pearce, 1948.

White, John Albert, *The Siberian Intervention*. Princeton, N.J.: Princeton University Press, 1950.

Zinner, Paul E., *Common Strategy & Tactics in Czechoslovakia, 1919-1948*. New York: Praeger, 1963.

Articles

Armstrong, Hamilton Fish, "Armistice at Munich." *Foreign Affairs*, XVII, January 1939, pp. 197-290.

Beneš, Eduard, "The New Order in Europe." *The Nineteenth Century and After*, XXX, September 1941, pp. 150-155.

——"The Organization of Postwar Europe." *Foreign Affairs*, XX, January 1942, pp. 226-242.

——"Czechoslovakia Plans for Peace." *Foreign Affairs*, XXIII, October, 1944, pp. 26-37.

——"Postwar Czechoslovakia." *Foreign Affairs*, XXIV, April 1946, pp. 397-410.

Bruce Lockhart, R.H., "The Second Exile of Eduard Beneš." *The Slavonic and East European Review*, XXVII, November 1949, pp 39-59.

Procházka, Theodore, "The Delimitation of Czechoslovak Frontiers After Munich." *Journal of Central European Affairs*, XXI, July 1961, pp. 200-218

Ripka, Hubert, "Principles of Czechoslovak Policy, Past & Future." *Central European Observer*, XIX, January 23, 1942

Seton-Watson, Hugh, "R.W. Seton-Watson's Einstellung zur Habsburger Monarchie, 1906-1914." *Österreich in Geschichte und Literatur mit Geograhie*, 1973, pp. 361-381.

Seton-Watson, R.W., "The German Minority in Czechoslovakia." *Foreign Affairs*, XVII, July 1938, pp. 651-666.

Skilling, Gordon H., "The Rediscovery of Masaryk." *Crosscurrents, A Yearbook of Central European Culture*, 1983, pp. 87-112.

Táborský, Edward, "Beneš and the Soviets." *Foreign Affairs*, XXVII, January 1949, pp. 302-314.

——"Beneš and Stalin, Moscow, 1943 and 1945." *Journal of Central European Affairs*, XIII, July 1953, pp. 154-181.

——"The Triumph and Disaster of Eduard Beneš." *Foreign Affairs*, XXXVI, July 1958, pp. 669-684.

Weinberg, Gerhard, "The May Crises, 1938." *Journal of Modern History*, XXIX, September 1957, pp. 213-225.

——"Munich After 50 Years." *Foreign Affairs*, LXVII, Fall 1988, pp. 165-178.

——"Secret Hitler-Beneš Negotiations in 1936-37." *Journal of Central European Affairs*, XIX, Jan. 1968.

Wiskman, Elizabeth, "Czechs and Germans After Munich." *Foreign Affairs*, XVII, January 1939, pp. 291-304.

Pamphlets

Eisler, Pavel, *Munich—A Retrospect.* Prague: Orbis.

Masaryk, Jan, *Statement on the Foreign Policy of Czechoslovakia: Speech Before the Provisional Assembly on March 6, 1944.* Prague: 1946.

——*Statement on the Foreign Policy of Czechoslovakia to Constituent Assembly, March 20, 1947.* Prague: 1947.

Odložilík, Otakar, *Masaryk's Idea of Democracy.* New York: Masaryk Institute, 1952, reprinted from the *University of Toronto Quarterly*, October 1951.

Price, N. Philips, *The Truth About Allied Intervention in Russia.* Moscow, 1918.

——*Russia in Turmoil, 1919.* Foreign Office 371/v. 3321, pp. 219-24.

Index

Abbéville Accord, 20, 24, 29, 32, 35
Abwehr (German Intelligence Agency), 94
Acheson, Dean, 290, 293, 306
Agram Treason Trial, 5
Agrarian Party, 9, 58, 60, 74, 82-83, 90, 110, 114, 219, 235
Alexander I, King of Yugoslavia, 88
Alexandrovsky 166
Alexeev, M., 261
Allen, D., 246
American Friends of Czechoslovakia, 189, 201
American Red Cross, 15, 45, 259
American Relief for Czechoslovakia, 259
Amur River, 41-42
Angara River, 40
Anschluss (Austrian) 64, 105-7, 111, 114, 118-26, 133
Antonescu, Ion, 151
Antonov, Alexei, 23 242
Apponyi, Count Albert 73
Archangel, 12, 15, 17-23, 27, 32, 35
Armstrong, Hamilton Fish, 178
Ashton Gwatkin, Sir Frank, 102, 131-34, 139, 149, 165, 167, 171
Asquith, Herbert, 8
Astor, Viscount Waldorf, 126, 130
Atlee, Clement, 248
Austro-Hungarian Empire, 1-6, 50-54, 57-58, 184

Bachmach, 13, 30
Baerlein, Henry, 49
Baikal, Lake, 41, 57
Baker, Newton D., 16, 25, 41-42, 62
Balfour, Sir Arthur James, 17, 22, 25, 27, 29, 56, 61-62
Banská Bystrica, 219, 222-23, 225
Barthou, Louis, 80-81, 88
Baruch, Bernard M., 61
Báta, Tomáš, 262
Beam, Jacob, 302-3, 307-8, 318
Beck, Jósef, 95, 115, 129, 152, 181
Beckendorff, Count, 2
Beneš, Bohuš, 174
Beneš, Eduard, 1-9, 17-18, 21-24, 31, 44, 49, 55-58, Foreign Minister: 60, 63, 65-68, 70, 76, 79-83; President: 85-89, 92-94, 104-24, 128, 132, 134-39, 144-46, 149, 151, 154-57, 164-66, 168, 171-85, 188, 191-214, 218-232, 235-37, 244-45, 248-61, 266-67, 274-80, 283, 292, 300-5, 312-17, 328-31
Beneš, Hana, 7, 9, 173, 256, 276, 301, 325, 330-32
Beran, Rudolf, 83, 90, 118, 172, 179, 219
Bergson, Henry, 62
Beria, Lavrenti, 312
Berle, Adolf A., 195, 203-4
Berlin, 13, 86, 96-99, 105, 115, 117, 120-21, 134, 138-39, 144-47, 153, 165, 175, 180, 191, 203

Bevin, Ernest, 246, 256, 271-72, 276, 287-89, 306, 313, 318
Biddle, Anthony Joseph Drexel, 194-97
Bílý, Josef, 190
Blomberg, Gen. Werner von, 103
Blum, Léon, 87, 96, 98, 106, 110-111, 144
Boček, Gen. Bohumil, 245
Bogomolov, Alexander, 199
Boncour. See Paul-Boncour
Bonnet, Georges, 111-116, 118, 121, 138-39, 141, 144-45, 151, 153, 155, 161, 181, 186
Boyd Orr, Sir John, 283-84
Brandeis, Louis D., 53, 59
Bratislava, 66, 174, 221, 225, 254, 266, 273, 283. See also Posony
Brest-Litovsk Treaty, 14, 17, 26, 181
Briand, Aristide, 9, 88
Bridges, Gen. George Tom M., 52
British Institute, Bratislava, 270, 273
Bruce Lockhart, Sir Robert, 12, 15-22, 29, 32-39, 46-48, 243, 311, 326-27, 332
Budapest, 3, 59, 64-68, 81
Bull, Gen., 252
Bullitt, William C., 178, 196
Butler, Nicholas Murray, 53, 174
Byrnes, James Francis, 247-48, 250-55, 264-73, 285-87

Cadogan, Sir Alexander George Montagu, 116, 128, 239
Caffrey, Francis, 313, 318-19
Cambon, Paul, 24, 25
Canaris, Admiral Wilhelm Franz, 105, 133
Carol, King of Romania, 110
Carl (Charles) Archduke of Habsburg, then King and Emperor, 9, 58-59, 68
Čas, 3-4, 8
Case Otto, 103
Case White, 177
Čatloš, Gen. Ferdinand, 219
Ceček, Stanislav, 39, 41
Cecil, Lord Robert, 8, 21-25, 27, 29
Chamberlain, Neville, 96, 98, 105-6, 110, 114, 116, 126-27, 131, 137, 144,

149-55, 158-59, 161-65, 168, 170-71, 175,176, 181
Charles IV, 169
Chautemps, Camille, 86
Chelyabinsk, 33-37
Chicherin, Georgyi, 27, 55, 80
Chilston, Viscount Aretas Akers-Douglas, 111, 122, 145, 150, 169, 226
Chita, 41
Choc, Dr. M., 216
Churchill, Winston, 27-28, 54, 86, 101, 103, 106, 109, 111, 121-22, 127, 136-37, 145, 149, 168, 171, 175-76; Prime Minister: 183, 185-86, 199, 207, 227, 231, 239-40, 245, 248, 269, 274-75, 290
Chvalkovský, František, 173, 183
CIA, 263, 313
Ciano, Count Galeazzo, 171
Clay, Gen. Lucius, 295
Clemenceau, Georges, 20, 22, 24, 26, 61, 156
Clementis, Vladimír, 236, 247, 254-55, 264, 284-86, 292, 314
Cliveden Set, 126
Cominform, 309-10
Comintern, 77, 80, 200
Communist Party (Czechoslovakia), 77, 80-83, 180, 172, 188, 209-11, 235, 300
Congress of Oppressed Nationalities, 54
Comnène, Nicholas, 152
Corbin, Charles, 104, 141, 144, 161
Corwin, Norman, 201
Cot, Pierre, 107
Court of International Justice, 67
Crane, Charles R., 16, 17, 51-53
Crane, Frances Anita, 321-22
Crane, Richard T., 17, 51
Curzon, Lord George Nathaniel (Earl of Keddleston), 17, 28, 29
Curzon Line, 181
Čvetisa, 3
Czech Word, 1
Czechoslovak Democratic Party, 55
Czechoslovak-French Treaty of Friendship (Jan. 25, 1924), 182
Czechoslovak Legions. See Legions

Czechoslovak National Committee. 7, 9, 34, 57, 182

Czechoslovak National Council, 7, 9-13, 18, 22-26, 30, 33-34, 38-39, 42-45, 55-58, 60, 197, 204

Czechoslovak National Council of America, 194

Czechoslovak National Union, 55

Czechoslovak Provisional Government, 184

Czechoslovak Refugee Institute (Fund), 188

Czechoslovak Refugee Trust, 188

Czechoslovak-Soviet Treaty of Alliance, 208, 231

Czechoslovak State Council, 212

Czernin, Count Ferdinand, 53, 192

Czernin Palace, 320, 325

Daily Review (London), 307

Daladier, Edouard, 111-12, 116, 138, 140-41, 144-45, 161-65, 168, 171, 174, 181

Daniels, Josephus, 61

Darlan, Admiral Jean, 162

Davenport, Marcia, 323-26, 329, 332

Davila, Charles A., 194

Davis, Elmer, 201

Davis, Jerome, 15

Delbos, Yvon, 98, 104, 106-7, 109

Deniken, Gen. Anton Ivanovich, 22, 39

Denis, Ernest, 2, 7, 8

Derby, Lord Edward Geoffroy, 24, 29, 35, 47

Dewey, Gov. Thomas E., 2, 4, 290

Dieterichs, Gen. Mikhail Konstantinovich, 13, 40-41

Dircksen, Herbert von, 154

Dixon, British Embassy, Prague, 319

Dmowski, Roman, 67

Dollfuss, Engelbert, 104

Douglas, Lewis W., 313

Doumenc, Gen. Joseph, 181

Drtina, Petr, 263-64, 299, 311

Druzinas, 11

Drysdale, Major Walter, 3, 8, 45. 48

Dukhonin, Gen. Alexieff, 12-13

Dulles, John Foster, 290

Dürich, Joseph, 9

Duriš, Julius, 260, 264

Duroselle, Jean-Baptiste, 117, 121-23, 149-50, 169-71

Economist, 102, 127

Eden, Sir Anthony, 96, 99-102, 105-6, 184, 196-97, 206, 208, 210-11, 213, 225-27, 237, 246

Eger, Col., 147, 168

Eisenhower, Dwight D., 239-40, 252-253

Eisenmann, Louis, 8

Eisler, Pavel, 311

Eliáš, Gen. Alois, 179, 190-91, 193

Eliot, Charles W., 53

Emerson, Colonel, 33, 36-37, 42-44

Engliš, Karel, 125

Entente, The Little, 3, 66-68, 70-71, 83, 86-88, 110, 122, 151

Espérey, General d', 64

Fahrquahr, 151, 169

Fajfr, Gen. Jaroslav, 143

Federer, I., 128, 130

Feierabend, Ladislav, 217

Feiling, Kenneth, 185

Ferdinand, Archduke, 1

Fierlinger, Zdeněk, 182, 206, 208, 225, 229, 231-32, Premier: 236, 243-45, 264, 280, 298

Fisher, 3

Flandin, Pierre-Étienne, 109

Fleming, D. F., 306

Foch, Gen. (Marshal) Ferdinand, 14, 61, 67

Fontaine, André, vol. I, 101, 185

Fourteen Points, 54

Francis, David R., 14, 26, 44

Franco, Francisco, 87, 107

François Poncet, André, 117, 138

Frank, Karl Hermann, 89, 132-33, 135, 140, 147-148, 153, 179, 192, 219, 277

Franz Josef, Emperor, 9

Freistadt, 129

Frejka, Dr. Ludwik, 284, 304

Fritsch, Gen. Werner von, 103

Gabčik, Josef, 192

Gajda, Capt. Rudolf, 36-42, 45, 78-79, 179, 235

Gamelin, Gen. Maurice Gustave, 106,

Gamelin, Gen. Maurice (continued) 107, 142-44, 160, 162
Gaulle, Gen. Charles de, 214-15, 225
Gehlen, Gen. Reinhard, 241, 246, 263
Geneva, 5, 7, 8, 60, 65, 80-81, 95, 145, 152, 169, 176, 179, 311, 322
Geysman, M., 31, 33, 46-47
Girsa, Vladimír, 39, 48
Godesberg Memo (Plan), 158-62, 166, 170
Goebbels, Josef, 118, 177,
Goldman, Josef, 284
Golián, Gen. Ján, 219, 222
Gömbös, Julius, 67, 76
Göring, Hermann, 81, 88, 107, 112, 120, 126-27, 138, 144, 146
Gottwald, Klement, 82, 207, 209, 212, 250, 264, 270, 277-78, 280, 283, 292, 296, 301-5, 311-16, 320, 328-29, 332
Graves, Gen. William S., 28, 36, 42-44, 47-49, 56-57, 62
Greece, 290-91
Greene, Sir Cecil, 47
Grew, Joseph, 250, 255
Guardian, Manchester, 16

Habsburg Monarchy, 9-10, 54, 68
Hácha, Emil, 172, 175-76, 179, 183, 189, 211, 219
Hájek, Jiří, 309
Halder, Gen. Franz von, 106, 163
Halifax, Lord Edward, 96, 98-99, 111, 115-16, 119-23, 126, 130, 132, 137, 139, 141, 146, 148, 150, 161, 166, 170, 180, 182-83, 185
Hankey, Maurice, 287, 307, 318
Harbin, 41
Harper, Samuel, N., 55
Harriman, William Averell, 209, 212, 216, 228-30, 233-34
Harris, Ernest L., 33, 40, 43
Heimwehr (German Home Guard), 107
Henderson, Loy, 178
Henderson, Sir Nevile, 99, 102, 117, 121, 123, 126-128, 130, 132, 140, 144, 146, 148, 150, 153
Henlein, Konrad, 82, 88-94, 100, 104,

113-19, 133-36, 139-40, 146, 148, 168, 171
Herald Tribune, New York, 306
Heydrich, Reinhard, 190-93, 267
Hicks, Capt. (British), 45, 48-49
Hitler, Adolf (or Führer) 76, 79, 81-82, 86, 89, 96, 98-99, 103-7, 110-11, 114-20, 124, 127-28, 131-32, 135-45, 148, 152-55,, 159-67, 170-71, 175-77, 181, 187, 192, 207, 222, 274
Hlasists, 73, 75
Hlinka, Father Andrej, 73, 76, 79, 100, 114, 118, 124, 172, 219
Hoare, Sir Samuel, 161
Hochman, Jiri, 122, 150, 169, 171
Hodža, Milan, 66, 83, 90-92, 96, 99, 114, 117-20, 124, 128, 131-32, 139, 147, 157, 174, 182, 195
Höfle, Hermann, 282
Hohenlohe, Prince Max von, 132-33, 135
Hopkins, Harry, 189
Hore-Belisha, Leslie, 120, 123
Horthy, Admiral Miklos, 67, 151
Houdek, Vladimír, 330
House, Col. Edward M., 52-53, 62
Houston, David Franklin, 53
Hradčany (Hrad), 83, 86, 92, 172, 305, 316, 325
Hromádko, Ing. Vilém, 180
Hull, Cordell, 195, 200-4, 212
Hurban, Olga, 325
Hurban, Vladimír, 26, 28, 30-31, 40, 46, 176, 183, 193, 196-97, 203, 325
Hus, Jan, 7, 161, 322
Husák, Gustav, 223
Hušek, Josef, 194
Hussite Reformation, 7, 46, 73, 301
Hutchins, Robert, 173

Ingr, Gen. Sergěj, 179, 182, 219
Ingram, E. B. M., 101
Irkutsk, 31, 33-34, 38-42 45-46, 49
Ismay, Sir Hastings, 239, 246
Izvestia, 221, 233

Jacomet, Gen. Robert, 106
Jaksch, Wenzel, 154

Janin, Gen. Maurice, 13, 45
Janoušek, Karel, 241, 245, 255
Jevtić, Bogoljub, 88
Jones, Elwyn, 273
Jordan, J. M., 48
Jusserand, Jean Jules, 51

Karl (German secret agent), 93-94
Karl, Prince. *See* Carl, Prince
Károlyi, Count Mihály, 64-65
Keans, Richard, 121
Keating, Maj. Gen. Frank, 296, 306
Keitel, Gen. Wilhelm von, 103, 167-68, 173, 177
Kennan, George, 27-28, 56, 183-84, 196, 229, 233
Kennard, 169
Kennedy, Joseph P., 178
Kerensky, Alexander, 12
Kerr, Sir Archibald Clark, 233-34
Khrushchev, Nikita, 281, 288
Kiakhovitch, 38
Kiev, 12-13, 32, 45
King, MacKenzie, 209
Klieforth, A. L., 246-47, 249-50, 255
Klinger, Dr. Oscar, 331
Klofáč, Václav, J., 1, 6, 9, 58, 191
Knight, Admiral, 25
Knox, Gen. Alfred W. F., 38
Knox, Philander, C., 200
Kolchak, Admiral Alexander, 22, 38, 45
Kole, Dr. Erwin, 274
Kollner, Deputy, 140
Konev, Gen. Ivan S., 239, 241-42, 277
Kopecký, Václav, 253, 264
Kornilov, Gen. Lavr G, 12
Košice, (Kassa), 66-67, 225, 230-32. 237, 241
Košice Program, 235, 237, 257
Kovanda, 5
Kramář, Karel, 1-3, 6, 9, 55, 57, 59-60, 64-65
Krejčí, Gen. Ludwik, 87, 93, 167, 172
Krofta, Kamil, 90, 110, 127, 132, 222
Kubiš, Jan, 192
Kuh, Frederick, 84
Kun, Béla, 67

Kundt, Deputy Ernst, 135-36, 139-40, 149
Kunta, Adolf, 3
Kursk, 13
Kusek, 7

Lacroix, Léopold Victor de, 138, 144, 155-57
LaGuardia, Mayor Fiorello H., 174, 201
Lamont, Thomas, 16, 28, 56
Langley, W., 29
Lansing, Robert, 17, 51, 55-59, 62
Lany, 329
Laušman, Bohumil, 264-65, 303, 315
Lavergne, General 19, 34
Lavička, 5
Law, Bonar, 22, 29
Layton, Margaret, 188
Layton, Sir Walter T., 127, 188
Lazacky, 192
League of Nations, 8, 65, 81-82, 85-86, 95, 119, 127, 145, 166, 176
Lebedov, Victor Z., 221
Léger, Alexis, 106, 116, 165, 171
Legions (Czechoslovak), 2, 11-15, 18-19, 22-23, 25-26, 30, 33, 35, 40, 45-46, 50, 52, 55, 57-58, 60-61, 78-79, 157, 316
Leith-Ross, Sir F., 96, 167
Lenin, Vladimir I., 14-17, 21-22, 78
Lidiče, 192, 201
Lie, Trygve, 320
Lindley, Francis Oswald, 13, 26, 34, 47
Link, Arthur, S., 27-28
Linnell, Irving, 188, 190, 202
Lippmann, Walter, 212
Litvinov, Maxim M., 80, 111, 119, 137, 145, 151-52, 177, 179
Lloyd George, David, 16, 54, 127
Lobcovicz, Princess Gillian, 326
Lobcovicz, Prince Max, 326
Locarno Conference (Oct. 16, 1925), 69, 80, 89
Lockhart, Robert Bruce. *See* Bruce Lockhart, Robert
Lodgmann, Rudolf, 63-64
Loevenstein, Karel, 75

London, 2-3, 7-10, 13, 16, 54, 61, 69, 95, 98, 117-18, 156, 159-61, 167-68, 174, 178, 182-87, 191, 196, 205, 209-13, 221-24, 231, 235, 238, 271, 287, 311, 322-23, 326-27, 329, 332
Lovett, Robert, 307, 310
Lublin Committee, 206, 224-26
Luža, Radomír, 84, 185, 256

Macchio, Baron, 5
Machar, Josef S., 3, 5
MacDonald, Callum, 203
Machnik, František 91
Mack, Judge Julian, 53
MacDowell, Lt. Col. Donald, 156
MacKenzie, 200
Maclay, Sir Joseph, 25
Maffia, 3-6, 50, 55
Maisky, Ivan, 136-37, 185
Majer, Václav, 264, 304
Malinovsky, Marshal Rodion, 242, 254
Malkin, William, 171
Mamatey, Victor S., 84
Mandel, Georges, 156
Mannstein, Fritz von, 167
Mara, 302, 307
March, Gen. Peyton C., 41, 53
Margerie, Roland de, 116
Marshall, George C. 290, 297, 307-8, 313, 317-19, 326
Marshall Plan, 296-97, 300-301, 310
Martin, Capt. Hugh S., 52
Masařik, Hubert, 164-65, 170-71
Masaryk, Alice G., 7, 9, 173, 311, 322. 325, 329, 332
Masaryk, Ana, 325, 329, 332
Masaryk, Charlotte G., 7, 321-22, 332
Masaryk, Herberta, 325, 329, 332
Masaryk, Jan G., 7, 98, 121, 145, 150, 159, 161, 164, 167, 170, 173-79, 182-85, 196-199, 202, 206, 213-14, 218, 221-28, 231, 235-388, 243, 251-53, 262-68, 272-73, 277-83, 286, 289, 291-93, 296-97, 300-303, 307-10, 314-32
Masaryk, Olga, 322
Masaryk, Tomáš G., 1-13, 17-19, 23-
24, 30, 39, 44-46, 50-61; President: 62-65, 69-70, 74-83, Resignation: 161, 176, 182, 323, 332
Mastný, Vojtech, 121, 165, 171, 190
Maxa, Dr. Procop, 13, 33
May, Deputy, 140
McCormack, Anne O'Hare, 212
McDonald, A. M., 149
McLarnen, Frances, 323
Merekalov, Alexei, 179
Mikolajczyk, Stanislaw, 208
Mikoyan, Anastas Ivanovich, 264
Millerand,, Alexandre, 69
Milner, Lord Alfred, 20, 22, 26
Molotov, Vyacheslav M., 177, 180-81, 196-97, 208, 226, 281, 296
Moravec, František, 86-87, 93, 98, 101, 173, 179
Morgenthau, Henry, 200
Morris, Newbold, 201
Moscow, 13, 17, 21, 25, 31, 35-36, 47, 82, 119, 180-82, 189, 198-99, 205-13, 225-31, 234, 243, 264-65, 276, 280, 296, 298
Munich, 157, 163-72, 175, 183, 187, 196-97, 200, 211, 245, 297, 311
Mucha, Jiří, 326
Muravieff, Gen. Mikhail, 12, 19, 30
Murmansk, 13-22, 32, 35, 39, 47, 56
Murphy, Robert, 251-52, 256, 292
Murray, Gilbert, 8
Mussolini, Benito, 79, 87, 104-5, 118, 153, 163, 166-67, 171-72

Nation Tcheque, 8
National Constituent Assembly, 280
National Democratic Party, 75, 79
National Social Democratic Party, 55, 60, 311, 315
National Socialist, 1-2, 55, 60, 293, 312-13
Nazi Party, 80-82, 89, 136, 140
Nečas, Jaromír, 144
Nejedlý, Zdeněk, 274
Neurath, Konstantin von, 103, 105, 179, 189-90
New Europe, 8
News Chronicle, 127, 188, 283

Newton, Basil C., 91, 93-94, 99-101,
    105-9, 113-14, 121-23, 130-32, 143,
    146-50, 155, 169-171
Nichols, Philip, 210-13, 224-28, 233-38,
    244-46, 254-64, 270-283, 286-89,
    294, 296-97, 300-7, 318
Nicolajevsk, 39-40
Nicolsk, 41
Noble, Sir A., 102, 169
Nosek, Václav, 236, 264, 311, 315

Office of Strategic Services (OSS),
    194, 198, 203, 222, 263
Olivova, Vera, 62, 121, 171
Omsk, 19-20, 28, 32, 35-36, 38, 46, 121
Operation Grün, 158
Osuský, Štefan, 110-12, 121, 155, 182,
    195-96
Otto, Archduke, 184, 194

Paderewski, Ignace, 59
Papánek, Betka, 321, 324
Papánek, Jan, 198, 320-21, 324
Paris, 3, 7-10, 12, 17, 21, 50, 57, 61, 69,
    73, 98, 118, 120, 154, 168, 178, 182,
    196, 297-98, 313
Patterson, Robert, 251-52, 256
Patton, Gen. George S., 239, 241
Paul, Prince of Yugoslavia, 88, 110
Paul-Boncour, Joseph, 106-7, 110
Pellé, Gen. Maurice 65, 67
Penza, 13, 19, 34, 35
Pergler, Charles, 50, 53
Peroutka, Ferdinand, 262-63
Pétain, Philippe, 106
Peter II, King of Yugoslavia, 88
Petka, 74
Petrograd, 11, 15, 21
Pflaum, Irving, 203
Phipps, Sir Eric, 97, 104, 109, 122, 140,
    144, 153-54, 160, 169-70
Pichon, Stephen Jean Marie, 23-24,
    51, 65
Pika, Gen. Heliodor, 255
Pilsen, 72, 75, 239, 254
Pilsudski, Jozef, 82
Pittsburgh Agreement (Convention),
    55, 65, 75, 100, 124

Poincaré, Raymond, 69, 88
Polk, Frank, 56, 62
Pollack, Major Richard, 243
Poole, DeWitt, C., 16, 43, 195, 203,
    214
Poole, Gen. Frederick C., 13, 17, 20-
    21, 32
Posony, (Pressburg then Bratislava),
    66
Potsdam Conference, 237, 248, 263,
    317
Prague, 1-8, 57, 59, 61, 63, 65, 67, 74,
    76-77, 80, 82, 91-92, 99, 104, 113,
    116-25, 128-29, 138-47, 155-56, 164,
    171, 173, 175, 178-79, 182-83, 191-
    92, 239-242, 245, 248, 263-66, 270,
    274, 278-82, 303, 305, 309, 311, 317,
    320-25, 329
Prager Tagblatt, 108, 122
Pratt, Major Sutton, 140, 143, 145, 147
Pravda, 180, 211
Pravo Lidu, 94
Preiss, Jaroslav, 75, 172
Presov, 225
Price, G. Ward, 112, 120, 122, 126-27
Price, M. Philips, 28
Prihoda, 330
Progressive (Realist) Party, 3

Rašín, Alois, 2, 6, 9, 78
Rauschning, Herman, 202
Reading, Lord Rufus Daniel Isaacs,
    17-18, 48, 52, 56, 62, 290
Red Army (and Guards), 12, 31, 33,
    37, 40-43, 76, 87, 201, 219-24, 229,
    235-36, 240, 255, 258, 270
Reichsrat, 2, 6, 9, 57, 64
Reichsstag, 105
Renondeau, Gen. Gaston, 117, 138
Revillod, Dr. Henri, 332
Rhineland Occupation, 86
Ribbentrop, Joachim von, 103, 117,
    129, 133, 154, 171, 173, 175, 181
Richter, Wolfgang, 94
Riddleburger, 307
Ripka, Hubert, 171, 182, 197, 199, 221,
    235-38, 264, 276, 308
Robb, Air Marshal, SHAEF, 241

Roberts, Frank, 116, 216
Robins, Col. Raymond, 15, 44
Rochat, Charles, 116
Rome, 4, 5, 54, 107, 118, 172
Roosevelt,, Franklin D., 61, 105-6, 137, 163, 173, 178, 189, 196-207, 213, 221, 227, 240, 248
Rose, Madame, 9
Ross, Sir F. *See* Leith-Ross, Sir F.
Rothschild, Baron Louis, 128
Rotterdam, 2
Rude Pravo, 77
Rumbold, Sir Horace George Montagu, 307
Runciman, Lord Walter, 121, 131-40, 147-49, 154-56, 159, 169, 170
Runciman Mission, 131-34, 138, 140, 147, 149-50
Russian Military Intelligence (OBZ), 255
Rutha, Heinz, 90, 94
Ruthenia, 66, 229, 244

Sabath, Adolph S., 53
Sadoul, Capt. Jacques, 15
Samara, 36, 39
Sarajevo, 1
Sargent, Sir Orme, 114, 116, 120, 123, 150, 170, 239, 246, 246, 274, 279, 287, 311, 318
Sasek, 3
Schacht, Hjalmar, 81, 88, 96, 98
Schieffelin, William J., 201
Schoenfeld, Rudolf, 215, 232-34
Schuschnigg, Kurt von, 104
Schuckburgh, 271, 288
Sebekowsky, Dr. Wilhelm, 139
Semonoff, Grigorii, 22, 25, 27, 31, 38, 48, 57
Seton-Watson, Robert William, 2, 3, 8, 9, 273
Seyss-Inquart, Arthur, 104, 113
Sezimovo Usti, 301, 317, 329-31
Shapiro, Ira, 324
Sherwood, Robert, 215
Siberia, 14, 17-19, 22-49, 56-62
Simon, Sir John, 161
Široký, Viliam, 236
Škoda, 72, 75, 88, 119, 157, 177, 179-80, 209

Slánský, Rudolf, 207, 209, 302, 329
Slávik, Juraj, 182, 294-95, 308
Slovak Communist Party, 218
Slovak Council of Organizations & Newspapers, 196
Slovak Democratic Party, 218, 278, 303-5, 313
Slovak League, 55, 194, 196
Slovak National Alliance, 194
Slovak National Council, 218-19, 222-24, 235, 237
Slovak National Party, 172
Slovak People's Party (Populist), 82, 100, 124, 172, 313
Slovak Uprising, 221-24
Šmeral, Bohumír, 3, 55, 76-78
Šmidke, Karol, 223
Smith, Gen. Walter Bedell, 262-63, 288
Smrkovský, Josef, 239, 240
Smutný, Jaromír, 198, 202, 208, 330-31
Smuts, Gen. Jan Christian, 20
Social Democratic Party (SdP), 55, 79-80, 89, 91, 100, 114, 117, 125, 133, 135, 140, 154, 278-79, 284, 302, 311, 315
Sokol, Dr., 100
Sokols, 64-65, 315-16, 331
Sosnowski, Kasimierz, 208
Soukup, František, 55, 58, 191
Soukup, Loumír, 330, 332
Špaček, Jiří, 39, 45, 48, 330
Šrámek, Monsignor Jan, 182, 236
Šrobár, Vavro, 55, 65, 67, 73, 236
Stachiewicz, Gen. Waclaw, 125
Stalin, Josef V., 83, 86, 177, 181, 189, 200, 205-8, 226, 230-231, 248, 253, 274-75, 280-81, 296, 312-14, 329
Stamboliski, Alexander, 68
Standly (U.S. Embassy, Moscow), 215
Steed, H. Wickham, 2, 9, 54, 115, 119-20, 123
Štefánik, Milan Rastislav, 8, 9, 11, 17, 23-24, 45, 50, 54, 58; War Minister: 60, 73
Steinhardt, Laurence, 249-51, 253-56, 259-60, 264-72, 275-76, 278, 282, 286, 292-295, 298-312, 317-19, 332
Sterling, Claire, 332

Stettinius, Edward, 201, 221, 245
Stimson, Henry, 200
Stoyadinović, Milan, 88,, 110, 151
Strang, Sir William, 116, 169, 180, 185
Stránský, Jaroslav, 236, 246, 264, 274
Stronge, Col. H. C. T., 143, 146, 150, 156
Students' British Assn., 249
Sub-Carpathian Rus (Ruthenia), 66, 229, 244
Sudeten Deutsche Heimatsfront or
Sudetendeutsche Partei (SdP), 82, 91, 100, 100, 114, 133, 135
Sudeten Nazis, 79, 82
Supilo, M., 5, 54
Supreme Headquarters Allied
   Expeditionary Force (SHAEF), 238, 241-42, 250
Svatkovsky, Vsevolod, 5
Švehla, Antonín, 1, 58, 74
Svoboda, Gen. Ludwík, 235-36, 241, 254, 264, 277, 315-16
Syrový, Gen. Jan, 157, 164, 166, 172, 181

Táborský, Edward, 198, 202
Taft, Sen. Robert, 290
Tardieu, André, 81, 88
Taylor, A. J. P., 121, 273
Taylor, John, 245
Tedder, Air Chief Marshall Arthur W., 244
Teheran Conference, 317
Teschen, 67, 71, 95, 102, 125, 166, 174, 207, 225-26, 232, 242, 281
Thomas, Albert, 12, 15
Thomas (U.S. Consul General), 37
Thompson, William Boyce, 15-16
Thomson, Hans, 176
Times (London), 29, 99, 109, 112-15, 122-23, 171, 316, 323, 330
Times, New York, 51, 212, 267, 275, 287, 306, 323, 330
Tiso, Father, 172, 174, 218-219, 224, 263
Titulescu, Nicholas, 115
Trade Union Congress, 314, 316
Trans-Siberian Railway, 19, 34, 40, 42-44, 57
Trotsky, Léon, 15-18, 21, 25, 27-30,
33-35, 44
Troutbeck, 102, 105, 122, 132
Truman Doctrine, 281, 291, 296
Truman, Harry, 248, 253-54, 290, 310, 316, 331
Trumbič, Ante, 5, 54
Tucker, Robert, 136, 149
Tuka, Vojtech, 76
Tukhacevsky, Gen. Mikhail, 86-87
Tumulty, Joseph Patrick, 53
Turčiansky Svätý Martin, 55, 222, 224
Turkey, 281
Turner, Henry Ashby, 85, 101
Tusar, Vlastimil, 75, 77

Ukraine, 12, 13, 21, 87, 201, 229, 244
Ullman, Richard H., 27-28
Unitarian Service Committee, 259, 276
United Nations, 232, 301-2, 313, 320, 330
United Nations Food and Agriculture
   Committee (later FAO), 283
United Nations Relief &
   Rehabilitation Administration
   (UNRRA), 258--59, 261, 276, 284, 286, 294, 296, 301
Unterberger, Betty Miller, 28
Ushakov, Gen., 42
Ussuri River, 41-42
Ustachi, 88
UTOK (Slovak National Council resistance), 222
UVOD (London Government resistance), 179, 189, 191

Vambery, Rustem, 194
Vancouver, 46, 50
Vandenberg, Sen. Arthur, 290
Vaněk, Vladimír, 330
Vansittart, Sir Robert, 116, 121
Versailles, 19, 63, 67-72, 85, 146, 285
Vickers-Armstrong, 113
Victor Emmanuel II, King of Italy, 61
Vienna, 3, 5-6, 9, 59, 64-65, 72, 81, 104, 106; Accord: 166, 243
Viest, Gen. Rudolf, 182, 222
Vinogradoff, Professor Pavel Gavrilovich, 3
Vinohrady, 5
Vishinsky, Andrei, 221, 229

Vladivostok, 12, 15, 17-24, 27, 30-32, 35-36, 38-42, 45-51, 56, 61
Vlasov, Gen. Andrei, 241
Vojta, Hugo, 190
Vologda, 21, 36
Voroshilov, Klementy, 160, 181, 208
Voska, Emanuel Victor, 2, 6, 10, 53, 57, 62
Vuillemin, Gen. Joseph, 138, 162

Wagner, Ferenc, 266
Wallace, Henry A., 200
Wardrop, Consul General, 26, 34-35
Warner, 256, 271-72
Webster, 45, 48-49
Weidemann, Capt. Fritz, 127, 130
Weidenfeld, A. G., 203
Weisäcker, Ernst von, 148, 154, 171
Welczek, Johannes von, 138-39
Welles, Sumner, 178, 193, 195, 197-204
Werth, Alexander, 104, 313
Wheeler-Bennett, John, 170-71
White Mountain, Battle of, 3, 72, 325
Wilkinson, Ellen, 188, 283
Williams, Albert Rhys, 15, 17, 27
Wilson, Sir Horace, 131, 154, 161-65, 171

Wilson, Woodrow, 16, 18, 27-28, 41-45, 50-62, 229, 301
Winant, John Gilbert, 184, 186, 239
Wise, Rabbi Stephen S., 53
Witkowitz Works, 76, 128-30
Wrangel, Gen. Petr, 22

Yalta Conference, 226-27, 231, 240, 302, 317
YMCA, 15
Yost, Charles, 303, 307
Young Czech Party, 2, 58
Young, Sir Robert F., 9
Yugoslavia, 51, 54, 64, 68, 76, 82, 133

Zápotocký, Antonín, 314
Zboroff Heights, Battle of, 12
Zeit, Die, 94
Zeman, General, 255
Zenkl, Petr, 191, 264, 293, 298-99
Zhdanov, Gen. Andrei, 254
Zilliacus, Konni, 273, 287
Žingor, Vilem, 224
Živnostenská Bank, 75, 172
Zorin, Valerian, 277, 312-13
Zürich, 5, 6, 133

About the Authors

JOHN O. CRANE (December 28, 1899–May 16, 1982) served as research and press secretary to the founding president of Czechoslovakia, Tomáš Masaryk. An historian, John Crane lectured on Central Europe for two summers at the University of Chicago and was the founder of the Institute of Current World Affairs. He was the author of *The Little Entente* (New York: Macmillan, 1931).

SYLVIA E. CRANE, historian and journalist, is the author of *White Silence: Greenough, Powers, and Crawford—American Sculptors in Nineteenth-Century Italy* (Miami: University of Miami Press, 1972). She has published widely abroad in such journals as *Le Monde Diplomatique, Esprit,* and *Témoignage Chrétien* in Paris, *Il Ponte* in Florence, *Astrolabio* in Rome, *The Humanist in Canada* in Ottawa, and *Transatlantik* in Munich.

During World War II, while engaged in public relations, she was requested by Czechoslovak ambassador Vladimír Hurban to arrange a public meeting in New York for President Beneš, in concert with John Crane. This collaboration between John and Sylvia was the beginning of a joint involvement with Czechoslovak affairs that deepened after their marriage in 1945 and continued until John's death in 1982. Sylvia then employed her training as an historian to research and complete this work.